CW00828952

Why Ethnic Parties Succeed

Why do some ethnic parties succeed in attracting the support of their target ethnic groups while others fail? In a world in which ethnic parties flourish in established and emerging democracies alike, understanding the conditions under which such parties succeed or fail is of critical importance to both political scientists and policy makers. Drawing on a study of variation in the performance of ethnic parties in India, this book builds a theory of ethnic party performance in "patronage-democracies." Chandra shows why voters in such democracies choose between parties by conducting ethnic head counts rather than by comparing policy platforms or ideological positions. Building on these individual microfoundations, she argues that an ethnic party is likely to succeed when it has competitive rules for intraparty advancement and when the size of the group it seeks to mobilize exceeds the threshold of winning or leverage imposed by the electoral system.

Kanchan Chandra is an assistant professor in the Department of Political Science at MIT.

Cambridge Studies in Comparative Politics

General Editor
Margaret Levi   *University of Washington, Seattle*

Assistant General Editor
Stephen Hanson   *University of Washington, Seattle*

Associate Editors
Robert H. Bates   *Harvard University*
Peter Hall   *Harvard University*
Peter Lange   *Duke University*
Helen Milner   *Columbia University*
Frances Rosenbluth   *Yale University*
Susan Stokes   *University of Chicago*
Sidney Tarrow   *Cornell University*

Other Books in the Series

Stefano Bartolini, *The Political Mobilization of the European Left, 1860–1980: The Class Cleavage*
Nancy Bermeo, ed., *Unemployment in the New Europe*
Charles Boix, *Democracy and Redistribution*
Carles Boix, *Political Parties, Growth and Equality: Conservative and Social Democratic Economic Strategies in the World Economy*
Catherine Boone, *Merchant Capital and the Roots of State Power in Senegal, 1930–1985*
Catherine Boone, *Political Topographies of the African State: Territorial Authority and Institutional Change*
Michael Bratton and Nicolas van de Walle, *Democratic Experiments in Africa: Regime Transitions in Comparative Perspective*
Valerie Bunce, *Leaving Socialism and Leaving the State: The End of Yugoslavia, the Soviet Union and Czechoslovakia*
Ruth Berins Collier, *Paths Toward Democracy: The Working Class and Elites in Western Europe and South America*
Daniele Caramani, *The Nationalization of Politics: The Formation of National Electorates and Party Systems in Europe*
Donatella della Porta, *Social Movements, Political Violence, and the State*
Gerald Easter, *Reconstructing the State: Personal Networks and Elite Identity*
Robert Franzese, Jr., *Macroeconomic Policies of Developed Democracies*
Roberto Franzosi, *The Puzzle of Strikes: Class and State Strategies in Postwar Italy*

Continued on page following the Index

Why Ethnic Parties Succeed

PATRONAGE AND ETHNIC HEAD COUNTS IN INDIA

KANCHAN CHANDRA

Massachusetts Institute of Technology

CAMBRIDGE UNIVERSITY PRESS
Cambridge, New York, Melbourne, Madrid, Cape Town, Singapore, São Paulo

Cambridge University Press
The Edinburgh Building, Cambridge CB2 2RU, UK

Published in the United States of America by Cambridge University Press, New York

www.cambridge.org
Information on this title: www.cambridge.org/9780521814522

© Kanchan Chandra 2004

First published 2004
This digitally printed first paperback version 2007

A catalogue record for this publication is available from the British Library

Library of Congress Cataloguing in Publication data

Chandra, Kanchan, 1971–
Why ethnic parties succeed : patronage and ethnic head counts in India / Kanchan Chandra.
　　p.　cm. – (Cambridge studies in comparative politics)
Includes bibliographical references and index.
ISBN 0-521-81452-9
1. Political parties – India.　2. Minorities – India – Political activity.　3. India – Ethnic
relations – Political aspects.　4. Patronage, Political – India.　I. Title.　II. Series.
JQ298.A1C43　2004
306.2´6´0954–dc21　　　2003048458

ISBN-13　978-0-521-81452-2 hardback
ISBN-10　0-521-81452-9 hardback

ISBN-13　978-0-521-89141-7 paperback
ISBN-10　0-521-89141-8 paperback

To my mother,
whose imagination creates mine.

For my father.

Contents

List of Maps, Figures, and Tables   *page* xi

List of Abbreviations   xiv

A Note on Terminology   xv

Acknowledgments   xvii

1   INTRODUCTION   1

Part I. Theory

2   LIMITED INFORMATION AND ETHNIC
    CATEGORIZATION   33

3   PATRONAGE-DEMOCRACY, LIMITED
    INFORMATION, AND ETHNIC FAVOURITISM   47

4   COUNTING HEADS: WHY ETHNIC PARTIES
    SUCCEED IN PATRONAGE-DEMOCRACIES   82

5   WHY PARTIES HAVE DIFFERENT ETHNIC HEAD
    COUNTS: PARTY ORGANIZATION AND ELITE
    INCORPORATION   99

Part II. Data

6   INDIA AS A PATRONAGE-DEMOCRACY   115

7   THE BAHUJAN SAMAJ PARTY (BSP) AND THE
    SCHEDULED CASTES (SCs)   143

8   WHY SC ELITES JOIN THE BSP   172

9   WHY SC VOTERS PREFER THE BSP   196

10 WHY SC VOTER PREFERENCES TRANSLATE INTO
BSP VOTES   222

11 EXPLAINING DIFFERENT HEAD COUNTS IN THE
BSP AND CONGRESS   246

12 EXTENDING THE ARGUMENT TO OTHER
ETHNIC PARTIES IN INDIA: THE BJP, THE DMK,
AND THE JMM   262

13 ETHNIC HEAD COUNTS AND DEMOCRATIC
STABILITY   287

Appendix A. Elite Interviews   293

Appendix B. Ethnographies of Election Campaigns   297

Appendix C. Content Analysis   299

Appendix D. Description of Survey Data   302

Appendix E. Description of the Ecological Inference (EI) Method   303

Appendix F. Method Used to Estimate Ethnic Voting Patterns   310

Bibliography   317

Index   337

Maps, Figures, and Tables

Maps

1.1 Scheduled Caste population across Indian states, 1991   *page* 19
1.2 Variation in Scheduled Caste vote for the BSP across Indian
     states, 1984–98 parliamentary elections   20
1.3 Hindu population across Indian states, 1991   24
1.4 Variation in Hindu vote for the BJP across Indian states, 1991
     parliamentary elections   25
1.5 Tamil-speaking population across Tamil Nadu districts, 1961   26
1.6 Variation in Tamil vote for the DMK across districts in Tamil
     Nadu, 1967 legislative assembly elections   27
1.7 Variation in vote for the JMM across districts in Jharkhand, 2000
     legislative assembly elections   28

Figures

1.1 Equilibrium of ethnic favouritism   12
4.1 The voting decision in a patronage-democracy   87
5.1 Stage I: party dominated by elites from group A   103
5.2 Stage II: competitive incorporation of elites from group B   104
5.3 Stage III: displacement of As by Bs   104
5.4 Stage I: party dominated by elites from group A   108
7.1 The Bahujan Samaj   156
8.1 Percentage of important cabinet portfolios allotted to
     Scheduled Caste ministers, 1951–92   179
8.2 Ratio of SC representation in Council of Ministers to SC
     percentage in population, 1951–92   179
9.1 Preference distribution of Scheduled Caste respondents
     in UP and Punjab, 1996 parliamentary elections   209

11.1 The Congress party organization   248
11.2 Incorporation of new elites through the multiplication
      of monoethnic factions   259
12.1 The organization of the Bharatiya Janata Party   273
12.2 The organization of the DMK   280

Tables

2.1 Data sources about ethnic and nonethnic identities   38
6.1 Dominance of the public sector in the organized economy in
     India, 1961–99   117
6.2 Relative growth rates of the public and private sectors in India,
     1991–99   118
6.3 Profile of central government employment in India, 1994   119
6.4 Profile of state government employment in Punjab, 1995   120
7.1 Efficacy of Scheduled Caste voters across Indian states, 1984   146
7.2 Stratified sample of Indian states: Uttar Pradesh, Punjab,
     Karnataka   159
7.3 Variables hypothesized to effect BSP performance among
     Scheduled Castes   162
8.1 Rise in literacy among Scheduled Castes in all three states,
     1961–81   173
8.2 Mean number of independent candidates in "reserved"
     constituencies, 1960–83   175
8.3 Profile of early joiners of the BSP   177
8.4 Representation in the BSP in Uttar Pradesh, 1984   188
8.5 Representation in the BSP in Uttar Pradesh, 1995–96   189
8.6 BSP candidates in Karnataka legislative assembly and
     parliamentary elections, 1989–98   193
9.1 Percentage of SC candidates fielded by all major parties/alliances,
     1996   198
9.2 Representational profile of major parties in Uttar Pradesh and
     Punjab at the state level, 1996   198
9.3 Relative weight of party and candidate in voter decisions in Uttar
     Pradesh and Punjab   200
9.4 Party issue positions, 1996   204
9.5 Scheduled Caste voter assessments of issue salience in Uttar
     Pradesh and Punjab, 1996   207
9.6 Party preferences of Scheduled Caste voters in Uttar Pradesh and
     Punjab, 1996   208
9.7 Party preferences of Chamar and non-Chamar voters in
     Uttar Pradesh and Punjab, 1996   210

Maps, Figures, and Tables

10.1	Demographic profile of Scheduled Castes across samples	232
10.2	Leverage and Scheduled Caste voting behaviour	233
10.3	Timing of decision: Scheduled Castes in Uttar Pradesh and Punjab	238
10.4	Timing of decision: Chamars in Uttar Pradesh and Punjab	240
10.5	Vote switching between Uttar Pradesh parliamentary and assembly elections, 1996	242
12.1	Profile of BJP vote, 1991–98	267
12.2	Representational profile of the DMK and Congress, 1968	278
12.3	Caste composition of Congress and DMK cabinets, 1957–67	279
A.1	Elite interviews by state and organization	294
B.1	Constituency studies during parliamentary and assembly campaigns, 1996–98	298
C.1	Words or phrases included in main issue categories in content analysis	300
D.1	Description of election surveys	302
F.1	Performance of the Bahujan Samaj Party by state, 1984–98 parliamentary elections	313
F.2	Performance of the Bharatiya Janata Party by state, 1991 parliamentary elections	315
F.3	Performance of the DMK in Tamil Nadu by district, 1967 legislative assembly elections	316
F.4	Performance of the JMM in Jharkhand by district, 2000 legislative assembly elections	316

Abbreviations

BJP	Bharatiya Janata Party
BJS	Bharatiya Jana Sangh
BKKP	Bharatiya Kisan Kamgar Party
BPP	Bihar People's Party
BSP	Bahujan Samaj Party
CPI	Communist Party of India
CPI(ML)	Communist Party of India (Marxist-Leninist)
CPM	Communist Party of India (Marxist)
DMK	Dravida Munnetra Kazagham
FPTP	First Past the Post
INC	Indian National Congress
JD	Janata Dal
JD(G)	Janata Dal (Gujarat)
JD(U)	Janata Dal (United)
NDA	National Democratic Alliance
NF/LF	National Front/Left Front
OBC	Other backward classes/other backward castes
PR	Proportional representation
RJD	Rashtriya Janata Dal
RPI	Republican Party of India
RSS	Rashtriya Swayamsevak Sangh
SAD	Shiromani Akali Dal
SC	Scheduled Caste
SJP	Samajwadi Janata Party
SP	Samajwadi Party
ST	Scheduled Tribe
VHP	Vishwa Hindu Parishad

A Note on Terminology

Throughout, I use the term "Scheduled Caste" to describe the Bahujan Samaj Party's target category rather than alternatives such as "Untouchable," "*Harijan*" or "*Dalit*." I employ this term because it was the most widely employed term of self-identification among my respondents. None of my respondents used the derogatory term "Untouchable" to refer to themselves. The term *Harijan*, meaning "children of God," a term coined by Gandhi to refer to those treated as untouchable, is now perceived as being patronizing. I do not use either of these terms, therefore, except when quoting verbatim from another source that does. Many of my respondents referred to themselves as "*Dalit*" (meaning "broken to pieces" or "oppressed"), a term popularized by the Dalit Panthers, a radical movement in the state of Maharashtra. But the more common term of self-identification was the term Scheduled Caste (SC), or the name of the caste category among the Scheduled Castes to which an individual subscribed.

I use the terms "other backward classes" (OBC) and "backward classes" interchangeably with the term "other backward *castes*" and "backward *castes*." The term "other backward classes" comes from a provision in the Indian Constitution that empowers the government to provide preferential treatment for "other socially and educationally backward classes." The Constitution does not lay down the criteria according to which the "backward classes" are to be identified, but the term "classes" in this phrase has come to be interpreted in everyday politics as a euphemism for castes. In 1990, the Indian government announced a decision to set aside 27 percent of jobs in central government institutions for the "Other Backward Classes," defined explicitly as a collection of castes. Especially since this policy decision, the terms "other backward classes" and "other backward castes" have come to be used interchangeably.

Acknowledgments

This book proposes a theory of ethnic party performance in "patronage-democracies," based on an analysis of ethnic party performance in India. It is intended for two overlapping audiences, which reflect also two of the intellectual communities to which I belong: those who are interested in the abstract principles that drive the particularities of politics anywhere; and those who are interested in the particularities of politics in India. My search for a way to use abstraction and particularity to illuminate each other was influenced especially by two books: David Laitin's *Hegemony and Culture* and Robert Putnam's *Making Democracy Work.*[1]

In its pages, the reader will encounter voters and politicians who are amateur mathematicians and statisticians. They count the heads of co-ethnics across parties and the electorate, use these head counts to attach probabilities to different outcomes, and choose their strategies according to the result of these calculations. This portrait of voters and politicians is based on ethnographic research on the Bahujan Samaj Party (BSP) and other political parties in India conducted between 1996 and 1998. The politicians and voters whom I interviewed in the course of this research had different, often complex, motivations. Political power was for many the principal channel for material advancement. For others, it was the principal route to self-assertion. Often, the desires for material advancement and for self-assertion were combined. But no matter what their motivations, they were engaged alike in sophisticated calculations of the chances of victory or influence, using numbers generated from ethnic head counts. Terms such as a "wave effect," a "plus factor," a "winning margin," "cutting votes" (i.e., votes

---

[1] David Laitin, *Hegemony and Culture* (Chicago: University of Chicago Press, 1986); Robert Putnam, *Making Democracy Work* (Princeton, NJ: Princeton University Press, 1993).

that cut into someone else's winning margin), and so on were a routine part of their vocabulary in almost every constituency that I visited.

I attempt in this book to theorize about the conditions that produce this systemic tendency toward calculated voting based on ethnic head counts, and to show how, in turn, these head counts determine the performance of ethnic parties. While I hope that the data on the behaviour of politicians and voters, drawn mainly from the 1996–98 period in India, provide sufficient evidence for its plausibility, this theory remains to be evaluated against new data from other time periods in India and from other patronage-democracies. Throughout, I use the term "ethnic identity" in a broad sense to describe identities based on ascriptive categories, including caste, language, tribe, and religion. In political discourse in India, the politics of caste, language, tribe, and religion are more often treated as separate phenomena. I use a common analytical category here, not because differences do not exist between these categories, but in order to highlight certain minimal similarities in politics based on any of them.

The book developed out of my doctoral dissertation in the Department of Government at Harvard University. Among my teachers, my debts start with Douglas Haynes, Nelson Kasfir, and Ian Lustick, then at Dartmouth College, who showed me how to think about ethnicity. At graduate school, I am grateful to the members of my dissertation committee: Samuel Huntington, for pushing me to think about the comparative implications of my argument; David Laitin, who has been an inspiration during this project and beyond it; Ashutosh Varshney, for sharing his enthusiasm for Indian politics; and Myron Weiner, who continued to influence many of the arguments I make here even after his death in 1999. In Delhi, Yogendra Yadav responded generously to my frequent requests for advice. I thank him also for involving me in the National Election Studies in 1996 and 1998, and for permission to use the data from the surveys conducted during those studies.

Financial support during writing and research was provided by fellowships from the SSRC-Macarthur Foundation on International Peace and Security; the Harvard Academy for International and Area Studies; a Mellon Grant for research on the performance of democracies; a Mellon Dissertation Completion Grant; the Department of Government, Harvard University; the Department of Political Science, MIT; and the Weatherhead Center for International Affairs, Harvard University. I am grateful also to the Harvard Map Collection for purchasing digital data on India's census districts and electoral constituencies at my request. The Center for

Acknowledgments

International Studies at MIT, directed by Richard Samuels and Stephen Van Evera, provided a generous grant to collect a cross-national database on ethnic parties to test the argument of this book more broadly. That project quickly expanded beyond the scope of this one, and its findings will be reported elsewhere. However, this book has benefited from the parallel concerns of that project.

For institutional support, I thank the Department of Political Science at MIT, the Harvard Academy, the Centre for the Study of Developing Societies (CSDS) in Delhi, the Institute for Development and Communication in Chandigarh, Wilder House at the University of Chicago, and the Weatherhead Center for International Affairs. Jean Anderson at Wilder House, Steve Baker at the Government Department at Harvard, Amy Frost at the SSRC-Macarthur Foundation, Beth Hastie at the Harvard Academy, and Pamela Clements and David Veritas at MIT made many difficult things easy. I am grateful to Rachel Gisselquist, Dan Metz, Dan Munro, Jessica Piombo, Bela Prasad, Chris Wendt, and Adam Ziegfeld for excellent research assistance.

I was humbled in the course of my research by the generosity of people to whom I offered little in return. Over several years, Yubaraj Ghimire and Saroj Nagi taught me the ethics and mechanics of field research in India and, with a light touch, gave me an invaluable education in Indian politics. Himanshu Bhattacharya, Sanjay Kumar, Kanchan Malhotra, and Chandrika Parmar at CSDS guided me in the design and interpretation of the NES surveys. My research on Uttar Pradesh is indebted to Ram Advani, Paul Brass, Zoya Hasan, Pappu Kumar, Noor Mohammad, Ashok Priyadarshi, M. V. S. Rami Reddy, Hemant Sharma, Nirmala Sharma, Anand Singh, Udai Sinha, T. Venkatesh, and Randeep and Priya Wahraich; on Punjab, to Vikram Balasubramaniam and Kavita Sivaramakrishnan, Gyan Chand, Dharmpal and Urmil Gupta, K. B. Kapoor, Harpreet Kaur, Pramod Kumar, P. N. Pimpley, A. S. Prashar, T. K. Ramasamy, Ravinder Sood, G. Vajralingam, Ramesh Vinayak, and Bhagwant Singh Ahluwalia and his family; and on Karnataka, to Shashidhara Bhat, G. K. Karanth, D. R. Nagaraj, Saritha Rai, Y. P. Rajesh, Sandeep Shastri, and O. Sreedharan. Most of all, I thank Professor Arun Chowdhury and his family.

I presented chapters from the manuscript at the following seminars and colloquia: the annual meetings of the American Political Science Association in 1999 and 2002; "India and the Politics of Developing Countries," a festschrift in honour of Myron Weiner, University of Notre Dame, 1999; the 2000 meetings of the Laboratory in Comparative Ethnic Processes

(LICEP); the Conference on Clientelism at Duke University, 2001; the MIT Political Science Faculty Colloquium, 2001; the Harvard Academy for International and Area Studies, 2001; the Comparative Politics Workshop, University of Chicago, 2001; the Center for International Security and Cooperation (CISAC), Stanford University, 2002; the Macarthur Preferences Network Meeting, University of Pennsylvania, 2002; the South Asia Seminar, Harvard University, 2002; the Southern Asian Institute Distinguished Lecture Series, Columbia University, 2002; the South Asia Conference at the University of Wisconsin, 2002; the Harvard-MIT Joint Seminar for Political Development, 2002; the Duke University Comparative Politics Workshop, 2002; and the UCLA Comparative Politics Seminar Series, 2002. I am grateful to the organizers of these events for their invitations to participate: Rob Boyd, Val Daniels, Jorge Dominguez, Lynn Eden, Samuel Huntington, Stathis Kalyvas, Devesh Kapur, Herbert Kitschelt, Mona Lyne, Philip Oldenburg, Carole Pateman, Daniel Posner, Scott Sagan, Susan Stokes, Narendra Subramanian, Ashutosh Varshney, and Steven Wilkinson. I thank also the participants at these meetings for their challenging and constructive comments, and especially the discussants: Robert Bates, Ellen Commisso, Gerry Digiusto, Valerie Funk, Akhil Gupta, Donald Horowitz, Michael Jones-Correa, Herbert Kitschelt, Lloyd Rudolph, and Richard Sisson. Materials from Chapters 5 and 11 were previously published in "Elite Incorporation in Multi-Ethnic Societies," *Asian Survey*, Vol. 40, No. 5 (2000): 836–855, and are reprinted here with permission.

The manuscript benefited from critiques by and discussions with several scholars. I thank Darshan Ambalavanar, Suzanne Berger, Chappell Lawson, Margaret Levi, Pratap Mehta, and the two anonymous reviewers for Cambridge University Press for their thoughtful comments on the entire manuscript. Michael Hechter gave me sound advice on the title. I relied often on Paul Brass's insight, both in his writing and in conversations with him. Linda Beck, Rogers Brubaker, Josh Cohen, Francisco Gil-White, J. P. Gownder, Anna Grzymala-Busse, Stathis Kalyvas, Devesh Kapur, Donna Lee Van Cott, and Steven Wilkinson provided detailed comments on individual chapters. Scott Desposato, Rachel Gisselquist, Rohini Pande, Jonathan Rodden, James Snyder, Chris Wendt, and David Woodruff offered useful feedback at an informal colloquium during the final stages of my work on the manuscript. I learned a great deal from conversations with Steve Ansolabehere, Robert Bates, Marc Busch, James Fearon, Mala Htun, Miriam Laugesen, Rory Macfarquhar, Barry Posen, Daniel Posner, Sanjay

Acknowledgments

Reddy, Lloyd Rudolph, Susanne Rudolph, Andy Sabl, Kenneth Scheve, Naunihal Singh, and Smita Singh. Gary King responded patiently to several questions about his ecological inference (EI) method. Karen Ferree was a generous tutor in EI. Lew Bateman at Cambridge University Press was a wise and patient editor.

My greatest debt is to the party workers and leaders of the BSP and other political parties in India. As politicians, they are also political scientists, historians, sociologists, ethnographers, and as I try to show here, mathematicians and statisticians. Their knowledge is the foundation for this study. In order to protect their confidence, I do not name in these acknowledgments individuals who spoke with me in their capacity as members of a political party. I also withhold or change the names of respondents whom I quote directly in the text, except when they are prominent public figures and the name or position is relevant to the interpretation of the quotation. This is an unfortunate omission, since it renders invisible those who should have been named as collective coauthors.

Needless to say, none of those whom I thank here necessarily agree with any or all parts of the manuscript. I alone am responsible for the argument and its errors.

1

Introduction

Why do ethnic parties succeed in obtaining the support of members of their target ethnic group(s)? Ethnic political parties now flourish across the democratic world. Canada, Spain, India, the United Kingdom, Israel, Sri Lanka, Macedonia, South Africa, and Russia are only a few examples of the established or emerging democracies in which they have taken root. For social scientists interested in explaining important political phenomena, the question is worth asking for its own sake. At the same time, the answer has broader implications for those with a stake in the survival of democratic regimes. Ethnic parties, and the politicization of ethnic differences more generally, are presumed to constitute a major threat to democratic stability.[1] An exploration of the processes by which such parties succeed or fail, then, illuminates also the processes that undermine or preserve democracy.

Drawing on a study of variation in the performance of ethnic parties in India, this book proposes a theory of ethnic party performance in one distinct family of democracies, identified here as "patronage-democracies." Voters in patronage-democracies, I argue, choose between parties by conducting ethnic head counts rather than by comparing policy platforms or ideological positions. They formulate preferences across parties by counting the heads of co-ethnics across party personnel, preferring that party that provides greatest representation to their co-ethnics. They formulate

[1] See, for instance, Robert Dahl, *Polyarchy* (New Haven, CT: Yale University Press, 1971); Donald Horowitz, *Ethnic Groups in Conflict* (Berkeley: University of California Press, 1985); Arend Lijphart, *Democracy in Plural Societies* (New Haven, CT: Yale University Press, 1977); Alvin Rabushka and Kenneth Shepsle, *Politics in Plural Societies* (Columbus, OH: Charles E. Merrill, 1972).

expectations about the likely electoral outcome by counting the heads of co-ethnics across the electorate. And they vote for their preferred party only when their co-ethnics are sufficiently numerous to take it to a winning or influential position.

This process of ethnic head counting is the foundation for the central argument advanced in this book: An ethnic party is likely to succeed in a patronage-democracy *when it has competitive rules for intraparty advancement* **and** *when the size of the ethnic group(s) it seeks to mobilize exceeds the threshold of winning or leverage imposed by the electoral system.* Competitive rules for intraparty advancement, other things equal, give a party a comparative advantage in the representation of elites from its target ethnic category. And a positive difference between the size of its target ethnic category and the threshold of winning or leverage indicates that the party has a viable shot at victory or influence.

The implications of this argument for the survival of democracy are paradoxical. At first glance, a politics of ethnic head counting appears to subvert democratic competition by producing predetermined results based on ethnic demography.[2] But a closer look yields a more optimistic prognosis. Ethnic head counts need not produce predetermined results, for the reason that the categories that voters employ in their counts are not predetermined. As constructivist approaches to ethnic identity have shown us, these categories are open to manipulation. And in an environment in which the choice of one category for counting over another means the difference between victory and defeat, we should expect competing political entrepreneurs to engage in such manipulation to the greatest extent possible. The determining role played by ethnic head counts in patronage-democracies, then, may well prevent the *pre*determination of election results.

I. Definitions

Ethnic Group and Ethnic Category

I take the term "ethnic group" to refer to the nominal members of an ascriptive category such as race, language, caste, tribe, or religion. As used here, the term "ethnic group" does not imply active participation in a common

---

[2] For an argument in this vein, see Horowitz, *Ethnic Groups in Conflict*, 84.

group identity. Wherever possible, I use the term ethnic "category" rather than "group" to emphasize this point.

Nominal membership in such ascriptive categories is inherited: I might, for instance, be born as a Sikh from the Mazhabi caste in Punjab, a Yoruba Christian from western Nigeria, or an African American Muslim from Chicago. As these examples illustrate, however, we are usually born as members of several categories, with a choice about which one we consider to be especially salient.

Ethnic Party

An *ethnic party* is a party that overtly represents itself as a champion of the cause of one particular ethnic category or set of categories to the exclusion of others, and that makes such a representation central to its strategy of mobilizing voters. The key distinguishing principles of this definition are those of *ascription, exclusion,* and *centrality*: The categories that such a party mobilizes are defined according to ascriptive characteristics; the mobilization of the "insider" ethnic categories is always accompanied by the exclusion of ethnic "outsiders"; and, while the party may also highlight other issues, the championing of the cause of an ethnic category or categories is central to its mobilizing efforts. A *multiethnic* party is defined here as a party that also makes an appeal related to ethnicity central to its mobilizing strategy but that assumes a position of neutrality or equidistance toward all relevant categories on the salient dimension(s) of ethnicity. A party that does not include and exclude categories mainly on the basis of ethnic identity, or that addresses ethnic demands but does not make such demands central to its political platform, is *nonethnic* by this definition.

In order to categorize a party as "ethnic," "nonethnic," or "multiethnic" according to this definition, it is necessary to examine the message that it sends to the electorate (what issues it highlights in its election campaigns and rallies, what policies it proposes or implements, how it promises to distribute resources).[3] Note that the message that a party sends to the

---

[3] The emphasis on a party's *message* distinguishes this definition from Donald Horowitz's in *Ethnic Groups in Conflict*, 291–3. For Horowitz, "the test of an ethnic party is simply the distribution of support" (291–2). What the party says and does, according to him, follows directly from its support base: "In practice, a party will serve the interests of the group comprising its overwhelming support or quickly forfeit that support" (291). This definition is not useful for the question driving this study. Incorporating the nature of a party's support base in the definition itself obscures the question of how it acquires such support in the

electorate might change over time. The same party that champions the cause of one ethnic category in one election may redefine its target ethnic category, or reinvent itself as a "multiethnic" or "nonethnic" party, in subsequent elections. Precisely for this reason, we should think of the classification of a party as an ethnic party as a time-specific classification that captures the character of the party in some time periods but may not do so in others.

Note that this definition characterizes a party as "ethnic" even if it claims to speak for more than one ethnic group. It would be useful here to underline the essential distinction between ethnic parties and multiethnic parties. The line separating the two cannot be drawn, as we might initially suppose, by separating parties that speak for one ethnic category from parties that speak for many. A close look at any supposedly "single" ethnic category would reveal that it is simultaneously an amalgam of others. The category "Yoruba" in Nigeria, for example, might be interpreted as a single ethnic category, or as a conglomerate of smaller categories, including "Oyo," "Ijebu," Egba," and "Ekiti," which are themselves conglomerates of still smaller units.[4] Similarly, the category "Hispanic" in the United States might be termed a "single" category, or an aggregate category consisting of the smaller categories of "Mexican," "Puerto Rican," "Cuban," and so on. The same is true of other ethnic categories in the United States, including "black," "white," "Asian American," and "Native American."[5] In a point to which I return repeatedly throughout this book, any ethnic party that claims to speak on behalf of a single ethnic category is typically trying to unify several previously disparate categories by claiming that such unity has always existed. The so-called subdivisions that nest within any supposedly "single" ethnic category are of critical importance in understanding the phenomenon of ethnic party success or failure.

The main distinction between an ethnic and a multiethnic party, therefore, lies not in the number of categories that each attempts to *include*, but in whether or not there is a category that each attempts to *exclude*. An ethnic party, regardless of how many categories it claims to speak for, always

---

first place. Defining an ethnic party based on its message, by separating the definition of the party from its base of support, makes it possible to investigate why a party obtains its support principally from some ethnic category or categories to the exclusion of others, and when it is able to expand this support to include the majority of its target ethnic category.

[4] David Laitin, *Hegemony and Culture* (Chicago: University of Chicago Press, 1986).
[5] Melissa Nobles, *Shades of Citizenship: Race and the Census in Modern Politics* (Stanford, CA: Stanford University Press, 2000).

identifies implicitly or explicitly the category that is excluded. A multiethnic party, while also invoking ethnic identities, does not exclude any group on the salient dimension(s) of identity.[6]

Let me illustrate with some examples. The Action Group (AG) in Nigeria in 1960 sought the support of all the tribal categories grouped together under the aggregate label of "Yoruba."[7] Should we classify it as an ethnic or a multiethnic party? According to the criterion just identified, the AG would be classified as an ethnic party to the extent that it excluded non-Yorubas from its appeal. Similarly, the Movimiento Revolucionario Tupaj Katari de Liberación (MRTKL) in Bolivia in 1985 sought the support of the several ethnic categories grouped together under the label "indigenous," including the Quechua, the Aymara, the Uru, and the Chipaya.[8] However, to the extent that it excluded non-indigenous categories from its appeal, it would be classified here as an ethnic party. On the other hand, the National Front in Malaysia, which in 1995 also mobilized several ethnic categories, would be classified here as multiethnic to the extent that it included parties from all salient ethnic categories, including Malays, Indians, and Chinese.[9] Similarly, the African National Congress in South Africa in 1994 would be defined as a multiethnic party to the extent that it did not exclude any salient ethnic category in its overt message.[10]

Success

I define the degree of success as the degree to which a party is able to capture the votes of members of its target ethnic category. A party is "successful" if it captures the votes of at least a majority of the members of its target ethnic

---

[6] For a somewhat similar point, see Horowitz, *Ethnic Groups in Conflict*, 299. Horowitz too argues that an ethnic party can serve the interests of more than one ethnic group. A party should be termed multiethnic, according to him, "only if it spans the major groups in conflict."

[7] John Mackintosh, *Nigerian Government and Politics* (London: George Allen and Unwin, 1966).

[8] For a general discussion of the MRTKL, see Xavier Albo, "And from Kataristas to MNRistas?," in Donna Lee Van Cott, ed., *Indigenous Peoples and Democracy in Latin America* (New York: St. Martin's Press, 1994), 55–82. For the composition of the category "indigenous," see the Minorities at Risk database: <http://www.cidcm.umd.edu/inscr/mar/data/latintbl.htm>.

[9] Based on a reading of campaign statements in 1995 as reported by FBIS (Foreign Broadcast Information Service).

[10] Based on a reading of ANC campaign statements during the 1994 elections as reported by FBIS.

category over successive elections, "moderately successful" if it captures the votes of a plurality, and "failed" if it is able to capture only a negligible percentage of votes from the members of its target category or categories. Note that the estimate of success is contingent upon the way in which an ethnic party defines its target ethnic category. If the ethnic category targeted by a political party changes, the estimate of success should be adjusted accordingly.

One could, by contrast, gauge success by the number of seats won by the party, its overall percentage of the vote, or its degree of influence in government. These definitions are not relevant to the theoretical purpose of this study. If an ethnic category is small or dispersed, a party that captures the entire vote of members of this category may still seem unsuccessful if we use the overall percentage of votes as a measure of success. However, the fact that it has managed to gather all the members of its target ethnic category into a single political mass is no small matter. It is this massing of ethnic groups behind ethnic parties, rather than behind their nonethnic or multiethnic competitors, that is the puzzle of interest to this study.

Patronage-Democracy

I use the term "democracy" in a minimal sense to mean simply a system in which the political leadership is chosen through competitive elections.[11] By the term "patronage-democracy," I mean a democracy in which the state monopolizes access to jobs and services, *and* in which elected officials have discretion in the implementation of laws allocating the jobs and services at the disposal of the state. The key aspect of a patronage-democracy is not simply the size of the state but the power of elected officials to distribute the vast resources controlled by the state to voters on an *individualized* basis, by exercising their discretion in the implementation of state policy. This individualized distribution of resources, in conjunction with a dominant state, I will argue, makes patronage-democracies a distinct family of democracies with distinct types of voter and elite behaviour. A democracy is not patronage-based if the private sector is larger than the public sector as a source of jobs and a provider of services, or if those who control the distribution of state resources and services cannot exercise discretion in the implementation of policies concerning their distribution.

---

[11] Samuel Huntington, *The Third Wave: Democratization in the Late Twentieth Century* (Norman: University of Oklahoma Press, 1991), 7.

The term "patronage-democracy" might be applied to a political system as a whole or to subsystems within it comprised of particular administrative areas or particular sections of the population. In the latter case, the relationship between these areas and/or sections of the population and the state would constitute a "pocket" of patronage-democracy within a larger system that is not patronage-based.

Currently available cross-national data do not permit a reliable operationalization of the concept of patronage-democracy within and across countries. The several available measures of government size can be misleading, since they typically underestimate the size of the state.[12] And there are no reliable measures of the degree of discretion available to state officials.[13] In order to construct trustworthy cross-national measures for the concept of patronage-democracy, therefore, it is necessary first to sift through country-specific data. I show here, on the basis of such data, that India is one example of a patronage-democracy. While conducting a similar analysis for other countries is beyond the scope of this work, secondary literature suggests that other examples of patronage-democracies are likely to abound particularly in Asia and Africa, where colonial rule left behind a legacy of state-dominated economies. Additional examples of patronage-democracies in these regions, apart from India, might include (intermittently) Nigeria, Zambia, and Senegal.[14] Patronage-democracies may also be found in the postcommunist world, because of the sprawling state

---

[12] The standard measure for size of government, with the most extensive coverage of countries, is government spending as a percentage of GDP, based on data published by the IMF *Government Finance Statistics Yearbooks*. This measure underestimates the size of the public sector for the following reasons: (1) it reports data only for central government spending and not for spending by subnational units; (2) it excludes a large sphere of public sector activity by not reporting data on expenditures by state-owned or state-managed enterprises that have even a partially commercial purpose; and (3) it does not capture the *regulatory* presence of the state. Other data on the size of the state are less comprehensive and less systematically collected.

[13] The closest proxy might be the Corruption Perception Index compiled by Transparency International, which measures the degree to which corruption is perceived to exist among public officials. However, the CPI is based on surveys that rely principally on the viewpoints of experts and the business community rather than of the general public. (See Transparency International, "Background Information to the CPI" <http://www.transparency.de/documents/cpi/2000/qanda.html>.)

[14] For Nigeria, see Richard A. Joseph, *Democracy and Prebendal Politics in Nigeria* (Cambridge: Cambridge University Press, 1987); for Zambia, see Daniel Posner, "The Institutional Origins of Ethnic Politics in Zambia" (Ph.D. dissertation, Harvard University, 1998); for Senegal, see Frederic Schaffer, *Democracy in Translation* (Ithaca: Cornell University Press, 1998).

apparatuses inherited from communist rule, and in some postindustrial states.[15] Finally, some large American cities have historically approximated the conditions for patronage-democracy during some periods, even when the United States as a whole might not qualify for such a classification.[16]

II. Background

Although political parties are among the central disciplinary preoccupations of political scientists, we have not so far identified the *ethnic* political party as a distinct phenomenon, or treated the question of ethnic party performance as a puzzle deserving theoretical attention. Instead, a voluminous literature addresses the rise of ethnic parties as part of the broader puzzle of ethnic "identification," a term used interchangeably with ethnic "participation," ethnic "mobilization," ethnic "collective action," ethnic "conflict," ethnic "competition," and ethnic "group formation."

Theories of ethnic "identification" and its purported synonyms fall into two broad families, distinguished by the assumptions that each makes about individual motivations. Materialist approaches, exemplified by the work of Robert Bates, Michael Hechter, Albert Breton, and Alvin Rabushka and Kenneth Shepsle, assume that individuals are motivated primarily by a desire for the material "benefits of modernity," such as land, jobs, and markets.[17] Donald Horowitz's influential study *Ethnic Groups in Conflict*

---

[15] Simona Piattoni, ed., *Clientelism, Interests and Democratic Representation* (Cambridge: Cambridge University Press, 2001).

[16] See, for instance, William Riordon, *Plunkitt of Tammany Hall* (Boston: Bedford Books, 1994), and Raymond Wolfinger, *The Politics of Progress* (Englewood Cliffs, NJ: Prentice Hall, 1974).

[17] Robert Bates, "Ethnic Competition and Modernization in Contemporary Africa," *Comparative Political Studies*, Vol. 6, No. 4 (1974): 457–483; Albert Breton, "The Economics of Nationalism," *Journal of Political Economy*, Vol. 72, No. 4 (1964): 376–386; Michael Hechter, "Group Formation and the Cultural Division of Labor," *American Journal of Sociology*, Vol. 84, No. 2 (1978): 293–318; Michael Hechter, "The Political Economy of Ethnic Change," *American Journal of Sociology*, Vol. 79, No. 5 (1974): 1151–1178; Michael Hechter, *Internal Colonialism* (Berkeley: University of California Press, 1975). Nonmaterial benefits, when acknowledged in this family of work, are treated as derivative from material benefits. Russell Hardin, *One for All: The Logic of Group Conflict* (Princeton, NJ: Princeton University Press, 1995) might arguably also be included among materialist approaches to ethnic mobilization. Hardin describes economic malaise, combined with a state that controls the allocation of scarce resources, as the single most important

presents an alternative, social-psychological theory of ethnic conflict.[18] Drawing upon social identity theory as developed by Henri Tajfel, Horowitz argues that individuals are motivated instead by a desire for greater self-esteem.[19] But despite their distinct assumptions about individual motivations and the distinct variables that they privilege in their analyses, both of these theoretical families assume, explicitly or implicitly, that the success of ethnic parties is a natural by-product of the process by which ethnic identities become politically salient.[20] As Horowitz puts it, political entrepreneurs who float ethnic parties in ethnically divided societies find "a ready-made clientele . . . waiting to be led."[21]

But ethnic parties often fail to attract the support of their target ethnic categories across space and time, even when the ethnic identities they seek to mobilize are politically salient. Consider the following examples:

- Although the pro-Yoruba Action Group in Nigeria was successful in obtaining majority support among Yorubas in the Western Region in 1960, it failed to win the support of Yorubas in Ibadan, Ilesha, and Oyo. And its vote share was cut in half four years later.[22] Yet Nigeria is among the textbook examples of ethnically divided polities, and divisions between the Yorubas, the Hausa-Fulanis and the Igbos were salient during this period.[23]

---

reason for ethnic conflict (228, 152, 179). While he also allows for individuals to be motivated by a desire for intangible benefits such as the "epistemological comforts of home," these intangible benefits are less important in Hardin's discussion than material interests.

[18] Horowitz, *Ethnic Groups in Conflict.*

[19] Horowitz also identifies "a sense of belonging" as a second desired psychic good. This good, however, is secondary to his analysis of ethnic group behaviour.

[20] See, for instance, the discussion of tribally dominated parties in Bates, "Ethnic Competition," 474. Hechter makes the same assumption in his *Internal Colonialism* (1975). In his later work, he recognizes the failure of the general theory of internal colonialism to account for variations in the patterns of support for the Scottish National Party in Scotland and revisits specifically the question of ethnic *party performance* in Margaret Levi and Michael Hechter, "A Rational Choice Approach to the Rise and Decline of Ethnoregional Parties," in Edward A. Tiryakian and Ronald Rogowski, eds., *New Nationalisms of the Developed West* (Boston: Allen and Unwin, 1985), 128–146.

[21] Horowitz, *Ethnic Groups in Conflict,* 308.

[22] John P. Mackintosh, *Nigerian Government and Politics* (London: George Allen and Unwin, 1966), 430, 514.

[23] See, for instance, Laitin, *Hegemony and Culture.*

- The pro-Buganda Kabaka Yekka (KY) obtained the support of the majority of the Ganda in Uganda in 1962, but lost influence quickly thereafter,
despite the salience of Ganda nationalism at the time.[24]
- The ethnoregional Scottish National Party (SNP) obtained the support
of only 20 percent of Scots in the 1992 and 1997 general elections in
Britain, with the rest voting for the Labour and Conservative parties.[25]
Yet in surveys conducted during these elections, over 60 percent of
Scots reported their "national identity" as more Scottish than British
or Scottish rather than British.[26]
- In Sri Lanka, close to 50 percent of Tamils did not vote for the two
principal Tamil parties, the Federal Party and the Tamil Congress, in the
1960s and 1970s.[27] Yet the Tamil-Sinhala cleavage dominated postcolonial politics.[28]
- In the 1994 and 1999 elections, the pro-Zulu Inkatha Freedom Party
(IFP) in South Africa obtained the support of a majority of Zulus in the
province of Kwazulu-Natal but not in the provinces of Gauteng and
Mpumalanga. And even in Natal, a substantial percentage of Zulus did
not support the IFP.[29] Yet a Zulu political identity has been among the
most salient political identities in post-independence South Africa.

[24] Nelson Kasfir, *The Shrinking Political Arena* (Berkeley: University of California Press, 1976), 124–126; Crawford Young, *The Politics of Cultural Pluralism* (Madison: University of Wisconsin Press, 1976), 254.

[25] James L. Newell "The Scottish National Party: Development and Change," in Lieven de Winter and Huri Tursan, eds., *Regionalist Parties in Western Europe* (London: Routledge, 1998); 105–124, p. 108 for 1945–1997. For 2001, BBC results as published at <news.bbc.co.uk/hi/english/static/vote2001>. For a discussion of the performance of the SNP, see Saul Newman, *Ethnoregional Conflict in Democracies* (Westport, CT: Greeenwood Press, 1996), 160–162, 166–169.

[26] Scottish national election studies 1992 and 1997, cited in Bonnie Meguid, "Understanding Policy Failure: The Overlooked Role of Ethnic Credibility in Party Strategic Success." Paper presented at the annual meeting of the American Political Science Association, Washington, D.C., September 2000.

[27] Estimated from election results for the Federal Party and the Tamil Congress between 1947 and 1977, as reported in A. Jeyaratnam Wilson, *Politics in Sri Lanka 1947–79* (London: Macmillan, 1979), 156–60, and the percentage of Tamils in Sri Lanka as reported by the 1971 census. See also Robert Kearney, *The Politics of Ceylon (Sri Lanka)* (Ithaca, NY: Cornell University Press, 1973), 118–119.

[28] Stanley Tambiah, *Sri Lanka: Ethnic Fratricide and the Dismantling of Democracy* (Chicago: University of Chicago Press, 1986).

[29] Estimated from election results published by the Independent Electoral Commission of South Africa at <http://www.elections.org.za/> and census data from *South African Statistics 1995* (Pretoria: Central Statistical Service, 1997). For a general discussion of Zulu support for the IFP, see Andrew Reynolds, ed., *Election '94 South Africa* (New York: St. Martin's

To the extent that general theories of ethnic identification cannot explain the *failure* of ethnic parties to obtain the support of their target ethnic categories across space and time, they cannot fully explain their success.

This book starts from the premise that in order to explain ethnic party performance, it is necessary first to detach the process of giving and seeking votes from the umbrella concept of ethnic "identification" and other interchangeably used terms. Such umbrella concepts group disparate types of ethnically motivated activity – including voting, protest, riots, war, and genocide – in the same analytical category. An explanatory strategy that disaggregates these concepts into their component parts allows us to investigate the specific variables and processes that explain each phenomenon. Separate models of voting, protest, riots, war, and genocide may well illuminate similarities in the processes that lead individuals to participate in them. Such similarities, however, should be demonstrated rather than assumed to exist.

III. Theory

Accordingly, this book develops a theory explaining when and why voters and elites in patronage-democracies privilege ethnic identities in their vote-giving and vote-seeking strategies. Synthesizing insights from both the materialist and social-psychological approaches, I assume that individual voters and elites in patronage-democracies are motivated by a desire for either material or psychic goods or some combination of the two. Regardless of the type of good they seek, however, I take them to be instrumental actors who invest in an identity because it offers them the best available means by which to obtain desired benefits, and not because such identification is valuable in itself. In this regard, the argument belongs to the family of "thin" rational choice explanations that abandon the narrow assumption that individuals are economically motivated but retain the assumption that individuals are instrumentally rational actors who pursue their objectives, however defined, by selecting those means that maximize their chance of obtaining them.[30]

In a patronage-democracy, the state is the principal means of obtaining both a better livelihood and higher status. For upwardly mobile "elites," by which I mean "modernizing individuals" – urbanized, educated, and

Press, 1994), and Andrew Reynolds, ed., *Election '99 South Africa* (New York: St. Martin's Press, 1999).

[30] Jon Elster, ed., *Rational Choice* (Oxford: Blackwell, 1986).

economically better off than the rest of the population – state employment or political office promises the best prospect of material advancement. And because individuals who control the state are in a position of power over the lives of others, it also brings with it higher status. For individuals who do not have the means to launch a bid for political office, proximity to those who seek state office becomes the principal source of both material and psychic benefits. Ties to a political patron increase a voter's chances of obtaining valued state resources and services. At the same time, they allow her the chance to bask in the reflected status of the patron. Patronage-democracies, therefore, produce an overwhelming preoccupation with politics on the part of both elites and voters seeking both material and psychic goods.

How do individual, benefit-seeking voters in patronage-democracies choose between competing elites vying for their vote? And how do individual, office-seeking elites decide whose votes to seek? The voting decision in a patronage-democracy is characterized by severe information constraints. These information constraints, I argue, force voters and politicians to favour co-ethnics in the delivery of benefits and votes. The result, described in Figure 1.1, is a self-enforcing and reinforcing equilibrium of ethnic favouritism. The remainder of the argument connects these individual microfoundations to a hypothesis explaining and predicting ethnic party performance in patronage-democracies. The logic underlying this hypothesis is as follows:

If a benefit-seeking voter expects to obtain the greatest material and psychic satisfaction from individual elites from her "own" ethnic group who occupy elected office, *she should be indifferent to the type of party that puts such elites in office.* As long as a political party installs co-ethnics in positions of power, the voter can expect to obtain access to both types of benefits, regardless of the platform of the party to which these elites belong. The most credible signal of whom a party expects to install in state office if it wins the election is, in turn, not *what it says* but *who it is.* Elites from those ethnic categories who are best represented in positions of power and prestige in the

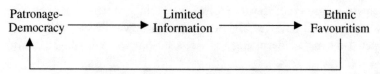

Figure 1.1. Equilibrium of ethnic favouritism.

party organization and previous governments are also most likely to capture the plum positions of state if the party comes to power. Elites from those ethnic categories who are in subordinate positions in the party organization and previous governments are least likely to capture state office if the party captures power. Faced with a choice between parties, therefore, an individual voter in a patronage-democracy should formulate preferences across parties by counting heads, preferring the party that represents elites from her "own" ethnic category to the greatest degree, regardless of whether it defines itself as an ethnic, multiethnic, or nonethnic party.

For an instrumental, benefit-seeking voter, however, preferences should not automatically translate into votes. A party that wins control of the government – or, at a minimum, obtains influence over the victory or defeat of its opponents – can distribute to its supporters both material benefits and the status benefits that come from establishing superiority in the political arena. A party without control of government and without influence over someone else's victory or loss, however, cannot distribute either material benefits or the status benefits that come from the acquisition of political power. The voter, therefore, should vote for her preferred party only if it has a reasonable chance of obtaining control or influence after the election and not otherwise. In other words, we should expect instrumental voters to also be strategic voters.

If voters formulate preferences across parties by counting the heads of co-ethnics across parties, then it follows that they can form a reasonable expectation about the likely electoral outcome by counting the heads of members of their own category and others in the electorate. This head count would allow voters to guess the numerical strength of others with the same preferences. If voters from their ethnic category are numerous enough to take their preferred party past the threshold of winning or influence, they will have a reasonable expectation that they can place the party in control of the state apparatus through coordinated action. However, if voters from their ethnic category are too few to take their preferred party past the threshold of winning or influence, they will have a reasonable expectation that even coordinated action on the part of all co-ethnics will not catapult their preferred party into state office. As a consequence, they should not vote for this party even if they prefer it to the others.

Based on the propositions just summarized, a preliminary version of the main hypothesis proposed by this book can now be stated: An ethnic party is likely to succeed in a patronage-democracy when it provides elites from across the "subdivisions" included in its target ethnic category or categories with greater opportunities for ascent within its party organization than the competition, and when voters from its target ethnic category or categories are numerous enough to take the party to a winning or influential position.

The optimal size of an ethnic category necessary to take a party past the threshold of winning and influence varies with the design of the government, party, and electoral systems, taken together. In general, proportional (PR) electoral systems with several parties and a coalition government allow small ethnic groups a greater degree of efficacy than first-past-the-post (FPTP) systems with two parties and a majoritarian form of government, which favour larger groups. As the number of parties in an FPTP system increases, other things being equal, however, the threshold of winning is reduced, increasing the efficacy of small groups. It follows that ethnic parties that seek the support of large ethnic categories, other things equal, are more likely to be successful across institutional contexts, while ethnic parties mobilizing small groups, other things equal, are less likely to succeed in pure FPTP systems with two parties and a majoritarian government, and more likely to succeed in FPTP systems with several parties or in PR systems with several parties and a coalition government.

I describe this hypothesis as "preliminary" because it raises a second, more fundamental question: What determines the ability of any political party to incorporate upwardly mobile elites seeking political office? Does an ethnic party not have a natural advantage in the representation of elites from across the spectrum of subdivisions in its target ethnic category?

The answer, I argue, is no. Just as benefit-seeking voters in a patronage-democracy are indifferent to the type of party that gives them access to benefits, office-seeking elites are indifferent to the type of party that offers them access to office. The incorporation of new elites, however, is a deeply intractable problem for any political party – ethnic, nonethnic, or multiethnic. The allotment of party posts to new elites usually means the displacement of their previous occupants. As a result, political parties seeking to induct new elites are faced with a collective action problem: Those already entrenched within the party apparatus are likely to support the idea of elite incorporation into the party as a whole but to resist the incorporation of such elites into their own party units. The ability of any political party to solve this collective action problem depends, I argue, on a combination of its probability of winning and its organizational structure. Given an equal probability of winning, parties with competitive rules for intraparty advancement are more successful at elite incorporation than parties with centralized rules for intraparty advancement, regardless of whether they are ethnic, nonethnic, or multiethnic.

The central hypothesis of this book can now be restated in final form: Ethnic parties are most likely to succeed in patronage-democracies when they have competitive rules for intraparty advancement and the ethnic group they seek to mobilize is larger than the threshold of winning or leverage imposed by the electoral system. The adoption of centralized rules for intraparty advancement, and/or a negative difference between the size of the target ethnic constituency and the threshold of winning or influence, increase the likelihood of failure.

To the extent that it depends upon the conjunction of organizational, demographic, and institutional variables, the success of an ethnic party is far from a foregone conclusion. Given the challenge of creating and maintaining a competitive intraparty organization, a favourable system of ethnic categorization, and a stable competitive configuration, creating and maintaining successful ethnic parties may, in fact, be an unusually difficult task.

IV. Method

Although I have just presented the theory in abstract terms, it was not developed in abstract fashion. Rather, it was built by conducting a comparative ethnography of the processes by which a single ethnic party went about building support across Indian states and theorizing about the mechanisms that made it successful in some states and unsuccessful in others. The mechanisms identified through ethnographic analysis were then tested against new sources of data from within the sample of Indian states, generated using new methods, including survey research, content analysis, and the ecological inference method developed by Gary King.[31]

The ethnic party that I focus on is the Bahujan Samaj Party (BSP) during the years 1984–98. The BSP takes its name from the word *Bahujan*, meaning "majority of the people." The BSP's long-term goal during this period was the political consolidation of caste and religious minorities in India, who collectively constitute a majority of the population, in opposition to

[31] Gary King, *A Solution to the Ecological Inference Problem* (Princeton, NJ: Princeton University Press, 1997).

the Hindu upper castes. Its immediate target constituency, however, were India's "Scheduled Castes" (SCs). The Scheduled Castes are over 400 castes that have historically been treated as "untouchable" by Hindu society. The term "Scheduled" refers to the government schedule in which they were originally listed as being eligible for affirmative action benefits. I restrict the analysis to the years 1984–98 since this is the period during which the BSP approximated most closely the definition of an ethnic party laid out earlier. Since 1998, the party has begun to eliminate the line of exclusion between the *Bahujan* and the Hindu upper castes, thus transforming itself from an ethnic to a multiethnic party.[32]

This close focus on the within-country variation in the performance of a single ethnic party is a valuable method for theory construction, which is the principal analytical burden of this book. Ethnographic analysis, by illuminating the processes by which an ethnic party courts and obtains voter support, makes it possible to identify the variables associated with success or failure and to model the mechanisms by which they produce one outcome rather than another. At the same time, combining ethnography with controlled comparison is more likely than an ethnographic study of a single case to produce a generalizable argument. Tracing a process in a single case may reveal several variables and mechanisms to be plausibly linked with the outcome of interest, some only coincidentally. Multiple ethnographies conducted across sites that are otherwise similar, by revealing which variables and mechanisms recur systematically across observations, are more likely to isolate key variables and mechanisms.

Three objections might be raised to the attempt to build a generalizable argument about ethnic parties from a study of the BSP. First, to the extent that the term "Scheduled Caste" originated as a government label, one might argue that it does not describe a "natural" ethnic category. But we know now from an extensive literature on historical institutionalist approaches to ethnic identities that the origin of many ethnic categories that appear to be "natural" lies in official classifications imposed by the state. In its official origins, then, the Scheduled Caste category is typical rather than exceptional, resembling "Hindus" in India, the "Yoruba" in Nigeria, the "Yao" in Malawi, the "Bemba" in Zambia, and "Hispanics" and "African

---

[32] I discuss this transformation in Kanchan Chandra, "Post-Congress Politics in Uttar Pradesh: The Ethnification of the Party System and its Consequences," in Paul Wallace and Ramashray Roy, eds., *Indian Politics and the 1998 Election* (New Delhi: Sage Publications 1999), 55–104.

Americans" in the United States.[33] Indeed, if we confer the label of an ethnic group only on "natural" categories, we may well be left with no ethnic categories at all.

According to a second objection, the BSP is better described as a multiethnic rather than an ethnic party on the grounds that it brings together several *individual* castes within the category Scheduled Caste, such as Chamars, Holeyas, and Balimikis. But, as I noted earlier, all ethnic categories have an essentially dual nature, existing simultaneously as single and composite categories. In this respect too, the Scheduled Castes are typical rather than exceptional. Indeed, the individual "subcategories" that make up the category "Scheduled Caste" do not escape this duality. As I will point out in Chapters 7 and 8, they can themselves be subdivided into further component units at the same time that they exist as "single" categories.

According to a third objection, "ranked" social systems such as caste, in which ethnicity and class coincide, are qualitatively different from unranked social systems and have different implications for political behaviour.[34] This may restrict the applicability of an argument developed from the study of a caste-based party to parties mobilizing other ethnic categories. It may well be the case that "ranked" societies are qualitatively different and deserve to be analyzed separately. Nevertheless, they are common. Examples of sets of ethnic categories with ranked relationships to each other might include Hutus and Tutsis in Rwanda and Burundi, earlier and later immigrants in American cities,[35] and Englishmen and others in the Celtic periphery.[36] An argument applicable only to ranked ethnic groups, therefore, should in principle apply to a significant family of cases.

---

[33] Bernard Cohn, *An Anthropologist among the Historians and Other Essays* (Delhi: Oxford University Press, 1987); Leroy Vail, ed., *The Creation of Tribalism in Southern Africa* (Berkeley: University of California Press, 1989); Melissa Nobles, *Shades of Citizenship* (Stanford: Stanford University Press, 2000); Daniel Posner, "The Institutional Origins of Ethnic Politics in Zambia," Ph.D. dissertation, Harvard University, 1998; Richard Fox, *Lions of the Punjab* (Berkeley: University of California Press, 1985); David Laitin, *Hegemony and Culture* (Chicago: University of Chicago Press, 1986); Gyanendra Pandey, "Which of Us Are Hindus?," in Gyanendra Pandey, ed., *Hindus and Others* (New Delhi: Viking, 1993), 238–272.

[34] Horowitz, *Ethnic Groups in Conflict*, 26.

[35] See, for instance, Ulf Hannerz, "Ethnicity and Opportunity in Urban America," in Abner Cohen, ed., *Urban Ethnicity* (London: Tavistock, 1974), 37–76.

[36] Michael Hechter, *Internal Colonialism* (Berkeley: University of California Press, 1975).

But the distinction between ranked and unranked social systems may be better seen as one of degree rather than type. Most modern societies, as one study of ethnic politics points out, are characterized by "asymmetrical, nonrandom, self-reproducing correlations between ethnic categories on the one hand and socioeconomic classes and political power on the other hand, that is, by structured inter-ethnic inequalities."[37] It might be more illuminating, then, to think of ranked and unranked systems as end points on a scale that orders ethnic groups according to the size of the correlation between class and ethnicity rather than as dichotomous categories. Scheduled Castes in India are likely to lie toward one extreme on this scale. But a study of such extreme cases may be useful in revealing, in bold relief, patterns that are muted in cases that lie closer to the centre.

Ultimately, the question of whether a hypothesis developed from the study of the BSP is more generally applicable can only be answered empirically. In this book, I apply this hypothesis to explaining the performance of three ethnic parties in India: the Hindu nationalist Bharatiya Janata Party (BJP) among Hindus across Indian states in 1991; the Dravida Munnetra Kazagham (DMK), a linguistic party, among Tamil speakers in Tamil Nadu in 1967; and the pro-Jharkhandi Jharkhand Mukti Morcha (JMM), a regionalist party, among "Jharkhandis" in 2000. These cases were chosen to maximize variation in time and space, the type of category (caste, religion, language, region, and tribe) targeted by the ethnic party, and the relative size of the ethnic category (majority and minority) that each party tried to mobilize. The studies of the BJP, DMK, and JMM indicate that the hypothesis developed from the study of a caste-based party can be useful in illuminating the variation in the performance of other types of ethnic parties in India. But a systematic attempt to evaluate and refine the hypothesis using new data from other ethnic parties in India and other patronage-democracies remains to be undertaken.

V. Data

The Scheduled Castes constitute 16.5 percent of the Indian population[38] and are found in varying proportions in almost all Indian states, with the

---

[37] Joseph Rothschild, *Ethnopolitics: A Conceptual Framework* (New York: Columbia University Press, 1981), 1–2.
[38] *Census of India 1991.*

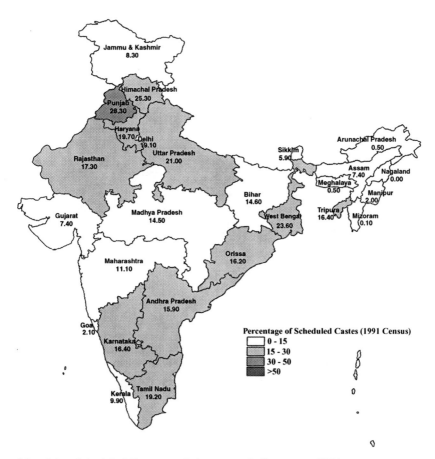

Map 1.1.   Scheduled Caste population across Indian states, 1991.

exception of the northeast.[39] Map 1.1 describes the percentage of the population made up by Scheduled Castes in each state, based on 1991 census figures.

In most states, the BSP is the principal party that stands explicitly and primarily for the cause of the Scheduled Castes against the Hindu upper castes.[40] The government is the principal provider of goods and services

[39] The five states where the population of Scheduled Castes is negligible are Goa (2.1%) in the West and Arunachal Pradesh (.5%), Manipur (2%), Meghalaya (.5%), Mizoram (.1%) and Nagaland (0%), all in the Northeast.

[40] Two exceptions are Tamil Nadu and Maharashtra, both of which have significant parties that target Scheduled Castes specifically.

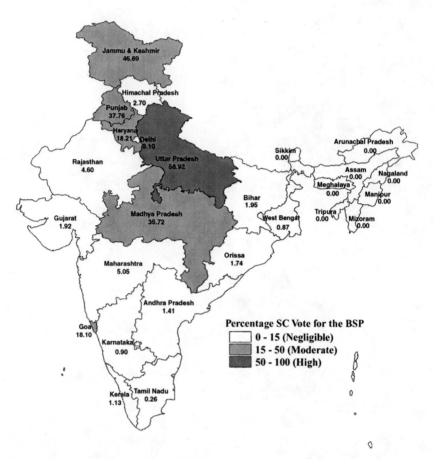

Map 1.2. Variation in Scheduled Caste vote for the BSP across Indian states, 1984–98 parliamentary elections.

in each state. The first-past-the-post electoral system is replicated in every Indian state. The majority of electoral constituencies in India are ethnically heterogeneous, and Scheduled Castes are found in a majority of constituencies. The BSP employs the same method to mobilize Scheduled Castes in each state. Yet, as Map 1.2 shows, the BSP has not obtained uniform support from the Scheduled Castes across Indian states (See Appendix F the data on which the map is based). A majority of Scheduled Castes massed behind the BSP in one state: Uttar Pradesh, in which 59 percent of Scheduled Castes, on average, voted for the BSP across five parliamentary elections.

Based on its support among Scheduled Castes, the party became a partner in coalition governments in Uttar Pradesh three times between 1984
and 1998. In a second class of states, the BSP has moderate levels of support among Scheduled Castes, ranging from 47 percent in Jammu and
Kashmir to 18 percent in the state of Haryana.[41] Finally, in the third and
largest class of states, the BSP has repeatedly drawn a blank across five
elections.

Why does the same party, employing the same strategy, operating in
states with identical institutional contexts, meet with such tremendous variation in outcomes? I examine the particular processes that led the BSP
to succeed or fail in otherwise similar environments in a sample of three
Indian states, selected according to the degree of success obtained by the
BSP among Scheduled Castes: Uttar Pradesh, in which the BSP obtained
majority support among Scheduled Castes; Punjab, in which it obtained
moderate levels of support; and Karnataka, in which it obtained negligible levels of support. Uttar Pradesh (UP), situated in northern India, is
the most populous of India's states. With a population of 139 million, it
is almost as large in population as the Russian Federation; if it were a
country by itself, it would be the seventh-largest country in the world.[42]
Punjab, situated in northwestern India, shares a border with Pakistan. With
a population of twenty million, it is one of India's smaller states, but its
population equals that of many large countries, including Ghana, Uganda
and Australia. Karnataka, situated in south India, has a population of almost
45 million. Of medium size among Indian states, it exceeds the population
of such major countries as Canada and South Africa. The criteria for case
selection are discussed further in Chapter 7.

I found that in each state, operating under the constraints of India's
patronage-democracy, Scheduled Caste voters and others believed that their
"own" man was most likely to favour them in the business of obtaining office
or distributing benefits. Given their trust in co-ethnics, therefore, Scheduled Caste voters preferred the BSP only when it gave greater representational opportunities to elites from their subdivision among the Scheduled
Castes in its party organization and government than the competition, and
not otherwise. And even when they preferred the BSP, Scheduled Caste

---

[41] The estimate for Jammu and Kashmir is based on four elections, since the 1991 parliamentary elections were not held in this state.
[42] World Bank, *World Development Indicators 1998* (Washington, DC: World Bank, 1998).

voters acted strategically, voting for the party only when it was in a winning or influential position, and not otherwise.

The variation in the performance of the BSP across the three states under study can be explained, therefore, either as the consequence of variation in the relative representational opportunities offered by the BSP and its competition to Scheduled Caste elites, or variation in the ability of Scheduled Caste voters to take the BSP past the threshold of winning or leverage through coordinated action, or by a combination of the two conditions.

- In Uttar Pradesh, the BSP gave greater representation to Scheduled Caste elites, especially those from the "Chamar" category, than the competition, and, through a series of electoral alliances in Uttar Pradesh's multiparty system, presented itself as a viable contender for control of, or influence in, coalition governments. Chamars constitute a majority among the Scheduled Castes in Uttar Pradesh. Consequently, a majority of Scheduled Castes massed behind the BSP in this state.
- In Punjab, Chamar voters, whose elites were best represented in the BSP organization, constitute a minority of Scheduled Castes in the state. Further, although the numerical strength of Chamar voters gave them leverage in some constituencies, the BSP's failure to negotiate electoral alliances made it difficult for the party to obtain a winning position. The combination of the limited representation given to non-Chamar elites in the BSP and the limited efficacy of Chamar voters resulted in only moderate success for the BSP among Scheduled Caste voters in Punjab.
- In Karnataka, the desire of Scheduled Caste voters to install co-ethnics in power had already been satisfied by the high degree of representation given to Scheduled Caste elites by other political parties. Consequently, Scheduled Caste voters had no incentive to vote for the BSP.

This argument constitutes a more compelling explanation for the variation in the performance of the BSP among Scheduled Castes than other, simpler arguments that attribute it to variation in organizational investment; linguistic and regional differences; differences in the degree of fragmentation of the Scheduled Caste category; differences in the composition of the Scheduled Caste category; and differences in the level of grievance of Scheduled Castes. These alternative explanations are discussed in Chapter 7.

Introduction

What explains, in turn, the differential incorporation of Scheduled Caste elites across different parties and across different states? In each state, the BSP's principal competition was the Congress party. Why did Congress incorporate Scheduled Caste elites in some states but not others? And why did the BSP, a party that specifically targeted Scheduled Caste voters, not provide representation to the entire spectrum of Scheduled Caste elites? The key variable determining whether or not either political party was able to give Scheduled Castes representation, I found, depended upon the design of the internal party organization combined with its control of government.

The argument is supported by comparative studies of the BJP, the DMK, and the JMM. Although the BJP openly championed the cause of India's Hindu majority in 1991, it obtained the support of only one-fourth of India's Hindus in that election. There was, furthermore, significant variation in the degree of support for the BJP among Hindus across Indian states. Maps 1.3 and 1.4 summarize the population of Hindus across Indian states and the variation in the degree of support obtained by the BJP among Hindus. The DMK openly championed the interests of Tamil speakers in the state of Tamil Nadu in 1967. It obtained the support of a near-majority of Tamils in that election. Significantly, however, a large percentage of Tamil speakers in Tamil Nadu, especially in the southern part of the state, did not vote for the DMK. Maps 1.5 and 1.6 summarize the population of Tamils across Tamil Nadu and the variation in the degree of support obtained by the DMK among Tamils across districts in Tamil Nadu in 1967. The JMM, finally, is a regionalist party that has, since its founding in 1972, called for the carving out of a separate state of Jharkhand from the districts of the Indian state of Bihar (and adjoining states). Yet even at the peak of its electoral performance, in the 2000 legislative assembly elections in Bihar, the party obtained the support of less than one-fifth of the Jharkhandis, concentrated mostly in the eastern belt of Jharkhand. Map 1.7 summarizes the percentage of support obtained by the JMM in the region of Jharkhand in these elections.

In each case, the relative opportunities for representation given to elites from across the spectrum of the target ethnic groups, combined with the expectations of the efficacy of the voters whose elites found representation, prove to be a more plausible explanation for the performance of these parties than the alternatives. Further, these cases show in even sharper relief the importance of the internal rules of intraparty advancement in creating these representational opportunities. The DMK, with a competitive organizational structure, was able to represent a broad spectrum of elites and

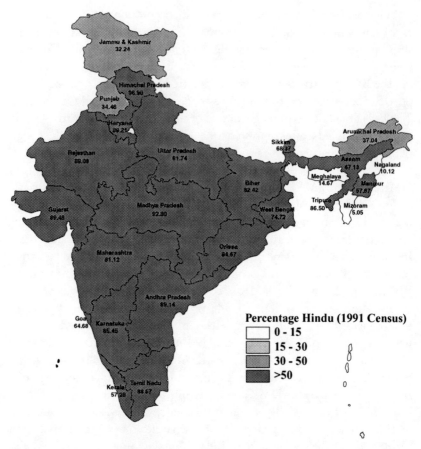

Map 1.3. Hindu population across Indian states, 1991.

so capture the vote of the largest percentage of its target ethnic category. The BJP, with a "semicompetitive" structure, made significant but limited progress in the race for elite incorporation. But the JMM, with the weakest and most centralized organizational structure of the three parties, was not able to broaden its ethnic profile beyond its founder elites.

VI. Sources

For information on elite motivations, I rely upon over 200 interviews conducted between 1996 and 1998 with leaders and workers of the BSP and its competition, conducted principally in the three states of Uttar Pradesh,

24

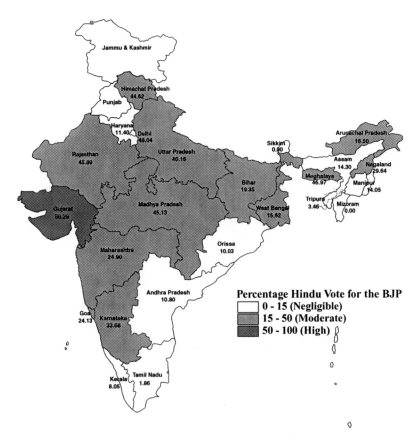

Map 1.4. Variation in Hindu vote for the BJP across Indian states, 1991 parliamentary elections. *Note*: No estimates for Punjab and Jammu & Kashmir.

Karnataka, and Punjab, and less intensively in the states of Delhi, Madhya Pradesh, Gujarat, West Bengal, Bihar, Andhra Pradesh, Maharashtra, and Rajasthan (described in Appendix A). I combine information gleaned from these interviews with an ethnographic study of four election campaigns stretching from 1996 to 1998 in twenty constituencies (described in Appendix B) and a content analysis of party pronouncements as recorded in newspaper sources and in tape recordings of party rallies that I attended (described in Appendix C).

For information on voter motivations and behaviour, I draw upon two principal sources in addition to the ethnographic data. First, I rely upon

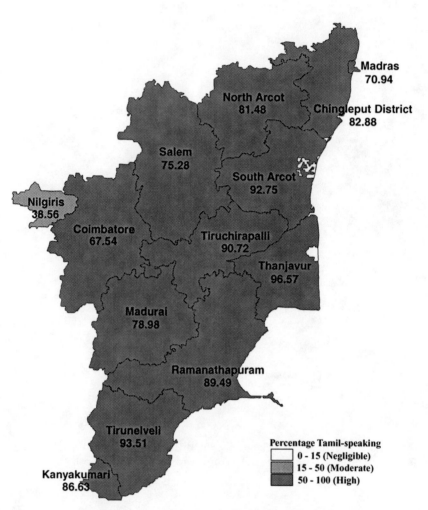

Map 1.5. Tamil-speaking population across Tamil Nadu districts, 1961.

election surveys conducted between 1996 and 1998 by the National Election Studies Project at the Centre for the Study of Developing Societies (described in Appendix D). These surveys represent the first large-scale effort to study the Indian electorate since 1971, and, as such, are a new and invaluable source of information on voting behaviour in India. Second, I undertake a quantitative analysis of a data set combining electoral and demographic variables for the 425 state assembly constituencies in Uttar Pradesh, drawing upon both census data and the election results published

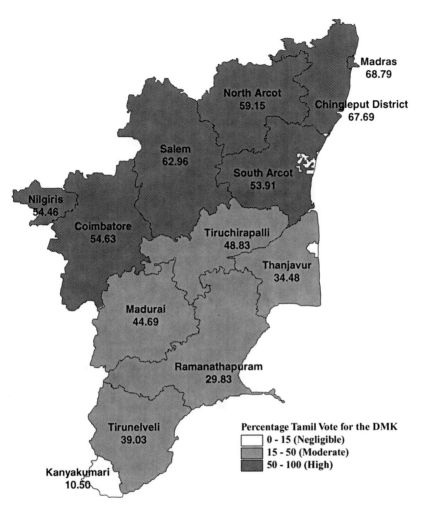

Map 1.6. Variation in Tamil vote for the DMK across districts in Tamil Nadu, 1967 legislative assembly elections.

by the Election Commission of India. In order to identify patterns of individual voting behaviour from aggregate-level data, I utilize King's ecological inference method (EI). The EI method opens up significant possibilities for research on ethnic voting, which I discuss in Appendix E.

I also draw on a variety of documentary sources, including (1) miscellaneous official data obtained from various government departments at the state level and from the National Commission for Scheduled Castes

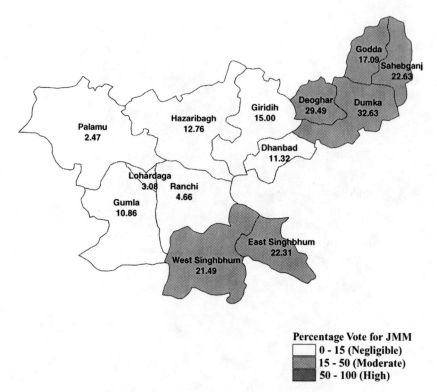

Map 1.7. Variation in vote for the JMM across districts in Jharkhand, 2000 legislative assembly elections.

and Scheduled Tribes in New Delhi; (2) official literature of the Bahujan Samaj Party, including back issues of the party magazine, *Oppressed Indian* (English), and its newspaper, *Bahujan Sanghatak* (Hindi); (3) official literature of other political parties; and (4) clippings obtained from the following newspapers: *The Times of India* (Delhi), *Hindustan Times* (Delhi), *Indian Express* (Delhi), *The Hindu* (Delhi), *Pioneer* (Lucknow/Delhi), *Tribune* (Chandigarh), *Ajit* (Jullundur), and *Deccan Herald* (Karnataka).

Finally, in addition to these primary sources, I rely on the well-developed body of secondary literature on Indian politics. Political parties in general, and ethnic parties in particular, have been the subject of sustained attention among scholars of Indian politics. The theoretical and empirical richness of this literature provides a particularly strong foundation on which to construct a theory of ethnic party success.

VII. Overview

The book is divided into two parts. Part I, comprised of Chapters 2–5, outlines the theoretical argument. Chapter 2 establishes the link between limited information and the bias toward ethnic categorization. Chapter 3 shows that when a patronage-democracy approximates the conditions of limited information, it is likely to be characterized by pervasive expectations of ethnic favouritism on the part of both voters and elites. Chapter 4 builds upon the propositions introduced in the preceding chapters to develop the hypothesis that an ethnic party is most likely to succeed in a patronage-democracy when it offers greater representational opportunities to elites from its target ethnic category than the competition, and when the size of its target ethnic category is large enough to take it past the threshold of winning or influence. Chapter 5 proposes a model explaining variation in representational opportunities across parties, arguing that, other things being equal, parties with competitive rules for intraparty advancement are more likely to incorporate new elites than parties with centralized rules.

Part II, comprised of Chapters 6–12, applies the argument to explaining the data. Chapter 6 establishes that the Indian political system is a patronage-democracy. This chapter sets the stage for the subsequent exploration of the performance of the BSP among Scheduled Caste elites and voters. Chapter 7 provides a general introduction to the Bahujan Samaj Party, the electoral context in which it operates, alternative explanations for the pattern of variation in its performance, and the states that I focus on in investigating this variation. Chapter 8 shows that a representational blockage for upwardly mobile Scheduled Caste elites existed in the two states of Uttar Pradesh and Punjab, but not in the state of Karnataka. As a consequence, the BSP was able to present itself as a viable option on the electoral market in Uttar Pradesh and Punjab, but not in Karnataka. Chapter 9 shows that Scheduled Caste voters and others formulated preferences across parties not by assessing their comparative issue positions, but by "counting heads" of elites belonging to their "own" ethnic categories across parties. Where the BSP had a monopoly on the representation of Scheduled Caste elites, Scheduled Caste voters were more likely to prefer the BSP than other parties. And even where the BSP had a monopoly on the representation of Scheduled Caste elites, voters from those Scheduled Caste categories whose elites were best represented in the BSP were more likely to prefer the BSP than voters from Scheduled Caste categories whose elites were less well represented. Chapter 10 shows that even when they preferred

the BSP, significant numbers of Scheduled Caste voters were strategic vot-
ers who voted for the BSP only when it was in a winning or influential
position, and not otherwise. Chapter 11 shows that the ability of both the
Congress and the BSP to incorporate Scheduled Caste elites depended,
other things being equal, upon their internal organizational structure.
Chapter 12 applies this hypothesis to explaining the performance of the
Hindu nationalist BJP in 1991, the pro-Tamil DMK in the state of Tamil
Nadu in 1967, and the regionalist JMM in the state of Bihar in 2000.

Chapter 13, the conclusion, draws out the implications of this argument
for democratic stability. This chapter shows, drawing on examples from
post-independence Indian politics, that politicians can transform election
results by reconstructing the categories with which voters identify. Such
heresthetical maneuvers, I argue here, are likely to sustain democracy in
patronage-democracies by introducing uncertainty into the final outcome.

PART I

Theory

2

Limited Information and
Ethnic Categorization

This chapter proposes a connection between limited information and the use of ethnic cues to identify and distinguish between individuals. I argue here that multiple sources of costless data about an individual's ethnic identities are available in most situations, while costless data on an individual's nonethnic identities (e.g., class, profession, income, place of residence, ideological affiliation, educational background) are less frequently available and then typically from fewer sources. Consequently, limited information settings bias observers who are distinguishing between individuals toward schemes of ethnic categorization. Limited information settings, I should emphasize, are *sufficient* to produce a tendency toward ethnic categorization, according to this argument, but not necessary. A similar tendency may also originate from other sources.

The term "limited information" has come to be used loosely to describe the information environment in all situations of political decision making. I use it here in a more precise sense. By a limited information situation, I mean a decision-making situation in which *observers are called upon to identify and distinguish between individuals* under severe information constraints. This chapter develops a logic by which this narrowly defined type of limited information setting should bias observers toward schemes of ethnic categorization. I am not concerned here, however, with settings in which individuals are called upon to make different types of decisions, such as distinguishing between groups, ascertaining the links between policy and outcome, identifying the main points of a party platform, and so on. These different types of limited information settings may well require different types of shortcuts.

Section I reviews the literature on the use of ethnic cues as information shortcuts; section II compares the availability of costless data about an individual's ethnic and nonethnic identities; and section III shows how the abundance of costless data on ethnic identities, combined with the scarcity of costless data on nonethnic identities, biases individuals toward schemes of ethnic categorization in limited information settings of the type just defined.

I. Background

The proposition that many consequential political and economic decisions are made under conditions of limited information is, by now, a familiar one. It has spawned entire fields of research in political science and economics on the use of information shortcuts.[1] The observation that ethnic cues are one among many commonly used types of information shortcuts is also now commonplace. However, this literature is concerned either with establishing that the use of ethnic cues as informational shortcuts is a rational strategy or with investigating the *impact* of the use of such cues. It does not address the cost of ethnic cues relative to the cost of other types of information shortcuts. And it does not identify situations in which one type of cue is more likely to be used than another.

Consider first the abundant literature in economics on the use of ethnic cues. George Akerlof argues, in a classic 1970 article, that employers often use the race of a job applicant as an information shortcut in assessing that applicant's quality. The article's principal concern is to establish that "this

---

[1] See, for instance, Anthony Downs, *An Economic Theory of Democracy* (Cambridge: Cambridge University Press, 1957); George Akerlof, "The Market for 'Lemons': Quality Uncertainty and the Market Mechanism," *Quarterly Journal of Economics*, Vol. 84, No. 3 (1970): 488–500; Anthony Pascal, ed., *Racial Discrimination in Economic Life* (Lexington, MA: Lexington Books, 1972); A. Michael Spence, *Market Signaling: Informational Transfer in Hiring and Related Screening Processes* (Cambridge, MA: Harvard University Press, 1974); George Akerlof, "The Economics of Caste and of the Rat Race and Other Woeful Tales," *Quarterly Journal of Economics*, Vol. 90, No. 4 (1976): 599–617; John Ferejohn and James H. Kuklinski, eds., *Information and Democratic Processes* (Urbana and Chicago: University of Illinois Press, 1990); Samuel Popkin, *The Reasoning Voter* (Chicago: University of Chicago Press, 1991); Bernard Grofman, ed., *Information, Participation and Choice* (Ann Arbor: University of Michigan Press, 1993); Melvin J. Hinich and Michael C. Munger, *Ideology and the Theory of Political Choice* (Ann Arbor: University of Michigan Press, 1994); Arthur Lupia and Matthew D. McCubbins, *The Democratic Dilemma* (Cambridge: Cambridge University Press, 1998); Arthur Lupia, Matthew D. McCubbins, and Samuel Popkin, *Elements of Reason: Cognition, Choice and the Bounds of Rationality* (Cambridge: Cambridge University Press, 2000).

decision may not reflect irrationality or prejudice – but profit maximization. For race may serve as a good *statistic* for the applicant's social background, quality of schooling, and general job capabilities."[2] In subsequent work, Akerlof explores the consequences of the use of caste as a predictor of individual economic behaviour.[3] But both works treat race and other ethnic cues as elements in a broader set of equivalent information shortcuts including age, class, profession, criminal record, organizational membership, friends, possessions, jobs, and so on.

Similarly, Spence's work on market signaling demonstrates that wage differentials can persist between individuals of equivalent productivity when employers attach different subjective probabilities to the productivity of individuals of equivalent education from different racial groups.[4] However, it does not ask why employers choose race as the relevant scheme of categorization rather than the alternatives. The extensive literature on the economics of racial discrimination makes the same omission. It establishes that racial discrimination can persist when employers use race as a relatively costless indicator of productivity.[5] But it assumes that cues other than ethnicity, such as school diplomas, are equally costless, and it does not identify situations under which employers are more likely to privilege one type over another.[6]

The literature on information shortcuts in political science is not much better. The early literature in this field overlooks entirely the use of ethnic cues as information shortcuts. In the pioneering work on the use of information shortcuts in voting behaviour, for instance, Anthony Downs identifies ideology as the voter's principal shortcut: "Ideologies help him focus attention on the differences between parties; therefore they can be used as samples of all the differentiating stands. With this shortcut a voter can save himself the cost of being informed upon a wider range of issues."[7] There is no discussion by Downs of ethnic cues or of any type of information

---

[2] Akerlof, "The Market for 'Lemons'," 494.

[3] Akerlof, "The Economics of Caste," 600.

[4] Spence, *Market Signaling*, 31–37.

[5] Kenneth Arrow, "Some Mathematical Models of Race in the Labor Market," in Pascal, ed., *Racial Discrimination*, 199; John J. McCall, "The Simple Mathematics of Information, Job Discrimination and Prejudice," in Pascal, ed., *Racial Discrimination*, 206.

[6] Kenneth Arrow, "Models of Job Discrimination," in Pascal, ed., *Racial Discrimination*, 83–120, 96.

[7] Downs, *Economic Theory*, 98.

shortcut other than ideology. Hinich and Munger develop Downs's argument further, providing a functional theory of ideology in politics according to which ideologies persist because they transmit useful information to voters about how candidates are likely to act on a range of issues. In their words: "The policy issues on which an elected official must decide are very difficult for voters to predict. Consequently, voters must depend on his ideological position, and his apparent commitment to it, as guides for judgment or comparison."[8] They do not, however, explain why voters in a limited information environment "must" depend on the candidate's ideological position rather than on other traits, including education, ethnic identity, character, reputation, and class.

More recent work identifies a wider range of shortcuts used by voters and explicitly names ethnic cues as one of them. Samuel Popkin is perhaps the strongest advocate of the position that "characteristics such as a candidate's race, ethnicity, religion . . . are important cues."[9] Similarly, Daniel Posner notes that ethnicity in Zambia is useful "because of the information it provides about the expected behaviour of elected officials."[10] However, this later literature is concerned simply with establishing the first-order propositions that voters use ethnic cues, among other types of cues, as information shortcuts and that the use of such cues is rational. The only ones to raise the second-order question of when and why voters use one type of cue rather than another are Lupia and McCubbins. In their words: "To understand why people cast the votes they do, we must understand how they choose among the cues available to them."[11] Ultimately, however, they beg their own question. Voters choose those cues, they argue, that are "better indicators of a candidate's or speaker's knowledge and trust than other available cues."[12] But they tell us little about which types of cues are more likely to convey information about knowledgeability and trustworthiness than others. The sections that follow identify one type of situation in which individuals should privilege ethnic cues over others.

---

[8] Hinich and Munger, *Ideology and the Theory of Political Choice*, 73.
[9] Samuel Popkin, "Information Shortcuts and the Reasoning Voter," in Grofman, ed., *Information, Participation and Choice*, 28.
[10] Daniel Posner, "The Institutional Origins of Ethnic Politics in Zambia" (Ph.D. dissertation, Harvard University, 1998), 125.
[11] Lupia and McCubbins, *Democratic Dilemma*, 208.
[12] Ibid.

II. There Are Typically Multiple Sources of Costless Data about an Individual's Ethnic Identities, while Costless Data about an Individual's Nonethnic Identities Are Scarce

The argument here builds upon Frederik Barth's insight that ethnic groups are characterised not by internal homogeneity, but by the possession of a limited set of "cultural differentiae" which separate insiders from outsiders.[13] These differentiae may be acquired involuntarily at birth (e.g., skin colour) or adopted voluntarily during a lifetime (e.g., language, or a change of name). Regardless of their initial origin, however, these differentiae are passed on to in-group members through descent. While some of these differentiae may be concealed (for instance, many Brahmins wear a sacred thread under their garments), all persons openly display a subset of these differentiae in their names, features, speech, and dress. An individual's nonethnic identities may sometimes also be associated with cultural differentiae. For instance, consumption patterns and tastes can often tell us a great deal about class or income. However, these cultural differentiae are typically displayed less often and less conspicuously.

This open display of ethnic markers means that *some* data about an individual's ethnic identity are costlessly available in any elementary interaction, no matter what the context of observation. Costless data about nonethnic identities, by contrast, are not typically available, and even then not in all contexts. Further, there are typically *multiple* sources of costless data about an individual's ethnic identities, while costless data about nonethnic identities, even when they exist, are likely to be from fewer sources. In order to obtain comparable information about an individual's nonethnic identities, therefore, the observer must pay the cost of conducting a background check. Such a cost entails securing the cooperation of the individual, or paying some third party to obtain and record answers to questions about profession, education, income, family background, place of residence, assets, tastes, organizational memberships, viewpoints, and other similar variables.

This argument is summarized in Table 2.1. The first column lists the different types of identities, often overlapping, that are most relevant in political and economic situations. Data sources such as name, features, speech, and dress are all categorized in the table as "costless," since the

---

[13] Frederik Barth, *Ethnic Groups and Boundaries* (Prospect Heights, IL: Waveland Press: 1969), 15–16.

Table 2.1. *Data sources about ethnic and nonethnic identities*

	Data Sources				
	Costless				Costly
Identity	Name	Features	Speech	Dress	Background Check
Ethnic	√	√	√	?	√
Class	?		?	?	√
Income	?		?	?	√
Profession			?	?	√
Education			√	?	√
Rural-urban			?	?	√
Ideology			?	?	√
Organizational affiliation			?	?	√

observer can obtain access to these data simply by observation, without even enlisting the cooperation of the person being observed. Data sources such as diplomas, résumés, individual records, interviews, biographies, and third-party testimonies are collectively categorized as "costly," since an individual needs to expend some effort in extracting these data. A check mark indicates that the source typically provides data about the identity in question; a question mark indicates that the source *sometimes* provides data about the identity in question; and a blank space indicates that the source does not usually provide data about the identity in question.

Name

Consider, first, the name. The name is typically packed with data about an individual's ethnic memberships. Simply by virtue of the language in which it is expressed, it carries encoded data about the linguistic categories to which a person belongs and does not belong. Because language can often be correlated with race, region, and/or religion, the name may also carry data about membership in these additional categories. For instance, Hindi names are likely to describe a nonwhite person, since Hindi speakers are mostly nonwhite; a north Indian rather than a south Indian, because Hindi is one of the languages spoken in northern rather than southern India; and so on. The surname, because it encodes data about membership in a descent group, also carries data about ethnic memberships. Naming conventions surrounding the last name are typically voluntarily adopted at some point. For instance, the last name "Kaur," which distinguishes Sikh women, originated in a religious movement whose purpose was to draw boundary lines between followers of the Sikh faith and others. Once adopted, however, the name is passed on to future generations at birth and becomes an ascriptive marker describing ethnic identities. First names, because they often celebrate some cultural hero or symbol, carry additional data about ethnic memberships. For instance, the name "Ram" carries the data that its bearer is Hindu, since Ram is a Hindu deity; the name "Gautam" carries the data that its bearer is Buddhist, since Gautama is another name for the Buddha; the name "Ali" carries the data that its bearer is Muslim, since Ali is the name of the grandson of Prophet Mohammad; and the name Peter carries the data that its bearer is Christian, since Peter is the name of one of Christ's disciples.

The name typically does not carry data, however, about nonethnic memberships. Take class as an example. We can infer data on class memberships from the name only when class happens to coincide with ascriptive or ethnic categories. In Britain, for instance, family name can often be a predictor of class. However, no independent data on class are systematically encoded in the name. Similarly, the name does not carry data on income. Prominent exceptions such as "Rockefeller" and "Rothschild" prove the rule. In these exceptional cases, income identity is fused with the ascriptive identity of family. In the more typical case in which income and family do not coincide, we obtain no information about income from the name. The same argument applies to other nonethnic identities. The name usually carries no data about professional identity, educational qualifications, rural or urban background, ideological beliefs, or organizational affiliations.

So far, I have simply stated that the name typically does not carry data about nonethnic identities. Can such data, however, not be acquired? Data on ethnic identities are often encoded in the name as a result of voluntary action initiated by missionaries, political entrepreneurs, or social reformers. Would it not be possible for entrepreneurs with an interest in organizing a population according to nonethnic identities to encourage the adoption of naming conventions that carry information about these nonethnic categories?

Some examples will serve to illustrate why names not only *are* not but *cannot* be bearers of data about nonethnic identities, even if some entrepreneur has an interest in creating such naming conventions. Imagine, for instance, the adoption of a naming convention encoding class identity, defined by an individual's relationship to the mode of production.[14] Once a set of individuals defined by their relationship to the mode of production adopts a distinct naming convention, they will retain these names even when their relationship to the mode of production changes. And their children will take these names even when their own relationship to the mode of production is different from that of their parents. As a result, over time the name will be emptied of the data that it initially carried on class identity.

Consider now the possibility of adopting a naming convention carrying data about professional identity. Again, once adopted and passed down to future generations, these names will become purely ascriptive markers and cease to carry information about the professional identity of their bearers. Take the case of Parsis in India, many of whom adopted last names during the nineteenth century that carried data on their professions. These names are now no longer informative about the profession of their bearer. Although the last name "Vakil" means "lawyer," for instance, its bearer Ardeshir Vakil is a writer; and even though he sports the last name "Contractor," Nari Contractor is really a cricketer.

Next, consider the case of ideological affiliations. A zealous parent might name a child after a revered ideological figure. Such a name, however, tells us more about the affiliation of the bearer's parents and the context in which she was born than about her own identity. For instance, the Indian politician M. K. Stalin is not a communist but a member of a Tamil regional party, the Dravida Munnetra Kazagham (DMK). By a similar logic, naming conventions adopted to carry data on rural-urban differences, educational qualifications, or income should cease to carry data about these identities over time and across generations.

Features

Let us move now to a second source of costless data: physical features such as skin colour, type and colour of hair, height, build, shape of eyes and nose, eye colour, shape of face, and so on. Physical features contain a great deal of independent data about ethnic identities. In large part, the

---

[14] For an account of a link between last name and property rights in England, see James C. Scott, John Tehranian, and Jeremy Mathias, "The Production of Legal Identities Proper to States: The Case of the Permanent Family Surname," *Comparative Studies in Society and History*, Vol. 44, No. 1 (2002): 4–44.

information about ethnic identities available in physical features has been put there by biological processes. Skin colour, for instance, carries information about race and region of origin. However, data on ethnic identities contained in physical features can also be put there by human processes, as in the case of tribal markings. Physical features typically do not contain independent information, inherited or acquired, about nonethnic identities.

Speech

Consider now speech as a source of data. The language in which a person speaks, and her accent, typically carry data about her ethnic memberships. At a minimum, they convey data about linguistic memberships. And because language is typically correlated with region and race, and sometimes with religion, speech may carry data about these other ethnic memberships as well.

Speech is also consistently informative about education, which can often produce a distinct accent and vocabulary. However, speech is less consistently informative about other identities. Speech patterns carry data on class to the extent that educational systems or ethnic categories are segregated by class. In the United Kingdom, for instance, class-segregated educational systems in public schools and universities have produced distinct upper-class and working-class accents. However, in the United States, where educational systems are not segregated to the same degree, speech tells us less about class. Similarly, the information about income, profession, rural-urban background, ideological and organizational identities contained in speech patterns depends upon the incidental fact of separate educational systems for the members of these categories, or on a coincidence of these categories with ethnic categories.

Dress

Conventions relating to dress (e.g., clothes, jewelry, accessories, hairstyle) are the one costless source that can carry comparable amounts of data about both ethnic and nonethnic memberships, depending upon the context of observation. Clothes and appearance can carry data about ethnic identities (for instance, a *burkha* carries the information that its wearer is Muslim, and a *yarmulke* the information that its wearer is Jewish). But appearance can also carry information about class. Take, for instance, the case of the United States. "There is an elite look in this country," writes Paul Fussell of the United States:

It requires women to be thin, with a hairstyle dating back eighteen or twenty years or so. . . . They wear superbly fitting dresses and expensive but always understated shoes and handbags, with very little jewelry. They wear scarves – these instantly betoken class, because they are useless except as a caste mark. Men should be thin. No jewelry at all. No cigarette case. Moderate-length hair, never dyed or tinted, which is a middle-class or high-prole sign. . . .[15]

Fussell's tongue-in-cheek account underlines the existence of a number of cues that give away class identity. The story of upwardly mobile individuals seeking entry into a higher-class stratum, in fact, is precisely the story of an attempt to drop "giveaways" associated with the lower stratum. Dress can sometimes carry data on profession (for instance, the uniforms of nurses, policemen, and firemen, or the dark suits that are the "uniforms" of lawyers and bankers). Educational qualifications are precisely encoded in academic regalia. Dress can also be informative about rural-urban identities: In developing economies, for instances, "westernized" clothes such as dresses and suits are commonly associated with the city and "traditional" attire with the countryside. Similarly, ideological and organizational affiliations can also be signaled by uniforms, badges, and emblems. Unlike other data sources, which carry the same information about the same identities regardless of the context of observation, however, the type of information carried by dress varies with the context. When on her way to work, a person may dress differently than when on her way to the synagogue. The type of identity signaled by her dress will therefore also be different.

III. Limited Information Settings Bias Observers toward Schemes of Ethnic Categorization

The multiple sources of costless data about an individual's ethnic memberships mean that an observer can typically guess an individual's ethnic identity on the basis of a relatively superficial interaction, even though such a guess may turn out to be erroneous. Further, observers can increase

---

[15] Paul Fussell, *Class: A Guide through the American Status System* (New York: Summit Books, 1983), 54.

the precision of an ethnic categorization by triangulating the evidence contained in these multiple data sources, even though the final categorizaton may well remain inexact.

Let me illustrate with a personal example. My name stores the information that I belong to at least the following categories: Asian/South Asian/Indian/north Indian/Hindu. Observers who come across my name in a newspaper or hear someone mention it might place me in any of these categories, depending upon the context and their own level of background knowledge. It also stores the information that I do not belong to a range of other categories: Sikh/Muslim/Jewish/Malayali/black/white. Even those observers who cannot place me in any of the categories to which I do belong might, at a minimum, be able to eliminate ethnic categories to which I do not belong. By looking at my skin colour, hair, and features, a relatively unsophisticated observer who encounters me on a Boston subway might guess that I am Asian, or at any rate of Asian origin, without a word exchanged. A more sophisticated observer, confronted with the same information in the same context, might classify me as South Asian, or of South Asian origin. And the same observer, confronted with the same information in Delhi rather than in Boston, would probably be able to use it to place me in narrower, more precise categories.

Note, first, that the possession of these markers does not yield any single or objectively correct classification. As the examples just mentioned illustrate, different spatial and temporal contexts may lead observers to code me differently. Second, different observers would code me differently depending upon the information they could bring to bear on the interpretation of the markers. Third, even if all observers used the same information, considerable uncertainty might remain. It is often difficult, for example, for even the most sophisticated observers to distinguish between individuals from India, Pakistan, and Bangladesh simply by looking at physical features or names. Fourth, regardless of, or even because of, her level of sophistication, the observer might simply get it wrong. Many Indians, for example, miscode me as Tamil or Bengali, when I am "really" north Indian. Fifth, the categories in which the observer places me need have no relationship to the categories with which I identify. I might think of myself primarily as a scholar, rather than as a Hindu or an Indian or a north Indian, or an Asian, or whatever. The key point here is that, notwithstanding such factors as the considerable heterogeneity within any single category, the differences in contexts in which the observation takes place, the different perspectives of different observers, the considerable room for ambiguity and error, and the individual's degree of identification with any of these categories, the name, features, speech, and dress convey enough information for most observers to classify the individual as belonging to some ethnic category or another on the basis of a relatively superficial interaction. Just as importantly, observers can also identify ethnic categories to which the individual does not belong.

Such sorting of individuals according to nonethnic identities is typically less likely in superficial interactions, *even when such identities are salient.* Imagine, for instance, a society in which all individuals can be objectively classified as either "rich" or "poor." We could get at this objective reality simply by looking at the income distribution of a population and categorizing those above a given income level as rich and those below it as poor. These categories may even have a subjective reality for those included in them. Political mobilization, for example, may make people aware of the categories in which they have been placed, so that those who are categorized as "rich" perceive themselves as being members of an imagined community of the rich, while those who are poor experience themselves as being "poor" and part of an imagined community of the poor. But how would observers sort individuals into these categories on the basis of superficial interactions? As I argued in section II, names do not permit inferences about their bearers' income, unless income and ethnic categories happen to coincide. Physical features, similarly, carry no information about income. Speech patterns and dress may, in particular contexts, convey some data about income, but the intermittent presence of such data is likely to be drowned out by the ubiquitousness and abundance of data on ethnic identities. The principal way to code the "rich" and "poor" would therefore be to procure personalized information on economic background and lifestyle. Other nonethnic categorizations (upper-class vs. working-class, urban vs. rural, landed vs. landless, farmer vs. peasant vs. worker) come with a similar lack of differentiating markers and therefore confront the observer with similarly higher costs if she is to obtain a coding based on these categories.

In any decision-making situation in which observers need to identify and distinguish between individuals under severe information constraints, therefore, the default scheme of categorization they are likely to use is ethnic. The schemes of categorization that observers are likely to employ in such interactions, as constructivist approaches to ethnic identity tell us, may be determined by several exogenous mechanisms, which are not necessarily mutually exclusive.[16] One variant of constructivism identifies macrohistorical processes such as modernization as the key variables determining the interpretation of markers,[17] another points to the role of a state-dominated economy,[18] a third to the role of institutions,[19] and a fourth to the role of political entrepreneurship.[20] Schemes of categorization might also emerge endogenously, by affixing a label to some systematic variation in ascriptive markers. For instance, observers who note a systematic regularity in skin colour among otherwise dissimilar individuals might systematically label them according to skin colour – e.g., white and black. Many ethnic categories often originate as no more than such a labeling, although they might later take on a life of their own.

I do not attempt here to offer a relative evaluation of the importance of the various determinants of these schemes of categorization, or to stipulate a priori that all observers must function within some uniform scheme. The multiple schemes through which individuals can be coded in principle, and the multiple mechanisms through which these schemes might be created, present those who would benefit from standardizing interpretations one way rather than another with a problem and an opportunity. The precise mechanism that these entrepreneurs employ, and the extent to which they succeed in getting individuals to coordinate in using the scheme of their choice, are likely to vary with the context in which they function.

IV. Conclusion

In the next chapter, I will argue that the voting decision in a "patronage-democracy" resembles a limited information setting of the sort described here, in which observers are called upon to identify and distinguish between

---

[16] For a review of constructivist approaches, see Kanchan Chandra, ed., "Cumulative Findings in the Study of Ethnic Politics," *APSA-CP*, Vol. 12, No. 1 (Winter 2001): 7–11.

[17] Benedict Anderson, *Imagined Communities* (London: Verso, 1983); Ernest Gellner, *Nations and Nationalism* (Ithaca, NY: Cornell University Press, 1983).

[18] Robert Bates, "Ethnic Competition and Modernization in Contemporary Africa," *Comparative Political Studies*, Vol. 6, No. 4 (1974): 457–483.

[19] Richard Fox, *Lions of the Punjab* (Berkeley: University of California Press, 1985); David Laitin, *Hegemony and Culture: Politics and Religious Change among the Yoruba* (Chicago: University of Chicago Press, 1986); Gyanendra Pandey, *The Construction of Communalism in Colonial North India* (Delhi: Oxford University Press, 1992).

[20] Nelson Kasfir, "Explaining Ethnic Political Participation," *World Politics*, Vol. 31, No. 3 (1979): 365–388.

individuals. Another example of a political setting to which the argument might also apply is the case of "founding elections" in new democracies. In the first competitive elections in new democracies, candidates often stand on a clean slate. They have not yet established a record of deeds and actions that voters can use to evaluate them. In such a setting, voters are likely to use a scheme of "ethnic profiling" to distinguish among candidates, using ethnic identity as a predictor of future actions – not because they are not aware that other predictors might be more accurate, but because they do not have access to data about these other predictors. Competitive environments with unstable party systems are also likely to resemble the type of limited information setting described in this chapter. In such systems, the cost of keeping track of changing candidate affiliations and platforms is likely to be high. The more fluid a party system, the more costly obtaining and analyzing such information is likely to be. Consequently, we should be more likely to see a propensity toward schemes of ethnic categorization.

At the same time, however, it is important to emphasize that many political decisions are *not* made under comparably severe information constraints. In competitive elections with stable party systems, for instance, ethnic markers need not be the only freely and ubiquitously available pieces of information about candidates. Rather, the party label sported by a candidate can be as costless an information cue as her name, providing information about the package of policies she is likely to support, just as her name provides costless information about her ethnic identities. Similarly, individuals operating in small settings, such as committees and neighbourhood associations, are likely to have accumulated intimate knowledge about each other in the course of previous interactions. This knowledge should eliminate the comparative advantage of ethnic cues, enabling individuals to combine ethnicity with other variables in order to develop more complex schemes of categorization.

3

Patronage-Democracy, Limited Information, and Ethnic Favouritism

This chapter builds upon the link between limited information and ethnic categorization to develop a theory of individual decision making among benefit-seeking voters and office-seeking elites in patronage-democracies. Confronted with competing elites, how does a voter in a patronage-democracy decide who is most likely to channel benefits to him individually? And confronted with different strategies for the distribution of benefits, how does an individual elite seeking to build a following decide whom to target? The voting decision in patronage-democracies, I argue, typically approximates a situation in which observers (voters) are forced to distinguish between individuals (the recipients of past patronage transactions) under severe information constraints. These severe information constraints produce a self-enforcing and reinforcing equilibrium of ethnic favouritism: voters expect co-ethnic elites to favour them in the distribution of benefits, and elites expect co-ethnic voters to favour them in the distribution of votes (see Figure 1.1, p. 12).

The tendency of patronage politics to go hand in hand with expectations of ethnic favouritism has been noted in other theoretical and empirical work. According to Kearney, a student of Sri Lanka: "A common expectation seems to be that a person holding a public office or other position of power will use his position for the near-exclusive benefit of his 'own' people, defined by kinship, caste, ethnic community or personal loyalty."[1] According to Haroun Adamu, a student of Nigerian politics: "It is strongly believed in this country that if you do not have one of your own kind in the local, state and/or national decision-making bodies, nobody would care

---

[1] Robert Kearney, *The Politics of Ceylon (Sri Lanka)* (Ithaca, NY: Cornell University Press, 1973), 8.

47

to take your troubles before the decision makers, much less find solutions to them."[2] Kenneth Post's description of elections in Nigeria emphasizes much the same point:

It was rare for a man to stand for election in a constituency which did not contain the community in which he was born. It did not matter if he had been educated elsewhere and had his business interests outside the community in which he was born, so long as he regarded it as his home. He would still be a better representative for it than someone who came from outside, who could not even speak in the same tongue.[3]

According to Chabal and Daloz, speaking of Africa in general: "All politicians, whether elected locally or nationally, are expected to act as the spokespeople and torchbearers of their community."[4] And Posner's investigation of voter expectations in Zambia in the 1990s found that the assumption that politicians in power will favour their own ethnic group was practically "an axiom of politics."[5] The principal variables proposed to account for this tendency in previous literature include (1) the functional superiority of ethnic networks, (2) institutional legacies that privilege ethnic identities, (3) a presumed cultural similarity that makes patronage transactions between co-ethnics easier than transactions between non-co-ethnics, and (4) the preexisting salience of ethnic identities. I depart from this literature here in proposing that the perceptual biases inherent in the patronage transaction are sufficient to generate self-fulfilling expectations of ethnic favouritism among voters and politicians even in the absence of networks, institutional legacies, cultural similarities between co-ethnics, and the preexisting salience of ethnic identities.

Section I lays out the theory identifying the link between limited information, patronage-democracy, and a politics of ethnic favouritism. Section II identifies factors that can mitigate the information constraints under which the voting decision is made in patronage-democracies and therefore reduce the likelihood of ethnic favouritism. And section III

[2] Cited in Richard Joseph, *Democracy and Prebendal Politics in Nigeria* (Cambridge: Cambridge University Press, 1987), 67.
[3] Kenneth Post, *The Nigerian Federal Election of 1959* (London: Oxford University Press, 1963), 391.
[4] Patrick Chabal and Jean-Pascal Daloz, *Africa Works* (Oxford: International African Institute, 1999), 99.
[5] Daniel Posner, "The Institutional Origins of Ethnic Politics in Zambia" (Ph.D. dissertation, Harvard University, 1998), 125.

evaluates the argument presented here against the alternatives. Recall that a patronage-democracy was defined in Chapter 1 as a democracy in which the state monopolizes access to jobs and services, and in which elected officials have individualized discretion in the implementation of policy distributing these jobs and services. Throughout, I use the terms "politician" and "political entrepreneur" to mean any individual seeking to obtain or retain elected office. In patronage-democracies, those who have the capital to launch a political career tend to be "elites" – that is, upwardly mobile middle-class individuals, better educated and better-off than the voters whom they seek to mobilize. I use the term "elite" interchangeably, therefore, with the terms "politician," "candidate," "incumbent," and "entrepreneur."

I. Theory of Voter and Elite Behaviour in Patronage-Democracies

This section introduces a series of testable propositions to explain why voters and elites in patronage-democracies are likely to organize their struggle along ethnic lines. Propositions 1–8 explain why voters in patronage-democracies should expect elites to favour co-ethnics in the distribution of material benefits. Proposition 9 explains why voters also expect to obtain psychic benefits from elites from their "own" ethnic group rather than from elites with whom they share other bases of group affiliation. Proposition 10 shows how these expectations result in a self-enforcing and self-reinforcing equilibrium of ethnic favouritism in patronage-democracies.

I.1. Politicians in Patronage-Democracies Have an Incentive to Collect Rents on Policy Implementation

In any society in which the state has monopolistic or near-monopolistic control over valued benefits, and in which elected officials have discretionary power in the implementation of policy concerning the distribution of benefits, these officials have incentives to market these benefits in return for private gain.[6] Basic goods and services, to which all citizens should have

---

[6] This section draws on the extensive literature on rent seeking and corruption, including Robert Bates, *Markets and States in Tropical Africa* (Berkeley: University of California Press, 1981); Douglass North, *Institutions, Institutional Change and Economic Performance* (Cambridge: Cambridge University Press, 1990); and James Scott, *Comparative Political Corruption* (Englewood Cliffs, NJ: Prentice-Hall, 1972).

automatic access, become commodities on which officials can collect rents. Officials who decide whose village gets a road, who gets the houses financed by a government housing scheme, whose areas get priority in providing drinking water, whose son gets a government job, whose wife gets access to a bed in a government hospital, and who gets a government loan are in a position to extract rents from beneficiaries for favouring them over other applicants. I have used here examples of the opportunities for rent seeking by elected officials in their dealings with the poor, who seek basic necessities. However, similar opportunities also exist in dealings with the rich. Industrialists, for example, who need access to land, permits for building, or licenses for marketing their products are similarly subject to the discretionary power of state officials, and so offer them similar opportunities for rent seeking.

In patronage-driven states that are not democratic, the rents that elected officials seek are likely to take the form of private wealth, such as money, assets, and land. In patronage-democracies, although rents may also be sought in these forms, votes are the most lucrative form of rent, since they provide the opportunity for continued control of the state. Wherever patronage-democracies exist, therefore, we should also see a black market for state resources, where the currency is votes and the buyers are voters. Incumbent and aspiring candidates in such democracies should court voter support by sending signals about whom they will favour in policy implementation if they win.

This black market, it is important to note, is comprised of *retail* transactions, in which customers are individuals, rather than *wholesale* transactions, in which customers are entire blocs of voters. Wholesale transactions can take place only through policy legislation, which applies simultaneously to large groups of individuals. Policy implementation, however, is of necessity a retail enterprise that applies piecemeal to individuals who come forward to claim the resources and services made available to some collective through policy legislation. Throughout the remainder of this book, I will refer to this retail black-marketing of promises to implement policy in return for votes as "patronage politics."

Before going further, let me clarify the relationship between the term "patronage politics" as used here and other terms that have slightly different meanings but are often used interchangeably: "rent seeking," "corruption," "clientelism," and "pork barrel politics."

The terms "rent seeking" and "corruption" typically refer to the sale of public goods for private gain, without specifying whether that private gain takes the form of wealth or political support. I use the term "patronage politics" here to refer to that form of rent seeking and corruption in which the returns to politicians take the form of votes rather than bribes.

The term "clientelism" is typically used to refer to a dyadic transaction between traditional notables and their dependents, who are bound by ties of reciprocity. While "patronage politics," as used here, certainly describes dyadic transactions between voters and politicians, the definition does not require them to be connected by traditional status roles or traditional ties of social and economic dependence. In fact, as I will show later, voters and politicians can end up in a relationship of mutual obligation without such preexisting ties.

Finally, the term "pork barrel politics" refers primarily to the practice of courting voter support through policy legislation (especially budgetary allocations).[7] The term "patronage politics," as used here, refers to an attempt to court support not by promising some group of voters favourable *legislation* but by assuring them of favourable *implementation*. For instance, an attempt to obtain the support of farmers by enacting a law providing them with subsidies on inputs would fall into the category of pork barrel politics. The term "patronage politics," as used here, does not describe the enactment of such legislation. However, let us imagine that in order to procure such a subsidy, farmers first have to obtain a certificate of eligibility from some politician with discretionary power over the distribution of such certificates. If such a politician courts the support of some farmers rather than others by promising to employ his discretionary power selectively in their favour, the transaction would be classified as a "patronage" transaction according to this study. Although the term "patronage politics" is often used interchangeably with "pork barrel" politics, the distinction that this study makes between the two terms is important. The collective transfer of goods to citizens through policy legislation produces different political outcomes than the individualized transfer of goods through policy implementation.

One immediate objection needs to be addressed before describing the features of this black market in policy implementation and its implications for the character of politics in patronage-democracies. Does a secret ballot not prevent the operation of such a black market? Under a secret ballot, there is nothing to deter voters from cheating by promising their votes

---

[7] For instance, see Barry Ames, *Political Survival: Politicians and Public Policy in Latin America* (Berkeley: University of California Press, 1987), 104.

to one candidate while casting them in favour of another. Knowing that they cannot enforce their contract, why should elected officials sell state resources on the electoral market?

Voting procedures in patronage-democracies, however, are unlikely to be secret, or perceived to be secret. Given the strong incentives that candidates in patronage-democracies have to obtain information about how voters vote, we should see regular attempts to subvert the secrecy of the ballot by exploiting loopholes in the design of the voting procedure. Such subversion is made possible by the difficulty of designing and implementing a "foolproof" secret ballot. Consider the following examples:

In municipal elections in the city of New Haven, Connecticut, a voter who voted for the party ticket for all fifteen municipal offices could do so simply by pulling a lever. Those who chose to split their votes between the two parties for individual candidates, however, could do so only through a time-consuming procedure. Even though the ballot was officially "secret," the method of casting the ballot provided a clear signal about how the individual had voted. As Wolfinger points out: "To observers in the polling place, the length of time the voter spent in the booth revealed the strength of his devotion to the party ticket, particularly since a bell would ring when either party lever was pulled. This arrangement...was an important inducement to straight-ticket voting."[8]

A second example comes from the procedure through which votes are counted. According to Schaffer's description of the 1993 elections in Senegal, each polling station accommodated an average of about two hundred voters. The ballots were then counted at each station and posted publicly. As Schaffer notes of this procedure: "While the electoral choice of each individual elector remained secret, the aggregate results for each (larger) village or group of (smaller) villages did not. Consequently, local level political patrons were still able to gauge the effectiveness of their efforts and the overall compliance of relatively small groups of voters."[9]

In both these cases, the secret ballot was implemented to the letter. However, politicians with an incentive to know how voters voted were able to subvert the secrecy of the ballot by exploiting loopholes in its implementation.

[8] Raymond Wolfinger, *The Politics of Progress* (Englewood Cliffs, NJ: Prentice-Hall, 1974), 23.
[9] Frederic Schaffer, *Democracy in Translation* (Ithaca, NY: Cornell University Press, 1998), 136.

But even in cases in which the secret ballot is somehow insulated from subversion, voters in patronage-democracies are unlikely to *believe* that their vote is secret. In a democracy in which elected officials enjoy discretion in the implementation of most laws, why should voters trust that voting procedures are somehow an exception? The *perception* that voting procedures are subject to the same type of discretion as other policies should deter cheating and encourage the sale of goods and services in return for votes just as if the ballot were in fact not secret.

I.2. Voters in Patronage-Democracies Have an Incentive to Use Their Votes as Instruments to Extract Material Benefits

Ever since the publication of Mancur Olson's *The Logic of Collective Action*,[10] we have presumed that there are few instrumental reasons to vote.[11] This presumption rests upon two propositions: (1) The benefit from voting is typically in the form of policy legislation, which all individuals benefit from regardless of whether or not they vote. (2) Any single vote is not likely to affect the electoral outcome. Since her vote is not likely to affect the outcome, and since she will benefit if her preferred candidate wins whether or not she votes, it always makes sense for a rational individual to abstain from voting. Consequently, we expect that those who vote do so for expressive reasons: perhaps because they think it is what good citizens should do, perhaps because their parents did, perhaps because they want to stand up and be counted for what they believe in, or perhaps because of the satisfaction of going to the polling booth with friends and companions. In each of these examples, it is the *act* of voting rather than the *outcome* that gives them satisfaction.

For most voters in patronage-democracies, however, a single motivation overrides the rest: the need to secure some of the vast material benefits at the disposal of those who implement policy. Such material benefits are highly valued, scarce, and, most importantly, private: As the examples given earlier illustrate, they are distributed in retail transactions to individuals (e.g., jobs,

---

[10] Mancur Olson, *The Logic of Collective Action* (Cambridge, MA: Harvard University Press, 1971).

[11] For attempts to explain the decision to vote within a rational choice framework, see Morris P. Fiorina, "The Voting Decision: Instrumental and Expressive Aspects," *The Journal of Politics*, Vol. 38, No. 2 (1976): 390–413; John Aldrich, "Rational Choice and Turnout," *American Journal of Political Science*, Vol. 37, No. 1 (1993): 246–278.

medical care, university admissions, housing loans, land grants) and to the micro-communities that they represent (e.g., roads, schools, electricity, water). And the vote is the currency through which individuals secure such goods for themselves or their micro-communities. The "expressive benefits" provided by the act of voting are ephemeral. The pleasure of doing the right thing, or of performing a traditional act, or of registering an opinion, or of participating in shared group activity does not last beyond the brief moment of casting the vote. The ephemeral expressive benefits provided by the act of voting are overshadowed by its utility as an instrument through which to secure the protection, services, and opportunities at the disposal of elected officials. While we might certainly find "expressive voters" in patronage-democracies, they are likely to be composed mainly of that minority of voters who, within these societies, are relatively independent of the state. The more dependent the voter is upon the state, the more likely he is to be an instrumental actor who uses his vote as a means through which to extract material benefits from competing candidates.

Voting in patronage-democracies, therefore, should not be viewed as a variant of the collective action problem. The collective action problem applies to voting only in cases in which the payoff from voting accrues to all individuals collectively, or to large groups. In patronage-democracies, however, the act of voting carries with it substantial, individualized benefits, and the act of not voting carries with it substantial, individualized costs. In patronage-democracies, where the value of the vote is so high, the problem is not explaining why individuals vote, but explaining why some do *not*.[12]

I.3. Benefit-seeking Voters Have an Incentive to Organize Collectively in the Pursuit of Individually Distributed Goods

The retail and informal nature of the patronage transaction poses a problem for voters: how to maximize the value of their investment and how to ensure delivery. Any individual voter knows that her capacity to purchase a job, a housing loan, or a university slot with her solitary vote is negligible. An

---

[12] One hypothesis suggested by the argument here is that there should be a positive relationship between the degree of dependence of voters upon the state and turnout rates. Within patronage-democracies, therefore, we should expect individuals dependent upon the state for their livelihood to turn out at higher rates than individuals who, because of greater education or greater preexisting wealth, are less dependent.

individual vote makes no difference to the overall outcome and so gives the candidate little incentive to provide goods and services in return. The voter, therefore, must find a way to magnify the purchasing power of her vote. Then, she must find a way to ensure that the goods that her vote purchases are delivered. Once the vote is cast, why should the candidate feel compelled to deliver on his promise?

Both problems are solved for the voter by organizing collectively. In throwing her lot in with a group, an individual agrees to vote for some politician even if she does not benefit herself, as long as the politician favours *some* group member over nonmembers. By joining a group, the voter magnifies the value of her vote. Because a bloc of votes can make a difference to the outcome, a number of individuals organized as a group can bargain more effectively with candidates than the same number of individuals voting individually. The price for this greater bargaining power is the possibility that some other member of the collective might obtain scarce benefits rather than the voter. However, those members who are denied benefits still have some expectation that their turn will come in the future. And to the extent that the politician favours her group over other groups and individuals, the voter is still better off than she would have been had she voted individually. Further, organizing as a group makes it easier for voters to ensure delivery. A candidate who does not deliver on his promise can be punished by the defection of the group as a whole, with a corresponding negative effect on his future electoral prospects.

While voters have an incentive to organize collectively in patronage-democracies, it is worth reiterating that the goods that they seek are individually, not collectively, distributed. Joining a group allows individual members to increase the odds that they or the micro-communities that they represent will receive greater priority in the allocation of benefits than individuals who are outside the group. However, all group members do not receive benefits simultaneously. In this sense, joining a group in order to obtain access to an individual benefit is analogous to buying a lottery ticket. Just as each individual must pay for her lottery ticket in order to be eligible for the prize, each group member must actually turn out to vote in order to be eligible for a benefit. But just as the prize is individually allotted to only a small number of those who buy lottery tickets, benefits are individually distributed to only a small number of group members. When an individual voter chooses to join one group rather than another, therefore, she is choosing one lottery rather than another. Given a choice, she will choose the group that promises her the best odds of obtaining benefits.

However, joining some group – any group – is always better than voting on her own.

I.4. Benefit-selling Candidates Have an Incentive to Target the Distribution of Individual Benefits to Group Members rather than to Free-floating Individuals

Just as the voter's problem is how to magnify the value of her vote and ensure delivery, the candidate's problem is how to magnify the purchasing power of the benefits at his disposal and how to monitor compliance. No matter how large the supply of jobs, licenses, loans, roads, and wells at his disposal, each job, license, well, or road can be given only to a single individual or to a single community represented by the individual. A procedure whereby each favour buys the vote of only the direct beneficiary would never produce the broad base of support required to win an election. How can the candidate multiply the value of his investment, so that each favour brings with it the support of others in addition to the direct recipient? And even if he were to purchase a large number of votes with a small number of favours, how might he ensure that voters pay him as promised?

Both problems are solved for the candidate by targeting favours to group members rather than to free-floating individuals. In dealing with individuals, a favour given to one individual would be a favour denied to another. It would cost the candidate as much as he would gain. In dealings with group members, however, a favour given to one member sends a signal to others that they too can count on him in the future. It also signals to all group members that he will favour individuals in their group over others. As such, it can win him support even from those denied favours in the present. Secondly, dealing with groups makes it easy for the politician to monitor compliance. Obtaining information about individual voting behaviour, which requires personalized knowledge of individual decisions and actions, is costly and often impossible. However, groups can be infiltrated more easily, and group voting behaviour can be monitored through collective institutions.

Electoral politics in patronage-democracies, therefore, should take the form of a self-enforcing equilibrium of "group voting," maintained by the incentives voters have to organize in groups and the incentives candidates have to encourage the organization of voters as groups. In principle, such groups might be organized on any basis: by place of residence, by class, by organizational affiliation, by ideology, and so on. In the propositions that follow, I show why patronage politics privileges *ethnic* group mobilization in particular.

I.5. Voters in Patronage-Democracies Evaluate the Promises of Candidates about the Distribution of Benefits in the Present by Looking at the Record of Past Patronage Transactions by Incumbents. Consequently, Incumbents Seek to Develop Records of Patronage Transactions that Will Help Them Most in the Future.

In any system in which there is a gap between legislation and implementation, voters have little reason to take the promises of candidates on faith. Candidates may openly declare their support for some category of voters. However, voters in patronage-democracies should believe only those promises that they can verify by surveying the record of past transactions. Where discretionary power in the implementation of state policy lies in the hands of elected officials, promises to enact policy legislation favourable to an individual or group are worthless unless accompanied by a verified record of implementation in favour of that individual or group.

Voters in patronage-democracies, therefore, should make their decision about whom to support by looking at the pattern of past patronage transactions. By probing for broad patterns in the history of patronage transactions by incumbents, they can identify the principle on which patronage benefits were distributed in the past, which is their best guide to how benefits will be distributed in the future.

Incumbents in patronage-democracies, therefore, will distribute patronage with an eye to future support, seeking to build the record that will help them most in obtaining votes in the future. And the credibility of promises that first-time candidates make will depend upon the record established by incumbents in the past. In this sense, previous incumbents have an agenda-setting power, determining which types of promises are more credible in the present and which less credible.

I.6. Voters Surveying the Record of Past Patronage Transactions Are Typically Forced to Distinguish between Individuals under Severe Information Constraints

Patronage transactions cannot be conducted openly in modern democracies. Any attempt by candidates to trade policy implementation for votes in the open market would constitute a serious violation of the norms of modern government and in all likelihood collide with the laws of most democracies. As an illustration, take the instance of public health facilities. A bed in a public hospital is a scarce commodity, and politicians in many developing countries are routinely called upon by favour seekers to secure beds for their friends and relatives. However, no politician could openly promise to favour some voters over others in the allocation of hospital beds. Selective allocation of basic services such as public health, to which all citizens should in principle have equal access, would be indefensible on both normative and legal grounds. The normative and legal constraints of modern democratic government ensure that politicians can send only surreptitious signals about whom they intend to favour in the implementation of policy, announcing their intent by unofficial action but not by open declaration in the official political sphere.

As a result, voters typically have very little background information about the beneficiaries of patronage transactions. Their main sources of data are reports in the newspapers or on television or radio about new appointments and promotions; rumours about who got rich under which government and who did not, whose sons got jobs and whose did not, whose villages got roads and electricity and whose did not; and actual observation of the personnel staffing a government office, either on television or in person. Even though politicians have an incentive to provide voters with as much data as possible on their past patronage transactions, the normative and legal constraints on such transactions prevent them from sending open messages; and even though voters have an incentive to acquire as much data as possible, the quality of the data sources available to them limits the information that they receive.

I.7. Consequently, Voters Are Biased toward Schemes of Ethnic Categorization in Interpreting How Past Patronage Benefits Have Been Distributed

For the reasons outlined in Chapter 2, the severe information constraints characteristic of patronage politics mean that voters concerned with assessing who benefited under which regime will always code beneficiaries on the basis of one of their many ethnic identities, whether or not these identities were actually relevant in securing benefits. Consider the following two examples:

"When in the middle of the nineteenth century," writes Wolfinger of politics in New Haven, "the first Irishman was nominated for public office, this was 'recognition' by the party of the statesmanlike qualities of the Irish, seen and appreciated by many Irishmen."[13] Apart from being Irish, the nominee was presumably many other things. Imagine, for instance, that he was a worker, or that he possessed particular professional qualifications for the office, or that he was known to be an influential neighbourhood leader. Those who knew him personally might interpret the nomination as an act that recognized his identity as a worker, or his qualifications, or his influence among his peers, or a variety of other considerations. However, those who did not know him but encountered him in a government office, or read his name in the newspaper, or heard him speak on the radio would have identified him purely on the basis of one of his ethnic identities, helped along by name, accent, manner, and any of the cultural differentiae that he happened to carry. It is not surprising, then, that the nomination was widely "seen and appreciated" as an act recognizing the Irish. Even if it had not been intended as such, it would be impossible for most voters to interpret it in any other way.

Consider another example, from Posner's study of patronage politics in Zambia. A newspaper column concerned with describing the extent of ethnic favouritism in Zambia noted: "There are organizations in this country, even foreign-owned for that matter, where almost every name, from the manager down to the office orderly, belongs to one region. . . . In this country, professionally qualified youngsters never find jobs if they belong to the 'wrong' tribes. When you enter certain . . . offices, you get the impression they are tribal establishments."[14] How did the author of this article know that certain tribes were being favoured and others were not? The article identifies two sources of information: names, and superficial observation of the staff in certain offices. Both these cues provide clues to the ethnic identity of the individuals concerned but say little or nothing about nonethnic identities. Even had he or she wanted to, the author of this article could not, based on these sources of information, have coded the beneficiaries on a nonethnic basis. Imagine that those given jobs in any one office, for example, were only coincidentally from the same ethnic group. Perhaps the real tie that got them their jobs was that they all went to the same school. Although the "true" criterion for distributing benefits in this case would have been membership in an old boy network rather than ethnic affinity, this criterion would be invisible to the outside observer.

[13] Wolfinger, *The Politics of Progress*, 36.
[14] *The Post*, January 24, 1996, cited in Posner, "Institutional Origins," 116.

In these and other examples, those who are intimately acquainted with the beneficiaries might code them in complex ways. However, most voters would only be able to sort them into ethnic categories. Consequently, watchful voters surveying patronage transactions "see" beneficiaries through an ethnic prism and conclude that politicians allot favours on the basis of ethnic identity, whether or not ethnic favouritism actually entered into the decision.

As I argued earlier, the categories that voters are likely to use to sort beneficiaries might be determined exogenously, by some previous process, or endogenously, by some striking systematic difference in ethnic markers. Further, such sorting need not be standardized. Different observers might assign the same beneficiary to different ethnic categories, or misidentify the individual as belonging to one category when he really belongs to another. Political entrepreneurs should attempt to manipulate this ambiguity, encouraging voters to code beneficiaries in categories that give them a political advantage. However, the key point here is that information about patronage transactions is transmitted through a process that amplifies signals revealing the ethnic identities of the beneficiary and suppresses his nonethnic identities. In an environment in which they receive exclusively ethnic signals, voters can ascertain whether benefits are being distributed randomly across their ethnic categories of choice, or whether they are being systematically directed toward some ethnic categories but not others. But they do not have the data to discern more complex patterns, employing variables other than or in addition to ethnicity, in the distribution of benefits.

I.8. When Voters Are Biased toward an Ethnic Categorization of Beneficiaries, Politicians Will Favour Co-ethnics in Their Distribution of Material Benefits, although They May Also Channel Leftover Benefits to Voters from Other Ethnic Categories

Consider now what this means for the strategy of politicians in patronage-democracies. In an environment in which voters at time $t + 1$ formulate expectations of benefits based on the history of patronage transactions at time t, and can interpret these past transactions only using schemes of ethnic categorization, incumbents at time t have no choice but to employ ethnic principles in the way in which they choose to distribute benefits. They may want, for whatever reason, to distribute benefits based on other principles, such as loyalty, ideological affinity, or income. And new candidates may also want, for whatever reason, to use these other principles in making their promises. However, these nonethnic principles, for the reasons already mentioned, are *unverifiable* on the ground. Watchful voters who are used to the gap between rhetoric and implementation in patronage-based systems will treat these unverifiable promises as mere noise. Consequently, incumbents have no choice but to send ethnic signals in their distribution of benefits.

Incumbents constrained by voter biases to distribute benefits on an ethnic basis have to decide how to distribute favours across ethnic categories. Should they distribute benefits equally across all ethnic categories? Or should they be selective, allotting a larger proportion of benefits to some categories than to others? And if they are selective, how do they decide which ethnic category or categories to favor? I will show why, paradoxically, incumbents in patronage-democracies should always elect to allot the lion's share of benefits to members of their "own" ethnic category, regardless of its size. They may *also* send leftover benefits in the direction of other ethnic categories, especially when their "own" is too small to be efficacious. However, the proportion of benefits that they distribute to members of their "own" category should always be larger.

In order to acquire a following, politicians need not only to promise to favour some distinct category of voters, but also to establish greater credibility than other politicians among this category of voters. A strategy of distributing favours equally across individuals from all ethnic categories does not give any candidate a comparative advantage. If an incumbent distributes favours equally to individuals from various ethnic categories at time t, voters will believe that other candidates are also likely to distribute benefits in the future according to impartial principles. In that case, since supporting any one candidate produces the same odds of obtaining benefits as supporting another, voters should be indifferent across candidates. Consequently, candidates should always avoid the strategy of equal distribution across ethnic categories in favor of selective targeting.

Consider now the strategy of selective targeting. We might initially suppose that an incumbent should distribute the lion's share of the benefits at her disposal to any ethnic category (or combination of categories) that is sufficiently numerous to take her to a winning position, whether or not the category is her own. But such a strategy is inadvisable, because it does not allow the incumbent to establish a comparative advantage. If incumbents distribute benefits at time t primarily to members of ethnic groups other than their own, voters surveying these past transactions will believe that a politician from one ethnic category can be trusted to deliver benefits to voters from another. In a competitive environment in which elites from one ethnic category can be trusted to deliver benefits to members of another, we should expect politicians of all hues to enter the race for support from the numerically dominant ethnic categories. The result would be a whittling down of the support that any one politician is likely to receive. This is not an optimal outcome from any politician's point of view.

But if incumbents distribute benefits primarily to members of their "own" ethnic category at time t, voters at time $t + 1$ will believe that those in power will help their "own" first and discount promises to distribute support on a cross-ethnic basis. In a field in which the only credible promises are those made by co-ethnics, all politicians from one ethnic category acquire a comparative advantage over others. Politicians from an "outside" category, because they do not have the right markers, will not be viable contenders for support. Playing ethnic favorites, therefore, gives politicians a "core" base of support, insulated from incursions by all but co-ethnic competitors.

The attraction of this core base of support should lead incumbents in patronage-democracies to allot the lion's share of benefits to their "own" category regardless of its size. However, the size of the difference between the benefits that they offer to their "own" and the benefits that they offer to "others" might well vary, depending upon the size of their "own" ethnic category. If their "own" ethnic category is large enough to be independently efficacious, they will have no incentive to distribute any benefits to members of other ethnic categories. However, if their "own" category is relatively small, they should be willing to spare a larger proportion of benefits for members of other ethnic categories in order to attract their support. Voters witnessing such behaviour will conclude that while politicians may help members of other ethnic categories at particular times under unfavourable competitive configurations, they are most consistent in helping their own. Consequently, voters should place the greatest trust in co-ethnics in their struggle for the delivery of patronage benefits.

At the same time that they have an incentive to favour their "own" ethnic category in an attempt to establish a comparative advantage over others, however, all politicians have an incentive to define their "own" category as large enough to take them past the threshold of winning or influence. The multiplicity of interpretations that can be attached to ethnic markers gives them this freedom in defining the boundaries and membership of this category. As I argued in Chapter 2, the correspondence between the "markers" that any individual possesses and the ethnic category membership that these markers signal is not given. It is changeable according to the context, knowledge, and interpretive frameworks of the observer. Consequently, a politician whose "own" category is initially too small to confer an electoral advantage has an incentive to manipulate the correspondence between markers and categories in order to produce a more advantageous definition of who her "own" people are. She may do this by reinterpreting her own markers in such a way that she qualifies for membership in a larger ethnic category than before, so that she can claim some larger section of the population as her "own"; by redefining the membership criteria for her "own" category in order to encourage more voters to identify with her than before; or by attempting to transform the prevailing system of categorization itself, changing the dimension on which voters attempt to categorize politicians in a way that gives her an advantage.

I.9. The Superior Visibility of Ethnic Identities in Limited Information Environments Also Drives Voters to Obtain Psychic Benefits from Co-ethnic Elites rather than Others

So far, I have discussed how the severe information constraints in a patronage-democracy should lead voters to expect greater access to *material* benefits from co-ethnic elites. Here, I discuss why the same mechanism should also lead them to expect psychic benefits from co-ethnics.

I build here upon the insights introduced by the social psychological approach that (1) individual self-esteem is a product of the socially recognized position of the groups of which one is a member, and (2) that in patronage-democracies, the principal source of collective social recognition is the state.[15] Groups whose elites control the state are likely to confer greater self-esteem upon voters who are their members than groups whose elites are less well represented in state institutions. In a world of multiple group affiliations, however, when and why does ethnic group membership, in particular, become a source of self-esteem?

I propose here that voters seeking self-esteem identify with their ethnic categories when information constraints make it difficult for third parties to detect other types of group affiliation. This proposition rests on the observation that in order to bask in the reflected glory of an elite

---

[15] Donald Horowitz, *Ethnic Groups in Conflict* (Berkeley: University of California Press, 1985).

who has obtained control of the state, a voter must be "seen" by others to be a member of the same group as the elite. In the absence of such third-party acknowledgement, the demonstrated superiority of the elite as an individual will not be interpreted as the demonstrated superiority of the group to which both elite and voter belong. In a personalized, information-rich setting, third parties possess the background data needed to sort voters and elites according to their non–ethnic group affiliations. In the impersonal environment of mass politics, however, the ethnic identity of each becomes the principal means that external observers have of ascertaining group affiliation. Voters should obtain greater self-esteem, therefore, principally from groups in which membership is signaled by widely observable ethnic identities, rather than by concealed nonethnic identities.

To illustrate, recall the effect of the nomination of an 'Irishman' in Wolfinger's study. That nomination conferred status on other Irishmen. However, it did not confer status on members of any of the nonethnic groups to which he might have belonged. The reason, I propose here, is that unlike his Irish identity, his nonethnic identities could not be "seen and appreciated" by those who shared them and by those who did not. Politicians in patronage-democracies, therefore, have an incentive not only to distribute material benefits to co-ethnic voters but also to portray their political successes as successes for their "own" ethnic category.

I.10. Consequently, We Should See a Self-enforcing and Self-reinforcing Equilibrium of Ethnic Favouritism in Patronage-Democracies

Once politicians, constrained by limited information conditions, bid for the support of co-ethnics, voters should follow suit by sorting themselves into ethnic blocs. In patronage-democracies, therefore, we should see a self-enforcing equilibrium of ethnic favouritism, in which voters mainly target co-ethnic politicians for favours, and politicians mainly target co-ethnic voters for votes. New politicians, faced with a playing field in which all others appear to be helping voters from their "own" ethnic category, will be forced to court the support of co-ethnics if they want to remain in the game. At the same time, however, they should attempt to propose as advantageous a definition of their "own" ethnic category as possible. Similarly, new voters, faced with a playing field in which all other voters appear to be best served by politicians from their "own" category, are forced to throw their support behind co-ethnics.

Once this equilibrium of ethnic favouritism is in place, we should also see a feedback loop, with ethnic politics strengthening the conditions of patronage politics that gave it birth. New voters entering the political arena should also mobilize on an ethnic basis and demand state largesse for their ethnic categories. We should expect the pressure from these newly mobilized ethnic categories to motivate politicians not only to guard jealously the discretionary power that they have but to seek an expansion of state services, and of their discretionary power over the allocation of such services, in order to maintain and expand their bases of support. Patronage politics and ethnic politics, therefore, should be locked in a stranglehold, with the one reinforcing the other.

Over time, this equilibrium should also generate additional reinforcing mechanisms that allow it to persist even after the initial information constraints that gave it birth are lifted.[16] For instance, both voters and politicians have an incentive to create and maintain ethnic networks and institutions in order to reduce the transaction costs of communicating demands and delivering benefits. Neither voter nor politician has a similar incentive to create or maintain nonethnic networks and institutions. Further, over repeated elections, voters should acquire a store of fairly precise information about the ethnic identities of political entrepreneurs and those whom they have favoured in the past, information that will assist them in predicting the behaviour of these entrepreneurs in the future. Similarly, politicians should acquire a store of information about the relative numerical strength of different ethnic blocs, defined on different dimensions, that will assist them in formulating profitable strategies. Neither voter nor politician has any incentive to collect and store comparable information about nonethnic categories. As a result, ethnic identities should become progressively more "real," and nonethnic identities progressively more invisible, over repeated interactions. Finally, the cycle of expectations built around patronage transactions during elections is likely also to spill over into the broader political arena, turning ethnic favouritism into a "basic axiom of politics."[17]

This equilibrium, I have argued, is maintained by information constraints, which are in themselves a product of the structural conditions defining a patronage-democracy. It is likely to break down only when the structural conditions that sustain these information constraints are altered.

---

[16] For a distinction between self-enforcing and self-reinforcing institutions, see Avner Greif, *Historical Institutional Analysis* (Cambridge University Press, forthcoming).

[17] Posner, "Institutional Origins."

For instance, a downsizing of the state sector would eliminate the root of the cycle of ethnic favouritism by removing the necessity for voters to use their votes as the means to secure their livelihoods. The reduction of discretionary power over the implementation of state policy, by legislating precise guidelines or introducing procedures for oversight, would have a similar effect. And, as I will argue later, even within the constraints of patronage-democracy, the vesting of control over the distribution of resources in politicians at the micro rather than the macro level of politics should erode the foundations of this equilibrium by replacing a limited information environment with an information-rich one. The effect of such structural changes may be impeded by the continued existence of ethnic networks and institutions, ethnically based statistics, and other reinforcing mechanisms that emerge as by-products of the equilibrium of ethnic favouritism. But over time, changes in the underlying structure should dismantle these reinforcing mechanisms and so gradually erode this equilibrium.

Before proceeding further, let me address the possibility of endogeneity. Might not the politics of ethnic favouritism itself produce patronage-democracy, rather than the other way around?

The argument here predicts that once the politics of ethnic favouritism is activated by the introduction of patronage-democracy, it should generate a feedback loop, strengthening and expanding the conditions that gave rise to it. In this sense, the discovery of reverse causal arrows *after* the introduction of patronage-democracy would confirm rather than disprove the argument. However, we should be less confident of the argument, in relation to the alternative, if we found that the *initial* establishment of patronage-democracy was systematically correlated with a preexisting politics of ethnic favouritism. A test of this argument awaits the collection of data tracking the establishment, expansion, and contraction of patronage-democracies over time. Here, let me note simply that there is no reason to expect that the two defining conditions of a patronage-democracy – a large state, and discretionary control over the implementation of state policy – are the systematic product of the politics of ethnic favouritism. The size of the public sector or the degree of regulation of the private sector might increase for a variety of reasons: as a consequence of ideology (e.g., communist or socialist regimes), because of a desire for accelerated economic development (e.g., the "developmentalist" state in India), or out of a concern for social welfare (e.g., welfare states in Sweden and Finland). And discretion over the distribution of jobs and services controlled by these large public sectors or regulated private sectors might be acquired by elected officials when the procedures for implementation are not well codified; or under conditions of widespread illiteracy or large-scale immigration, where an inadequate understanding of the letter of the law among citizens gives state officials discretionary power in practice; or under conditions of extreme job scarcity, where an excess supply of identically qualified applicants gives state officials the power to select from among them arbitrarily in allocating jobs and services.

II. Factors Mitigating the Likelihood of Ethnic Favouritism in Patronage-Democracies

I have argued so far that the propensity of patronage-democracies to produce the politics of ethnic favouritism is a product of the degree to which the voting decision in patronage-democracies approximates a setting in which observers have to distinguish between individuals under severe information constraints. When the voting decision does not approximate this type of setting, other things being equal, we should not see patronage-democracy produce the politics of ethnic favouritism. Here, I identify four conditions that, by altering the information environment, can lower the likelihood of ethnic favouritism in patronage-democracies.

Vesting of Control over the Distribution of Patronage at the Micro Level

Micro levels of politics (e.g. family, village, ward, neighbourhood, and municipality) are information-rich environments, in which individuals know each other personally and have engaged in repeated interactions over a long period of time. Macro levels of politics (state, province, region, nation, large district) are information-poor environments, in which individuals do not have personal knowledge about each other and do not have a history of repeated interactions. The level at which control over the delivery of benefits is vested varies across political systems. In some systems, it is politicians at the macro level of politics (e.g., national legislators, provincial legislators) who pull the strings by which benefits are released at lower levels of politics. In others, control over these benefits is vested directly in elected officials at these lower levels (e.g., with municipal councilors or village headmen).

When control over patronage transactions is vested in politicians at the micro level, voters surveying a politician's record of past patronage transactions are faced with the task of classifying only a small number of individuals about whom they typically have additional sources of information based on previous interactions. This allows them to supplement the limited data that usually accompanies patronage transactions. Simply by hearing the name of some individual who has been denied a favour, for instance, voters may be able to ascertain, by drawing upon the store of information collected through previous interactions, whether this person was denied a favour because of her personal rivalries with a politician, or her character, or economic circumstances, or family feuds. As a result, they can code beneficiaries of previous patronage transactions in complex ways. When patronage is distributed at the macro level of politics, however, voters are called upon to classify larger numbers of individuals of whom they have no personal knowledge and with whom they do not have any history of prior interactions. Consequently, they are more likely to code them on an ethnic basis. Other things being equal, therefore, we should be more likely to see ethnic favouritism in patronage-democracies in which control over patronage is vested in politicians at the macro rather than the micro level. Further, if institutional reforms in patronage-democracies transfer control over the distribution of patronage from the macro to the micro level of politics, we should see a decline in the likelihood of ethnic favouritism, other things being equal; and if institutional reforms transfer control over patronage from the micro to the macro level, we should see an increase in the likelihood of ethnic favouritism, other things being equal.

Mediated Democracy

"Mediated democracies," in which only a small number of voters are autonomous, also reduce the likelihood of ethnic favouritism in patronage-democracies by increasing the sources of information available to voters about the beneficiaries of patronage transactions. When only some voters are autonomous and control the votes of the rest, politicians can target benefits to a small and select pool of beneficiaries. With a small number of beneficiaries, the cost of obtaining information about each is also reduced. As a result, voters can formulate hypotheses that do not rely solely on ethnic characteristics. Examples of mediated democracies include "traditional" polities in which landed or other powerful classes are the autonomous voters and control the votes of subordinate groups through ties of deference and coercion. As these ties of deference and subordination are eroded, however, and political participation increases, we should see the likelihood of ethnic favouritism increase in patronage-democracies.

Aggregate Beneficiaries

The likelihood of ethnic favouritism is also reduced when the customers in patronage transactions are aggregates rather than individuals. As I argued in the previous chapter, observers are likely to be biased toward ethnic categorization under limited information constraints only when they are concerned with distinguishing between individuals. When called upon to distinguish between groups, observers should not be biased toward ethnic categorization even under severe information constraints, since groups do not sport ethnic markers as individuals do. Consequently, regimes in which voters are required to code aggregate rather than individual beneficiaries should not necessarily be characterized by expectations of ethnic favouritism.

Examples of cases in which the principal beneficiaries of patronage are aggregates rather than individuals abound, particularly in Latin America, which exhibits a distinct pattern of "corporate" or "collective" clientelism.[18] According to Robert Gay's ethnographic study of patronage politics in two *favelas* in Brazil, for instance, candidates sought voter support by paying off the entire neighbourhood of Vila Brasil – providing collective goods such as paved roads, uniforms for the neighbourhood soccer team, and public bathrooms in the neighbourhood association building.[19] With some exceptions, the candidates did not barter with individuals.[20] Susan Stokes's study of shantytown politics in Peru reveals the same pattern: Residents of the shantytown of Independencia bargained with politicians not as individuals but as communities, and sought from these politicians not individual goods – such as jobs, university slots, and loans – but community goods – such as water, electricity, and land titles conferred collectively to the shantytown as a whole.[21] Jonathan Fox's study of patronage politics

---

[18] Gerrit Burgwal, *Caciquismo, Paralelismo and Clientelismo: The History of a Quito Squatter Settlement* (Urban Research Working Papers no. 32) (Amsterdam: Institute of Cultural Anthropology/Sociology of Development, Vrije Universiteit, 1993); John D. Martz, *The Politics of Clientelism: Democracy and the State in Colombia* (New Brunswick, NJ: Transaction Publishers, 1997). For a recent ethnography that traces these forms of collective bargaining, see Javier Auyero, *Poor People's Politics: Peronist Survival Networks and the Legacy of Evita* (Durham, NC: Duke University Press, 2000).

[19] Robert Gay, *Popular Organization and Democracy in Rio de Janeiro: A Tale of Two Favelas* (Philadelphia: Temple University Press, 1994), Chapters 2 and 4.

[20] Ibid., Chapter 2.

[21] Susan Stokes, *Cultures in Conflict: Social Movements and the State in Peru* (Berkeley: University of California Press, 1995), 64.

in Mexico, similarly, identifies collectives rather than individuals as the beneficiaries of patronage transactions: Food was made available to entire villages in the form of food stores, or to collectively organized region-wide community food councils; Regional Solidarity funds were provided not to individuals but to "project proposals submitted from the organizations of the region"; and public works programmes were provided to local committees.[22]

The designation of aggregates rather than individuals as the beneficiaries of patronage transactions depends on several factors. First, it depends upon the nature of the goods over which elected officials have discretionary control. States in which elected officials have discretionary control over collective goods (e.g., roads, sanitation, drinking water) but not over individual goods (e.g., licenses, permits, land titles, loans) will designate aggregates rather than individuals as beneficiaries. Second, it depends upon the way in which economic activity is organized. In societies with a tradition of individual land ownership and cultivation, for instance, elected officials can distribute land titles or agricultural loans on an individual basis. But in societies with a tradition of collective ownership and cultivation, elected officials are forced to conduct business with collectives rather than with individuals. Third, it depends upon the extent to which the rules that govern distribution of patronage permit or prevent individual targeting. For instance, the distribution of Regional Solidarity funds in Mexico, guided by a rule book written by a crusading president and the World Bank – both of whom had an interest in undermining clientelism – established procedures by which officials were forced to direct funds to organizations rather than to individuals. No matter what its origin, however, the distribution of patronage benefits to aggregate rather than individual beneficiaries eliminates the link between patronage politics and the politics of ethnic favouritism.

Perfect Homogeneity and Perfect Heterogeneity

When a population is perfectly homogeneous (i.e., all individuals have identical ethnic markers) or perfectly heterogeneous (i.e., all individuals have unique ethnic markers), voters surveying the beneficiaries of past patronage transactions will be unable to detect any pattern in the distribution of patronage. In such situations, politicians will be hampered in their

[22] Jonathan Fox, "The Difficult Transition from Clientelism to Citizenship: Lessons from Mexico," *World Politics*, Vol. 46, No. 2 (1994): 164, 168, 172.

attempt to use their discretionary control over state jobs and services as a strategy for obtaining votes. Even though they have an incentive to market these jobs and services in return for votes, they will be unable to send meaningful signals to their target voters. We might expect politicians in such situations to transfer control of patronage from the macro to the micro level of politics and so enable themselves to send nonethnic signals about the distribution of patronage. Alternatively, we might expect them to switch to a different method of courting votes and to divert their discretionary control of state resources in order to seek rents in forms other than votes. In either case, we should be less likely to see the politics of ethnic favouritism.

III. *Alternative Explanations for Ethnic Head Counts*

In this section, I evaluate the argument presented here against the alternatives found in commonsensical understandings of politics or explicitly proposed in the literature on ethnic mobilization. This literature is not directly concerned with explaining the emergence of such a cycle. The questions it asks are related but different: When and why do ethnic groups form? When does one type of cleavage become politically salient rather than another? When do ethnic groups fight? When does ethnic identity become a basis for political coalition building? However, directly or indirectly, this literature offers different hypotheses for the link between patronage politics and ethnic politics, with different observable implications.

Networks

Perhaps the most compelling of all the hypotheses discussed here lays the primary explanatory burden for the cycle on the "dense social networks" presumed to bind together members of ethnic groups. Such dense networks might result from kin connections, from the spatial concentration of ethnic groups (in urban neighbourhoods, in village hamlets, and in artificially constructed "homelands"), or from shared membership in ethnic organizations, including churches, mosques, language clubs, and tribal and caste associations. Such networks might facilitate a patronage transaction by providing "ready-made" channels through which requests can be made and benefits distributed. They might convince voters that the most efficient way to get their voices heard is to approach co-ethnics, and convince politicians that the most efficient way to obtain votes is to approach co-ethnics. We see

71

this mechanism at work, for example, in machine politics in American cities, where the "gangs, firehouses, secret societies and saloons" in ethnically homogeneous wards became the principal places where voters and politicians interacted and where patronage transactions were conducted.[23] Alternatively, they might work by providing both voters and politicians with the means to enforce compliance with patronage contracts, thus leading both to conclude that co-ethnics are the most suitable partners in a patronage transaction.

The utility of kinship networks in explaining the politics of ethnic favouritism is likely to be limited. Kinship networks, constituted by individuals related to each other by blood, are too small to facilitate patronage transactions in modern democracies. The argument that the politics of ethnic favouritism might be best explained by ethnic networks based on patterns of residence or organizational membership, on the other hand, is a powerful one, and it was among my initial working hypotheses. However, it is also unsatisfying upon closer analysis, for the reason that it suffers from an endogeneity problem. As I will show in the following discussion, the dense social networks that characterize ethnic groups – whether they are spatial, organizational, or extended kinship networks – are an *outcome* of a process by which individuals privilege their ethnic identifications over others, rather than the cause of that process. Once individuals choose to invest in them, these networks undoubtedly facilitate patronage transactions. But we can, in principle, imagine some initial point when individuals might equally well have invested in nonethnic networks but chose not to. If this is the case, then we cannot argue that the cycle of self-fulfilling expectations of ethnic favouritism develops out of these networks – rather, the cause of this cycle must be traced to the variable that leads individuals to form and maintain these ethnic networks in the first place.

Consider the "fact" of spatial clustering of ethnic categories, which in turn leads to the formation of dense social networks among those who share a common space. If we look carefully at "ethnically homogeneous clusters," it soon becomes clear that the homogeneity we perceive is an artifact of the boundaries we draw. Take an example from Jones-Correa's study of neighbourhoods in northwestern Queens. Jones-Correa found that the "natural" boundaries that demarcated ethnic communities were not dictated by geography but were generated and maintained by perceptions of difference.

---

[23] Ira Katznelson, *City Trenches: Urban Politics and the Patterning of Class in the United States* (New York: Pantheon Books, 1981), 56.

As he points out of Roosevelt Avenue, which divided "white ethnics" from "new immigrants": "Why should Roosevelt Avenue or Junction Boulevard be considered natural boundaries? Roosevelt has two lanes of traffic, with the number 7 train built overhead – a major transportation route into Manhattan. The street is lined with shops, restaurants, and travel agencies. It is a vibrant and congested street, and an important space for pedestrians."[24] While, objectively speaking, Roosevelt Avenue does not constitute a "natural" dividing line, it has nevertheless become one in the minds of those who live on either side: "Roosevelt has become the main thoroughfare for newer immigrants in the area, but most older white ethnic residents avoid it. For them it has "a completely different lifestyle. It's South American, Hispanic . . . completely different."[25] If we, as external observers, treated Roosevelt Avenue as an objective boundary, we would see two ethnically homogeneous clusters, composed of whites on the one side and Hispanic immigrants on the other. However, if we drew a different boundary line, we would see ethnically mixed clusters. This example illustrates that the appearance of spatial concentration among ethnic groups and the social networks that rise out of such concentration are themselves a product of some process that compels individuals and observers to organize their world by privileging certain ethnic identities over others.

Consider now the following additional examples, each of which describes the tendency of individuals in initially mixed populations to sort themselves and others into ethnically homogeneous clusters.

In a "natural experiment" conducted in Zambia (then Northern Rhodesia) from 1951 to 1954, the anthropologist J. C. Mitchell attempted to explore whether single men who migrated to industrial centres chose to live with co-ethnics or ethnically proximate individuals or whether they chose to cluster together on the basis of some other criteria. As he notes:

When unattached men migrate to industrial centres they frequently do so in groups from the same village or district in the rural areas, and therefore seek accommodation together. If they are allocated accommodation with others they usually seek the first opportunity they can to move into rooms where the company is more congenial to them. The administrative officials do not usually raise objections to this procedure since for them it involves merely a transfer within the same type of accommodation. Over time, therefore, the composition of groups of men occupying single quarters

---

[24] Michael Jones-Correa, *Between Two Nations: The Political Predicament of Latinos in New York City* (Ithaca, NY: Cornell University Press, 1998), 25.

[25] Jones-Correa, *Between Two Nations*, p. 25, citing an interview with a white respondent.

reflects to a large extent their choices of the companions with whom they prefer to live. The composition of single quarters therefore provides one means of examining whether or not behaviour is influenced by ethnic identity.[26]

Mitchell found that, over time, men indeed tended to cluster into living arrangements that included either co-ethnics or members of ethnically proximate categories.

In a field study of Pakistani immigrants in Great Britain, Badr Dahya describes the arrival in Birmingham in 1940 of "some thirty-odd Asian merchant seamen (among whom were Sikhs and Muslims from undivided India and Yemenis)." Upon visiting Birmingham in 1956, Dahya found that

... [t]he immigrants had already "sorted" themselves out on the basis of national origins and ethnicity (that is, on factors such as language/dialect, religion/sect, and area of origin). Pakistanis had moved across to Moseley/Sparkbrook, and to Small Heath and Aston; most of the Jat Sikhs (landowning castes by origin) had moved to places such as Smethwick and Wolverhampton and a few had gone to Sparkbrook, whereas Ramgarhia Sikhs (artisan castes by origin) had settled a little to the south of the primary area and established themselves in two or three streets off Edward Road where they are found to this day with their *Gurdwara* on the corner of Mary and Hallam Streets.... Similarly most of the Yemenis moved to the area south of Edward Road and to parts of Moseley....[27]

Robert Ernst's description of the residential choices made by newly arriving, initially mixed immigrant populations in New York City reveals a similar drive among individuals to sort themselves and others using ethnic classifications rather than others:

Whether in shanty towns or in the commercial districts, whether along the waterfront or in the Five Points, immigrant settlers drew to their area others having the same nationality, language, religion or race. Once a nucleus was established toward which later arrivals were attracted, the cohesive bond resulting from consciousness of similarity tended to replace the magnetic forces of cheap shelter and ready employment.[28]

The several examples just cited all point to the same process: Initially heterogeneous populations, placed in an initially mixed space, quickly sort themselves into ethnically homogeneous clusters. Once these clusters are

---

[26] J. C. Mitchell, "Perceptions of Ethnicity and Ethnic Behaviour: An Empirical Exploration," in Abner Cohen, ed., *Urban Ethnicity* (London: Tavistock, 1974), 9–10.

[27] Badr Dahya, "The Nature of Pakistani Ethnicity in Industrial Cities in Britain," in Cohen, ed., *Urban Ethnicity*, 96.

[28] Robert Ernst, *Immigrant Life in New York City* (New York: King's Crown Press, 1949), 38, cited in Katznelson, *City Trenches*, 51.

formed, it is not surprising that individuals interact closely with those who reside within the clusters and only intermittently with those who reside outside. And once such dense social networks spring up within ethnically homogeneous clusters, they no doubt facilitate patronage transactions. However, these networks are endogenous to the explanation. If we are to explain why ethnic identity is favoured in patronage transactions, we must explain why individuals favour co-ethnics in their choice of whom to interact with most closely. The hypothesis that I have advanced in this section offers such an explanation. In all the examples cited here, individuals, motivated by the desire for familiarity in a strange place, sought to associate with others like themselves. Had they possessed extensive information about each others' backgrounds, they might have been able to discover similarities based on occupation, temperament, education, interests, background, or a range of other characteristics. However, in each of these examples, they had limited information about the strangers they found themselves with. In a classificatory enterprise with limited information, as I argued earlier, ethnic identity is all they have to work with in deciding who is "one of them" and who is not. To the extent that the greater "visibility" of ethnic identities explains the decision by individuals to invest in intraethnic networks, it should be viewed as the root cause of the cycle of self-fulfilling expectations described here.

Let me move now from spatial to organizational networks. Although intraethnic organizational networks may certainly favour patronage transactions, we may well find, by looking far enough, that individuals who invest in ethnic organizational networks have available to them the option of investing equally in nonethnic networks as well. However, we typically find nonethnic networks to be less attractive to both voters and politicians than the ethnic alternatives. Take, for example, Foner's description of trade unions in New York:

Quite often, several nationalities united within the same labor organization, as in the Upholsterers Union in New York, which had among its membership in 1850 German-American, Irish American, French-Canadian, English, and native American workers. The Tailors Union of New York was made up of native American and German-American workers. At first they were not on the best of terms, but police brutality, impartial as to a worker's national origin, during a strike made for greater understanding."[29]

---

[29] Philip Foner, *History of the Labour Movement in the United States, Vol. 1* (New York: International Publishers, 1972), 224, cited in Katznelson, *City Trenches*, 55.

We have no reason to imagine that the ties that bind co-members together in a trade union should be any less strong than the ties that bind co-members in a church, in a language association, or in some other ethnic association. Union members spend long hours together throughout the work week, experience the same working conditions, and often have a shared enemy in the management. In fact, those who share membership in a trade union are more likely to know each other intimately, by dint of working together on a daily basis, than those who share membership in an ethnic association, which typically meets intermittently. Surprisingly, however, such trade unions do not provide potent channels for patronage transactions. As Katznelson points out, parties concerned with distributing patronage in New York City bypassed the trade union as a channel for distributing patronage and concentrated instead on ethnic networks.[30] The greater political salience of ethnic organizational networks, despite the nonethnic alternatives, is not simply a New York phenomenon. Varshney's study of agricultural politics in India, to cite another example, revealed that farmers' unions were crippled in their political struggles by the greater appeal that caste, linguistic, and regional identities held for their members.[31] Given the choice, why do individuals invest more heavily in intraethnic rather than cross-ethnic networks? I argue here that it is because ethnic identity provides them with an easy way to distinguish who is like them and who is not.

Historical Institutionalist Arguments

A second hypothesis explaining the politics of ethnic favouritism comes from "historical-institutionalist" approaches to ethnic politics.[32] The policies followed by the colonial administration, according to this body of literature, imposed a set of categories upon colonized populations that privileged ethnic identities over nonethnic identities. The precise ethnic categories privileged by the colonial state differed across cases: In Yorubaland, it privileged tribal identities; in northern Nigeria, it privileged

---

[30] Katznelson, *City Trenches*, 58.

[31] Ashutosh Varshney, *Democracy, Development and the Countryside* (Cambridge: Cambridge University Press, 1995), 187.

[32] David Laitin, *Hegemony and Culture* (Chicago: University of Chicago Press, 1986); Posner, "Institutional Origins"; Richard Fox, *Lions of the Punjab* (Berkeley: University of California Press, 1985); Gyanendra Pandley, *The Construction of Communalism in Colonial North India* (Delhi: Oxford University Press, 1992); Nicholas Dirks, *Castes of Mind* (Princeton, NJ: Princeton University Press, 2001).

religious identities;[33] in India, it also privileged religious identities at the national level, while caste identities were privileged in some provinces;[34] and in Zambia, it privileged tribal and linguistic identities.[35] Once imposed, however, these administrative categorizations came to dominate the commonsensical framework of both citizens and political entrepreneurs concerning which identities were politically relevant and which were not, a framework that persisted into the postcolonial period.

This body of work suggests that there is nothing inherent in the nature of the patronage transaction that produces expectations of ethnic favouritism on the part of either politicians or voters. Rather, it tells us that the expectations of ethnic favouritism have their roots in the institutional legacy of colonial rule, which forces citizens and politicians alike to treat only ethnic identities as politically relevant and blinds them to the political potential of nonethnic identities. Had the colonial state privileged nonethnic identities, this reasoning implies, then voters and elites in postcolonial states would have treated nonethnic identities as politically relevant, and they would have formed expectations of in-group favouritism where the reference group was nonethnic in nature. In its most general form, this argument suggests that any political system in which institutional structures play a role in "classifying" the population in the way that colonial states did in Asia and Africa should display patterns of identity salience that reflect these past categorizations.

Historical institutionalist arguments do not, however, provide a compelling explanation for the origin of the politics of ethnic favouritism to the extent that they too are characterized by an endogeneity problem. Although the claim is that the privileging of ethnic over nonethnic identities *followed* from the structures of classification imposed by the colonial state, the analyses suggest that the structures of classification imposed by the colonial state at least in part *reflected* perceptions on the part of the state and the colonized populations about which identities were already salient. In Laitin's account of northern Nigeria, for example, the menu from which the British chose included only two options: tribe and religion. There is no reference to their relying upon individuals or groups defined by nonethnic categories to perpetuate their rule. Once the policy of the colonial administration was in place, it undoubtedly further strengthened tribal identity in

---

[33] Laitin, *Hegemony and Culture*.
[34] Pandey, *Construction of Communalism*.
[35] Posner, "Institutional Origins."

relation to religious identity. However, nonethnic identities do not appear to have even been on the initial menu of options that they perceived to be relevant. Similarly, in India, historical institutionalist accounts successfully show that colonial policies classified heterogeneous populations with localized and fragmented identities into religious categories – and to a lesser extent, caste-based categories – at the national level. At the same time, however, these accounts describe the British as operating within a conceptual framework that "saw" ethnic communities as the principal interest groups in India, and that chose religion from a menu of purely ethnic options. If we accept that the colonial state was, even in part, *reacting* to the *perceived* importance of the cleavages it found at some initial point, then the institutional legacy of colonial rule cannot be treated as an exogenous variable explaining the subsequent dominance of ethnic categorizations in postcolonial politics. Rather, this simply takes us a few decades back, to the question of why it is that ethnic cleavages appeared to be more important than nonethnic cleavages at some initial point.

The argument that I have made here offers a different explanation for these initial perceptions. It suggests that the cultural diacritica that uniquely accompany ethnic identities render them more visible than nonethnic identities and so more amenable to classificatory enterprises by external observers. This greater "visibility" may account for the tendency among colonial administrators, operating initially under severe information constraints about the societies that they encountered, to privilege ethnic identities in their initial classificatory systems.

To argue that colonial classifications may be endogenous to the salience of ethnic identifications is not to deny the enormous historical impact of colonial rule in other respects. Colonial rule, I should point out, has been of critical importance in building many of the sprawling states that later gave way to patronage-democracies. And once theories of ethnic group favouritism have been established, colonial institutions may play an important role in creating incentives for political entrepreneurs to favour some ethnic categories over others.

Culture

A third explanation for the politics of ethnic favouritism runs as follows: Members of an ethnic category share a common culture, or at least have more in common with each other than with members of other ethnic categories. Voters and politicians in patronage democracies may favour co-ethnics, therefore, not because of information constraints but because cultural similarities lower the transaction costs of interacting with co-ethnics, and cultural differences raise the transaction costs of interacting with non-co-ethnics.

This explanation is based on an understanding of ethnic groups as distinct "cultural communities" that does not hold up to closer analysis. If we look closely at the members of a given ethnic category, it quickly becomes clear that they are often characterized by a high degree of cultural difference rather than by cultural similarity. The category "Serb," for instance, includes individuals who differ from each other in multiple ways: there are urban Serbs and rural Serbs, Bosnian Serbs, Krajina Serbs, and "Serbian Serbs," all with distinct regional identities, political histories, language patterns, and social customs.[36] Tamils in Sri Lanka are divided on the basis of religion (Hindu, Muslim, and Christian), caste, class, and region.[37] Similarly, Hindus in India are divided on the basis of language, caste, class, religious doctrine and practice, region, and social custom.

At the same time, members of nonethnic categories can often share cultural similarities. E. P. Thompson's study of the English working class shows us, for instance, that class can be "a cultural as much as an economic formation," "embodied in traditions, value-systems, ideas and institutional forms."[38] Luc Boltanski makes a similar point, showing that cadres in French society shared acquired cultural similarities in behaviour, professional training, professional experience, consumption patterns, tastes, behaviour, and manner.[39] In fact, by choosing to organize on an ethnic basis, individuals often reject fellowship with culturally proximate individuals in order to band together with culturally distant ones. Cultural similarity, therefore, cannot be viewed as an explanation for why voters and politicians favour co-ethnics in patronage transactions.

Preexisting Patterns of Identity Salience

Finally, a fourth alternative explanation for the politics of ethnic favouritism runs as follows: Voter preferences across rival politicians depend, not on

---

[36] Misha Glenny, *The Fall of Yugoslavia: The Third Balkan War* (New York: Penguin, 1992).

[37] Stanley Tambiah, *Sri Lanka: Ethnic Fratricide and the Dismantling of Democracy* (Chicago: University of Chicago Press, 1986).

[38] E. P. Thompson, *The Making of the English Working Class* (New York: Vintage, 1963).

[39] Luc Boltanski, *The Making of a Class: Cadres in French Society* (Cambridge: Cambridge University Press, 1987).

information constraints, but on preexisting and exogenously determined patterns of identity salience.[40] In societies in which ethnic identities have been salient in the past, for whatever reason, voters should formulate preferences across rival politicians by ascertaining their ethnic memberships, whether or not they are in a patronage-democracy. But in societies in which nonethnic identities have been salient in the past, for whatever reason, voters should formulate preferences across rival politicians based on their nonethnic characteristics, whether or not they are in a patronage-democracy.

This explanation may account for ethnic favouritism during some initial period of political competition. However, it leaves unanswered the question of why the politics of ethnic favouritism might persist over time. Any explanation that relies upon the past to explain the present must identify the mechanism that keeps these historical patterns locked in place and the conditions under which these patterns might be transformed. The argument of this chapter is an advance over previous explanations to the extent that it identifies a set of conditions under which the patterns of the past will be retained or transformed. If the distinguishing characteristics of a patronage-democracy are introduced in a political system in which all types of identities are initially equally salient, according to this argument, it should intensify the salience of ethnic identities and depress the salience of others; if it is introduced in an environment in which nonethnic identities are more salient than ethnic identities, it should reverse this pattern; and if it is introduced in an environment in which ethnic identities are already more salient than others, it should have a reinforcing effect, intensifying this salience and maintaining it, even after the conditions that initially led to it have lapsed.

IV. Conclusion

I have argued here that severe information constraints are an important and neglected variable explaining the politics of ethnic favouritism. Although the argument has been developed specifically with reference to patronage-democracies, it should also be applicable to other settings in which voting

[40] I owe this point to a discussion with Barry Posen. It has also been developed by Karen Ferree in a dissertation on voting patterns in South Africa. See "A Cognitive Framework for Ethnic Census Elections," paper presented at LICEP (Laboratory in Comparative Ethnic Processes), Dartmouth College, October 2001.

decisions are made under comparable information constraints, such as "founding elections" and elections in unstable party systems.

Other variables, such as institutional legacies and ethnic networks, may *reinforce* the politics of ethnic favouritism once it emerges. However, I have suggested that these additional variables are not independent but endogenous to conditions of limited information and should persist only as long as the underlying information constraints persist. Let me highlight in conclusion some testable implications that result from the argument.

First, to the extent that politicians are able to manipulate the interpretation of ethnic markers, we should expect them to propose interpretations that produce ethnic categories of optimal size, given their electoral objectives. If the politics of ethnic favouritism is produced by information constraints, therefore, we should expect a systematic correlation between the size of an ethnic category and its degree of political salience. On the other hand, if the politics of ethnic favouritism is produced by preexisting networks and institutions, then there should be no systematic correlation between the size of an ethnic category and its political salience. In this case, the ethnic categories that are salient should be a straightforward reflection of preexisting structural and historical patterns, regardless of size.

Second, if the politics of ethnic favouritism is produced by information constraints, then, given a choice between ethnic categories of equivalent size, politicians should mobilize voters around those ethnic categories that are most *visible*.[41] On the other hand, if the politics of ethnic favouritism is produced by networks or institutions independent of information constraints, then there should be no systematic correlation between visibility and the political salience of an ethnic category.

Finally, if the politics of ethnic favouritism is produced by information constraints, then administrative reforms such as decentralization, by shifting the locus of patronage to information-rich environments such as the neighbourhood and village, should result in a deactivation of ethnic identities. Conversely, if the politics of ethnic favouritism is independently produced by networks or institutions, then decentralization should not result in any change in the salience of ethnic identifications unless it also simultaneously transforms the character of networks or institutional legacies.

---

[41] I owe this point to a discussion with Susan Stokes.

4

Counting Heads

WHY ETHNIC PARTIES SUCCEED IN PATRONAGE-DEMOCRACIES

This chapter builds upon the individual microfoundations introduced in the previous chapter to propose a hypothesis predicting ethnic party success and failure in patronage-democracies. Voters in patronage-democracies, I argue here, decide whether or not to vote for any type of party – ethnic, multiethnic, or nonethnic – based on a comprehensive process of ethnic head counting. They formulate preferences across parties by counting the heads of co-ethnics in positions of power and prestige in party organizations. They decide to vote in accordance with these preferences only when they expect their preferred party to win or to exercise influence after the election. And they formulate expectations about the probable electoral outcome by ascertaining, after counting the heads of co-ethnics and ethnic outsiders in the electorate, that members of their "own" ethnic category are numerous enough to take the party past the threshold of winning or influence. Ethnic parties are likely to succeed, therefore, only when they have a comparative advantage in the representation of elites from their target ethnic category *and* when members of their target ethnic category are numerous enough to affect the outcome. When either of these two conditions is not met, ethnic parties are likely to fail.

This chapter is organized as follows: Section I outlines the proposition that voters in patronage-democracies formulate preferences across political parties by counting heads belonging to their "own" ethnic category rather than by assessing party issue positions; section II outlines the proposition that these benefit-seeing voters are also strategic actors who will vote for their preferred party only if it is likely to win or to exercise influence after the election, and not otherwise; section III outlines the proposition that voters formulate expectations about the electoral outcome by counting the heads of co-ethnics across the electorate; section IV outlines the proposition

82

that party strategy in patronage-democracies should give primary emphasis to developing advantageous systems of ethnic categorization rather than to developing advantageous issue dimensions; section V, based on these previous propositions, outlines the hypothesis predicting the success of ethnic parties; and Section VI elaborates on the paradox of ethnic party failure. The argument presented here also generates a range of additional hypotheses about elite strategy and voting behaviour in patronage-democracies. These are identified but not tested here, since they are tangential to the main subject of this study.

I. Voters in Patronage-Democracies Formulate Preferences across Political Parties by Counting Heads Belonging to Their "Own" Ethnic Category rather than by Assessing Party Issue Positions

If voters are motivated by the desire for benefits, and expect to obtain these benefits from politicians who belong to their "own" ethnic category, then it follows that they will formulate preferences across political parties not by comparing the positions that the parties assume on issues during the election campaign, but by counting the number of heads belonging to their "own" ethnic category across parties. Because individuals belong to multiple ethnic categories, however, we cannot stipulate a priori which category (or categories) voters will choose to identify with as their "own." That category (or categories) will vary across cases, and it may be endogenously transformed by political competition. This section elaborates upon this proposition and its implications.

To some extent, we might expect voters everywhere to discount parties' issue positions for two reasons. First, it requires a significant investment of time and resources for voters to familiarize themselves with party platforms. Second, party platforms typically include exaggerated promises that often go unfulfilled. "Citizens," Fiorina reminds us, "are not fools. Having often observed political equivocation, if not outright lying, should they listen carefully to campaign promises?"[1] However, voters in patronage-democracies have even more reason to be skeptical of party promises on various issue dimensions. Such promises typically describe some collective good (responsible government, law and order, economic reform) to be delivered through new policy legislation or better policy enforcement. But for

---

[1] Morris P. Fiorina, *Retrospective Voting in American National Elections* (New Haven, CT: Yale University Press, 1981), 5.

patronage-seeking voters, such promises are beside the point. A decision to pass new policy legislation or to enforce policy at the macro level is of little value to them unless they have a reasonable expectation that the local government official will favour them in the implementation of that decision. And an unfavourable decision on policy legislation or enforcement at the macro level, similarly, is of little relevance if the local government official is willing to bend the rules in their favour. Even if they care deeply about issue dimensions, even if they are well informed about party positions on these issue dimensions, and even if they believe that such platforms reveal sincere intentions, benefit-seeking voters have little reason to treat these data as relevant. Rather, they will look for guarantees that the benefits that flow from the implementation of the promised policies will be directed toward them.

The ethnic identity of party personnel, for the reasons outlined in the previous chapter, provides exactly such a guarantee. The more that members of their "own" ethnic category are represented at key levels in the party apparatus, the more confident voters can be of obtaining access to patronage benefits from this party. The less elites from their "own" category are represented at the appropriate levels in the party, the less confident voters can be of obtaining access to patronage benefits from this party. As I argued earlier, the nonethnic identities of party personnel or their personal qualifications – such as character, reputation, and influence – simply do not provide credible guarantees about access to patronage benefits. Patronage-seeking voters in patronage-democracies, therefore, will formulate preferences between competing parties by counting heads belonging to their "own" ethnic category across parties and ignoring party issue positions.

At which level of party organization, however, should we expect benefit-seeking voters to count heads? Party personnel include local candidates, members of local organizational units, state leaders, and national leaders, and the ethnic identity of individuals holding different posts might differ. How do we know which of these posts are most important to voters in conducting their head counts across different contexts? If the tendency to count heads is driven by expectations of access to patronage benefits, then it follows that *rational voters will count heads at that level of the party organization where the power to distribute patronage resources is concentrated.* The level at which they count heads will vary with the design of the party organization. In regionalized or federalized parties, where regional party officials decide how these resources are distributed, voters will count heads at the regional level. In centralized parties, where decision-making power is concentrated at higher levels, voters will count heads at these higher levels. And where the regional and central leadership share authority, voters will assign some weight to party personnel at both levels in their assessment.[2] In all cases, they will prefer that party that has the most heads belonging to members of their "own" ethnic category at the appropriate level, regardless of its issue position. If heads from their "own" category are distributed equally across parties, they will be indifferent, equally inclined toward all parties, regardless of the issues they stand on. And if heads from their "own" ethnic category are not found in any party, they will also be indifferent, equally alienated from all parties, regardless of the issues they stand on.

Case studies of patronage-democracies provide ample support for the plausibility of this proposition. Chabal and Daloz note of voters in Africa: "They do not vote because they support the ideas, even less read the programmes of a particular political party."[3] Posner, similarly, argues that voters identify with parties based on the ethnic identity of those who lead the party, even if the official platforms of political parties do not emphasize the ethnic identity of their leaders: "The identification of the party with a particular ethnic group was less an outcome of active self-definition by party organizers than a consequence of an unprompted equation in peoples' minds of the party with the ethnic group of the party's president."[4] The focus on the ethnic identity of the personnel and the ignorance of issues is so strong, according to Posner, that "not only do Zambian political parties take on the ethnic affiliations of their leaders, but when the party leaders change, so too do the perceived orientations of the parties."[5] Wolfinger makes much the same point in his description of the "issue-free quality" of elections in New Haven and other cities dominated by machine politics.[6] He points out that the indifference of voters to issues and policies in patronage-based systems, ironically, creates possibilities for greater policy innovation, since politicians are relatively unhampered by constituents' views on policy positions.

---

[2] The design of the party organization, in turn, is likely to parallel the design of the governmental structure. Federal systems should have regionally powerful parties.

[3] Patrick Chabal and Jean-Pascal Daloz, *Africa Works* (Oxford: International African Institute, 1999), 89.

[4] Daniel Posner, "The Institutional Origins of Ethnic Politics in Zambia" (Ph.D. dissertation, Harvard University, 1998), 129.

[5] Ibid.

[6] Raymond Wolfinger, *The Politics of Progress* (Englewood Cliffs, NJ: Prentice Hall, 1974), 1, 121; Robert Dahl, *Who Governs?* (New Haven, CT: Yale University Press, 1961), 98–99.

II. Voters in Patronage-Democracies Are Strategic Actors, Voting for Their Preferred Party Only If It Is Likely to Win or Exercise Influence after the Election, and Not Otherwise

So far, I have argued that benefit-seeking voters in patronage-democracies are rational actors who use the vote as an instrument to secure patronage benefits. I have also argued that they prefer the party that represents members of their own ethnic category to the greatest degree and so promises them the greatest access to patronage benefits. In this section, I argue that the rational benefit-seeking voter is also a strategic voter. He will vote for his preferred party only if he expects his preferred party to win the election or to exercise leverage over the electoral outcome. When he has no reasonable expectation that his preferred party will do either, he will vote instead for the competition. In this section, I outline the logic underlying this proposition.

The precise threshold for winning control of government or exercising influence over someone else's victory or loss varies with the design of the government, party, and electoral systems taken together. Consider first the threshold for *winning*. In a first-past-the-post system with a parliamentary form of government and two parties, for instance, the threshold for winning control of the government is high. A party must obtain *at least* 51 percent of the vote in at least 51 percent of the seats in order to win. As the number of parties increases in an FPTP system, however, other things being equal, the threshold for winning control of government goes down. In a multiparty system, other things being equal, a party can get away with obtaining less than 51 percent in a majority of the constituencies and still form a government. And in an FPTP system in cases where the party system is so fragmented that no single party wins a majority, a party can win only a plurality of votes in a small number of seats and still share control of the government. In List PR systems with multimember districts and coalition forms of government, the threshold for winning control of or participation in the government is generally lower than in FPTP systems.

The variation across electoral systems in the threshold at which a party obtains *influence* over someone else's victory or loss is harder to predict. In FPTP systems with a parliamentary form of government, influence may be exercised either during the election in the contest for victory in individual constituencies, or after the election in the contest for the formation of government. In general, the closer the race for victory at the constituency level

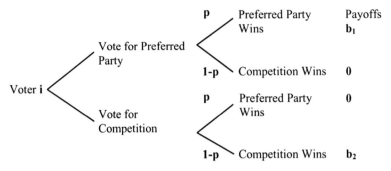

Figure 4.1. The voting decision in a patronage-democracy.

during the election or for the requisite number of seats after the election the more a party is likely to have influence over the electoral outcome. In PR systems, one party can exercise influence over another's electoral fortunes by cutting sufficiently into its overall vote share to influence its participation in government. The threshold of influence in this case depends upon the precise formula for the conversion of votes into seats, and for the conversion of seats into participation in government.

Imagine a voter in a patronage-democracy faced with the choice between two parties. Figure 4.1 captures the decision problem faced by voter i.

Voter i has two possible courses of action: to vote for his preferred party or for the competition. The preferred party has a probability p of winning the election or exercising leverage over someone else's victory or loss. The competition has a probability $(1 - p)$ of winning the election or exercising leverage over someone else's victory or loss.

Voter i's access to benefits depends upon the electoral outcome. A victorious party has control over state resources and so has the means to "pay" him for his vote. At the same time, the capture of political power by co-ethnics, by establishing their superiority over other ethnic categories, provides the voter with a source of pride and status. A party that does not win but influences someone else's victory or loss can bargain for the resources with which to reward its supporters. At the same time, exercising influence over the fate of a candidate from a different ethnic group also gives voters a sense of superiority. A party that neither wins nor exercises leverage has nothing to offer its supporters. Without access to state power, it has no material benefits to distribute. And as a party without power or influence, it also cannot provide status rewards. Rather, its loss is likely to compound feelings of inferiority among the ethnic categories that prefer it.

The benefit-seeking voter, therefore, has an incentive to end up on the winning side. If his preferred party is victorious or influential after the election, and he votes for his preferred party, he obtains the net benefit b_1. This is the best possible scenario for him, since his expectation of access to benefits is greatest from his preferred party, populated by his own co-ethnics, than from the competition. If the competition is victorious or influential after the election, and he votes for the competition, the voter obtains the net benefit b_2. This benefit is likely to be small, since, as I argued in Chapter 3, the competition will be responsive primarily to voters from some other ethnic category. However, it is better than nothing. In other words, $b_1 > 0$, and $b_2 > 0$, but $b_1 > b_2$.

The worst-case scenario for the voter is to vote for a party that is neither victorious nor influential. If he votes for his preferred party and it emerges neither victorious nor influential after the election, it will have nothing to distribute to its supporters. The voter in this scenario will obtain a payoff of zero, and his vote will have been wasted. And if he votes for the competition and it emerges neither victorious nor influential, he also obtains no benefits. Politicians from his preferred party will not "pay" him, since he did not vote for them, while the competition will have nothing to offer. In some cases, furthermore, this payoff might even be negative, if there is a threat of retaliation from either the competition or the preferred party.

This voter will vote for his preferred party only when the expected payoff from voting for his preferred party is greater than the expected payoff from voting for the competition. This will be true when the following condition is fulfilled:[7]

$$\frac{(p)}{(1-p)} > \frac{b_2}{b_1}$$

We can draw the following conclusions from this model:

When $p = 0$ (the preferred party has no probability of securing either victory or influence after the election), voter i will not vote for his preferred party. The reasoning is as follows: The only condition under which voter i will vote for his preferred party when $p = 0$ is if $b_2/b_1 < 0$. However, given

[7] The expected payoff for voter i for voting for the preferred party is $p(b_1) + (1-p)(0) = pb_1$; the expected payoff for voter i for voting for the competition is: $p(0) + (1-p)(b_2) = b_2 - pb_2$. The expected payoff for voting for the preferred party will exceed the payoff for voting for the competition when $pb_1 > b_2 - pb_2$, which simplifies to the expression above.

the stipulation that $b_1 > 0$, and $b_2 > 0$, this will never be the case. When $p >= .5$ (the preferred party has a 50 percent chance or better of securing either victory or influence after the election), voter i will always vote for his preferred party. The reasoning is as follows: The condition under which voter i will vote for his preferred party when $p >= .5$ is if $b_2/b_1 < 1$. But given the stipulation that $b_1 > b_2$, this is always the case.

When $0 < p < .5$, the voting decision of the voter depends upon the degree to which b_1 is greater than b_2. The more substantial the difference, the lower the value of p must be for the voter to vote for his preferred party. The smaller the difference between b_1 and b_2, the higher the value of p must be for the voter to vote for his preferred party. For example, when $p = .25$, the voter will vote for his preferred party only if b_1 is more than three times as large as b_2 (i.e., $b_2/b_1 < .33$), and so on. In other words, if the competition offers only negligible benefits to voters from ethnic categories not well represented in its party organization, these voters will defect to the party that represents their co-ethnics even when it has a very low threshold of winning or leverage. However, the more the competition offers to such underrepresented voters, the higher the threshold of winning or leverage for their preferred party has to be before they are likely to defect. In this situation, even though such voters do worse under the competition than they would have under a party that represents members of their ethnic category, a sizable "payment" in benefits can prevent them from defecting.

It is not necessary to describe voting behaviour under all possible scenarios. The main point that I wish to make here is that the rational benefit-seeking voter is also a strategic voter. His voting decision, in other words, depends upon an assessment of the probability that his preferred party will obtain victory or leverage after the election. When this probability is high enough, he will vote in a manner consistent with his preferences. When this probability is low, however, he will vote contrary to his preferences in order to secure at least some access to benefits.

Note that I have so far been discussing the behaviour of an *individual* benefit-seeking voter in a patronage-democracy. Two qualifications are necessary in moving from predicting the behaviour of an individual voter to predicting the behaviour of the entire population of voters in a patronage-democracy. First, although *most* voters in a patronage-democracy are dependent upon the state for benefits, *all* are not. Even in the most state-dominated of polities, there are always some sections of the population who are able to exist in relative autonomy from the state. These individuals, who are not dependent upon the state, may well have the luxury of voting expressively. Second, even though the model predicts that most voters in a patronage-democracy should vote strategically, it does not stipulate that all such strategic voters will behave identically. Although the model assumes that $b_1 > b_2$ for all individuals in all cases, it allows the precise value of both quantities and the magnitude of the difference between them to vary for different groups of voters. The values of p at which different groups of voters might vote for their preferred party, therefore, may well differ, leading to differences in their voting behaviour.

III. Voters in Patronage-Democracies Formulate Expectations about the Likely Electoral Outcome by Counting Heads of Co-Ethnics and Outsiders in the Electorate

How, in turn, might voters in patronage-democracies formulate expectations about the likely electoral outcome? How, in other words, do they estimate the value of p in the model just discussed? Studies of strategic voting suggest that voters formulate expectations about the competitive position of "their" party based on opinion polls.[8] Opinion polls, the argument runs, provide information about the preferences of other voters. And based on this revealed information, individual voters formulate expectations about how others will vote and so adjust their own behaviour accordingly. Where such polls do not exist, or where voters do not have access to these polls, the argument implies that voters cannot formulate these expectations.

However, if voters formulate preferences by counting heads belonging to their "own" ethnic category across parties, then sufficient information is available about other voters' preferences and likely voting behaviour independent of opinion polls and election surveys. Voters from any one ethnic category know that just as they prefer the party that represents members of their own ethnic category to the greatest degree, so will voters from other ethnic categories prefer those parties that represent members from *their* own categories. By counting heads from each ethnic category in the population and imputing to them preferences across parties, they can guess at the relative positions of the parties if all voters vote according to their

---

[8] Gary Cox, *Making Votes Count* (Cambridge: Cambridge University Press, 1997), 79. See also Stephen Levine and Nigel S. Roberts, "Elections and Expectations: Evidence from Electoral Systems in New Zealand," *Journal of Commonwealth and Comparative Politics*, Vol. 29, No. 2 (1991): 129–152; and Mark Fey, "Stability and Coordination in Duverger's Law: A Formal Model of Preelection Polls and Strategic Voting," *American Political Science Review*, Vol. 91, No. 1 (1991): 135–147.

preferences. They can then guess whether, if all voters from their "own" ethnic category were to coordinate on voting for their preferred party, they would be sufficient to make this party a possible winner or kingmaker. They also possess sufficient information to guess whether such coordination on their part would be sufficient to take their preferred party past the threshold of winning or leverage.

Formulating expectations in this way, it should be obvious, is a process that can carry with it a great deal of uncertainty. In a world of multiple ethnic identifications, there may not always be agreement on which lines of cleavage and which categories to use in counting heads across the population and across parties. Second, even in those situations in which there is agreement on the relevant ethnic cleavages and categories, the relative numerical strength of each category may be contested. Third, even where the categories are agreed upon and the numerical strength of their members is clear, uncertainty may remain about turnout rates across different ethnic categories. Fourth, while the preferences of those who are best represented in each of the parties can be inferred with confidence, the preferences of voters from ethnic categories that are underrepresented in all parties are likely to be highly uncertain. The "unrevealed" preferences of such voters may make it more difficult to predict the electoral outcome. Fifth, where there is more than one party representing members of one ethnic category, it may not be clear which way members of that ethnic category might lean. However, the main point is that counting heads provides voters with the information to make *some* prediction about the electoral outcome (although this prediction may be uncertain or even wrong) and to adjust their voting decision accordingly. In fact, we should expect political parties courting strategic voters to manipulate this uncertainty to their advantage, proposing favourable ethnic demographies, inflating the proportions and turnout rates of their target ethnic categories, and claiming to be the party of choice of voters with "unrevealed" preferences – all with a view to influencing voters in their favour by influencing their expectations.

If benefit-seeking voters vote strategically, then we should expect an en masse vote by voters from any given ethnic category in favour of their preferred party if they believe it to be a likely winner or kingmaker. Conversely, where even an en masse vote by co-members of an ethnic category is not likely to result in victory or influence for their preferred party, we should not expect to see many of them vote for their preferred party. As a result, the voting behaviour of particular ethnic categories is likely to change with the competitive configuration. Where the competitive position of the preferred party is stable across elections, the voting behaviour of its target ethnic category should also be stable. But where the preferred party's competitive situation fluctuates, we should also see considerable volatility in voting behaviour.

IV. Party Election Strategies in Patronage-Democracies Should Focus on Identifying Advantageous Systems of Ethnic Categorization Rather than on Identifying Advantageous Issue Dimensions

In a world in which all individuals belong simultaneously to multiple ethnic categories, and where all choose some ethnic category to identify with independently and arbitrarily, the distribution of preferences across parties would be indeterminate. Imagine, for instance, an election with two competitors: Party X and Party Y. Imagine further that the total set of ethnic categories available to individuals in this society consists of four dichotomous pairs, $\{a, \sim a, b, \sim b, c, \sim c, d, \sim d\}$, and that each party is composed of individuals with identical repertoires of ethnic categories. The ethnic profiles of elites in Party X and Party Y are summarized below:

Party X	Party Y
$X_1 = \{a, \sim b, c\}$	$Y_1 = \{\sim a, b, c\}$
$X_2 = \{a, \sim b, c\}$	$Y_2 = \{\sim a, b, c\}$
$X_3 = \{a, \sim b, c\}$	$Y_3 = \{\sim a, b, c\}$
.....	.....
$X_n = \{a, \sim b, c\}$	$Y_n = \{\sim a, b, c\}$

Imagine a voter with the following repertoire: $\{a, b, d\}$. If this voter arbitrarily identified ethnic category a as her own, she would prefer Party X. If she identified category b as her own, she would prefer Party Y. If she identified category d as her own, she would be equally alienated from, and therefore indifferent between, the two parties. In this case, she would be potentially available for mobilization by a challenger party, one with d's well represented in its organization. Imagine now an entire electorate where each voter has an identical repertoire of categories. If each voter decided independently and arbitrarily which ethnic category to identify as her own, the resulting preference distribution would be unpredictable. Imagine, finally, a heterogeneous electorate with variation in the ethnic repertoires of individual voters. Once we introduce the fact of ethnic heterogeneity, the preference distribution becomes even more difficult to predict ex ante.

The multiplicity of possible categorizations presents political parties with a problem and an opportunity. On the one hand, it raises the possibility of arbitrary coding by voters, which puts many (but not all) political parties at a disadvantage. However, it also gives these political parties an incentive to restrict the set of categorizations that voters employ. This restricted set of alternatives disciplines the choice. E. E. Schattschneider's observation about the organization of the American electorate by political parties is relevant here:

> Anyone watching the crowds move about Grand Central Station might learn something about the nature of party organization. The crowds seem to be completely unorganized. What the spectator observes is not chaos, however, because the multitude is controlled by the timetables and the gates. Each member of the crowd finds his place in the system (is organized by the system) because his alternatives are limited. The parties organize the electorate by reducing their alternatives to the extreme limit of simplification.[9]

Schattschneider's observation is a precursor to a now extensive literature that employs social choice theory to illuminate the role that political parties play in restricting the set of alternatives among which voters choose.[10] This literature, while it has typically focused on the restriction of the set of policy alternatives, contains important insights for the way in which politicians can restrict the set of ethnic categories that voters identify with.[11] If all parties signal themselves as representing either members of category a or members of category ∼a, then all voters in the earlier example who have a in their repertoire should prefer Party X, and those who have ∼a in their repertoire should prefer party Y. The fact that these voters simultaneously belong to other ethnic categories is irrelevant in a political arena where the set of alternatives is restricted to a and ∼a. The argument in Chapter 2 suggests that the *mechanism* by which political entrepreneurs should attempt to send such signals is the manipulation of the interpretation of ethnic markers. Political entrepreneurs, thus, should attempt to provide voters with a "standardized" interpretation of ethnic markers so that any

[9] E. E. Schattschneider, *The Semisovereign People* (New York: Holt, Rinehart and Winston, 1960), 58.

[10] Particularly William Riker, *Liberalism against Populism* (Prospect Heights, IL: Waveland Press, 1982); William Riker, *The Art of Political Manipulation* (New Haven, CT: Yale University Press, 1986); William Riker, *Agenda Formation* (Ann Arbor: University of Michigan Press, 1993).

[11] I explore these implications in Kanchan Chandra, "Ethnic Bargains, Group Instability and Social Choice Theory," *Politics and Society*, Vol. 29, No. 3 (2001): 337–362.

given marker is coded either as a or ~a by all voters, even though it might, in principle, signal membership in many different categories.

For any given set of alternatives, the argument suggests that the effective strategy of political parties in patronage-democracies should consist of marketing themselves as the best representatives of some ethnic category within this set. And where possible, political strategies should consist of transforming the set of alternative categories. Parties that stand to gain from the current set of alternatives should strive to maintain it, while parties that stand to lose should strive to transform it. At the same time, we should see relatively low investment by political parties in distinguishing themselves on issue dimensions in patronage-democracies. Party issue positions in patronage-democracies should be broadly similar, and weakly emphasized in election campaigns. Furthermore, the emphasis on representation of ethnic categories rather than issues should be true of all parties – ethnic, nonethnic, and multiethnic.

Here, then, lies the importance of the overt message sent by a political party in a patronage-democracy. The essential purpose of this message lies, not in signaling *what* a party will do when in power, but *whom* it will serve when in power. Political parties in patronage-democracies, as I argued in the previous chapter, cannot make open declarations about how they intend to use their discretionary power. However, they can, by their public rhetoric, influence voters to use some modes of categorization and not others.

I have suggested that by manipulating the set of alternatives, political parties can induce individuals to identify politically with different ethnic identities in their voting decision. Isn't ethnic identity too deeply held, however, to be manipulated so easily? Do voters simply switch identities as politicians decide? They do not. For two reasons, it would be erroneous to assume that the voter, in choosing one ethnic category to identify with as her "own" in a voting decision, is discarding any of her other identities:

First, the decision to vote on the basis of one category rather than another does not constitute a total identity shift. It is a phenomenon qualitatively different from other acts that activate ethnic identity. The decision to participate in a civil war or a riot, for example, may require an irrevocable decision about which identity an individual values most highly. The decision about whether to assimilate with the dominant language category, similarly, requires decisions about educational investments that have binding consequences in the future.[12] Over the course of even a single

[12] David Laitin, *Identity in Formation* (Ithaca, NY: Cornell University Press, 1998).

generation, this decision privileges some linguistic identities and eliminates others decisively. The act of voting, however, consists of a *partial* activation of some identity category in the electoral arena. It does not necessarily lead to the renunciation of other categories available in an individual's repertoire. These other categories might well continue to be relevant in other arenas and at other times. Kasfir's example of Nigerian workers "who participated in a general strike in June 1964 only to vote along ethnic lines the following December"[13] is a case in point. When participating in the general strike, the workers deactivated but did not renounce their ethnic identity, just as when voting in December they deemphasized but did not give up their class identity. The choice of an ethnic category in the one event was independent of, and nonbinding upon, the other.

Second, as Barth points out, the act of identification with any ethnic category consists only of a change in the *boundary* of the category within which individuals place themselves rather than a change in the *content* of their identity. Individuals who place themselves in any single category, therefore, change only the nature of those whom they identify as "outsiders," without effecting any change in their own sense of self.

If the argument presented here is supported by the data, it has significant implications for research on party politics and voting behaviour. A prominent strand in this research, influenced by the publication of Hotelling's 1929 article on spatial competition and Downs's work on *The Economic Theory of Democracy* in 1957, has attempted to model voter choices by identifying the salient issue dimensions on which parties position themselves and the preference distributions of voters on these issue dimensions.[14] Over the course of a half-century, this literature has produced sophisticated spatial models and increasingly refined techniques of data collection that allow researchers to identify salient issue dimensions as well as party positions and the distribution of voter preferences.[15] The

[13] Nelson Kasfir, "Explaining Ethnic Political Participation," *World Politics*, Vol. 31, No. 3 (1979): 365–388, p. 374.
[14] Anthony Downs, *An Economic Theory of Democracy* (Cambridge: Cambridge University Press, 1957); Harold Hotelling, "Stability in Competition," *The Economic Journal*, Vol. 39 (1929): 41–57.
[15] See, for instance, Ian Budge, Ivor Crewe, and Denis Farlie, *Party Identification and Beyond* (London: Wiley, 1976); Ian Budge, David Robertson, and Derek J. Hearl, eds., *Ideology, Strategy and Party Change: Spatial Analyses of Post-War Election Programmes in 19 Democracies* (Cambridge: Cambridge University Press, 1987); John Huber and Ronald Inglehart, "Expert Interpretations of Party Space and Party Locations in 42 Societies," *Party Politics*, Vol. 1, No. 1 (1995): 73–111; Frances Castles and Peter Mair, "Left-Right Political

proposition advanced here suggests that, rather than concentrating on issue dimensions, research on party politics and voting behaviour in patronage-democracies should turn its attention to developing or adapting techniques of modeling and data collection tailored to the manipulation of alternative dimensions of identity.

V. Why Ethnic Parties Succeed in Patronage-Democracies

A hypothesis about the conditions under which ethnic parties succeed or fail can now be constructed from the propositions just outlined. If voters prefer parties that represent their "own" men to the greatest degree, vote for their preferred parties only when they expect them to win or to exercise influence, and form expectations about the probable electoral outcome by counting the heads of co-ethnics across the electorate, then it follows that an ethnic party is likely to succeed among voters from its target ethnic category only (1) when it gives greater representational opportunities than the competition to elites from all "subdivisions" from its target ethnic category and (2) when voters from its target ethnic category are numerous enough to affect the electoral outcome through coordinated action. Conversely, an ethnic party is likely to fail under two conditions: (1) If elites from all or some "subdivisions" among its target ethnic category are also well represented in the competition and/or (2) if voters from its target ethnic category are not numerous enough to affect the outcome through coordinated action. The precise level of the political system at which voters should count heads, the threshold of winning or influence, and the size of the ethnic category required to take a party past it will vary with the nature of the governmental, party, and electoral systems in patronage-democracies. However, the *mechanism* explaining ethnic party success or failure should be the same across these different institutional contexts.

This hypothesis is not unique to explaining the success of *ethnic* parties but applies generally to all parties in patronage-democracies – ethnic, non-ethnic, and multiethnic. All parties in patronage-democracies, I argue here, succeed based on an ethnic head count. The difference between them lies only in the nature of the coalitions whose support they seek. Ethnic parties seek uniform coalitions of support, with the same "insiders" and the same "outsiders" across constituencies and across levels of the political system

Scales: Some Expert Judgments," *European Journal of Political Research*, Vol. 12 (1976): 73–88; David Robertson, *A Theory of Party Competition* (London: Wiley, 1976).

(local, regional, and national). Consequently, they can afford to declare their allegiance to some ethnic category, and their opposition to others, openly. Multiethnic and nonethnic parties, however, seek the support of differentiated ethnic coalitions, with different sets of insiders and outsiders across different constituencies and levels. For such parties, declaring an open allegiance to one ethnic category but not another would be sure to alienate some component of their target support base. Consequently, in their overt messages such parties are forced to use nonethnic or multiethnic appeals as a "cover" for targeted ethnic messages in particular contexts.

VI. The Paradox of Ethnic Party Failure

If the formula for ethnic party success requires the identification of a target ethnic constituency of "optimal" size and provision of greater opportunities for representation for elites from this target ethnic constitutency, and if political entrepreneurs learn this formula over time, then why should ethnic parties fail at all? Should political entrepreneurs not simply adjust their behaviour over time, forming only ethnic parties that mobilize ethnic categories of the right size, and adjusting the ethnic profile of the party leadership accordingly?

Indeed, the argument implies that we should see a trend toward the formation of ethnic parties in patronage-democracies that target ethnic constituencies of optimal size. Ethnic parties that seek to mobilize ethnic categories that are indisputably smaller than the optimal size in any given political system should be winnowed out over time. Elites from "small" ethnic categories, therefore, should either throw in their lot with elites from other ethnic categories in order to form nonethnic or multiethnic parties, or attempt to "resize" the definition of their "own" ethnic category in order to produce memberships of an optimal size.

While political entrepreneurs might attempt to construct a new ethnic category of optimal size, however, historical and institutional constraints may prevent the success of such an effort. Further, even when these categories can easily be *constructed*, it may not be as easy to "*tailor*" them to be of uniformly optimal size across time and space. Imagine, for instance, a political system with several provinces: An ethnic category may be of optimal size in some of these provinces but not in others. Consequently, even if political entrepreneurs do the best they can to design an ethnic category of optimal size for the political system as a whole, such an ethnic category may often fall below optimal size in particular regions and provinces, resulting in the failure of the ethnic party in particular regions but not in others. Similarly, imagine a political system in which the threshold of winning or influence changes across elections: An initially low winning threshold, given a fragmented party system in an FPTP electoral system, may suddenly be transformed into a high winning threshold by the coalescence of previously fragmented parties in a bipolar alliance. An ethnic category that was of optimal size in the earlier context may be reduced to suboptimal status in the new one. Foresight on the part of political entrepreneurs, therefore, should limit but not preclude the emergence of ethnic parties that seek to mobilize ethnic categories of suboptimal size.

Further, even when ethnic parties succeed in designing an ethnic category of optimal size, creating the correct ethnic profile is by no means a simple matter. Despite its desire to obtain the exclusive support of an ethnic category, an ethnic party is not automatically able to provide greater representational opportunities than the competition to elites from across the spectrum of subdivisions among its target ethnic category. The conditions under which it is likely to offer such representational opportunities and the conditions under which it is likely to fail are the subject of the following chapter.

5

Why Parties Have Different Ethnic Head Counts

PARTY ORGANIZATION AND ELITE INCORPORATION

What determines the initial differences in relative opportunities that a political party in a patronage-democracy offers to elites from different ethnic groups? And, regardless of these initial differences, once it is clear that success depends upon acquiring the correct head count, why might unsuccessful parties fail to adjust their ethnic profiles over repeated elections?

These questions raise a broader theoretical question: Under what conditions are political parties in multiethnic democracies able to incorporate new elites, and under what conditions are they likely to fail? General theories of party politics in multiethnic societies propose a sociological answer to the problem of elite incorporation, according to which success or failure in elite incorporation is determined by the pattern of conflict or harmony between ethnic categories in society. Where ethnic categories are in conflict in society, according to these theories, elites belonging to these categories will not be able to coexist in the same political party. Consequently, multiethnic parties are described as "inherently unstable."[1] Conversely, ethnic parties, which bring together elites from a single ethnic category, or from socially harmonious ethnic categories, are posited to enjoy a more stable existence.[2]

This chapter proposes a model of elite incorporation that explains the successful incorporation of elites by any political party – whether multiethnic, nonethnic, or ethnic – as a consequence of the internal organizational structure of the party. The model builds upon Myron Weiner's study of

---

[1] Alvin Rabushka and Kenneth Shepsle, *Politics in Plural Societies* (Columbus, OH: Charles E. Merrill, 1972).

[2] Donald Horowitz, *Ethnic Groups in Conflict* (Berkeley: University of California Press, 1985); Rabushka and Shepsle, *Politics in Plural Societies*.

the incorporation of new elites in the Congress party in India.[3] According to the model, parties with competitive rules for intraparty advancement, other things being equal, are able to continually incorporate new elites while keeping old ones acquiescent. Such parties are stable parties, better able to retain the allegiance of elites during "lean" periods when they are out of government. Parties with centralized rules of intraparty advancement, other things being equal, are "closed" to the entry of new elites. Such parties are unstable, deeply vulnerable to defections by old elites when they are out of power. The internal organizational structure, I propose, is more influential than the degree of conflict between ethnic groups in society. Where a competitive structure exists, it promotes coexistence even between elites from warring groups in the same party. Where a centralized organizational structure exists, however, we are likely to see splits and defections even within a party dominated by elites from the same ethnic category.

The chapter is organized as follows: Section I redefines the problem of elite incorporation as a variant of the collective action dilemma. Section II models the process by which competitive party organizations overcome this dilemma. Section III shows why centralized party organizations are less likely to overcome this dilemma.

I. Elite Incorporation in Competitive versus Centralized Party Organizations

I assume that new and old elites from any ethnic category are motivated by the desire to obtain political office in the long term and are instrumentally rational. They may desire office for material reasons, or for psychic reasons, or both, but they will affiliate themselves with the political party that promises them the best chance of obtaining office in the long term. New elites, faced with a choice between political parties, will join the one that gives them the best long-term chance of obtaining office. Elites already entrenched in any political party organization, faced with a decision about whether to remain or to defect, will also choose the party that maximizes their chances for obtaining office in the long term.

For any individual elite, the expected probability of obtaining office through any given political party is the product of two independent probabilities: (1) the probability of the party's winning an election in the

---

[3] Myron Weiner, *Party Building in a New Nation* (Chicago: University of Chicago Press, 1967).

long term, which in turn affects the number of offices at its disposal, and (2) the probability of their obtaining a position in the party organization high enough to guarantee them one of the limited offices. The following equation represents this calculation:

$$EP(Office) = P(Win)^*P(Org)$$

EP(Office) represents the expected probability of obtaining office in the long term, **P(Win)** the probability of the party's winning an election in the long term, and **P(Org)** the probability of obtaining a suitable position in the party organization for any individual elite. For new elites, **P (Org)** is a measure of how high they can expect to rise within the party organization. For old elites already in positions of power in the party, **P(Org)** is a measure of how much they can count on recapturing their position or an equivalent one if they are displaced. It follows that political parties that offer elites a high value of **P(Org)** can afford to promise them a relatively low value of **P(Win)**. In other words, political parties that offer new elites a high probability of ascent within the organization and old elites a high probability of return, but have a low probability of winning, can be as attractive to each set of elites as political parties with a high chance of winning but a low probability of ascent within the ranks or return to old positions.

The intractability of the problem of elite incorporation should be immediately clear from the equation above. In order to incorporate new elites while retaining the allegiance of old ones, a political party must promise a high value on **P(Org)** to both groups simultaneously. In other words, it must promise new elites a high probability of ascent within the organization, at the same time that it promises old elites a high probability of retaining their positions or advancing to higher ones. This appears, on the face of it, to be impossible. The number of posts in any political party is limited. Promising new elites access to these posts must necessarily entail the displacement of their previous occupants. How is it possible for political parties to simultaneously satisfy both old occupants and new aspirants? This is the essence of the problem of elite incorporation.

The problem may be restated as a variant of a collective action dilemma. The success of political parties in attracting the support of voters from any ethnic category, as I have argued so far, depends directly upon their ability to incorporate office-seeking elites from newly modernizing ethnic categories. If it is clear that the electoral success of the party depends upon elite incorporation, therefore, we should expect to see rational office seekers within each political party taking steps to incorporate these elites. However, what is rational for the party as a whole is not rational for individual office seekers within the party. The incorporation of new elites usually means the displacement of those who already hold positions of power in the party organization and are therefore first in line for the spoils of victory. And so office-seeking elites already entrenched within the party organization are likely to be free riders, cheering for incorporation of new elites into the party as a whole, but resisting the incorporation of new elites into their own local party units. In this situation, we should expect localized resistance by each elite individually to prevent the process of elite incorporation, even though this costs the party as a whole the election and each is worse off individually than if the party had won.

The ability of any party to incorporate new elites successfully depends, therefore, on the invention of a mechanism that circumvents the collection action dilemma by tying the individual interests of office-seeking elites within the party to the incorporation of new elites from the outside. The introduction of competitive rules for intraparty advancement, provides one such mechanism. Competitive rules of intraparty advancement induce elite incorporation by forcing those elites already entrenched in the party apparatus to recruit new elites if they are to safeguard their own positions. At the same time, they prevent the displacement of old elites by creating a system of alternation, so that those displaced have a stable expectation of returning. Party organizations where posts are allotted through competition, therefore, permit elite incorporation into a party with even a low probability of winning. A centralized internal structure, on the other hand, prevents elite incorporation by divorcing the incentives for those elites already entrenched within the party organization from the recruitment of new ones. Party organizations where posts are allotted through centralized coordination, therefore, are closed to new entrants even when they have a high probability of winning the election. The remainder of this chapter develops this argument.

II. Competitive Party Organizations

At some initial point, imagine a political party organization dominated by elites from a single ethnic category A, the earliest ethnic category to modernize. Competition within the party takes the form of factions within group A. The process of modernization throws up new elites from new ethnic categories looking for a channel to office. For the reasons outlined in Chapter 3, these office-seeking elites should mobilize bands of co-ethnic followers in

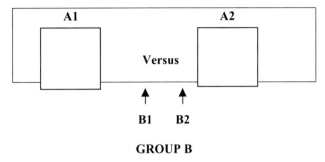

Figure 5.1. Stage I: party dominated by elites from group A.

order to increase their bargaining power vis-à-vis the dominant elites in the parties in which they seek entry. In order to increase their chances for incorporation into the party, they should emphasize the identity that allows them to build the largest following among co-ethnics. Suppose that these elites define themselves as members of group B (see Figure 5.1).

This party organization is characterized by competitive rules for intraparty advancement, which I define as follows: (1) intraparty elections for all organizational posts by majority rule and (2) open membership policies. Taken together, the two rules produce an incentive structure in which the survival and advancement of those at higher levels in the party is systematically tied to the induction of new members, first into the party and then into leadership positions. The *system of intraparty elections* for all organizational posts creates an incentive for factional leaders from category A seeking to improve or maintain their positions within the party hierarchy to mobilize broad coalitions of support from below. The *open membership rules*, by making it relatively easy for nonmembers to be converted into voting members of the party, creates an incentive for competing factional leaders to recruit new elites from outside the party in order to increase the size of their coalitions of support within. In order to purchase the support of new elites, competing factional leaders are forced to concede a limited amount of power in the form of party posts or election tickets. The acquisition of this limited amount of power, in turn, gives new elites a foothold that they use to pull themselves up the party hierarchy. When cracks open up among factions at the top, these members move up from subordinate levels to replace the old factional leadership, using the same mechanisms that had led to their own recruitment. At the same time, the competitive mechanism promises displaced elites some predictable probability of return.

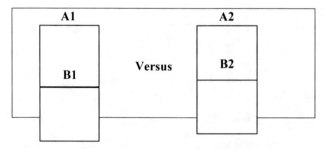

Figure 5.2. Stage II: competitive incorporation of elites from group B.

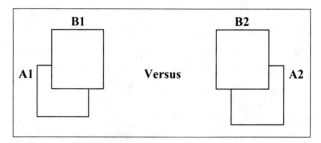

Figure 5.3. Stage III: displacement of As by Bs.

Note that the system of elite incorporation described here depends upon the conjunction of both rules. A system of intraparty elections without open membership would produce internal elite circulation within the party, but it would not result in the incorporation of new elites from outside. Similarly, a party that permitted open membership but disallowed intraparty elections would not be able to promise new elites a probability of ascent within the organization. I will return to this point in my discussion of centralized party organizations.

Figures 5.2 and 5.3 illustrate the working of the incorporative mechanism created by competitive rules of intraparty advancement. Given the rules of intraparty advancement, there is a coincidence of interests between dominant elites A1 and A2 and rising elites B1 and B2. A1 and A2 seek additional support to bolster their positions relative to each other and offer in return some limited power within the party organization. B1 and B2 are looking for posts of influence within the party and can offer the votes of members of their following of co-ethnics to whichever faction leader bids highest for their support. The result, at stage II, is the incorporation of B1 and B2 into leadership positions within the party, bringing co-ethnic followers in their wake. At this stage, B1 and B2 remain subordinate to A1 and A2, and their followers are concentrated at the bottom of the vertical chain of factional networks. The leadership of the factional networks continues to lie with members of ethnic category A.

At stage II, competition within the party takes the form of competition between two multiethnic factions, composed of As and Bs. There are now two axes of competition: Elites from each faction have an incentive to improve their relative positions *across* factions, but elites from both A and B also have an incentive to bolster their relative positions *within* the factions. Over time, therefore, B1 and B2 use their footholds within the party to improve their positions in the subsequent rounds of intraparty elections. Stage III illustrates the displacement of A1 and A2 and their followers by B1 and B2 and their followers (Figure 5.3).

The displacement of the As by the Bs within the factional networks shown in Figure 5.3 is not an inevitable outcome. The capacity of elites from category B to displace elites from category A depends upon the relative size of the modernizing pool within each ethnic category and on the number of factions competing for support. With only two factions, both initially dominated by As, the probability that elites from ethnic category B will ascend to leadership positions is correlated with their number. If ethnic category B has a large pool of modernizing elites, it will have the numerical strength to overthrow the As within the party organization. If the pool of modernizing elites from category B is small, however, elites from category B are likely to remain in a subordinate position in the organization. However, as the number of factions within the party increases, the importance of the relative size of each ethnic category decreases. The more intense the factional competition, the greater the bargaining power of each new elite and therefore the greater the likelihood of his ascending to plum positions within the party. Other scenarios, therefore, are also compatible with the model, depending upon the numerical strength of the modernizing elites in each group and the number of factions: The Bs might be able to replace the As in only one faction; the Bs and As might be equally balanced within factions; or the Bs might continue to be subordinate to the As.

Regardless of whether displacement or subordination is the outcome, however, neither can be assumed to be permanent in a competitive party organization. Because their position within a faction depends simply upon the degree of support from below, displaced factional leaders may regain their position to the extent that they are able to mobilize alternative coalitions of support. And elites who are subordinate within the faction during any single time period can reasonably hope to ascend further, either as the modernizing pool of elites within their party increases or as factional competition within the party increases, thus raising the value of their vote.

As new waves of elites outside the political party modernize, the same mechanism should lead also to their incorporation. Imagine now the creation of a new pool of elites from category C. The size of the modernizing pool in category C and the intensity of factional conflict should determine the rate at which Cs rise up the party hierarchy.

I have assumed so far that different ethnic categories modernize one at a time, and so elites from each category enter the party sequentially. The same logic should apply, however, to the incorporation of elites from ethnic categories that modernize simultaneously. Suppose that categories B and C modernize at equal rates, producing identical proportions of office-seeking elites. In this case, B1 and B2 and C1 and C2 would be simultaneously rather than sequentially incorporated into the party. Over time, therefore, even though all elites mobilize monoethnic followings in order to increase their bargaining power, these monoethnic followings should be incorporated into multiethnic factions, thus broadening the representational profile of the competitive political party.

Note that the process of continuous elite incorporation that I describe here is driven entirely by the internal power struggles within the party and is therefore *independent* of electoral incentives. However, even though it is generated by an incentive structure internal to the party, successful elite incorporation serves the party well in the electoral arena. For one thing, it steadily expands the party's base of support. The more elites the party incorporates, the wider the circles of support it has among the broader population. For another, it preempts the emergence of a strong opposition party by absorbing those elites who might otherwise have fed the competition.

Is the party described here stable? There is no mechanism here that halts the process of incorporation at the level where elites from "enough" ethnic categories have been incorporated to guarantee electoral victory. Rather, as long as the competitive rules are in operation, the process of incorporation will continue unchecked, so that the party will become swollen over time, absorbing more and more new entrants. We might initially conclude, therefore, that a competitive party organization will become unstable over time to the extent that it generates "oversize coalitions," far in excess of what is necessary to win.[4]

The logic that suggests that such a coalition is unstable runs as follows: We know that for office-seeking elites, the expected probability of obtaining a government office depends upon the joint probability of the party's winning in the long term and the probability that the elite will obtain a position in the party organization. The number of offices available in the government and in the party organization are limited. We would expect the probability of obtaining a post in the party organization to decline with each new entrant. Even if the party continued to win elections, we should find that as the probability of obtaining a post in the party organization approaches zero, the expected probability of obtaining office for any individual elite goes to zero as well. Consequently, after some turning point, elites should have an incentive to defect to the competition, or to found a new party.

But this process can indeed produce a stable party, for the following reason: As new elites enter the party, they are integrated into a system of factional competition. Each faction is composed of some subset of the party membership as a whole. What we should see, then, is not a single "oversize" coalition but a collection of alternative "minimum winning coalitions," with each faction representing a single coalition aiming for office. With each new entrant, therefore, the probability of obtaining an office is certainly diminished, but not to the degree that we might expect if we thought of the party membership as a single coalition competing for office.

Consider now an elite faced with a choice between joining a faction within this "swollen" party and joining a new political party of the same size and structure as the faction. The choice is not equivalent. As a member of a faction within the swollen party, the individual has a much higher chance of obtaining office than as a member of a new party of the same size as his faction. This is because as a member of a faction, she benefits from the votes mobilized by each of the other factions in the party at election time. Once the party has won the election, this individual then faces competition for office from the other factions. A party of the same size as her faction, however, would not be able to win an election on its own. As a member of this party, therefore, the elite would almost certainly be denied office.

[4] Rabushka and Shepsle, *Politics in Plural Societies*, 84; Horowitz, *Ethnic Groups in Conflict*, 309.

This argument suggests that the competitive party is stable because the threshold at which individuals might begin to defect from factions within the swollen party to an opposition party is extremely high. The opposition party would have to be, at its inception, large enough to win the election on its own. It is unlikely that a single opposition party could amass this kind of strength at its first election. One condition under which an opposition force of this size might form at its first election would be through an alliance of several opposition parties, but this presents a difficult coordination problem.

III. Centralized Party Organizations

Let me move now to centralized rules of intraparty advancement, which I define as follows: All posts within the party are allotted through a centralized directive, issued either by a single leader or by some collective. Figure 5.4 illustrates this system at stage I. Again, competition within the party takes the form of factions within group A. Outside the party, in the larger society, elites from category B seek entry into the political system. The difference, however, is that competing faction leaders from group A obtain and maintain their positions by appealing to the leader or to some selectorate at the top. The rewards in this scenario come solely from currying favour with the central leadership.

At first glance, we might expect a centralized organizational structure to be capable of solving the problem of elite incorporation. A single leader

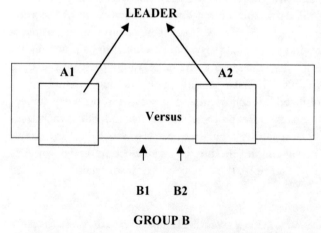

Figure 5.4. Stage I: party dominated by elites from group A.

108

has a strong incentive to do what it takes to get the party to win, since her own fortune depends upon the fortunes of the party. The same is true of a selectorate. Consequently, we might expect the leader or selectorate, looking out for their own interests, to solve the collective action dilemma through one of two mechanisms: (1) by allotting party positions solely on the basis of demonstrated support from below, which would in effect reproduce the incentive structure of the competitive system outlined earlier in this section, or (2) by forcibly inducting new elites in spite of the dissent of old ones. However, neither of these two mechanisms is likely to be effective under a centralized system.

Just as the interests of individual elites do not always coincide with the interests of the party as a corporate whole, the interests of the central leader do not always coincide with the interests of the party as a whole. On the one hand, the central leader has an interest in ensuring the electoral victory of the party and therefore an interest in incorporating new elites. On the other hand, she must also ensure her own survival. Actions that ensure the first objective do not always ensure the second. And in a conflict between the two objectives, the second is always paramount. The paramountcy of personal survival makes the systematic replication of the competitive incentive structure by a centralized system difficult. For a leader interested in personal survival, awarding posts solely on the basis of demonstrated support from below carries with it the risk of the emergence of an intraparty challenger. Any self-interested leader, therefore, has an incentive to intervene when such an intraparty challenger emerges and to award the post to a less threatening aspirant, regardless of the support the aspirant enjoys from below. The fear of such a challenger, furthermore, gives the leader an incentive to launch a preemptive effort to prevent her emergence by awarding posts to loyalists or, at a minimum, to weak figures. Finally, a leader seeking to ensure personal survival also incurs debts for services rendered by loyalists, which she must pay through the use of party posts in order to retain her own hold on the party. The imperative of personal survival means, therefore, that even the wisest – or especially the wisest – leader has an incentive to substitute other, arbitrary criteria for the criterion of allotting posts in return for popular support. The same logic applies to a selectorate.

How often the leader or the selectorate subverts the competitive mechanism might vary across party organizations. Where the leadership is secure, it is likely to subvert the process sparingly or not at all, recognizing that the interest of the party as a whole lies in allotting posts using competitive criteria. Where the leadership is insecure, we should see frequent subversion. However, the incentive that the leadership, whether an individual or a selectorate, has to subvert the competitive process means that it cannot credibly provide the same guarantee of advancement within the party to old and new elites that a competitive system can. Recognizing the incentive to subvert, old elites cannot reliably estimate their probability of return if they are displaced. New elites, similarly, cannot form reasonable expectations of advancement within the party if they join. The fact of a centralized leadership with an interest in its own survival introduces an element of arbitrariness that is absent in the impersonal competitive system. And this element of arbitrariness prevents the expectation of return for displaced elites, and of ascent for rising elites, on which the solution to the collective action problem depends.

Let me address now the second mechanism through which a centralized system might solve the dilemma of elite incorporation: coercion. A centralized leadership can easily induct new elites forcibly when the need arises, overriding the resistance of those elites already entrenched within the party. Why would this mechanism not be effective? The answer is that it cannot ensure the compliance of old elites. Displaced elites, in the absence of credible guarantees of reinstatement, have no reason to stay. They are likely to respond to their displacement either by switching allegiance to the competition or by forming a new political party. Where the criteria for advancement within the party organization are arbitrary, furthermore, new elites also cannot reasonably gauge their chances of advancement once they have accepted an initial post. Consequently, new elites also have less incentive to affiliate themselves with the centralized party.

If the centralized party becomes a governing party, the incentives for old elites to defect, and for new elites to avoid the party, might be arrested. Obtaining control of the government results in a massive increase in the number of posts and allows a party to accommodate more people. During "lean" periods, however, when the centralized party is not a likely winner, we should see a greater propensity among elites to exit in centralized parties than in competitive party organizations. Centralized parties, therefore, are likely to be more unstable than competitive ones.

IV. Conclusion

The argument presented here implies that even when it targets an ethnic category of optimal size, the success of an ethnic party is contingent upon

110

its organizational structure. A competitive internal structure would allow an ethnic party to broaden its elite profile beyond its initial founder elites, giving additional opportunities for representation to elites from all "subdivisions" within its target ethnic category. As a result, it should increase the likelihood of obtaining votes from members of its target ethnic category. By the same logic, even when it targets an ethnic category of optimal size, an ethnic party is most likely to fail when it has a centralized organizational structure. A centralized structure renders an ethnic party unable to broaden its elite profile beyond its founder elites. As a result, even when an ethnic party makes an open bid for the support of some ethnic category, voters from subdivisions within this category whose elites are less well represented should have less reason to vote for it. Subsequent chapters investigate this hypothesis against the data.

PART II

Data

6

India as a Patronage-Democracy

The state is everywhere. Life chances are influenced by the state. If you don't have access to the state, life is difficult.[1]

Those who rule have everything. Those who do not rule have nothing.[2]

The state is widely perceived as a 'grace and favour' state; state officials tend to be seen, and see themselves, as dispensers of favours. It is widely assumed that if an official wishes to do something for you he can, and the problem is how to make him want to.[3]

In Part I, I argued that the patronage-democracy was a distinct type of democracy, with distinct patterns of voting behaviour and therefore distinct conditions leading to ethnic party success. In this chapter, I propose an interpretation of the Indian political system as a patronage-democracy. This interpretation applies broadly to postcolonial India, from independence in 1947 until the present. The Indian state is currently undergoing two major structural changes: the deregulation of the Indian economy and the decentralization of political power. So far, however, these changes have not been of sufficient magnitude to alter the nature of India's patronage-democracy.

---

[1] Satyam Patel, Congress party member, in an interview with Atul Kohli in Ahmedabad, cited in Atul Kohli, *Democracy and Discontent* (Cambridge: Cambridge University Press, 1990), 266.
[2] BSP campaigner in a village corner meeting, Hoshiarpur, January 28, 1997.
[3] Robert Wade, "Politics and Graft: Recruitment, Appointment and Promotions to Public Office in India," in Peter Ward, ed., *Corruption, Development and Inequality: Soft Touch or Hard Graft?* (New York: Routledge, 1989), 103.

Virtually every major study of Indian politics and political economy has remarked upon India's dominant state and the extent to which voting behaviour in India is conditioned by expectations of access to the state.[4] This chapter builds upon this previous literature in order to advance two further arguments. First, it argues that the essential element influencing voting behaviour in India is not simply the dominance of the state, but the ability of those who control the state to exercise discretion in the *implementation* of state policy. Second, whereas previous studies have analyzed state dominance and ethnic politics as two parallel processes, this chapter proposes a connection between the two: The individualized distribution of benefits at the disposal of those who control the dominant state, I argue here, produces and sustains ethnic politics in India.

Section I describes the discretionary control of the Indian state over jobs, livelihoods, and living conditions and shows that those who hold state office have considerable opportunity for rent seeking in the implementation of state policy. Section II describes the opportunities for rent seeking open to politicians in particular. Section III describes the marketing of state resources and services by politicians in return for political support on an ethnic basis, and section IV describes the availability of information about voting patterns that makes such marketing possible.

I. Discretionary Control over Jobs, Livelihoods, and Living Conditions

This section describes the discretionary control of the state over the jobs, livelihoods, and living conditions of the majority of the Indian population, and the opportunity to collect rents that this discretionary control creates for public officials. Let me begin with jobs in the organized economy, where the term "organized economy" refers to all establishments in the public sector and all nonagricultural establishments in the private sector employing ten or more persons. Only 27 percent of the labour force is employed in the

---

[4] Kohli, *Democracy and Discontent*; Pranab Bardhan, *The Political Economy of Development in India* (Oxford: Basil Blackwell, 1984); Lloyd I. Rudolph and Susanne H. Rudolph, *In Pursuit of Lakshmi* (Chicago: University of Chicago Press, 1987); Pradeep Chhibber, *Democracy without Associations* (Ann Arbor: University of Michigan Press, 1999); Myron Weiner, *Party Building in a New Nation* (Chicago: University of Chicago Press, 1967); Paul Brass, *Theft of an Idol* (Calcutta: Seagull Books, 1998); Paul Brass, *Factional Politics in an Indian State* (Berkeley: University of California Press, 1965).

Table 6.1. *Dominance of the public sector in the organized economy in India, 1961–99*

Year	Public Sector (%)	Private Sector (%)
1961	58.3	41.7
1971	61.4	38.6
1981	67.7	32.3
1991	71.3	28.7
1999	69.1	30.9

Source: Statistical Outline of India 1997–98 for the years 1961–1991; *Economic Survey of India 2000–1,* Table 3.3, for 1999.

organized economy.[5] I will discuss the "unorganized" economy, in which the bulk of Indian labour force is employed, later in this section.

The Indian state controls most jobs in the organized economy. Table 6.1 summarizes the percentage of the labour force in the organized economy working in the public sector from 1961 to 1999. As the table indicates, the public sector provides the lion's share of employment opportunities in the organized economy. This share was on an increasing trajectory between 1961 and 1991: From little more than half the jobs in 1961, the public sector had acquired control over two-thirds of the available jobs by 1991. Significantly, the dominance of the state has not shrunk appreciably since the economic reforms introduced by the ruling Congress party in 1991 and continued by the coalition governments that have ruled India since 1996. While these successive governments have attempted to limit the expansion of public sector enterprises and the bureaucracy, they have shied away from downsizing the public sector. In 1999, therefore, almost a decade after the economic reforms were first introduced, the dominance of the public sector in the organized economy stood relatively unchanged, at 69 percent.

While the absolute share of the public and private sector in employment has remained relatively stable, however, the relative rates of growth of the two did change following the economic reforms. The greater opportunities and incentives now provided by the government in the private sector, combined with restrictions on the expansion of the public sector, mean that the private sector is now growing at a faster rate. Table 6.2 summarizes the growth rates of employment in the organized sector since 1991. In the

[5] *Statistical Outline of India 1997–8.*

Table 6.2. *Relative growth rates of public and private sectors in India, 1991–99*

Year	Public Sector (%)	Private Sector (%)
1991	1.52	1.24
1992	.8	2.21
1993	.6	.06
1994	.62	.01
1995	.11	1.63
1996	−.19	5.62
1997	.67	2.04
1998	−.09	1.72
1999	0	.11

Source: Economic Survey of India 2000–1, Table 10.3, p. 192.

longer run, if government policy continues to encourage the expansion of economic activity in the private sector, we should expect its relative share of employment to increase even in the absence of privatization efforts. In the present and for the immediate future, however, the state continues to dominate employment opportunities in the organized economy in India.

Public sector jobs are classified into four categories based on an income criterion: Class I (or Group A), Class II (or Group B), Class III (or Group C), and Class IV (or Group D). The Class I category is the highest-paid category and includes employees of the prestigious Indian Administrative Service (IAS), the Indian Foreign Service (IFS), the Indian Police Service (IPS), and related central government services. Class II employees, who fall into the next income bracket, include, among others, officers of the state civil service cadre. The Class III and Class IV categories include relatively low-income posts such as primary school teachers, revenue inspectors, constables, peons, clerks, drivers, and sweepers.

Selecting authorities have relatively little discretion in the recruitment of Class I and Class II positions, which are typically filled by competitive exams and an interview conducted by a collective body. The exams produce a first cut of applicants based on educational and technical qualifications. Although a further elimination takes place at the interview stage, the influence of any individual member of the interview board over the selection of candidates is limited, since each needs the consent of others to approve any candidate. Class III and Class IV jobs, however, are low-skill, low-qualification jobs, filled according to less rigorous procedures. In a survey of employees in four government agencies, for instance, Panandikar

118

Table 6.3. *Profile of central government employment in India, 1994*

Class	Employment (%)
Class I or Group A	2.2
Class II or Group B	3.3
Class III or Group C	66.8
Class IV or Group D	27.2
TOTAL	99.5*

* The figures do not add to one hundred percent because of rounding error.

Source: *Report of the Fifth Central Pay Commission, January 1997*, p. 223.

and Kshirsagar reported that only 3.2 percent had been selected through competitive examinations. As many as 81.2 percent of the employees had been recruited directly by the offices concerned, through advertisements or notifications at the employment exchange and a single interview.[6] It is in the allocation of these Class III and Class IV jobs, therefore, that the selecting authorities and those who influence them can exercise the greatest discretion.

The significance of this discretion in the allocation of Class III and Class IV jobs becomes clear when we look at the sheer volume of these jobs. Table 6.3 provides a snapshot of the distribution of jobs across the four categories of central government employment. As the table indicates, the overwhelming majority of public sector jobs in the central government (94 percent) lie in the Class III and Class IV categories.

The profile for state government employment is identical. Table 6.4 summarizes the profile of government jobs by category for Punjab state, which we may take as typical. As the table shows, state government employment is also dominated by these lower-level positions. Discretionary control over Class III and Class IV jobs translates, therefore, into discretionary control over the bulk of government employment.

As an illustration, consider the procedure for appointment to the post of police constable. The district superintendent of police advertises at the local level for "qualified young men," where the qualifications are minimal (the candidate should be literate, in good physical condition, and from a "good

[6] V. A. Pai Panandikar and S. S. Kshirsagar, *Bureaucracy and Development Administration* (New Delhi: Centre for Policy Research, 1978), 170, Table G.

119

Table 6.4. *Profile of state government
employment in Punjab, 1995*

Class	Employment (%)
Class I or Group A	2.37
Class II or Group B	1.55
Class III or Group C	67.64
Class IV or Group D	16.77
"Contingency" workers	11.67
TOTAL	100

Source: Statistical Abstract of Punjab, 1995, p. 445.

family") and often waived. From among these men, "selection is apt to be rough and ready – a tape measure for height and chest expansion, cursory physical examination by a civil surgeon, attestation of literacy or education, and some indication of earnestness and integrity usually by means of a written "chit" from a village headman or influential neighbour or a verbal recommendation from another policeman."[7] The district superintendent (SP) is the single official responsible for the selection of constables. He is the sole judge of which personal recommendations ("chits") to weigh more heavily than others, and of how to combine these recommendations with other criteria for selection. The minimal physical and educational requirements for a secure government job mean that there is usually a large number of applicants. The large number of applicants, the minimal qualifications required, and the absence of guidelines about how much weight to give each qualification all give the SP the power to arbitrarily allot these posts to some individuals and to deny them to others. Police constables constitute over 90 percent of the states' police forces.[8] Most police posts at the state level, in other words, are filled according to discretionary procedures.

In the absence of adequate secondary data, it is difficult to measure the scope of discretion in other, comparable jobs. If we look simply at outcomes, however, it appears that politicians and bureaucrats have considerable freedom in appointing candidates to many of these jobs. Take, for instance, the appointment of primary school teachers. "Primary school teachers," according to a recent World Bank study, "comprise the largest, most steadily growing profession in India, with nearly 2.8 million primary and upper

[7] David H. Bayley, *The Police and Political Development in India* (Princeton, NJ: Princeton University Press, 1969), 90.
[8] Bayley, *Police and Political Development,* 76.

primary teachers employed in 1993. In 1991, teachers accounted for 11.8% of all government employees."[9] The appointment of primary school teachers is reportedly one of the principal levers of patronage available to the state government, which is responsible for decisions on qualifications and recruitment procedures.[10] Jobs in the health department are similarly described as a valuable pool of discretionary resources that can be used to feed a political support base. According to one of Weiner's respondents:

> I have managed to find employment for thousands of Bengali boys in the government during the last ten years. Many of them are employed as clerks or nurses in the health department. These jobs do not fall under the pubic service commission but are given simply on the basis of interviews. The head of the health department loves me and my activities very much because of what I have done in hospitals to eliminate the Communists who were giving much trouble there. The health department is rapidly expanding and so needs many people. Whenever there are openings I send my boys down for interviews.[11]

In general, the lower we go down the hierarchy of government jobs, the greater the discretion we might expect to find in the procedures by which they are filled.

Public sector employment, however, covers only a minority of India's labour force. Let me move now to the agricultural sector, where most of the labour force is employed. Over a third (39 percent) of the "main workers"[12] in India are "cultivators," meaning that they have access to land, either as owners or tenants. Agriculture is a private enterprise in India, and cultivators are self-employed. However, public officials exercise discretionary control over the livelihoods of cultivators through the power they wield over the supply of inputs.[13]

---

[9] World Bank, *India: Primary Education Achievement and Challenges* (Washington, DC: World Bank, 1996), 114.

[10] Jean Dreze and Haris Gazdar, "Uttar Pradesh: The Burden of Inertia," in Jean Dreze and Amartya Sen, eds., *Indian Development: Selected Regional Perspectives* (Delhi: Oxford University Press, 1998), 79; Weiner, *Party Building*, 25; Hilton Root, "A Liberal India: The Triumph of Hope over Experience," *Asian Survey*, Vol. 37, No. 5 (1998): 510–534. Root points out that "even the recruitment of teachers can become part of the spoils system. Highly decentralized school boards offer excellent patronage opportunities" (523).

[11] Weiner, *Party Building*, 347.

[12] The term "main worker" refers to individuals who "were engaged in any economically productive activity for 183 days or more during the year" (Census of India 1991).

[13] Ashutosh Varshney, *Democracy, Development, and the Countryside* (Cambridge: Cambridge University Press, 1995), 199.

Consider land security. The cultivator obtains state recognition of his right to his land by registering it with the officials concerned and obtaining a title. But getting land registered and securing titles is no routine matter. Those officials who are in charge of assessing the amount of land owned may underestimate that amount in order to assist wealthy landlords in subverting land reform legislation.[14] They may also exploit economically vulnerable populations by refusing to grant titles, or by extorting bribes in exchange for registering them as the rightful owners of their land.[15] Not surprisingly, therefore, the *patwari* (official keeper of land records) and the land-settlement officer are powerful men, whom wealthy and poor cultivators alike must either appease, by paying bribes, or control, by cultivating influence among their superiors.[16]

Consider, further, the provision of water, which is provided to the cultivator through government-run irrigation schemes.[17] Given the great demand for irrigation, "water is perennially scarce."[18] Such scarcity gives the officials who control irrigation schemes (the village headman, the tubewell operator, the engineer) and those with the ability to influence these officials the power to collect rents through selective allocation. According to Wade, "there is a fairly standard amount that vulnerable villagers can expect to pay and on top of that an additional amount that varies with weather conditions and the propensities of officials."[19] The power to allocate water selectively, furthermore, prevents villagers from successfully protesting such rent-collecting activities, even when they are blatant. As an assistant engineer reportedly told villagers who threatened to complain to

[14] See, for instance, Weiner, *Party Building*, 89; and Francine Frankel, *India's Political Economy 1947–1977* (Princeton, NJ: Princeton University Press, 1978).

[15] As one of Gupta's respondents noted, in a common complaint, "There is so much deception going on. They don't allow plots to be registered, just keep the paperwork unofficial. . . . They have made it a business." Akhil Gupta, *Postcolonial Developments: Agriculture in the Making of Modern India* (Durham, NC: Duke University Press, 1998), 147. See also Miriam Sharma, *The Politics of Inequality* (Honolulu: University Press of Hawaii, 1978), 58.

[16] Myron Weiner, *The Politics of Scarcity* (Chicago: University of Chicago Press, 1962), 12. For a discussion of the tampering with land records as a source of rents for politicians and bureaucrats in both urban and rural areas, see Rob Jenkins, "The Developmental Implications of India's Federal Institutions," paper presented at the annual meeting of the American Political Science Association, Washington, DC, August 1997, 12–16.

[17] This section draws on Sharma, *The Politics of Inequality*, and Wade, "Politics and Graft."

[18] Sharma, *Politics of Inequality*, 185.

[19] Wade, "Politics and Graft," 85.

his superior about his performance: "If you complain to the EE [Executive Engineer], next time I will give you no water."[20]

Rural credit is dominated by public lending institutions, comprised of nationalized banks and credit cooperatives.[21] The pivotal figure in these lending institutions is the manager, "who has the effective power to sanction loans, and to override official eligibility conditions if necessary."[22] The manager, thus, is in a position to extract bribes or other favours from those who seek loans. Voters who cannot provide a bribe might seek to influence the manager through political intervention. It is unlikely, however, that they would secure a loan without either political clout or the payment of a bribe.

Roads may be diverted selectively in order to favour those with political influence.[23] In one district that I studied, I found a striking example of such diversion. The BSP government sanctioned a road construction scheme with several binding guidelines attached, one of which was that the road could only be built in a Scheduled Caste–majority village. Even though the official guidelines were followed to the letter, the locally powerful elite still managed to intervene in its implementation. A "village" is often an artificial census construct, made up of several hamlets at some distance from each other. Thakur voters in one hamlet were able to use their influence with the local bureaucracy to ensure that the road, while nominally built in the Scheduled Caste–majority "village," was diverted to their own hamlet rather than to the hamlets populated by Scheduled Castes. Electricity connections, similarly, may be selectively provided or repaired. In these and other ways, therefore, even though they are self-employed, cultivators are subject to the power of the discretionary state in hundreds of everyday transactions.

Finally, let me address the remaining component of the agricultural labour force, which consists of agricultural labourers,[24] marginal workers, and others who have no access to land. One way in which the government

---

[20] Ibid., 92.

[21] Peter Lanjouw and Nicholas Stern, *Economic Development in Palanpur over Five Decades* (Delhi: Oxford University Press, 1998).

[22] Lanjouw and Stern, *Economic Development in Palanpur*, 522. For the use of credit as an instrument of patronage, see also Weiner, *Party Building*, 284.

[23] Root, "A Liberal India," 521; Hans Schenk, "Corruption . . . What Corruption? Notes on Bribery and Dependency in Urban India," in Peter M. Ward, ed., *Corruption, Development and Inequality: Soft Touch or Hard Graft?* (London: Routledge, 1989), 114.

[24] According to the 1991 census, agricultural labourers constitute 26 percent of the "main workers" in India.

influences the livelihoods of the landless population is through regulating wages in the agricultural sector. Most states in India have passed legislation regulating wages in the agricultural sector, and the responsibility for enforcing these laws falls upon the local bureaucracy, including the block development staff and the staffs of the Revenue and Labour Departments.[25] Locally powerful elites, however, have been able to frustrate the implementation of the minimum wage policy and other policy legislation aimed at empowering the landless through their contacts in the state legislature and the local bureaucracy.[26] Even in order to ensure effective implementation of minimum wage legislation, therefore, the landless require a friendly administration with a commitment to enforcing the letter of the law.

A second way in which the government influences the livelihoods of the landless population is through its several poverty alleviation programmes, designed to augment the income of the landless or to assist them in switching to a more lucrative occupation. The principal poverty alleviation programme is the Integrated Rural Development Programme (IRDP).[27] The IRDP functions as a subsidized credit programme with the objective of helping selected rural families living below the poverty line to take up self-employment ventures. The beneficiaries of IRDP loans are selected on the basis of income criteria. Given that household income is difficult to verify, those in charge of identifying beneficiaries have enormous discretionary power. Estimates of ineligible beneficiaries selected under IRDP, according to one study, range from 5 to 40 percent.[28] Dreze, Lanjouw, and Stern, in their ethnographic study of the implementation of the IRDP in Palanpur, found that it was possible for the village development officer, who was in charge of drawing up a list of eligible beneficiaries, "to recommend virtually anyone he wishes."[29] In other cases, where the responsibility for the selection of beneficiaries lies not with a government functionary but with an elected *panchayat* (village council), rent seeking in the selection of beneficiaries was equally rampant.[30]

[25] Frankel, *India's Political Economy*, 553.
[26] Ibid., 577.
[27] Lanjouw and Stern, *Economic Development in Palanpur*, 200.
[28] World Bank, *India: Achievements and Challenges in Reducing Poverty* (Washington, DC: World Bank, 1997), 31.
[29] Lanjouw and Stern, *Economic Development in Palanpur*, 201.
[30] See, for instance, Raghav Gaiha, P. D. Kaushik, and Vani Kulkarni, "Jawahar Rozgar Yojana, Panchayats and the Rural Poor in India," *Asian Survey*, Vol. 72, No. 10 (1998): 928–949.

The government also targets the rural poor through the Jawahar Rozgar Yojna (JRY). The objectives of the JRY are to generate additional employment opportunities for the rural poor and to create a durable infrastructure in rural areas.[31] As in the case of the IRDP, employment under the JRY scheme is frequently allotted on the basis of discretionary criteria. The World Bank survey cited earlier found that in some states elected officials contracted out JRY projects to private contractors, who were free to hire anyone they chose instead of giving preference to those eligible under the programme guidelines.[32] Similarly, in his study of the National Rural Employment Programme (NREP), which was the precursor to the JRY, Echeverri-Gent found that political parties often intervened in the implementation of the NREP, giving employment or designating projects selectively in order to elicit political support, or channeling program funds to party organizations.[33] In a general summing up of the poverty alleviation programmes, the World Bank noted that "discretion is enormous and information is asymmetric – criteria for granting or refusing a benefit are often not known to the applicant and change frequently. There is no transparency – no reasons need be given for refusal and there is generally no appeal except to the same person who took the initial decision."[34]

Let me move now from livelihoods to living conditions, in order to describe the extent to which the state dominates the everyday business of existence, especially in rural India, and especially for the poor. Births, if they take place in a hospital at all, take place in a government hospital. Access to a hospital bed is not routinely granted. In an environment of scarcity, this access is a highly prized commodity obtained through the intervention of the district medical officer or some other influential government functionary. In order to purchase food at subsidized rates from government-run fair price shops, the poor need "ration cards," often obtained by paying a bribe to the government clerk in charge of issuing the cards. Beneficiaries of affirmative action policies need "certificates" attesting to their caste identity before they can claim subsidies for school education or entry into the university system.[35] Those government officials who perform the routine function of issuing or signing such certificates are also in a position to extract returns in

[31] This section draws on John Echeverri-Gent, *The State and the Poor* (Berkeley: University of California Press, 1993).

[32] World Bank, *India: Achievements and Challenges*, 30.

[33] Echeverri-Gent, *The State and the Poor*, 153.

[34] World Bank, *India: Achievements and Challenges*, 32–33.

[35] Weiner, *Party Building*, 412.

the form of money or political support. Protection from arbitrary violence, which should in principle be routinely guaranteed to all citizens by the state, is itself selectively provided and selectively withheld. As Brass points out,

The police do not automatically come to any village upon request, even where there are good reasons to believe that a breach of the peace is taking place. It is usually necessary in such circumstances, as in all dealings with government authorities and agencies in India, that the persons filing a complaint be known to the police. Often enough, it also means that a payment is made or has been made in the past or that some profit is likely to come to the police for doing their duty.[36]

Even in death, citizens are not free from the discretionary power of the state. As one politician boasted to Weiner, voters sought his intervention even in the conduct of post mortems:

There is much difficulty with the police about post mortems. Hindus don't like to have this done to bodies but sometimes the police require this if there is an unnatural death. I have had to handle many problems like this. I have handled four post mortem examinations in the last four months. In each case I have been able to get the body released....[37]

To argue that most individuals in India must encounter the discretionary power of the state in one way or another in the simple business of survival and advancement is not to imply that *all* individuals are equally dependent upon the discretion of state officials. In general, those with wealth and education have the means to purchase an exit option from the patronage-based economy, or to challenge the use of such discretion. However, the poor and those with less education are more reliant on state services and more vulnerable to rent seeking.[38] Scheduled Caste voters are among those

---

[36] Brass, *Theft of an Idol*, 194. Brass is not the only one to point to widespread corruption among the police. A survey conducted by David Bayley, in what is the standard text on the police in India, reports that between 7 percent (in rural areas) and 25 percent (in urban areas) of the population had themselves seen bribery occur, while a majority believe that the police are corrupt. As he notes: "So convinced is the general public of the venality of the police that, even in order to obtain assistance in the normal course of duty, one-fifth of all respondents would provide themselves with money so as to be in a position to grease a palm." Bayley (1969), 286. Police reports themselves note that "the majority of the subordinate ranks are corrupt" (cited in Bayley [1969], 289). "The forms of corruption are almost infinite. Police may exact money for doing something, for not doing something, for doing something properly, for misdoing something, for maintaining goodwill and for seeing that something is done speedily" (290).

[37] Weiner, *Party Building*, 350.

[38] Further, the discretionary capacity of the state might vary across Indian states as a consequence of institutional reforms adopted by state governments. In Kerala, for instance,

most dependent on the largesse of those who control the state. Let me illustrate their degree of dependence by drawing on the story of one such voter, recounted by Dreze, Lanjouw, and Sharma in Lanjouw and Stern's study of Palanpur village in Uttar Pradesh. Mahavir is a good example of the median Scheduled Caste voter in Uttar Pradesh, who is rural, illiterate, landless, and poor. Dreze, Lanjouw, and Sharma describe their meeting with him in the following terms:[39]

On 9 January 1987, during one of our sojourns in Palanpur, we received the visit of a man called Mahavir. The first half of January is a time of slack labour demand, and Mahavir, a landless labourer, had been unable to find work for several days. He told us that he had spent the whole morning trying to find someone who would lend him one rupee, so that he could at least feed his two children in the evening.

Mahavir is a well-known resident of Palanpur, who is in no danger of leaving the village, and, poor as he is, he would have had no difficulty in repaying a one-rupee loan later in the season. But no one agreed to lend him a rupee. He commented, *"garib aadmee ko koi naheen deta,"* "no one lends to a poor man." Eventually, he was able to obtain one kg of wheat (worth two rupees) from one of the village moneylenders with an interest of 50 percent in kind after the harvest – four months from then.

At that time, the local branch of the Prathma Bank (a state-run rural bank) was implementing the "Integrated Rural Development Programme," a scheme of subsidized credit intended for households below the poverty line. Loans of several thousand rupees could be obtained under this programme, at a nominal interest rate of 12 percent per year. The Scheduled Castes, of which Mahavir is a member, were one of the main target groups, and had to repay only two-thirds of the principal according to the programme's official guidelines. We asked Mahavir why he had not applied for a loan from Prathma Bank, but he dismissed this fanciful idea. To start with, he did not have the resources to bribe the headman, the village development officer, and the bank manager. Besides, he was afraid of being cheated. "These people," he said, referring to the bank managers, "they tell you something and write something else."

Even though a government-sponsored credit programme existed that was tailored to his needs, Mahavir could not count on obtaining such credit

"decentralized planning" at the local level is reported to have had some impact on reducing the level of rent-seeking by elected officials and salaried employees. Thomas Isaac, "Campaign for Democratic Decentralization in Kerala," paper presented at the Conference on Experiments in Empowered Deliberative Democracy, University of Wisconsin–Madison, January 2000. While I do not investigate the varying degrees of dependence of individuals of different incomes and of different educational and regional backgrounds on the discretionary power of the state here, this is a subject worthy of independent research.

[39] All references to Mahavir in the following paragraphs are from Lanjouw and Stern, *Economic Development in Palanpur*, 506–507.

without having either the material resources to bribe the government employees responsible for credit allocation or, presumably, the political influence with which to sanction them. Further, all available opportunities to improve his position led him back toward the discretion of public officials. He might have attempted to obtain additional employment during the period of slack labour demand, under the government-run JRY employment scheme. However, the village headmen in charge of implementing these schemes routinely violated the programme guidelines for employing skilled labour, and he would have needed the material or political resources with which to influence them.[40] Had he tried to escape his circumstances by securing regular employment in the public sector, he would have needed "contacts."[41] The option of securing a government loan that would permit him to pursue a more lucrative occupation was, as we have seen, foreclosed already. The government in Palanpur possessed land, confiscated during the first land consolidation operations in the 1950s, for distribution to Scheduled Castes. However, any attempt to secure a land grant under policy legislation that earmarked such land for Scheduled Caste beneficiaries would have required him "to bribe the *lekhpal* [the record-keeper], the *kanungo* [revenue inspector], and the *tehsildar* [the subdivisional district magistrate, responsible for the administration of the tehsil, or district subdivision]."[42] Had he obtained land, he would have needed influence to ensure that it was secure. As another study of a UP village points out, Scheduled Caste beneficiaries of land grants or housing plots allotted by the village headman continued to wait for the registration papers that would make their control over the property official.[43] And had he managed to obtain secure control of land, he would be dependent upon the discretionary power of public officials to ensure access to water, seeds, fertilizer, farming equipment, credit, electricity, and so on.

Further, Mahavir's and his family's access to routine social services in Palanpur also depended upon influence with the administration. Subsidized food and provisions were sold by the manager of the government fair price shop for a fee.[44] Health care was available only to those with "clout."[45] Even access to education depended to some degree upon influence over

---

[40] Ibid., 195–196.
[41] Ibid., 129.
[42] Ibid., 191.
[43] Gupta, *Postcolonial Developments*, 147.
[44] Lanjouw and Stern, *Economic Development in Palanpur*, 193.
[45] Ibid., 195.

the appointment of teachers. Scheduled Caste children in Palanpur had lower rates of school attendance than those from other caste groups, in part because of the attitude of the upper-caste village teacher, who "considers any form of direct contact with Jatab children as repulsive."[46] The teacher's job, however, was safeguarded through political connections: He was the son of the headman. He could not be challenged, therefore, without some rival source of political influence.

As Mahavir's story shows, Scheduled Castes' access to any of the basic necessities of survival and advancement depends upon the discretionary power of the local and state administration. Those among them who possess material resources may be able to use them to bribe state officials in their favour. For most who, like Mahavir, do not have such resources, the best chance of obtaining these benefits is through political intervention.

II. The Capacity of Politicians to Collect Rents

So far, I have argued simply that public officials, because of the discretion at their disposal, have a multitude of opportunities to collect rents from citizens. Does the power to collect rents lie, however, with salaried government employees or with politicians? In most cases, it is salaried government employees who are directly responsible for the allocation of jobs and services: The district superintendent gives out jobs as "police constable," the assistant engineer distributes water, the bank manager makes decisions on loan eligibility, and the *patwari* is influential in the settlement of land disputes. As a result, these salaried employees have the opportunity to extract rents directly from the public at the point of contact. As I will show, however, the control and influence that politicians exert over government employees gives them *additional* power to collect rents from voters who seek their intervention.

Politicians control salaried employees in part through administrative oversight or coordination: IAS officials in any state are responsible to the ministers in their respective departments; members of the state legislature (MLAs) and MPs both have seats on the District Board, where the district collector must consult with them on the allocation of development funds; lower-level bureaucrats may answer to the district *panchayats*, and so on. However, the most important tool of influence that politicians have over

[46] Ibid., 63–64.

salaried employees, and therefore in the collection of rents, is the power to transfer government employees.[47]

The transfer of senior civil servants in any state is the responsibility of the chief minister. Ministers in the state government can transfer senior civil servants within their own departments. The chief minister and other ministers, furthermore, share the power of transfer with other politicians in the party and the state legislature. In order to preserve support among his own faction in the party and to weaken others, the chief minister or ministers can "farm out" the power to transfer salaried employees to MLAs.[48] The MLAs, in turn, may be obligated to locally influential politicians or to party functionaries. As a result, political control over the bureaucracy is widely dispersed. Those civil servants whose transfers are controlled by the MLAs and their political allies are in turn responsible for the transfers of government employees lower down the income scale within their areas of jurisdiction. Consequently, politicians exert a chain of influence that runs down to the lowliest employee at the local level. As de Zwart describes it:

The District Education officer is responsible for deciding on the transfer of teachers.... The district education officer can take decisions on his own account but because he himself can be transferred by the state minister of education, he has to bear in mind the wishes of certain local politicians – in particular those who belong to the same faction as the minister of education and can therefore influence the minister.[49]

Some indication of the importance of the transfer as a tool for exerting political control comes from the sheer volume of such transfers. In Madhya Pradesh, for instance, an estimated 30,000 transfers were carried out in one month in 1988.[50] There is no quantitative study of such transfers, and so no way of telling whether these figures are typical. Qualitative studies of such transfers, however, report that the volume is substantial.[51] Politicians are able, through their power to promise favourable postings to malleable officials and unfavourable ones to others, to pressure salaried government employees to respond to their wishes. In turn, pressure successfully applied on any one employee *magnifies* the power of the politician, rendering

---

[47] Wade, "Politics and Graft"; Frank de Zwart, *The Bureaucratic Merry-Go-Round: Manipulating the Transfer of Indian Civil Servants* (Amsterdam: Amsterdam University Press, 1994); Bayley, *Police and Political Development*.
[48] de Zwart, *Bureaucratic Merry-Go-Round*, 7.
[49] Ibid., 99.
[50] *India Today*, August 31, 1988, cited in Ibid., 80.
[51] de Zwart, *Bureaucratic Merry-Go-Round*; Wade, "Politics and Graft."

others dependent on him. In a typical example of such a transaction, a head constable might approach a politician in hopes of avoiding a disciplinary sentence.[52] The head constable's fate depends upon the district superintendent, an IPS officer who can be transferred by the state government. The politician may intervene with the superintendent, using his control over the superintendent's position to extract a favour for the head constable. At the end of the transaction, the head constable is also directly obligated to the politician. At election time, the politician is able to draw on a network of such obligations created through the threat of transfer to promise some voters favourable treatment from the bureaucracy and to withhold it from others in return for votes.

How, in turn, is the capacity to seek rents distributed across politicians at different levels of the state apparatus? The "state" in India is a three-tiered structure, consisting of the national government, the state governments, and the local governments. Does the power to distribute state resources and services for private return lie with those who head the local governments, the state government, or the national government?

To some extent, politicians at all three levels have some patronage resources at their disposal. Especially since 1993, when the seventy-third and seventy-fourth amendments to the Constitution introduced a uniform structure of local self-government across India, local governments have acquired greater control over such resources. Their precise responsibilities vary across states: They might be responsible for the transfer of school teachers in their areas, for the allocation of funds to development projects, for decisions on where these projects should be located, for the selection of IRDP beneficiaries, or for the allocation of common land.[53] Those who belong to the central government also have some ability to affect the lives of individuals at the local level. Under the MP Local Area Development Scheme, for instance, all members of Parliament have discretionary control over how funds amounting to Rs. two crore (20 million rupees) per year are spent in their constituencies. MPs, furthermore, sit on the District Board and so have some influence on decisions on district development projects.

[52] This is adapted from Bayley, *Police and Political Development*.
[53] Maitreya Ghatak and Maitreesh Ghatak, "Grassroots Democracy: A Study of the Panchayat System in West Bengal," paper presented at the Conference on Experiments in Empowered Deliberative Democracy, University of Wisconsin–Madison, January 2000; Isaac, "Campaign for Democratic Decentralization in Kerala."

But while some capacity to collect rents is found among politicians at all levels, it is at the level of the *state* government that the greatest capacity to collect rents currently lies. The Indian Constitution gives state governments exclusive responsibility for most of the areas that affect the daily lives of citizens: law and order, police, agriculture, water supply, power supply, urban development, education, state public services, agriculture, cooperatives, and public health.[54] Further, it is the state government that decides on the transfers and postings of bureaucrats within state boundaries. As a result, it is politicians at the state level who have the greatest control over the distribution of patronage and the collection of rents, although party linkages might force them to share some of this power with politicians at other levels.[55]

Because the state looms so large in India, and because control over the state offers individuals the capacity to obtain both material goods and status, public office – either in the bureaucracy or in representative institutions – is one of the most sought-after career opportunities in India.[56] Elected office is a particularly attractive channel for upward mobility because of the relative ease through which it can be attained. An individual attempting to build a career as an economic entrepreneur requires capital in the form of wealth, natural resources, or technical know-how – access to which is typically restricted by birth and educational opportunities. An individual attempting to build a career as a political entrepreneur, however, labours under no such restrictions. The capital required to launch a bid for entry into the state apparatus is simply a demonstrated popular following, which can be built from nothing. No wonder, then, that elections in India, especially

---

[54] Constitution of India, seventh schedule.

[55] For further evidence on the importance of the state/central government as opposed to the local level, see Chhibber, *Democracy without Associations*. Chhibber himself does not distinguish between state and central governments. For examples of the importance of the MLA compared to the MP, see Bayley, *Police and Political Development*, 371; and Lelah Dushkin, "Scheduled Caste Politics," in J. Michael Mahar, ed., *The Untouchables in Contemporary India* (Tucson: University of Arizona Press, 1972), 194.

[56] As Weiner noted, those who joined the Congress party were motivated by the desire for both status and material advancement: "The Congress party is simply one object of power, along with the District Local Board, the taluka development boards, and the banking and credit institutions. The desire to maintain control over land, to have access to credit, to influence the local market, and to obtain licenses and permits for oneself and more often for one's relatives and friends constitutes a powerful motive. Nor should we dismiss the desire to maintain one's status within one's community in a society in which access to power, along with caste, wealth and education, constitutes a source of prestige." Weiner, *Party Building*, 274.

at lower levels of government, have the character of job fairs, with hundreds of upwardly mobile elites queuing up in front of party offices, seeking party tickets to contest the elections.

III. The Sale of State Resources and Services in Return for Votes

In this section, I focus on the use of state resources and services by politicians to garner political support. While politicians also seek rent in other forms, including monetary gain, status, and reciprocal obligations, voter support is an important form of rent, since it allows political entrepreneurs to retain control of the state.

The allocation of public sector jobs, even though they constitute only a small proportion of the total number of jobs in the economy, is one valuable means of obtaining voter support. These jobs are highly valued as channels for upward mobility, for their economic as well as their status returns. As a result, although the number of jobs is small, the number of aspirants for these jobs is considerably larger.[57] Further, these jobs are significant because of the number of people each government employee actually supports.[58] The dependents of government employees include not just their immediate kin but the entire communities from which they come. One IAS officer I interviewed related proudly that he was the first IAS official from his village and described the expectations that his village had of him as a provider of developmental resources and additional jobs for unemployed village youth.[59] We can get some idea of the political importance of the limited number of government jobs if we consider that even four or five government jobs per village can make a difference in the lives of a much larger pool of people. The average government employee does not have the power to get developmental resources diverted to his community or village. However, he does serve as a point in a network through which others from the same community or village can pull themselves up.[60] Because those who allot this limited number of jobs are bargaining effectively with a significantly larger pool of aspirants, and because each job allocated affects not

[57] On this, see Gupta, *Postcolonial Developments*, 143; and Lanjouw and Stern, *Economic Development in Palanpur*, 128.
[58] Gupta, *Postcolonial Developments*, 143.
[59] Interview, Lucknow, December 1997.
[60] On this, see Lanjouw and Stern, *Economic Development in Palanpur*, 130.

only the direct recipient but also his dependents, the selective allocation of these few jobs brings politicians magnified results.

Government jobs, however, are only one of the several resources that can be allocated selectively by politicians in return for voter support. As the preceding section illustrated, politicians are also able to offer a variety of other selective benefits, including wells, housing, roads, land security, schools, telegraph lines, power connections, water, loans, hospital beds, police protection, ration cards, university admission, and any number of development benefits intended in principle to be allocated on the basis of impersonal criteria. They might extract votes by delivering such benefits, or by withholding them. The use of such "short-term highly specific induce-ments to localized groups of voters"[61] in return for votes has been noted in the several general studies on which I draw in this chapter. I illustrate it here by drawing mainly upon the work of Myron Weiner, whose 1967 study illuminates the individual-level transactions between politicians and voters in the most detail.

In one of the several descriptions of election campaigns in which such transactions took place, Weiner describes the following two election meet-ings in the state of Andhra Pradesh:

Meeting #1:
A group of fifteen or twenty villagers met us at the panchayat office. We all crowded into a small room. It was a blazing hot sunny afternoon. Prasada Rao [the vice president of the district Congress committee] asked them how the village was going to vote. They said that some of the prominent persons in the village had decided to go to Swatantra [a competing party]. He asked them what they were going to do. They said that they hadn't decided. Prasada Rao grew visibly angry, raised his voice, and waved his hands emotionally. He said that these big men never suffer no matter how they vote, but they [the people in the room] would. He said that the Congress MLA would naturally help those people who were with him and that if they should go to him or to some ministers with their problems, they shouldn't expect any help. He grew even more angry and told them he didn't care what they did but he was only telling them what the situation was. Then he walked out of the panchayat office, accompanied by the Congress candidate (who had remained silent) to the car and we drove off. When we reached the outskirts of the village, he asked one person in the car, a local Harijan [a commonly used term for Scheduled Castes, which many now see as derogatory] leader, who had once been an MLA to return to the village and see what effect his remarks had had.[62]

[61] Wade (1989), 81.
[62] Weiner, *Party Building*, 195

134

Meeting #2:
We then went to the nearby hamlet of Itemkampadu, which shares the same polling station as Upparapalem. The village contains mostly Muslims and Harijans. The president of the panchayat is a Muslim and the vice president a Harijan. Both men, along with other villagers, met us under a large shady tree at the edge of the village. The panchayat president told us that they would vote for Congress but that they didn't know the Congress assembly candidate personally. He said that that he wanted an assurance from Prasada Rao that if they had any problems or needs they could go to him, since they knew him, rather than to the MLA. They wanted to know if Prasada Rao would take care of their problems. On that assurance he said that they would vote for Congress. Prasada Rao then said a few words about what Congress had already done for them, then said that he would personally see to it that their problems were taken care of.[63]

The two incidents illustrate the essence of patronage politics in India: The politician uses promises of tangible material benefits, and threats to withdraw such benefits, in order to induce political support. Voters, meanwhile, are equally instrumental. In Itemkampadu, voters negotiated a straightforward exchange of votes in return for benefits and sought guarantees for the informal contract. In Upparapalem, the fact that voters took the trouble to arrange a meeting with the Congress campaigner to indicate that they were thinking of defecting to the competition suggests that they too were using the threat of withdrawal of support in order to extract promises of benefits. As Weiner points out, in his own analysis of the two incidents: "Clearly, the party politicians and village factions play the game of politics in much the same way."[64] And as he emphasizes throughout his study: "It is a mistake to think that villagers are constantly being exploited by political parties, for it is no less true that political parties are exploited by village factions seeking to maximize their own interests by associating themselves with district political organizations."[65]

However, since all voters are not equally dependent upon state resources and services, all voters may not be equally instrumental in their use of the vote. Those with wealth and education may be indifferent to the allocation of these goods, since, as I pointed out earlier, they have the means to ensure their access to such goods in the private economy. However, the more dependent the voter is on the state, the more we should expect him to make instrumental use of his vote. The stakes for such a voter are high,

[63] Ibid., 196.
[64] Ibid., 200.
[65] Ibid., 168, 309, 189.

and the vote is his principal means of obtaining a favourable outcome.[66] Weiner's own study points to fierce bargaining for resources by Scheduled Castes and other vulnerable groups. As he points out: "Harijans want to know if the candidate is willing to look into their request for permits for housing sites. Another group wants to know if he can provide fertilizers, help them obtain irrigation, tanks, drinking water facilities, grain storage facilities or more loans."[67] Similarly, Wade notes that it is particularly "the numerically preponderant low caste and Scheduled Caste voters" who "tend to vote according to a calculus of material gain."[68]

In assessing their degree of access to patronage benefits under different governments, voters expect to benefit most from politicians from their "own" ethnic groups. The reaction of a Scheduled Caste youth in Uttar Pradesh facing resistance from a local bureaucrat in obtaining an appointment letter for a government job is illustrative of these expectations. The government at the time was headed by the BJP, which is dominated mainly by upper castes, and to a lesser extent by backward castes. His attitude was philosophical: "Its because *our* government has fallen. If *our* government was in power, he would have given me that letter in two minutes."[69] By "our" government, he meant a BSP government headed by a Scheduled Caste chief minister. The statement is remarkable because of the unquestioned acceptance of the idea that those in power will serve members of their "own" group first. For this respondent, it was natural that a government headed by his "own" group would be responsive to his needs, and that one headed by some other group would, just as naturally, be responsive to some other group's needs. For another Scheduled Caste voter, having a government populated by his "own" men in the state capital meant the concrete acquisition of a hand pump. The upper-caste-dominated BJP government, he complained, could not be trusted to deliver benefits. "When Mayawati [the BSP leader and several times the chief minister of the state of Uttar Pradesh] became chief minister," he reported, "we went twice and got the

---

[66] The argument here suggests that literacy is not a prerequisite for rational action. Rather, it is precisely because those who are illiterate are also more vulnerable that we should expect them to calculate carefully the costs and benefits of voting one way rather than another. On the rationality of subordinate groups, see especially Samuel Popkin, *The Rational Peasant: The Political Economy of Rural Society in Vietnam* (Berkeley: University of California Press, 1979).
[67] Weiner, *Party Building*, 189.
[68] Wade, "Politics and Graft," 93.
[69] Interview, November 19, 1997, Lucknow (italics mine).

handpump."[70] A third respondent in Uttar Pradesh described the firm reputation that Mulayam Singh Yadav, who belonged to the Yadav caste, had as a champion of Yadav interests. "The minute Mulayam Singh Yadav [from the Yadav caste] becomes Chief Minister, the Yadavs will put on their best clothes and show up at the door of the district magistrate, demanding that he do their work . . . and just to get rid of them he will do it."[71] A member of the legislative assembly from the Nishad caste described the impact of his election among his constituency: "*My* people [by which he meant fellow Nishads as well as "backward castes" more generally] come directly to me, they do not go to the constable or the rest of the administration. Of course, they can go to them directly, but they trust me more."[72] In general, as Root points out in a discussion of voting behaviour in India in previous elections: "Voters sought leaders who came from their own caste or subcaste – people more like themselves."[73]

These expectations of in-group favouritism certainly appear to have an objective basis. In Uttar Pradesh, in one of many instances of in-group favouritism, 720 out of 900 teachers appointed by Mulayam Singh Yadav reportedly belonged to the Yadav caste.[74] In Bihar, observers have noted that when Jagannath Mishra, a Maithil Brahmin, was chief minister, "the Maithil Brahmins acquired important positions in the political system."[75] Such acts of in-group favouritism pervade the system from top to bottom. In Akhil Gupta's study of Alipur, for instance, the manager of a state-owned farm, "like other low-level bureaucrats acted as a patron, using his position as an officer of the state to help his own people. Most of the daily labourers he hired (at state-stipulated wages, which were above the prevailing market rates) were people of his own caste."[76]

But, as I argued in Chapter 2, the basis for this objective reality lies in the greater "visibility" of ethnic identities, which lead both voters and politicians to support co-ethnics. A reporter or an ordinary observer might easily ascertain, from a list of names, the caste identity of Mulayam Singh's

---

[70] *New York Times*, February 25, 2002.
[71] Interview, November 14, 1997, Allahabad.
[72] Interview, December 19, 1996, Delhi.
[73] Root, "A Liberal India," 519.
[74] *India Today*, October 15, 1994, 37, cited in Christophe Jaffrelot, "The BJP and the 1996 General Election," paper presented at the National Conference on Political Sociology of India's Democracy, New Delhi, November 14–16, 1996.
[75] *Economic and Political Weekly*, May 4, 1991.
[76] Gupta, *Postcolonial Developments*, 144–5.

appointments, or Jagannath Mishra's cabinets, or the farm manager's employees. However, it would be difficult to ascertain, on the basis of such superficial information, what the other bases for these appointments might have been. No wonder, then, that the calculus of voters in India is routinely described as "voting for the surname."[77]

One final question that arises from the account so far is why politicians centre their electoral strategy on the "retail" sale of particular inducements to individual voters. Why not simply court voter support by promising collective goods in the form of policy legislation? Why, in turn, should voters demand selective goods in return for their votes? Why not demand, instead, collective goods in the form of policy legislation? Politicians have greater incentives to promise patronage benefits rather than policy goods for two reasons. Policy legislation is a one-time good that might bring the party responsible for such legislation one-time voter support, but there is no guarantee that such support will not disappear once the policy is in place. The particularized sale of benefits, on the other hand, ensures their providers continuous support. When politicians tell voters that they will withdraw such benefits if not elected, the threat is credible. Further, the interests of any individual politician are far better served by the politics of patronage rather than by the politics of policy. The credit for policy legislation, and therefore the returns in the form of voter support, goes to the party as a whole or to a single leader. Credit for the individualized distribution of patronage, however, accrues to individual politicians. As a consequence, patronage politics allows each individual within a party to build up a distinct following. It is for this reason that we find high-level politicians, including chief ministers and cabinet ministers, personally involving themselves in seemingly trivial transactions such as the provision of hand pumps, licenses, and appointment letters.

For voters, different incentives drive the demand for specific rather than collective goods. Voters in India and in other patronage-democracies are well aware of the yawning gap between policy legislation and implementation. As the previous section showed, almost every major developmental policy adopted by the Indian government has been tampered with in its implementation in order to favour some individuals and to deny others. Such voters, therefore, are likely to believe promises of policy legislation

---

[77] *The Week*, January 18, 1998.

from a party only if the presence of co-ethnic elites in its past organization and governments gives them a credible guarantee that they will be favoured individually in its implementation.

IV. The Availability of Information about Voting Patterns

The sale of state resources and services in return for votes that I have described so far can take place only when politicians can obtain information about how voters have voted, or equivalently, when voters believe that politicians can obtain such information.

One method through which politicians obtain such information is the right of political parties to designate "polling agents" at each voting booth. The function of the polling agent is to assure each candidate of a free and fair poll, and to assist voters by locating their names on the voter list. In practice, however, the polling agents are also the means by which candidates exercise surveillance. The polling agents are usually men from the village itself, or from close by, who know the identity of each voter. While they do not witness the actual vote, they know who shows up to vote and can report on turnout figures. The presence of polling agents serves, furthermore, as a warning to the voter as he or she enters the polling booth that the candidate expects loyalty.

In the past, information about voting patterns was also made available through the system of counting ballot papers and announcing each candidate's votes separately for each polling station. A polling station covers a very small section of the electorate, usually comprising no more than one or two villages. Combined with information about turnout rates gathered by polling agents, this system of counting permitted candidates to construct a fairly detailed picture of how particular communities vote. As Subramanian notes in his study of ethnic mobilization in South India:

Party representatives are intimately aware of the social composition of the population voting in their booth, and note the approximate numbers and social background (caste/class) of those who vote at different points in the day.... Contrary to official rules, poll officials often empty ballot boxes "carefully" before counting so that votes are counted approximately in the order in which they were cast – The parties' election agents are given updates of the party-wise breakdown for the booth as the counting proceeds as well as the final tally. When correlated with notes about the

139

groups which voted at different points, these figures give activists a fairly accurate picture of the sources of support for the major parties.[78]

This system of counting was eliminated by election reforms introduced during T. N. Seshan's term as election commissioner, and votes are now counted by mixing the ballot papers for the entire assembly constituency.[79] These reforms make it more difficult for politicians to monitor voting behaviour. However, it may be more difficult to establish the *credibility* of these reforms in a political system in which the implementation of state policy is routinely subverted.

Third, because monitoring the act of voting is so important, political parties invest in creating a network of informers who inform them about voting behaviour in particular communities. The candidates whom I interviewed reported that they were able to obtain information about voting behaviour retrospectively with relative ease, through *panchayats*, religious organizations, or neighbourhood leaders. As one candidate put it: "See, for individuals it is very difficult. But for groups it is easy. In villages, castes live in different localities. Our workers see which locality is for whom."[80] According to another: "We know which caste voted for whom in which village."[81]

Fourth, although a vast state machinery exists to safeguard the secret ballot, this machinery is frequently allied with the locally influential ethnic groups in each district.[82] The individual voter casts his or her vote at polling booths staffed by polling parties appointed by the state and guarded by a small police force. The polling parties, including the presiding officer, are local men, employed in petty government positions (clerk, schoolmaster, postman, watchman) in the district. Their relations with leaders from the dominant parties in the district are deferential, based on their inferior social and economic status.[83] As a result, they are vulnerable to attempts

---

[78] Narendra Subramanian, *Ethnicity and Populist Mobilization: Political Parties, Citizens and Democracy in South India* (Delhi: Oxford University Press, 1999), 66, 39n.

[79] Election Commission of India, *Handbook for Counting Agents* (Delhi: Election Commission of India, 1997).

[80] Interview, May 1, 1996.

[81] Interview, April 11, 1996.

[82] For detailed descriptions of the ties between locally influential elites and the state, see Brass, *Theft of an Idol*, and Brass, *Factional Politics in an Indian State*. See also Schenk, "Corruption ... What Corruption?," and Weiner, *Party Building*.

[83] Schenk, "Corruption . . . What Corruption?"

at intimidation or bribery from the locally powerful elite.[84] Voters from subordinate groups, therefore, are less likely to trust that their vote will be secret, whether or not such intimidation and bribery actually occurs.

Finally, the actions of the state, even when informed of such intimidation or bribery, are unpredictable. As a result, elites can either find out how voters voted or, even more importantly, create the *perception* that they might find out. One incident from a polling day in the course of an election between 1996 and 1998 is instructive.[85] At one polling booth during these elections, voters from the locally dominant caste prevented Scheduled Caste voters from entering the booth and stuffed the ballot boxes with bogus votes. The police constable stationed at the booth complained to the zonal magistrate in charge of overseeing the elections. When the zonal magistrate arrived at the spot, however, the polling party appointed by the state was unwilling to register an official complaint. By lodging an official report, the presiding officer knew that he would expose himself to reprisals by those who had stuffed the boxes, especially if they ended up on the winning side after the votes were counted. The zonal magistrate decided not to take punitive action for two reasons: (1) He guessed that he had arrived in time to prevent large-scale ballot stuffing. In his experience of fraudulent voting across repeated elections, this was a relatively small-scale event. (2) Without an official complaint from the presiding officer, he lacked firm justification for taking punitive action. He left the polling place after issuing a general warning to the crowd clustered outside the booth, and in all likelihood the ballot stuffing continued as before.

The critical point underlined by this incident, and by others like it, is not that the state machinery is equally likely to look the other way in all cases. Indeed, the Election Commission of India has become more aggressive in safeguarding the secrecy of the ballot. And politicians and officials are held accountable by the press, which routinely reports incidents of vote fraud, along with accounts of the actions taken or not taken by government authorities in response. But the *possibility* of subversion of the secret ballot is common enough, especially in "small-scale incidents" of the type just described, for voters to believe that politicians can enforce compliance with voting contracts.

[84] For an account of voter intimidation in the state of Bihar, see Kohli, *Democracy and Discontent*, especially p. 214.
[85] This account is based on my own observation and on interviews with the zonal magistrate, the polling parties, and the polling agents of the parties.

V. Conclusion

The argument of this chapter offers one explanation for the rising rates of both office-seeking activity (measured by the number of contestants per seat) and voter participation (measured by looking at voter turnout rates) that characterize democracy in India.[86] This high level of politicization has been idealistically interpreted as the "maturing" of Indian democracy, implying that some kind of normative commitment to the democratic idea has taken root among the Indian electorate.[87] It has also been indulgently interpreted as a ritual, a celebration, and even "in a beautiful way . . . the greatest sport in India."[88] The argument here suggests the more cynical interpretation that the expansion of participation in Indian politics represents less a normative commitment or a spirit of celebration and more the intensification of a struggle over the scarce resources provided by the state, where the stakes are high and the outcome makes an immediate difference to the lives of elites and voters alike. In subsequent chapters, I explore the attempts of Scheduled Caste elites and voters to gain access to the state through the Bahujan Samaj Party and its competition.

---

[86] Yogendra Yadav, "Reconfiguration in Indian Politics," *Economic and Political Weekly*, Vol. 31, Nos. 2 and 3 (January 13–20, 1996): 95–104.

[87] See, for instance, "The Maturing of a Democracy," *India Today*, August 31, 1996.

[88] Shiv Vishwanathan, "Thinking about Elections," *Seminar 440* (April 1996): 72–75.

7

The Bahujan Samaj Party (BSP) and the Scheduled Castes (SCs)

This chapter describes the Bahujan Samaj Party (BSP) and its target ethnic category, the Scheduled Castes.[1] Section I provides a brief history of the BSP and locates it in the context of Indian politics. Section II discusses the Scheduled Castes. Section III describes the platform on which the BSP appeals to the Scheduled Castes and contrasts its platform with that of the Congress party, its principal competitor. Section IV describes the method that I employ to develop the hypothesis proposed in this book. Section V evaluates this hypothesis against the principal explanations for the variation in support for the BSP among Scheduled Castes proposed by informed observers of the BSP, including social scientists, media analysts, and BSP activists themselves. Subsequent chapters then develop and test the separate propositions contained in this argument.

I. History

The Bahujan Samaj Party was founded in 1984 by Kanshi Ram, a Ramdassia Sikh belonging to the Chamar caste category among the Scheduled Castes.

---

[1] There are few secondary sources available on the BSP, which, although founded in 1984, has only recently begun to attract significant scholarly and media attention. For recent studies of Dalit politics that also discuss the BSP, see Sudha Pai, "Politicization of Dalits and Most Backward Castes," *Economic and Political Weekly*, June 7, 1997; Gail Omvedt, *Dalit Visions* (New Delhi: Orient Longman, 1995); Oliver Mendelsohn and Marika Vicziany, *The Untouchables* (Cambridge: Cambridge University Press, 1998); Ghanshyam Shah, ed., *Dalit Identity and Politics* (Delhi: Thousand Oaks, 2001); Walter Fernandes, *The Emerging Dalit Identity: The Reassertion of the Subalterns* (Delhi: Indian Social Institute, 1996); Christophe Jaffrelot, "The Bahujan Samaj Party in North India," *Comparative Studies of South Asia, Africa and the Middle East*, Vol. 18, No. 1 (1998): 35–52; and Ian Duncan, "Dalits and Politics in Rural North India: The Bahujan Samaj Party in Uttar Pradesh," *The Journal of Peasant Studies*, Vol. 27, No. 1 (1999): 35–60.

Born in 1934 in a rural district in the north Indian state of Punjab,[2] Kanshi Ram obtained a B.Sc. degree from a local college. He then entered one of the government positions "reserved" for Scheduled Caste candidates, first with the Survey of India and then with the government-owned Explosives Research and Development Laboratory in the city of Pune in the western state of Maharashtra.[3]

Although he did not initially aspire to a political career, incidents of caste discrimination during his tenure in government service pushed him toward politics.[4] While employed in the Pune Laboratory, Kanshi Ram became involved in an agitation by Scheduled Caste employees protesting the cancellation of an official holiday commemorating the birthday of Dr. B. R. Ambedkar, India's most prominent Scheduled Caste leader during the movement for independence from the British.[5] He was suspended following an altercation with an upper-caste superior over this incident.[6] He resigned from his job altogether in 1971 and, in 1973, founded the Backward and Minority Community Employees Federation (BAMCEF), a local association of government employees with the explicit purpose of increasing the political influence of the ethnic categories that they represented.

In its initial years, BAMCEF supported the activities of the Republican Party of India, then India's best-known Scheduled Caste party, with a base mainly in the state of Maharashtra.[7] It also sought the support and participation of Scheduled Caste and other politicians from all political parties.[8] By the early 1980s, however, Kanshi Ram's goal shifted from seeking influence for Scheduled Castes to creating a channel for direct political participation. In 1981, he founded the Dalit Shoshit Samaj Sangarsh Samiti (DS-4). Ostensibly the "agitational" wing of BAMCEF, the DS-4 soon evolved into a political party, contesting elections with the limited objective of obtaining

[2] Ambeth Rajan, *My Bahujan Samaj* (Delhi: ABCDE, 1994), 1.
[3] Ibid.
[4] Interview with Kanshi Ram, February 24, 1997, Ludhiana.
[5] Ambeth Rajan, *My Bahujan Samaj Party*; interview with Kanshi Ram, February 24, 1997, Ludhiana.
[6] Interview with an old associate of Kanshi Ram from this period, November 21, 1996; Mendelsohn and Vicziany, *The Untouchables*, 220.
[7] Interviews with early BSP activists.
[8] Early BAMCEF functions were addressed by member parties across the political spectrum, including Jagjivan Ram, the most prominent Scheduled Caste leader from the Congress party, and Ram Vilas Paswan, who then belonged to the Lok Dal. Mendelsohn and Vicziany, *The Untouchables*, 221; interview with senior BSP activist, November 23, 1996.

official recognition[9] and organizing voters from the Scheduled Caste and other minority groups through "cadre camps," "awakening squads," and "bicycle marches." In 1984, Kanshi Ram officially announced the creation of a new political party, the Bahujan Samaj Party. BAMCEF provided the BSP with its initial base of cadres and considerable infrastructural support. The explicit goal of the BSP, in contrast to its predecessor organizations, was to obtain political power. According to Kanshi Ram, "Political power is the master-key with which you can open any lock, whether it is [a] social, educational or cultural lock."[10]

II. The BSP's Primary Target Constituency: Scheduled Castes

In defining his new party's target ethnic constituency, Kanshi Ram faced a dilemma. For the reasons outlined in Chapter 3, his best chance of obtaining a political following was to mobilize members of his "own" ethnic category. The principal salient categories that he could identify as his own were "Ramdassia," "Chamar," "Punjabi," "Sikh," and "Scheduled Caste." Of these, the Scheduled Caste category was the only one that had a nation-wide membership. His motivation for entering politics, furthermore, had to do specifically with the grievances of the Scheduled Castes. However, the population of Scheduled Castes is not sufficient to bring about a victory in the struggle for power either at the centre or in any of the Indian states.

India has a parliamentary form of government at both the central and state levels: The national government is formed by the party that wins a majority in nationwide parliamentary elections, and the state-level government are formed by the party that wins a majority in separate statewide elections for the state legislative assembly. The electoral system for both types of election is a first-past-the-post (FPTP) system with single-member constituencies. This means that any party seeking to form the government at the national level must obtain a plurality of votes in a majority of India's 542 parliamentary constituencies. And any party seeking to form a government

---

[9] The criteria for official recognition of a political party in any state when the BSP was founded were (1) its existence and participation in political activity for a period of five years or (2) its securing at least four percent of the votes cast in the state in Lok Sabha or Vidhan Sabha elections (after excluding the votes polled by the party's candidates who forfeited their deposits). David Butler, Ashok Lahiri, and Prannoy Roy, *India Decides: Elections 1952–1995* (Delhi: Living Media, 1995).

[10] Rajan, *My Bahujan Samaj Party*, 32.

Table 7.1. *Efficacy of Scheduled Caste voters across Indian states, 1984*

Country/State	ENPV*	MWT*	%SC*
All India	5	21	16.3
Andhra Pradesh	4	26	15.9
Arunachal Pradesh	4	26	0.5
Assam	5	21	7.4
Bihar	7	15	14.6
Goa	5	21	2.1
Gujarat	4	26	7.4
Haryana	6	17	19.7
Himachal Pradesh	4	26	25.3
Jammu and Kashmir	4	26	8.3
Karnataka	5	21	16.4
Kerala	6	17	9.9
Madhya Pradesh	4	26	14.5
Maharashtra	5	21	11.1
Manipur	10	11	2
Meghalaya	7	15	0.5
Mizoram	6	17	0.1
Nagaland	6	17	0
Orissa	5	21	16.2
Punjab	4	26	28.3
Rajasthan	5	21	17.3
Sikkim	6	17	5.9
Tamil Nadu	5	21	19.2
Tripura	4	26	16.4
Uttar Pradesh	6	17	21
West Bengal	4	26	23.6

* ENPV = effective number of parties; MWT = minimum winning threshold; SC = Scheduled Caste.

Source: Election Commission of India, various years; *Census of India 1991* (for Jammu and Kashmir, *Census of India 1981*).

at the state level must obtain a plurality of votes in a majority of assembly constituencies in the state concerned. The percentage of votes that a political party needs to obtain a plurality of votes in the majority of seats in each election is inversely related to the number of competitors in the fray: The more competitors in a first-past-the-post system, the smaller the number of votes that any one party needs in order to win.

Table 7.1 provides a snapshot of the efficacy of the Scheduled Castes in each state in 1984, the year in which the BSP was formed, based on the degree of competitiveness in each state. The measure of competitiveness employed here is the "effective number of parties" (ENPV). This measure weights competitors in proportion to their vote share. The general formula for the effective number of parties in any election is as follows: If v_j is the vote share of the jth party, then the effective number of parties is $1/(\Sigma v_j{}^2)$.[11] In order to ascertain the degree of competitiveness of the party system in each state, including the BSP, I calculate the effective number of parties as $[(1/(\Sigma v_j{}^2)) + 1]$, where the term v_j refers to the vote share obtained by each party in the election immediately previous to 1984, and the 1 is added to the standard formula to reflect the entry of the BSP, which did not participate in the preceding election but is assumed to have a weight of 1 prior to the 1984 election. The second column lists the effective number of parties at the national level in the parliamentary elections and in the legislative assembly elections for each state, including the BSP. The third column summarizes the minimum winning threshold (MWT) in each election given the effective number of parties. The minimum winning threshold refers to the *minimum* percentage of the vote (in whole numbers) that a party must obtain in order to win a plurality, given the effective number of competitors. If two parties are in the fray, for example, any one party must obtain at least 51 percent of the vote in order to win, although it may well win more. Similarly, if three parties are in the fray, any one party must obtain at least 34% of the vote in order to win. As the effective number of competitors in the electoral arena increases, the minimum percentage of the vote that any one party needs to win the election falls. Finally, the fourth column summarizes the percentage of Scheduled Castes in each state and at the all-India level.

The Scheduled Caste population is dispersed across both parliamentary and assembly constituencies in India. It typically constitutes no more than a third of the electorate. Let us assume for the sake of simplicity that the effective number of parties and the percentage of Scheduled Castes in each constituency mirrors the effective number of parties and the percentage of Scheduled Castes in the state as a whole. A look at the table quickly reveals that the Scheduled Caste population was not sufficient to put a new political party in power in any state in India in 1984, with three exceptions: Haryana, Punjab, and Uttar Pradesh. And even in these states, the Scheduled Caste population was large enough not necessarily to assure victory, but to barely

---

[11] Marku Laakso and Rein Taagepera, "Effective Number of Parties: A Measure with Application to Western Europe," *Comparative Political Studies*, Vol. 12 (1979): 3–27.

permit a political party with Scheduled Caste support to cross the *minimum* threshold necessary for victory.

Consistent with the theory proposed in Chapter 3, therefore, Kanshi Ram sought to manufacture a new definition of his "own" category that would be more efficacious. He introduced the category "Bahujan," which he defined as an ascriptive category consisting of a collection of subordinate ethnic categories, hitherto considered separate, that constitute a majority of the Indian population. The term "Bahujan" entered political discourse around the turn of the century through the Satyashodhak Samaj, a lower-caste social and religious reform movement in Maharashtra that attacked Brahmanic Hinduism. "Bahujan" literally means "majority" in Marathi, its language of origin, and in Hindi, the language in which Kanshi Ram popularised it.[12] The Satyashodhak Samaj used the term to refer to the majority of Hindu castes, including untouchables, who were not Brahmins and not merchants, and it became one of the categories used by subordinate caste groups to identify themselves in the politics of colonial Maharashtra.[13] By 1984, the Satyashodhak Samaj no longer existed, and the term "Bahujan" had fallen into disuse. Kanshi Ram resuscitated the term, and at the same time redefined it to refer not only to subordinate Hindu castes in Maharashtra but to groups throughout India defined by caste, religion, and tribe whom he described as being united in sharing a history of humiliation and subordination at the hands of the Hindu upper castes. In his words: "Bahujan Samaj is comprised of Scheduled Caste, Scheduled Tribes, Other Backward Classes and converted minorities."[14]

The term "Scheduled Tribe" refers to "tribal" populations that are eligible under the Indian Constitution for affirmative action in government employment, education, and representative institutions. Scheduled Tribes make up 8 percent of the population of India.[15] The term "Other Backward Classes" (OBCs) refers, misleadingly, to a collection of subordinate *caste* categories identified by the government-appointed Mandal Commission in 1980 as "backward" and therefore deserving of affirmative action in government employment. Although the census does not collect data on the population of OBCs, as they are now called, they

---

[12] Gail Omvedt, *Cultural Revolt in a Colonial Society* (Bombay: Scientific Socialist Education Trust, 1976), 4.

[13] Omvedt, *Cultural Revolt.* Also see Rosalind O'Hanlon, *Caste, Conflict and Ideology* (Cambridge: Cambridge University Press, 1985).

[14] *Oppressed Indian,* April 1985.

[15] *Census of India 1991.*

are estimated to make up 52 percent of the Indian population.[16] Finally, the term "converted minorities" refers to India's religious minorities: Muslims, who make up 12 percent of the Indian population; Christians, who make up 2.34 percent; Sikhs, who make up 1.94 percent; and Buddhists, who make up .76 percent.[17] The BSP refers to the Bahujan Samaj as constituting 85 percent of the population of India. The 85 percent figure, while not precise, underlines its claim to speak for the majority of the Indian population.

The strategic motive behind this attempt to enlarge the definition of his "own" ethnic category is evident in Kanshi Ram's decision to change the name of the party from the Dalit Shoshit Samaj Sangharsh Samiti to the Bahujan Samaj Party. The term "Dalit," also a Marathi word, literally means "ground" or "broken to pieces."[18] It was popularized as a term of self-identification for Scheduled Castes by the Dalit Panthers, a militant organization formed in Maharashtra and named after the Black Panthers. Although there have been subsequent attempts to broaden the definition of the term "Dalit" to mean any oppressed group, the term has generally come to be understood as a synonym for the Scheduled Castes. By naming his first political organization as he did, Kanshi Ram had sought to mobilize all "oppressed and exploited people," including Scheduled Castes but also other minorities. However, the use of the term "Dalit" immediately signaled an overt primary orientation toward Scheduled Castes. By replacing the term "Dalit" with "Bahujan" in the name of his new party, therefore, Kanshi Ram was making a significant strategic move. He himself alluded to the significance of this move at the opening convention of the BSP, noting that the new name was arrived at after "deep study and contemplation."[19] According to one of his early associates, the contemplation given to the name centered specifically around the issue of winning. As he put it, relating conversations with Kanshi Ram: "It was a very conscious decision. He talked to me a lot, six months before the party was launched. He said: we need a party that can win (*Jeetne wali party chahiye*). And 'Bahujan' means 'majority.'"[20]

Manufacturing this new ethnic category, however, was not an easy task. The term "Bahujan" had no political resonance in India in the 1980s outside

---

[16] *Mandal Commission Report of the Backward Classes Commission 1980* (Delhi: Akalank Publications, 1980).

[17] All figures are from the *Census of India 1991*.

[18] Eleanor Zelliot, *From Untouchable to Dalit* (Delhi: Manohar, 1996), 267.

[19] Speech at the Inaugural Convention of the BSP, quoted in *Oppressed Indian*, October 1984.

[20] Interview, November 23, 1996.

the state of Maharashtra. A further difficulty lay in the socioeconomic, cultural, and historical disparities between the various groups that Kanshi Ram grouped together under the label "Bahujan Samaj." Kanshi Ram attempted to bridge these disparities by creating a common history of the Bahujan Samaj, drawing on personalities and symbols from across the categories included under the label. He organized periodic "cadre camps" in which selected BAMCEF cadres were instructed in this imagined history. These BAMCEF cadres then organized cadre camps of their own at lower levels, training workers from the BSP to repeat these lessons to mass audiences.

The manufacture of this new category was arrested in 1985 by a nationwide split in BAMCEF. The split cost the BSP the infrastructure on which it had relied for the construction of a new identity category. Following the split, Kanshi Ram conceded that the mobilization of the Bahujan Samaj was no longer a viable goal in the short term. The BSP's immediate and primary target in every electoral battle became the Scheduled Castes. As Kanshi Ram put it at a rally in Uttar Pradesh in 1996: "85% of the people in this country belong to the Bahujan Samaj. This 85% is our ultimate target. But realistically, we can aim for about 41% in U.P.... We have 50% of all the SC votes. If all the SCs vote for us, our target will be fulfilled."[21] The BSP also seeks the support of other sections of the Bahujan Samaj in its electoral battles, but it does so selectively, seeking the support of *only as many* categories within the Bahujan Samaj as are sufficient to take it to a winning position *when added to* the votes of the Scheduled Castes. As one BSP leader in Uttar Pradesh put it, describing BSP's strategy in his constituency: "The Scheduled Caste vote was our base vote, plus the Yadav vote.... this caste combination was a winning combination. Similarly in other areas, our combinations are SC + Minorities [a euphemism for Muslims]; SC + Yadav; SC + Rajbhar and so on."[22]

III. The BSP's Message to Scheduled Castes

In Chapter 1, I defined an ethnic party as one that overtly aligns itself with an ethnic category or categories to the exclusion of another or others and that makes such an alignment central to its electoral strategy. In this section, I describe the content of the message that the BSP sent to Scheduled Castes between 1984 and 1998, showing the extent to which it fit this definition

---

[21] Speech by Kanshi Ram at a rally at Begum Hazrat Mahal Park, Lucknow, July 30, 1996.
[22] Interview, Lucknow, November 20, 1997.

during that period. In order to highlight the distinctiveness of the BSP's election platform, I contrast it here with the platform of the Congress party, its principal competitor for Scheduled Caste votes.

The Congress party has historically courted Scheduled Castes through coded appeals, signaling a commitment to Scheduled Caste interests but rarely stating this commitment openly. In a rally organized to bolster its sagging fortunes in Uttar Pradesh in 1997, for instance, the party featured Meira Kumar as one of the three chief speakers. The daughter of Jagjivan Ram, one of Congress's most prominent leaders from the Scheduled Castes, Kumar assumed the mantle of Scheduled Caste leadership in Congress after his death. Speakers at the statewide rally were carefully selected to appeal to the party's target constituencies. Meira Kumar's presence on the dais signaled that Congress took Scheduled Castes in Uttar Pradesh seriously. However, this commitment was not articulated in words. Kumar did not align herself with Scheduled Castes in her own speech, portraying herself instead as a national leader, devoted to the many groups and many causes that Congress espoused.[23] Although in her speech she twice raised grievances associated with Scheduled Castes, such as untouchability, she raised these issues as a national leader concerned with the problems of one of the many groups that made up her constituency, rather than as a champion of the Scheduled Castes. Significantly, even in everyday conversations about Scheduled Castes, Kumar prefers to use the term "they" rather than "we."[24]

By contrast, the BSP loudly identified itself as a champion not of the nation as a whole, but of the Bahujan Samaj and the Scheduled Castes in particular. As Kanshi Ram put it, in a typical statement: "I am the agent of the backwards and weaker sections and the minorities who constitute 85% of the population of the country."[25] Among this 85 percent, the party openly declared itself in support of the Scheduled Castes. BSP workers admit that in any electoral constituency, they first approached the Scheduled Castes.[26] They often treated the terms "Dalit" and "Bahujan" as interchangeable.[27] At most election rallies, furthermore, Kanshi Ram and other BSP activists typically called for the support of each Scheduled Caste category by name, appealing individually to the Chamars, the Mahashahs, the Satnamis,

---

[23] Congress rally in Allahabad, November 14, 1997.
[24] Interview, Meira Kumar, November 14, 1997, Allahabad.
[25] Kanshi Ram, quoted in Rajan, *My Bahujan Samaj Party*.
[26] Interviews with BSP workers across constituencies.
[27] See, for instance, BSP rally at Dabri Palam, Delhi, December 8, 1996.

BSP election posters featuring party leaders Kanshi Ram and Mayawati, 1998 parliamentary elections.

Congress campaign vehicle featuring Meira Kumar (left), Congress candidate from Karol Bagh, along with Gandhi and various Congress leaders, including Jawaharlal Nehru, Indira Gandhi, Rajiv Gandhi, and Jagjivan Ram.

One of many statues of Dr. Ambedkar installed by the BSP government in Uttar Pradesh. Ambedkar was the chairman of the Drafting Committee for the Indian Constitution, which he clutches in his hand. The BSP describes its mission as implementing the Constitution.

Posters of Rajiv and Sonia Gandhi, among the Congress leaders to which the Congress party traces its lineage.

BSP leaders Kanshi Ram and Mayawati speaking at an election rally in Sahranpur (Uttar Pradesh), 1998 parliamentary elections.

Bhanwar Singh Gangwar, the BSP's thirty-year-old candidate, campaigning door to door in Ujjain (Madhya Pradesh), 1998 parliamentary elections. Gangwar's relative youth is typical of BSP candidates and office-bearers.

154

the Balmikis, the Pasis, and so forth, for their support. They also did not shy away from identifying the category to which they themselves belonged.[28] In a 1985 by-election campaign against Meira Kumar in the parliamentary constituency of Bijnor, for instance, the BSP candidate (and now one of its two most prominent leaders) Mayawati noted flatly: "I am born of a Chamar mother."[29] Underlining the difference between her open allegiance to Scheduled Castes and Meira Kumar's reticence, she declared: "I have not forgotten my Dalit and oppressed brothers the way that others, who live as slaves in Brahminical parties, have forgotten them."[30]

The contrast between the messages to Scheduled Castes of the two parties becomes even clearer when we look at the degree to which they excluded other ethnic categories from their appeals. Congress was careful not to exclude any other category, ethnic or otherwise, in the process of championing the interests of the Scheduled Castes. Kumar's speech at Allahabad, for instance, began by invoking a common sense of nationhood and depicting the Congress as a party of all individuals who made up the nation. Subsequently, she identified Scheduled Castes as one of many fluid and overlapping social groups that constitute the Indian nation, along with the poor, women, and religious minorities, all of which were represented by Congress. Far from opposing Scheduled Caste interests to those of other groups, she assumed a commonality, applauding the effort of Congress to bring them "into the mainstream."[31]

Between 1984 and 1998, however, the BSP drew a clear line separating Scheduled Castes and others from the upper castes, whom it portrayed as outside and opposed to the Bahujan Samaj. Perhaps the clearest illustration of this separation of insiders from outsiders is the diagram shown in Figure 7.1, routinely reproduced in BSP publications and speeches to communicate the definition of the category "Bahujan" to BAMCEF cadres and to popular audiences.

The vertical line represents the traditional status hierarchy according to which caste groups are conventionally believed to be ranked.[32] The

---

[28] Based on attendance at several rallies. See, for instance, BSP rally in Hoshiarpur, January 25, 1997.

[29] *Bahujan Sangathak*, March 9, 1987.

[30] Ibid.

[31] Congress rally at Allahabad, November 14, 1997.

[32] This representation of caste has been challenged by scholars who argue that it is an artificial construction imposed by colonial rule on a highly differentiated system.

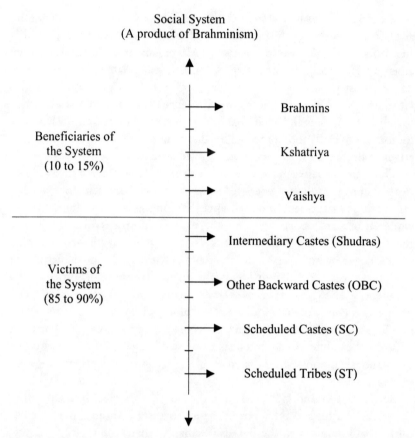

Figure 7.1. The Bahujan Samaj. *Source: Oppressed Indian*, February/March 1986.

BSP expanded this hierarchy to include the Scheduled Tribes, normally not thought to be part of the caste system, and also religious minorities, whom it defined as former low-caste Hindus who sought to escape the oppression of the caste system by changing their religion. The BSP argued that political and economic power coincides with the status hierarchy, so that those who rank high on this hierarchy were better off on all dimensions than those who ranked low. The horizontal line separates

See, for instance, Nicholas Dirks, *Castes of Mind* (Princeton, NJ: Princeton University Press, 2000), and Dipankar Gupta, *Interrogating Caste* (Delhi: Penguin, 2000). Despite its constructed origins, this has become the subjective understanding of caste in the imagination of political entrepreneurs and those whom they mobilize.

156

those lower-ranked groups who belong to the Bahujan Samaj from those higher-ranked groups who do not. It was routine in BSP rhetoric to find references to these upper castes, and especially to Brahmins and "Brahminism," as the "enemies" of the Bahujan Samaj.[33] The slogans used by BSP workers and their own explication of the party's ideology underlined this exclusion. Explaining the meaning of the Bahujan Samaj in an interview, for instance, one worker defined it as "all those not included in the three Hindu upper castes."[34] And politics was portrayed throughout this period as a zero sum game, in which the more the upper castes received, the less was left for the Bahujan Samaj and the Scheduled Castes. As Kanshi Ram put it in a speech in 1988, "The minority is eating the share of the majority."[35]

A third major difference between the two parties lies in the degree to which Scheduled Caste interests were treated as central to the party's election campaign. For the Congress, the championing of Scheduled Caste interests, even in coded and inclusive language, was marginal to its overall election message. Kumar's speech in Allahabad, for instance, was devoted to such themes as the removal of poverty, religious harmony, and the glorious nationalist history of Congress. An end to untouchability was only one item in a laundry list of items on the agenda of Congress. "On 15 August 1947," she said, "we tick marked the first item on our agenda because we had obtained independence. But ending poverty, bringing about social harmony, ending untouchability, ending communalism, establishing secularism, these items on our agenda remained."[36] Her campaign slogans emphasized the rule of the poor (*aarthik svraj, garib ka raj*), distinguished the Congress as the only party able to provide stability (*Jan Sab Ka Yahi Vichaar, Congress hi degi sthayi sarkar*), called for unity in diversity (*Anekta Mein Ekta*), or praised the leadership of the Gandhi family (*Rajivji ke sapne sach karne soniaji aage aiyee hain*). For the BSP, however, the championing of Scheduled Caste interests, and to a lesser extent those of the Bahujan Samaj, was its raison d'être. Unlike the Congress and most other political parties in India, it did not publish a manifesto or take positions on issues. It described itself as having a single-point programme: bringing political power to the Scheduled Castes and others in the Bahujan Samaj. And even when

---

[33] See, for instance, the *Bahujan Sangathak*, March 17, 1986.
[34] Interview with BSP worker, Lucknow, August 1996.
[35] Kanshi Ram, speech at Allahabad, *Bahujan Sangathak*, March 30, 1988.
[36] Congress rally at Allahabad, November 14, 1997.

asked to respond to issues such as terrorism, poverty, and communalism, on which other parties took positions, Kanshi Ram interpreted each of these problems as being the product of the political powerlessness of the Bahujan Samaj.

A Scheduled Caste voter listening to the overt campaign of the Congress party during this period would have had to strain to ascertain the extent and nature of the Congress commitment to his particular group. He would have had to recognize, further, that Congress also had a commitment to other groups against whom it would balance his own concerns. Listening to the message of the BSP between 1984 and 1998, however, would have left him in no doubt about whom the party stood for. Although its overall and long-term purpose was to champion the cause of the Bahujan Samaj, the BSP conveyed unambiguously that Scheduled Castes were its immediate and most favoured target constituency.

IV. Research Design

Why, then, did the Scheduled Castes in all states not flock to vote for the BSP? I explore this question based on data from three states: Uttar Pradesh, Punjab, and Karnataka. The strategy for case selection is to maximize the range of variation on the dependent variable. The three states were selected by classifying Indian states into three strata, based on the BSP's performance among Scheduled Castes in each state, and selecting one state from each stratum. No single state is entirely representative of the stratum from which it is selected, and each choice made some trade-off necessary. The three strata and the state selected from each are listed in Table 7.2.

The choice of Uttar Pradesh from stratum I was simple: It is the only state in which the BSP has won a majority of Scheduled Caste votes. The choice of a state from stratum II involved greater trade-offs. The choice of Jammu and Kashmir from this stratum, because of its unique position as a border state and its history of conflict, would have run the risk of selecting an "atypical" state. Of those remaining, Madhya Pradesh, the state with the largest population of the five states here, would have been more representative. However, the timing of legislative assembly elections in Punjab, which were held in 1997, afforded the opportunity to obtain ethnographic data on the BSP's election campaign, whereas the timing of the Madhya Pradesh assembly elections, which were held toward the end of my field work in 1998, did not. I selected Punjab for this reason, but

Table 7.2. *Stratified sample of Indian states: Uttar Pradesh, Punjab, Karnataka*

No.	Level of Support for BSP	States Included in Stratum	State Selected
I	High	Uttar Pradesh	Uttar Pradesh
II	Moderate	Punjab, Madhya Pradesh, Haryana, Jammu and Kashmir, Goa	Punjab
III	Negligible	Delhi, Himachal Pradesh, Rajasthan, Gujarat, Maharashtra, Bihar, Orissa, West Bengal, Andhra Pradesh, Karnataka, Kerala, Tamil Nadu, northeastern states	Karnataka

supplemented the study of Punjab with less intensive research on Madhya Pradesh.

The choice of a single state from stratum III, which contains the largest and most diverse group of states, was the most difficult, since no state is adequately representative of the stratum as a whole. I selected Karnataka as representative of the four south Indian states, the largest family of states within this stratum. This choice among south Indian states was arbitrary: Any of the four would have done as well. Even so, this leaves out two other important families of states, those in the West (Gujarat and Maharashtra) and the East (Bihar, Orissa, West Bengal), as well as scattered others. While including states from either or both these families would undoubtedly have broadened the scope of this study, the trade-off in time and resources made it inadvisable. As before, however, I supplement the study of Karnataka with less intensive research on these excluded states.

The state-level data summarized here represent a very high level of aggregation. If we probe the patterns of support for the BSP in constituencies or administrative subdivisions within these states, we will notice a similar pattern of variation in the performance of the BSP across and often *within* these smaller units. Systematic data on plausible independent variables, however, are unavailable at the constituency level: Record-keeping procedures in the BSP, and indeed in most political parties, are rarely good enough to permit a systematic exploration of variables that might plausibly be linked to variation in party performance at the constituency level; and government data, including data from the census, are reported by administrative subdivisions (district, *tehsil*, and bloc), which do not coincide with

159

constituencies. Individual-level data on the variation in Scheduled Caste voting patterns, which might have been another alternative, are available following the large-scale election surveys carried out by the Indian National Election Study. However, comparable data for the 1984–96 period do not exist. I use these survey and constituency-level data to supplement analyses from aggregate data to the greatest extent possible in my study of individual states. I also explore variation in the performance of the BSP within a single district elsewhere, through an ethnographic analysis.[37] The state remains, however, the basic unit for which we have systematic data on the dependent and independent variables and which therefore permits us to explore the sources of variation in the performance of the BSP.

In their influential methodological treatise, King, Keohane, and Verba criticize a research design that selects cases on the dependent variable as unlikely to yield valid causal inferences.[38] The criticism rests on two claims: (1) While such a design may generate a hypothesis, it cannot confirm the hypothesis unless it is supplemented by a study in which observations are selected only on the explanatory variable of interest, and (2) even the unconfirmed hypothesis is likely to be flawed, since, according to them, "such a design is useless for making descriptive inferences about the dependent variable," and the "absence of systematic descriptive data and the increased possibility of other problems caused by possible nonlinearities or variable causal effects means that this procedure will not generally yield valid causal inferences."[39]

The logic of the first claim is self-evident. However, the fact that selection on the dependent variable is likely to be more helpful in "generating" than in "confirming" a hypothesis recommends rather than disqualifies this design. King, Keohane, and Verba portray hypothesis testing as the central task of political science. But in many research enterprises within political science, as in this study, the analytical burden is on hypothesis construction rather than hypothesis testing.[40] Before we can test hypotheses, we need to complete

---

[37] Kanchan Chandra, "The Transformation of Ethnic Politics in India: The Decline of Congress and the Rise of the Bahujan Samaj Party in Hoshiarpur," *Journal of Asian Studies*, Vol. 59, No. 1 (2000): 26–61.

[38] Gary King, Robert Keohane, and Sidney Verba, *Designing Political Inquiry* (Princeton, NJ: Princeton University Press, 1994), 141.

[39] Ibid.

[40] In an APSR symposium, David Laitin argued that King, Keohane, and Verba should recognize that the criteria for case selection may be different when theory is strong as opposed to when theory is weak. David Laitin, "Disciplining Political Science," *American Political*

the prior tasks of constructing concepts, identifying the variables relevant to an ethnic party's success, and describing the process by which these variables are linked together. Once we have identified plausible explanatory variables, we can then "confirm" hypotheses that link them to the dependent variable by selecting new observations based on the values that these explanatory variables take.

When the plausible explanatory variables are not known in advance, selecting systematically on the dependent variable, as I do here, is a prudent research strategy. By tracing the process by which the BSP builds support individually in each of my cases, I ascertain whether the same variables explain the same outcomes in each case. Because I select a stratified sample of cases based on the entire range of values of the dependent variable, I have some confidence that my sample is relatively representative of the universe from which it is selected. And because I use explicit criteria to select cases within each stratum, I have some measure of whether and how the exclusion of some cases biases the analysis, and some idea of how to compensate for this bias. Once this research design has yielded a plausible hypothesis, I then attempt to test the plausibility of this hypothesis by conducting tests using new sources of data from states within the sample and from out-of-sample states.

The logic of the second claim is less obvious. In this study, descriptive data on the dependent variable can be procured or estimated for all states, and the cases for intensive research have been selected after the range of variation on the dependent variable has been adequately described. Selecting to maximize the range of variation on the dependent variable, therefore, does not impede the collection of systematic descriptive data. And the "problems caused by possible nonlinearities or variable causal effects" are not specific to this research design but are inherent in all comparative research.

V. Alternative Explanations

Based on my study of the three states, I argue that the explanation for the variation in the performance of the BSP lies in the conjunction of two variables: a comparative advantage in the representation of Scheduled Caste elites within the BSP, *and* the presence of Scheduled Caste voters

---

Science Review, Vol. 89, No. 2 (1995): 454–460. The method for case selection that I employ here develops this insight.

Table 7.3. *Variables hypothesized to affect BSP performance among Scheduled Castes*

State	(1) % SC	(2) Strength of BAMCEF in 1984 1 = Strong 0 = Weak	(3) Effective No. of SCs (Rounded)	(4) Chamars as % of SC Population	(5) % SC Below the Poverty Line (1983–84)	(6) Average Number of Atrocities (1989–91)	(7) % SC Literate	(8) % SC Landless[a]	(9) Average Vote for BSP among SCs (1984–98)
Andhra Pradesh	15.9	0	3	0.16	51	696.67	25.89	37.44	1.41
Arunachal Pradesh	0.5	0	7	0.00		9.00	46.20	1.31	0
Assam	7.4	0			21.9	39.33	43.33	8.99	0
Bihar	14.6	0	5	29.37	71.1	797.33	15.12	27.67	1.95
Delhi	19.1	1	5	36.67		5.33	45.71	0.68	8.1
Goa	2.1	1	3	0.00		4.00	49.76	6.88	18.1
Gujarat	7.4	1	4	27.25	39.9	979.00	50.49	18.47	1.92
Haryana	19.7	1	3	52.65	27.9	75.33	30.79	18.11	18.21
Himachal Pradesh	25.3	1	5	29.81	23.5	53.33	43.73	10.40	2.7
Jammu and Kashmir	8.3[b]	1	4	24.59	32.9	79.67			46.69
Karnataka	16.4	0	6	6.31	54.1	695.00	30.71	23.93	0.9
Kerala	9.9	0	7	0.01	43.9	759.67	69.38	24.19	0.13
Madhya Pradesh	14.5	1	3	52.25	59.3	7,550.67	27.72	19.47	35.72
Maharashtra	11.1	1	4	19.32	55.9	710.33	45.93	22.26	5.05

162

	1	2	3	4	5	6	7	8	9
Manipur	2	0	2	0.00		5.00	46.81	9.22	0
Meghalaya	0.5	0	7	0.00			35.46	6.36	0
Mizoram	0.1	0	7	0.00			71.49	3.76	0
Nagaland	0	0	0	0.00		3.33			0
Orissa	16.2	0	10	2.83	54.9	561.67	30.19	20.63	1.74
Punjab	28.3	1	5	27.07	21.8	21.00	33.36	18.79	37.76
Rajasthan	17.3	1	7	32.07	44.9	2,228.67	20.57	13.97	4.6
Sikkim	5.9	0	2	0.00		10.00	41.16	4.20	0
Tamil Nadu	19.2	0	4	0.00	59.4	526.67	39.47	32.05	0.26
Tripura	16.4	0	5	2.20			45.54	9.39	0
Uttar Pradesh	21	1	3	55.09	57.3	5,221.00	21.08	15.46	58.92
West Bengal	23.6	0	9	5.92	52	19.00	34.27	15.02	0.87

[a] "Landless" refers to those classified as either agricultural workers or marginal workers in census data.
[b] 1981 census figures.

Sources: Columns 1, 7, 8: *Census of India 1991*; column 2: rating by Tejinder Singh Jhalli, a prominent BAMCEF leader in 1984, interviewed on December 25, 1997, confirmed by interviews with other former BAMCEF officers; columns 3, 4: *Census of India 1981*; column 5: *Basic Rural Statistics 1996*; column 6: National Commission for Scheduled Castes and Scheduled Tribes, New Delhi; column 9: Election Commission of India, various years. Note that the percentage of SC literates in column 7 has been calculated on the basis of the total SC population in each state.

in numbers large enough to take the BSP past the threshold of winning or leverage through coordinated action. The chapters that follow develop this argument. Here, I evaluate the principal alternative explanations that suggest themselves from the pattern of variation or that are proposed by informed observers of the BSP. The variables identified by these hypotheses are summarized in Table 7.3.

Organization

One obvious explanation for the BSP's success is simply its initial invest-ment in building an organization in each state. When the BSP was founded in 1984, BAMCEF and DS-4, whose cadres formed the backbone of the new party, were strongest in the North and West. Column 2 in Table 7.3 describes the variation in organizational strength of BAMCEF across states in India in 1984.[41] The organizations were entirely absent in the Northeast and had a weak to negligible presence in southern and eastern India. The BSP continued to place north India high on its list of investment priorities early in its history as a political party, and devoted fewer resources to other regions. At the opening convention of the party in Delhi in 1984, Kanshi Ram was reported to have told one of the few delegates from the South that he was not immediately concerned with building a base for the BSP in the South: "It is from Uttar Pradesh that we can rule India. After the North, I will come to the South."[42] Party units in the four south Indian states were formally inaugurated only in 1989, five years after the BSP was established in the north Indian states.[43] And in 1997, thirteen years after the party was founded, Kanshi Ram continued to place the South low on his list of priorities.[44] In addition to the South, the BSP also did not devote time or resources to building an organization in the East or the Northeast. "We reap as we sow," one economist reminds us, "and in particular, we do

---

[41] The ratings are based on rankings provided by Tejinder Singh Jhalli, one of the most im-portant leaders of BAMCEF and formerly in charge of the northwest zone of BAMCEF. Interview, December 25, 1997, Ghaziabad. Jhalli became the national president of BAMCEF after BAMCEF and the BSP split in 1985. The ratings are confirmed by in-terviews with other BAMCEF activists.

[42] Interview with S. Gopal, the first convenor of the Bahujan Samaj Party in Karnataka, Bangalore, March 18, 1997.

[43] *Deccan Herald*, July 18, 1989; interview with an early associate of Kanshi Ram's, April 6, 1997, Hyderabad.

[44] Interview with Kanshi Ram, February 24, 1997, Ludhiana.

not reap what we do not sow."[45] Is the BSP simply doing better where it has tried to build a party organization and worse where it has not?

It is true that the failure to create a party organization in the South and the East has hurt the BSP's electoral prospects in these regions. Creating a party organization, as I argue in subsequent chapters, is a necessary precondition for electoral success. A probe into the prehistory of the BSP, however, reveals organizational investment to be endogenous to the explanation. Kanshi Ram decided how to allocate resources to organization building by gauging the expected response from every region in India after more than a decade of experimental mobilization. The Northeast, geographically remote and with a negligible Scheduled Caste population, was ruled out from the outset. The decision not to invest in the South and East, however, came after several years of fruitless effort among government employees in these regions. Kanshi Ram had begun establishing contacts in the South at least as early as 1974, when he wrote to a prominent Scheduled Caste activist in Karnataka seeking support for BAMCEF.[46] However, he was unable to find a critical mass of joiners. As one of Kanshi Ram's early associates described it: "In the beginning, we tried very hard in the south. But our movement did not take hold."[47] By 1978, therefore, when BAMCEF was officially launched, its target regions were northern and western India. Once established, this organizational imbalance contributed to the variation in the performance of the BSP across these states: The states in which the BSP has done best – Uttar Pradesh, Punjab, Haryana, Jammu and Kashmir, Madhya Pradesh, and Goa – are all states in which it developed an early organizational presence. While organizational investment is an important intervening variable in the causal chain that leads to the success or failure of the BSP, therefore, it is not among the fundamental causal variables explaining the variation in the party's performance. Rather, it is itself part of the puzzle that needs to be explained.

Organizational investment, furthermore, has not been sufficient to bring success. When the BSP was formed in 1984, as Table 7.3 shows, BAMCEF had developed strong organizational roots in eleven states in the North and West. However, it was able to achieve a significant following among Scheduled Castes in only six of these: Punjab, Haryana, Uttar

---

[45] Amartya Sen, "Indian Development: Lessons and Non-Lessons," *Daedalus* (Fall 1989): 387.
[46] Interview with the activist who tried and failed to organize BAMCEF in Karnataka, March 23, 1997.
[47] Interview, April 6, 1997, Hyderabad.

Pradesh, Madhya Pradesh, Goa, and Jammu and Kashmir (see Map 1.2). In the remaining states (Rajasthan, Delhi, Himachal Pradesh, Maharashtra, and Gujarat), the BSP made little electoral headway despite a strong organization. Further, there is significant variation in the degree of support for the BSP even in those states in which it was successful and had a comparably strong organization. The substantial variation in support for the BSP among Scheduled Castes, even controlling for organization, indicates that other variables are necessary to account for its success.

Language

A second explanation emphasizes the major linguistic divisions between north India and other regions in the east, south, and west. The successes of the BSP have been in Hindi-speaking states (Uttar Pradesh, Haryana, and Madhya Pradesh) or in states where the regional language is proximate to Hindi (Punjab, Jammu and Kashmir). The failures have been concentrated in states in which the regional languages are more distant from Hindi. Linguistic and cultural differences, however, are not insurmountable barriers for parties with pan-Indian aspirations. The Congress party built an all-India organization by knitting together a coalition of regional party units, as did the Janata Dal and the BJP. Why has the BSP not been able to do the same?

It is not that the BSP did not try. In the state of Karnataka, for instance, the BSP attempted to surmount linguistic differences between its Hindi-speaking national leadership and the Kannada-speaking Scheduled Castes[48] by building a regional unit staffed by local men. It attempted to expand this regional organization by merging it with the Dalit Sangarsh Samiti (DSS), an initially nonpolitical organization founded to fight for the rights of Scheduled Castes in Karnataka. The DSS was a regional organization, founded and staffed by Kannada speakers. However, even after the merger with the DSS, the BSP was not able to win support from among the Scheduled Castes in Karnataka.

Further, this explanation does not permit us to understand the major variation in the performance of the BSP *within* the Hindi belt. Why, if linguistic similarities determine electoral performance, has the BSP had little success in Bihar, Rajasthan, Delhi, and Himachal Pradesh, all

[48] Most Scheduled Castes in Karnataka speak Kannada, although there are also linguistic minorities among them speaking Tamil, Telugu, and Marathi.

166

Hindi-speaking states? To the extent that the BSP does badly even in Hindi-speaking states in the North, and to the extent that it was not able to expand in the South even after the creation of regional party units, linguistic differences between the North and other regions in India cannot explain the variation in the performance of the BSP among Scheduled Castes across geographic regions.

Fragmentation

A third explanation points to the high degree of fragmentation within the nominal "community" of Scheduled Castes. Column 3 in Table 7.3 records the "effective number of Scheduled Castes," using a standard measure of group concentration. This measure is calculated using the formula $1/(\Sigma p_j{}^2)$, where the term p_j refers to the percentage of the Scheduled Caste population made up by the caste category j. These caste categories differ in language, region, religion, and cultural practice. It could be argued, therefore, that the "Scheduled Castes" exist as a category only in official documents and are not available for ethnic mobilization on the basis of a common identity. Failure rather than success is likely to be the norm, according to this argument, which appears to be borne out by the large number of states in which the BSP has found no support.

This argument is not compelling, in this simple form, for the following reason: As I argued in Chapter 1, fragmentation is typical of most ethnic categories prior to political mobilization. The Hindu "majority" in India, for example, which, according to the Indian census, constitutes 82 percent of the Indian population, has frequently been described as "an artifact of categorization," encompassing "a diversity of gods, texts and social practice and a variety of ontologies and epistemologies."[49] Yet this fragmentation has not prevented large numbers of Hindus in some states from organizing as a political community behind the pro-Hindu BJP since the 1980s. Sikhs in Punjab are fragmented on the basis of caste, cultural practice, and economic status. Yet, although this has not always been the case, the majority of Sikhs in contemporary Punjab are supporters of the Shiromani Akali Dal. The DMK in Tamil Nadu, as I will argue in a subsequent chapter, was highly successful in bringing together a range of groups from within its target category of "Tamils." Fragmentation, then, does not in itself constitute an

---

[49] Lloyd I. Rudolph and Susanne H. Rudolph, *In Pursuit of Lakshmi* (Chicago: University of Chicago Press, 1987), 37.

explanation for ethnic party success or failure. Rather, these examples prod us to ask: What are the conditions under which the BSP might overcome the problem posed by fragmentation, as other ethnic parties have in other time periods and states in India, and what are the conditions under which it might not?

According to the argument of this book, fragmentation is relevant to explaining the success of the BSP *when combined with attention to its party organization.* Fragmentation, I argue here, can be overcome by a competitive party organization that allows elites from the different "subdivisions" within an ethnic category to coexist under one political roof. As a highly centralized party, however, the BSP has been unable to expand its representational profile beyond the subdivision or subdivisions that constitute its initial pool of cadres. The larger the number of effective Scheduled Caste categories in each state, therefore, the larger the pool of Scheduled Caste elites not given representation in the BSP, and therefore the larger the pool of Scheduled Caste voters who are likely not to vote for the BSP.

Chamar Population

A fourth explanation reiterates the presumption that ethnic groups are "naturally" attracted to their "own" ethnic parties. It suggests, however, that Scheduled Caste voters are more likely to think of their *individual* caste category as their "own" than the aggregate category "Scheduled Caste." Both Kanshi Ram and Mayawati, as well as much of the early leadership of the BSP, come from the "Chamar" caste category. Consequently, according to this argument, the BSP should do better in those states that have a substantial Scheduled Caste population than in others.

The *prediction* of this argument finds some support in the data. Column 4 in Table 7.3 describes the percentage of the Scheduled Caste population in each state constituted by the "Chamar" category. As the table indicates, the states in which the BSP has done well all have a substantial Chamar population. The *logic* underlying this prediction, however, is erroneous. The category "Chamar" is an aggregate rather than an individual category, no different from the category "Scheduled Caste." In the state of Punjab, for instance, the "Chamar" category is constituted by the still smaller categories of "Adharmis" and "Ramdassias," among others. There are clear and subjectively perceived differences in religion and custom between these two categories. The majority of Adharmis are clean-shaven, and while they sometimes accept the label "Hindu" and sometimes distinguish "Ad-Dharm" as a religion distinct from Hinduism, most Adharmis describe themselves as non-Sikh. Ramdassias unambiguously define themselves as Sikhs. Adharmis are followers of Bhagat Ravi Das, a sixteenth-century saint. Ramdassias are followers of Guru Ram Das, one of the ten Sikh gurus.[50] Adharmis and Ramdassias do not intermarry. When asked to distinguish between Adharmis and Ramdassias, one Adharmi worker in the BSP put it starkly: "Adharmis follow Guru Rabidas and are usually Hindu. Ramdassias follow Ramdas, and are always Sikh. Their traditions are absolutely different."[51] Yet both share in a common Chamar identity and both vote for the BSP in Punjab. The political coalescence of Chamars behind the BSP, therefore, cannot be said to be natural, given the high degree of differentiation among Chamars at the social level.

Further, there is substantial variation in support for the BSP even among individuals categorized as "Chamar." In three states with a substantial Chamar population – Gujarat, Rajasthan, and Bihar – the BSP has done poorly. And even in those states in which the BSP has done well, not all Chamars vote for it. In the state of Madhya Pradesh, for instance, the Scheduled Caste base of the BSP is largely among Satnamis, one of the castes in the Chamar family concentrated in the Chattisgarh region of Madhya Pradesh. Chamars living in the Malwa region of Madhya Pradesh, however, think of themselves as having a distinct identity as "Malwi Chamars," even though they do not exist as a separate census category. They do not share a sense of community with the Satnamis and vote for Congress rather than for the BSP.[52]

Given that Chamars are not themselves a united category, and given that there is substantial variation in the degree of support for the BSP among Chamars, the question remains of why some Chamars are able to come together politically under the BSP's roof, and not others. The argument here provides one answer. Chamars are among the categories of Scheduled Castes that modernized earliest. Consequently, Chamar elites were among the first Scheduled Caste elites to obtain posts within the BSP and, when possible, within other political parties. In those states in which they became

---

[50] Mark Juergensmeyer, *Religion as a Social Vision* (Berkeley: University of California Press, 1982), 84, 89; K. S. Singh, *The Scheduled Castes* (Delhi: Anthropological Survey of India and Oxford University Press, 1995), 316–317.

[51] Interview with BSP worker, Hoshiarpur district, January 30, 1997.

[52] Based on fieldwork in Ujjain District in Madhya Pradesh, February 1998.

entrenched within the BSP's organization, Chamar elites then prevented the incorporation of elites who emerged subsequently from other caste categories among the Scheduled Castes. Consequently, the BSP was successful in attracting Chamar support. In those states in which Chamars as a whole, or subdivisions among Chamars, were better incorporated in the competition, however, Chamar voters were more likely to vote for the competition. The BSP, in other words, does not do well among Chamars because Chamars are naturally attracted to it. Rather, it obtains the support of Chamar voters only when it supersedes the competition as a channel to office for Chamar elites from across subdivisions among Chamars, and not otherwise.

Grievance

A fifth explanation commonly proposed by BSP activists themselves explains the variation in the performance of the BSP as a function of the level of grievance experienced by the Scheduled Castes across states. According to one version of this argument, the greater the grievances experienced by Scheduled Castes, the more likely these Scheduled Castes are to seek an exit option by voting for a Scheduled Caste party. Consequently, the BSP should do better in those states and constituencies in which Scheduled Castes experience greater levels of material and social oppression. A second version of this argument predicts the opposite: The better the material and social conditions of the Scheduled Castes, according to this argument, the more resources they would have to support a new political party. Consequently, the BSP should do better in those states and constituencies in which Scheduled Castes are better off.

This simple relationship between grievance and performance is not supported by the data. Columns 5–8 in Table 7.3 describe the variation in several different measures of subordination among Scheduled Castes across Indian states: Column 5 reports on the percentage of Scheduled Castes estimated to live below the poverty line in each state; column 6 reports on the average number of "atrocities" committed against Scheduled Castes across Indian states; column 7 reports on the percentage of the Scheduled Caste population that is illiterate across Indian states; and column 8 reports on the percentage of the Scheduled Caste population that is landless across Indian states. The data indicate no relationship, positive or negative, between the vote obtained by the BSP among Scheduled Castes and the material and social circumstances of the Scheduled Castes.[53] The BSP obtained the support of a majority of Scheduled Castes, on average, in the state of Uttar Pradesh, which ranks among the highest in its incidence of violence, poverty, and illiteracy among Scheduled Castes. However, it also did well among Scheduled Castes in the state of Punjab, in which Scheduled Castes are better off on all dimensions than Scheduled Castes in most other states. And even within Uttar Pradesh, the party obtained early and high levels of support both in western Uttar Pradesh, in which Scheduled Castes are relatively prosperous, and in eastern Uttar Pradesh, where the level of grievance is higher.

The argument of this book proposes a more complex relationship between the material and social subordination of Scheduled Castes and their propensity to vote for the BSP. The degree of subordination among Scheduled Caste voters should affect the political outcome, according to this argument, through the mechanism of strategic voting. The greater the level of subordination of a Scheduled Caste voter, the argument suggests, the higher must be the probability of the BSP's acquiring influence or victory to induce the voter to switch to the BSP. As a result, if we probe individual-level voting patterns, we should find that the less subordinate among Scheduled Caste voters should switch early to the BSP, even when it has a small chance of winning. Such voters are also more likely to be faithful supporters, able to withstand limited fluctuations in the party's probability of winning or obtaining influence. The more subordinate among Scheduled Caste voters, however, should defect to the BSP only when it has established its influence in the electoral arena. Furthermore, their support for the BSP should be more volatile, quickly withdrawn when the party's electoral prospects waver. A study of individual-level data should reveal this more complex pattern even when it does not show up in the aggregate data summarized in Table 7.3. Subsequent chapters probe such individual-level patterns.

---

[53] A simple OLS regression does not reveal any correlation between these variables and the dependent variable. Regardless, I do not report these results here, since the number of observations is too small to permit reliable conclusions.

8

Why SC Elites Join the BSP

This chapter describes the formation of the BSP in Uttar Pradesh, Punjab, and Karnataka. In Part I of this book, I argued that upwardly mobile elites in patronage-democracies seek a channel to political office in the long term but are indifferent regarding the type of party – ethnic, multiethnic, or nonethnic – that offers them such a channel. Here, I describe how, in the states of Uttar Pradesh and Punjab, a representational blockage in the competition diverted these elites toward the BSP and so enabled it to acquire the critical mass of support from elite activists necessary for party formation. In Karnataka, however, representational "openness" in the competition for these Scheduled Caste elites prevented the BSP from obtaining their support. As a consequence, the party has not been able to present itself as a viable option on the electoral market in Karnataka, despite repeated attempts.

The chapter is organized as follows: Section I describes the emergence of a class of upwardly mobile, office-seeking elites among Scheduled Castes in each of the three states under study. Section II describes the variation in opportunities for representation available to these elites in the major parties in each of these states. It shows that the Congress party and the rest of the party system in Uttar Pradesh and Punjab blocked the entry of these Scheduled Caste elites. In Karnataka, however, the Congress party and other political parties were able to incorporate these elites successfully. Section III describes the link between the representational blockage of Scheduled Caste elites and the formation of the BSP in Uttar Pradesh; Section IV does the same for Punjab; and Section V describes the link between representational "openness" and the failure of the BSP to take root as a viable political party in Karnataka.

Table 8.1. *Rise in literacy among Scheduled Castes in all three states, 1961–81*

State	Variable	1961[a]	1971	1981
Uttar Pradesh	Scheduled Caste literacy rate (%)	7.14	10.2	14.96
	Number of SC literates per village[b]	7.54	12.63	25.20
Punjab	Scheduled Caste literacy rate (%)	9.64	16.12	23.86
	Number of SC literates per village	24.58	27.33	67.55
Karnataka	Scheduled Caste literacy rate (%)	9.06	13.89	20.59
	Number of SC literates per village	5.75	9.93	24.83

[a] Figures for 1961 are for Punjab prior to the linguistic reorganization of the state in 1966.
[b] Calculated by dividing the absolute number of *rural* SC literates by the number of inhabited villages.
Source: *Census of India 1961, 1971,* and *1981.*

I. The Emergence of Office–seeking Elites among Scheduled Castes

At independence from the British in 1947, Scheduled Castes in India partic-ipated in electoral politics mainly as benefit seekers. Less than 10 percent of the Scheduled Caste population was literate, whereas the literacy rate among the general population was at least twice as high.[1] In addition, the Scheduled Castes were economically dependent upon other caste categories for their livelihood. With illiteracy and economic subordination came de-pendent political participation. While the Scheduled Castes sought benefits from upper-caste patrons who dominated the political system, few among them sought elected office themselves.[2]

By the 1980s, however, affirmative action policies in education had pro-duced a growing class of literate, upwardly mobile Scheduled Caste elites who sought to participate in the political system as office seekers rather than as benefit seekers. Table 8.1 describes the rise in literacy rates among

[1] Since the 1951 census did not report literacy rates for Scheduled Castes separately, these figures are extrapolated from the 1961 census.
[2] See Lloyd I. Rudolph and Susanne H. Rudolph, *The Modernity of Tradition* (Chicago: University of Chicago Press, 1967), and Sidney Verba, Bashiruddin Ahmad, and Anil Bhatt, *Caste, Race and Politics* (Beverly Hills, CA: Sage, 1971), for a description of the de-pendent political participation of Scheduled Castes. The voting behaviour of Scheduled Castes during this period corresponds to the model of "vertical mobilization" developed by Rudolph and Rudolph, where Scheduled Castes were mobilized by upper-caste local notables through patron-client networks. Verba, Ahmed, and Bhatt rely on survey evi-dence to establish that Scheduled Castes had lower levels of political activism than other categories.

Scheduled Castes in each of the three states under study between 1961 and 1981. As the table indicates, the percentage of Scheduled Castes who were literate more than doubled in all three states between 1961 and 1981. The magnitude of the change between 1961 and 1981 might be clearest if we look at the change in the absolute number of Scheduled Caste literates per village in each of these three states. In Uttar Pradesh, the number of literates in each village tripled, from seven in 1961 to twenty-five in 1981. In Punjab, the number of literates per village in 1961 was already significantly high, at twenty-five. By 1981, it had almost tripled, to sixty-eight. In Karnataka, the rise in the absolute number of literates per village paralleled that of UP: From six literates per village in 1961, it rose to twenty-five in 1981. Even in 1981, educated Scheduled Castes were only a minority of the Scheduled Caste population, which continued to be illiterate and economically dependent. However, they now constituted a sizable class in each state. It is this class of literate Scheduled Castes who sought elective office rather than mere benefits.

Why should upwardly mobile Scheduled Caste elites seek an entry into elective office after leaving school or college? In Chapter 6, I argued that the attraction of elective office in India lies, on the one hand, in the degree to which the Indian state dominates the opportunities for economic and status advancement and, on the other, in the relative ease with which these opportunities can be captured. Let me now develop this argument with respect to the Scheduled Caste elites.

Educated Scheduled Castes sought careers that would give them both better economic opportunities than their parents and higher status. Obtaining control of the state presented them with more opportunities for obtaining both than the private sector. As the first generation of upwardly mobile elites from an economically and educationally disadvantaged ethnic category, they did not, in most cases, have the financial capital that would allow them to set up independent enterprises.[3] As relatively unskilled individuals with only a general college degree or a professional diploma, neither did they possess the intellectual capital that can often substitute for material resources in launching a private enterprise. Finally, they did not have access to caste-based networks that might allow them to gain access to

---

[3] There are some prominent exceptions to this rule, notably a minority of Chamars in Western Uttar Pradesh who have been able to convert their traditional skills into successful entrepreneurship in the leather-working industry.

Table 8.2. *Mean number of independent candidates in "reserved"*
constituencies selected legislative assembly elections, 1960–83

State	1962[a]	1971–74	1980–84
Uttar Pradesh	1	2.4	3.1
Punjab	2	1.5	2.7
Karnataka	1.1	1.1	2.9

[a] Figures for 1961 are for Punjab prior to the linguistic reorganization
of the state in 1966.

Source: Election Commission reports (various years); Singh and Bose
(1985).

desirable private sector employment.[4] The experience of Gopal, one such
educated Scheduled Caste job seeker, is a typical example of the difficulties
that educated Scheduled Castes faced in moving into the private sector.
After finishing his education, Gopal moved from his village to the city in
search of a job. However, the only jobs he found were as a domestic servant
or restaurant help, which paid little and which he found degrading. As he
put it: "When I don't clean my own utensils at home, (my mother does it),
why should I do it for other people here?"[5]

Relatively speaking, therefore, government employment and elective office are attractive and accessible channels for upward mobility for Scheduled
Castes. Both promise them a regular income. Simultaneously, both promise
the increase in status that comes from being in a position of power over
others. Some of these upwardly mobile elites were absorbed into government employment through affirmative action policies immediately after
finishing their education. At the same time, these elites also sought elected
office in large numbers.

Table 8.2 describes one measure of the rise in office-seeking activity
among Scheduled Caste elites: the rise in the number of Scheduled Caste
candidates contesting as independents in the state legislative assembly elections in all three states. The Indian Election Commission does not publish information on the caste identity of candidates separately. However, a
certain number of constituencies in each state are "reserved" for Scheduled

---

[4] For the importance of caste networks in securing employment opportunities, see Peter
Lanjouw and Nicholas Stern, *Economic Development in Palanpur, over Five Decades* (Delhi:
Oxford University Press, 1998), especially Chapter 3.
[5] Interview, December 5, 1996, New Delhi.

Caste candidates. The table describes the mean number of independents running for election in Scheduled Caste constituencies in each of the three states, for selected elections in each decade. It does not capture Scheduled Caste candidates running for election in "open" constituencies. However, the number of independents running for election in Scheduled Caste constituencies constitutes an accurate measure of the *minimum* number of Scheduled Castes running for election as independents.

All three states recorded an increase in the average number of Scheduled Caste candidates contesting elections as independents between the 1960s and the 1980s. In Uttar Pradesh and Karnataka, the number of Scheduled Caste independents tripled. In Punjab, the increase was more modest. The slower rate of increase in office-seeking Scheduled Caste elites in Punjab, despite higher rates in literacy, is consistent with the argument presented in this chapter. Of the three states under study, Punjab offers the greatest opportunities for nonstate employment, in part because of the "Green Revolution" in agriculture. While Scheduled Castes in Punjab continue to be more disadvantaged in entering the private sector than other ethnic categories, they have greater private sector opportunities in Punjab than in the other states.[6] As affirmative action policies produced increasing numbers of upwardly mobile elites, therefore, a greater proportion was likely to be siphoned off into the private sector in Punjab than in the other two states.

The increase in the number of Scheduled Castes contesting as independents in elections for the state legislative assembly measures only the tip of the iceberg of office-seeking activity among Scheduled Caste elites. It requires considerable resources to be considered a viable candidate in a state legislative assembly election, and this is likely to have served as a deterrent to many aspiring candidates. The greatest volume of office-seeking activity, therefore, is likely to be found at the lower levels of the political system, in elections for local bodies and student unions. Other arenas where we might see an increase in office-seeking activity are the ostensibly nonpolitical organizations (trade unions, employee federations, cultural associations) that are often used to build the following required to launch a career in politics.

Finally, even those Scheduled Caste elites who made it into government employment found that they required political clout in order to ensure favourable posts and promotions. Access to political clout, in turn, depended upon having members of their own ethnic category in elective

[6] Bhupindra Yadav and Anand Mohan Sharma, *Economic Uplift of Scheduled Castes* (Chandigarh: Institute for Development and Communication, 1995), 34–36.

Table 8.3. *Profile of early joiners of the BSP*

	N	Yes (%)	No (%)	Unknown (%)	Total (%)
Born after 1947?	52	71.2	17.3	11.5	100
Professional diploma or higher level of education?	52	82.7	3.8	13.5	100
Previously involved in political or associational activity?	52	75	9.6	15.4	100

Source: Interviews (see Appendix A for details).

office. In a typical incident described by Khare, a Scheduled Caste clerk employed at the Uttar Pradesh State Electricity Board was able to resolve a dispute with an upper-caste superior only after appealing to a Scheduled Caste politician.[7] Several of my respondents related incidents of disputes over promotions where their principal weapon was invoking the name of an influential politician from their caste category. To the extent that influential politicians belonging to Scheduled Castes were relatively scarce, these government employees found themselves at a disadvantage compared to employees from other ethnic categories.[8] Faced with the need for political influence, therefore, Scheduled Caste elites in government employment developed a shared interest with those outside.

By the 1980s, therefore, a class of Scheduled Caste elites emerged who sought elective office themselves or had an interest in supporting Scheduled Caste office seekers in each of the three states under study, and across the country more generally. The BSP's initial activists and voters came overwhelmingly from this class of upwardly mobile office seekers. Kanshi Ram, as described in Chapter 7, was himself a government employee who abandoned his job and began mobilizing support for a political party after a dispute with his upper-caste superiors. And the majority of the early members of the BSP were already engaged in an attempt to build some form of political capital before Kanshi Ram came along – contesting elections to student unions, to local bodies, or to the legislative assembly; organizing Scheduled Caste employee organizations; and founding caste associations. Table 8.3

[7] R. S. Khare, *The Untouchable as Himself* (Cambridge: Cambridge University Press, 1984), 116. See also Simon Charsley and G. K. Karanth, eds., *Challenging Untouchability* (Delhi: Sage, 1998), 102.

[8] Charsley and Karanth, *Challenging Untouchability*, 102.

summarizes the ages, educational backgrounds, and office-seeking activities of a sample of the early joiners of the BSP. It includes Scheduled Caste respondents at all levels of the party (national, state, and local) from five states (Uttar Pradesh, Karnataka, Punjab, Delhi, and Madhya Pradesh) who joined the BSP on or before the date it was officially launched in the state (1984 in the first four states, 1989 in Karnataka). While the sample itself is small, it is representative across geographical areas and across levels of the party hierarchy.

Although most of the BSP's initial supporters were educated Scheduled Caste office seekers, educated Scheduled Caste office seekers did not always join the BSP. In two of the three states, Punjab and Uttar Pradesh, these office seekers converged upon the BSP in their search for a channel to office. In Karnataka, however, they scattered among the existing political parties. In the section that follows, I describe the variation in the opportunities for representation for office-seeking Scheduled Caste elites in the major parties in all three states. Later in the chapter, I will establish the link between the variation in representational opportunities and the variation in the performance of the BSP across states.

II. Variation in Representational Opportunities across the Three States

This section describes the representation given to Scheduled Caste elites at the state and local levels in each of the major parties in the three states from 1951 to 1992. The BSP was officially launched in Uttar Pradesh and Punjab in 1984 and in Karnataka in 1989. At the point at which the BSP entered, other parties in Uttar Pradesh and Punjab gave a low degree of representation to Scheduled Castes, and Karnataka a high degree. Following the entry of the BSP, the degree of representation given to Scheduled Castes by the competition in Uttar Pradesh and Punjab remained unchanged. In Karnataka, however, it continued to rise.

Since the Indian Constitution reserves a proportionate number of seats for Scheduled Caste candidates in all legislative bodies, each party was compelled to allot a certain number of tickets to Scheduled Caste candidates in all three states under study. However, there was significant variation in the degree to which these Scheduled Caste legislators were given positions of importance in the parties and in government across the three states. Figures 8.1 and 8.2 describe the variation in representation given to Scheduled Castes in the cabinets and councils of ministers of the parties

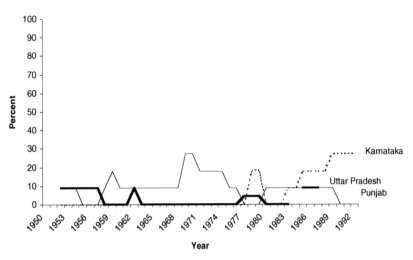

Figure 8.1. Percentage of important cabinet portfolios allotted to Scheduled Caste ministers, 1951–92. *Source:* Members of the cabinet, Council of Ministers, and their portfolios are from *India Annual* (various issues) and *Journal of Parliamentary Information* (various issues). Scheduled Caste ministers are identified from Scheduled Caste candidates as listed in Election Commission of India reports (various issues) and in Singh and Bose (1987–88).

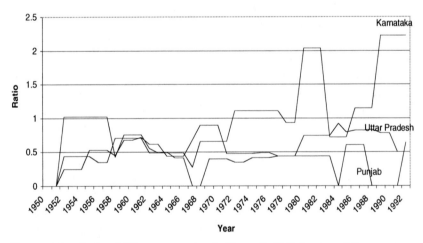

Figure 8.2. Ratio of SC representation in Council of Ministers to SC percentage in population, 1951–92. *Source:* Members of the cabinet, Council of Ministers, and their portfolios are from *India Annual* (various issues) and *Journal of Parliamentary Information* (various issues). Scheduled Caste ministers are identified from Scheduled Caste candidates as listed in Election Commission of India reports (various issues) and in Singh and Bose (1987–88).

179

for each of the three states. I use two separate indicators to measure the degree of representation given to Scheduled Castes, one measuring the importance of the cabinet posts ceded to Scheduled Castes and the other the simple numerical presence of Scheduled Castes in the councils of ministers of the major parties. Figure 8.1 describes the percentage of important portfolios allotted to Scheduled Castes in each state between 1951 and 1992. I identify the important portfolios on the basis of Bueno De Mesquita's 1969–70 survey asking party leaders to identity the most desirable portfolios.[9] The portfolios cited in this survey include: chief minister, home, finance, agriculture, education, labour, revenue, irrigation and power, and industries. I have added two portfolios (cooperatives and public works) to Bueno De Mesquita's list, based on alternative assessments.[10] A single individual holding more than one important portfolio is counted twice. Figure 8.2 describes the ratio of the percentage of Scheduled Castes in the council of ministers as a whole to the percentage of Scheduled Castes in the population.

In Uttar Pradesh, the Congress party was the ruling party for the entire period from 1951 until the entry of the BSP in 1984, with two brief exceptions during 1967–68 and 1977–80. In almost all Congress cabinets, only 9 percent of the important portfolios (one out of eleven) were allotted to Scheduled Caste individuals. The degree of representation enjoyed by Scheduled Castes soared for a brief period in 1969, when they held 27 percent (three out of eleven) of the important portfolios. However, by the time the BSP began mobilizing Scheduled Castes in Uttar Pradesh, it had dropped back down to the previous low level of 9 percent. The low level of representation in important portfolios is replicated when we look at the simple numerical representation given to Scheduled Castes in Congress party cabinets in Uttar Pradesh. Scheduled Castes have been underrepresented in relation to their population in every Congress party council of ministers. The degree of representation given to Scheduled Castes in non-Congress parties in Uttar Pradesh before the entry of the BSP was equally low. In the first non-Congress cabinet, led by a coalition of opposition parties between 1967 and 1969, only one important cabinet portfolio

[9] Bruce Bueno de Mesquita, *Strategy, Risk and Personality in Coalition Politics* (Cambridge: Cambridge University Press, 1975), 103.

[10] Paul Brass, *Factional Politics in an Indian State* (Berkeley: University of California Press, 1965); Sandeep Shastri, *Towards Explaining the Voters' Mandate: An Analysis of the Karnataka Assembly Elections* (Bangalore, 1995).

was allotted to a member of the Scheduled Castes, and the overall per-centage of Scheduled Castes in the cabinet continued to be less than their percentage in the population. In the second cabinet, from 1977 to 1980, no important portfolios were allotted to Scheduled Castes, and the ratio of Scheduled Caste representation in the council of ministers to the percent-age of Scheduled Castes in the population continued to be less than one.

The situation remained unchanged even after the entry of the BSP. The Congress cabinet from 1985 to 1988 allotted only one important cabinet portfolio to a Scheduled Caste minister. In 1989, the Janata Dal snatched control of the state government from the Congress party. The degree of representation given to Scheduled Castes in the Janata Dal government plunged even further: Not a single important portfolio was allotted to a Scheduled Caste minister. The same was the case with the Bharatiya Janata Party government between 1991 and 1992. In every council of ministers following the entry of the BSP, furthermore, Scheduled Castes continued to be underrepresented in relation to their percentage in the population.

The degree of representation given by major political parties to Sched-uled Castes in Punjab was lower than that in Uttar Pradesh. In Punjab, too, the Congress was the ruling party for most of the period before the entry of the BSP in 1984, except for a brief interlude between 1967 and 1972 when the state had a series of non-Congress governments, led by a coalition of opposition parties. Whether the Congress or the opposition was in power, however, the degree of representation given to Scheduled Castes remained equally low. Scheduled Castes were not given any important portfolios in either Congress or non-Congress governments for most of the period between 1951 and 1984, except for three brief periods: in two Congress governments during the 1950s and 1960s, when a Scheduled Caste minis-ter held the agriculture portfolio, and in one non-Congress government in 1977, when a Scheduled Caste minister shared the public works portfolio with an upper-caste minister. The situation changed only marginally after the rise of the BSP. The Akali Dal–led government in Punjab between 1985 and 1987 allotted one important portfolio to a Scheduled Caste minister. However, the Congress government, which took power in 1992, did not allot any important portfolios to Scheduled Caste ministers. In both the Akali Dal and Congress governments, the ratio of Scheduled Caste repre-sentation in the council of ministers to the percentage of Scheduled Castes in the population rose only slightly, from .4 to .6.

In Karnataka, the degree of representation given to Scheduled Castes by the time the BSP entered the state was significantly higher than in the other two states. The Congress party was in power in Karnataka from 1951 until 1983, for the entire period prior to the rise of the BSP. Until 1972, Scheduled Castes were as underrepresented in Congress governments in Karnataka as they were in the other two states. Except for a one-year period from 1962 to 1963, no important portfolios were ceded to Scheduled Caste ministers between 1951 to 1972. And during this one-year interlude, a Scheduled Caste minister held only one important cabinet portfolio. Scheduled Castes were represented in proportion to their population in only one Congress government, between 1952 and 1957. In all other years, they were underrepresented.

Starting in 1972, however, we see the beginnings of a remarkable surge in the representation of Scheduled Castes in both Congress and non-Congress governments. In 1972, no important cabinet portfolios were allotted to a Scheduled Caste minister. However, the numerical representation of Scheduled Castes in the cabinet rose significantly, so that Scheduled Castes were slightly *overrepresented* in relation to their population. Following 1972, the degree of representation given to Scheduled Castes in the Congress party followed a rising trend in both importance and numbers. By 1989, when the BSP was launched in Karnataka, the Congress party had lost control of the government. Scheduled Castes continued to be overrepresented in relation to their population in the governments of the opposition Janata Party and were allotted important portfolios. Two of eleven (18 percent) of the important portfolios were held by Scheduled Caste ministers in the Janata government, including the critical home portfolio, which is second only to the chief ministership in prestige and in the patronage resources that it commands. Following the entry of the BSP, the degree of representation given to Scheduled Castes in both parties continued to rise. In the Congress government between 1989 and 1994, Scheduled Castes were the single largest category in the council of ministers, given more than twice their representation in the population. They occupied, furthermore, 27 percent (three out of eleven) of the important posts. In 1994, the Janata Dal, a descendant of the former Janata Party, succeeded Congress as the governing party in Karnataka. The proportion of Scheduled Castes was lower in the Janata Dal government than in Congress. However, they continued to be overrepresented numerically and occupied two out of eleven important portfolios.

The data I have presented so far refer purely to representation at the state level. Less systematic data are available on representation at the local level in each of these states. What evidence there is, however, confirms the state-level picture. In Uttar Pradesh, several ethnographic studies reveal local-level politics to be dominated by members of the upper and intermediate castes from among all parties. Notable among these is Paul Brass's study of factionalism in five districts across the state in 1965 (Meerut, Aligarh, Gonda, Deoria, and Kanpur).[11] In 1965, Brass found that the local party organizations of Congress and the opposition parties were controlled by the dominant proprietary castes. In 1982, when Brass revisited two of the five districts that he had studied in the 1960s, he found these castes (Brahmins and Bhumihars) still firmly in control of the local bases of power.[12] And in my own fieldwork in Uttar Pradesh in 1996 and 1998, I found that Scheduled Caste elites were still excluded from the Congress party and all other parties. In 1997, of the 114 presidents of the district and town Congress committees for which data were available, 61 percent (70) were from the upper castes, while 3 percent (3) were from the Scheduled Castes.[13] Of the BJP's sixty district presidents, not a single one was from the Scheduled Castes.[14] And of the ninety-six district and town unit presidents from the Samajwadi Party, only two belonged to the Scheduled Castes in 1997.[15]

While comparable district-level studies of political parties in Punjab are scarce, state-level studies refer to both Congress and the Akali Dal as historically dominated by upper and intermediate castes, both Hindu and Sikh.[16] The local-level data that I collected in 1997 confirmed this pattern. Of the nineteen district Congress committee presidents in Punjab in 1997, only one belonged to the Scheduled Castes.[17] Of the twenty district presidents of the Shiromani Akali Dal, none belonged to the Scheduled

[11] Brass, *Factional Politics in an Indian State*; see also Harold Gould, *Grassroots Politics in India* (Delhi: Oxford and IBH Publishing, 1994); and Angela Sutherland Burger, *Opposition in a Dominant Party System* (Berkeley: University of California Press, 1969).

[12] Paul Brass, "National Power and Local Politics in India: A Twenty Year Perspective," *Modern Asian Studies*, Vol. 18, No. 1 (1984): 89–118.

[13] Coded through interviews at the Congress office in Lucknow in December 1997, on the basis of a list of district presidents provided by the party office.

[14] Coded through interviews at the BJP party office in Lucknow in December 1997, on the basis of a list of district presidents provided by the party office.

[15] Coded through interviews with state SP president Ram Sharan Das in Lucknow in December 1997, on the basis of a list of district presidents also provided by Mr. Das.

[16] Atul Kohli, *Democracy and Discontent* (Cambridge: Cambridge University Press, 1991); Baldev Raj Nayar, *Minority Politics in the Punjab* (Princeton, NJ: Princeton University Press, 1966).

[17] Coded through interviews at the Congress party Office in Chandigarh in February 1997, on the basis of a list of district presidents provided by the party office.

Castes.[18] And of the twenty-three district presidents of the BJP, only one belonged to the Scheduled Castes.[19]

In Karnataka, however, there is some evidence of a shift in local-level representation for Scheduled Castes that corresponds to the picture at the state level. In Weiner's study of Belgaum district (in northwestern Karnataka), conducted between 1961 and 1963, for example, Scheduled Castes were hardly to be found in the local Congress organizations. Weiner's caste profile of 115 party officers in Belgaum, including members of the DCC executive, MLAs and MLCs, Mandal presidents and Taluka presidents, reveals only four Scheduled Caste officers.[20] Atul Kohli, returning to Belgaum district in 1986, reported a dramatic change in the power structure at the local level: Whereas Scheduled Castes had simply been absent from the local-level leadership of the party organization in 1961, Kohli found that the leader of one of the two main Congress factions in Belgaum in 1986 was from the Scheduled Castes.[21] Jalali confirms the beginnings of a shift in local-level power structures in favour of the Scheduled Castes after 1972. Scheduled Castes, who had no representation in Taluka development boards in 1960 and 1968, managed to get four Taluk board presidents elected in 1978.[22]

The low degree of representation given to Scheduled Castes by all major parties at all levels in Uttar Pradesh and Punjab sent a signal to the emerging class of office-seeking Scheduled Caste elites that they would have no chance of advancement if they affiliated themselves with any of these parties. Searching for a channel to office, they responded immediately when the BSP entered these states in 1984. In Karnataka, however, the high degree of representation given to Scheduled Castes in the Congress and Janata governments at both the state and the local levels sent these office-seeking elites an opposite signal. It indicated that they could reasonably hope to ascend the ranks of the party hierarchy into positions of power in the state apparatus if they joined either of these parties. Consequently, they did not

[18] Coded through interviews at the Akali Dal party office in Chandigarh in December 1997, on the basis of a list of district presidents provided by the party office.
[19] Coded through interviews at the BJP Party office in Chandigarh in February 1997, on the basis of a list of district presidents provided by the party office.
[20] Myron Weiner, *Party Building in a New Nation: The Indian National Congress* (Chicago: University of Chicago Press, 1967), 273.
[21] Kohli, *Democracy and Discontent*, 113.
[22] Rita Jalali, "The State and the Political Mobilization of the Disadvantaged: The Case of the Scheduled Castes in India" (Ph.D. dissertation, Stanford University, 1990), 132.

respond to the BSP, despite its repeated and sustained efforts over at least a decade. The sections that follow provide evidence of the link between representational opportunities in the competing parties and the response to the BSP for each of the states in turn.

III. The BSP in Uttar Pradesh: Representational Blockage and Party Formation

The population of Uttar Pradesh can be classified according to at least four different ethnic cleavages: religion, caste, language, and region. Eighty-two percent of the population is Hindu, and 17 percent Muslim. Ninety percent, mainly Hindu, speak Hindi, while 10 percent, mainly Muslim, speak Urdu. The state is divided into at least six historic and cultural regions: Poorvanchal, Rohillkhand, Bundelkhand, Uttarkhand, Western Uttar Pradesh, and Central Uttar Pradesh.[23] The population, both Hindu and Muslim, is distributed among hundreds of castes that have been combined under different aggregate categories at different points in time. The Scheduled Castes, one such aggregate category, constitute 21 percent of the population of Uttar Pradesh.[24] The Scheduled Caste category in Uttar Pradesh includes sixty-six individual categories as listed in the census.[25] The two largest of these census categories are Chamars, who constitute 56.6 percent of the Scheduled Caste population, and Pasis, who constitute 14.6 percent. However, as Chapter 7 pointed out, each of these census categories is itself composite in nature. The "Chamar" category in Uttar Pradesh, for example, includes four categories – Chamar, Dhusia, Jhusia, and Jatava – whose members sometimes describe themselves collectively as Chamars and sometimes emphasise their distinct identities. And a sense of shared ethnic identity among individual castes often spills over the census categories, so that Koris, listed separately in the census and numbering 5.9 percent of the Scheduled Caste population, also describe themselves as Chamar and are understood as such by the rest of the population.

The BSP launched its first major electoral effort in the state in the 1985 elections for the Uttar Pradesh state legislative assembly, although its predecessor organizations had been active in the state since 1978. By 1985,

---

[23] Based in part upon Brass, *Factional Politics in an Indian State*, 6–8.
[24] *Census of India 1991.*
[25] Ibid.

as section I described, we saw the emergence of an office-seeking class of Scheduled Caste elites in Uttar Pradesh. The BSP became a lightning rod for these elites immediately upon entry. The earliest cadres of the BSP reported finding an overwhelming response in their efforts to set up local party units. As one described it: "If there was a community leader in the village, someone educated, we caught hold of him. If he was not useful, we found another, preferably his rival. Then we added on others. We found ready made community leaders wherever we went."[26] In the very first assembly election that it contested in the state, the BSP put up candidates for 272 out of Uttar Pradesh's 425 assembly seats (more than 50 percent) and established party units throughout the sprawling state (especially in western and eastern Uttar Pradesh).

The biographies of some of these early BSP members in Uttar Pradesh reveal them all to be college educated, in their twenties and thirties, and engaged in some form of political or associational activity before joining the BSP. Raj Bahadur, the first BAMCEF convenor for the state of Uttar Pradesh, was the first college graduate from his village. He was employed as a clerk in the telegraph department when approached by Kanshi Ram, where he was the president of the Scheduled Caste employees federation.[27] He joined BAMCEF in 1978, at the age of thirty-five. And following the first election, he abandoned his government job to pursue a political career. Guru Sharan, a BSP activist from eastern Uttar Pradesh born in 1958, ran in the assembly elections in 1984 as an independent. He sought the BSP's support for his electoral debut and joined the party formally immediately after the election.[28] Bali Ram, a BSP MP when I met him in 1996, was a twenty-six-year-old student and the president of the Scheduled Caste Student Union at Banaras Hindu University when he first started attending functions organized by the BSP's predecessor organizations.[29] When the BSP was officially launched in 1984, he became one of its official cadres. Each of these men was seeking better economic opportunities and higher status recognition than his parents, and each found these in politics.

The BSP's success in attracting these elites was a direct consequence of the representational blockage in the Congress and other political parties. In 1984, Congress was the dominant party in Uttar Pradesh politics, having

[26] Interview, November 27, 1997, Lucknow (UP).
[27] Interview, December 13, 1997, Lucknow.
[28] Interview, November 30, 1997, Gonda (UP).
[29] Interview, December 12, 1996, New Delhi.

won almost every state legislative assembly election since 1951. Given the dominance of upper castes in positions of power in the Congress organization and previous governments, however, these office-seeking elites could see clearly that they had little hope of obtaining access to offices in the state apparatus through the Congress party. All other parties in the Uttar Pradesh party system offered the same dim prospects for obtaining state office, regardless of which party won the election. Consequently, they affiliated themselves instead with the BSP.

Congress leaders themselves readily acknowledge that the representational blockage for Scheduled Caste elites in their own party pushed them toward the BSP. According to one Scheduled Caste politician and former minister in the Congress party:

If they had made me Chief Minister, SCs [Scheduled Castes] would not have left. There has never been a Scheduled Caste or Muslim Chief Minister in Uttar Pradesh. In the South, there was D. Sanjivaiah, in Rajasthan, Jagannath Pahadia. In Uttar Pradesh, they took the power but did not share it. The formula for the cabinet was usually 12 brahmins, 12 thakurs [both upper castes], 3 SCs, 2 minorities [a euphemism for Muslims]. Scheduled Caste youth felt slighted – they did not like it.[30]

Viewed in isolation, this statement might be interpreted as a case of sour grapes for not being given the chief minister's post rather than an objective assessment of why Congress lost the support of young Scheduled Caste elites. However, it is part of a chorus of voices that offer the same conclusion. According to a Congress office-bearer, who was a Brahmin:

In the beginning, Scheduled Castes felt that they had a promise from the Congress.... But then later they felt, my son now has an education, he wants a job or a political post, and Congress could not give. Congress said, we will have only 2 SC ministers, one Chamar, one Pasi. But an SC could never become the Chief Minister. Chaudhury Girdhari Lal [a Scheduled Caste minister in UP in the 1950s] was an important leader but could never become Chief Minister. A Bania [upper caste] might be the Congress Chief Minister, maybe a Brahmin, but never a Scheduled Caste. Scheduled Castes wanted active participation, power to be shared, but Congress was not able to understand.[31]

The Congress man's statement illustrates the crux of my argument. On the one hand, in Uttar Pradesh there were rising Scheduled Caste elites looking for a "job or a political post." It is worth noting that he lumps

---

[30] Interview, November 20, 1997, Lucknow.
[31] Interview, December 27, 1997, Lucknow.

Table 8.4. *Representation in the BSP in Uttar Pradesh, 1984*

	Number of Posts	SC	Chamar	Pasi	Other SC	Non-SC	Total
National	1	100%	100%	0%	0%	0%	100%
State	10	90%	80%	10%	0%	10%	100%
Local	272	57%	40%	6%	10%	43%	100%

Source: For national and state posts, interviews (see Appendix A for details). For local posts, *Oppressed Indian*, March 1986.

the two together, equating politics with employment. On the other hand, a representational blockage in the Congress party and the rest of the party system meant that no political party in Uttar Pradesh gave them a viable channel to office. The result was the diversion of these elites to the BSP.

Significantly, however, the BSP did not absorb elites from all Scheduled Castes equally. Literacy rates among different Scheduled Castes in Uttar Pradesh varied: Sixteen percent of Chamars in Uttar Pradesh were literate in 1981, compared to only 10 percent of Pasis.[32] The unevenness in literacy rates meant that when BSP organizers went looking for educated elites to staff the party organization, those that they found were overwhelmingly from the "Chamar" category. Once the party had developed a core leadership composed of Chamar elites, this core prevented the incorporation of new elites from other Scheduled Caste categories.

Table 8.4 summarizes the BSP's own representational profile in 1984, revealing the domination of elites from the "Chamar"[33] category throughout the party hierarchy. The BSP had only an ad hoc organizational structure in 1984. The posts counted at the national and state levels, therefore, were identified by determining through interviews the most powerful individuals at either level. At the local level, the identification of important posts was relatively straightforward. There was an almost total overlap between the legislative and organizational wings of the BSP in 1984. Those who headed local party units were also typically the party's election candidates. The list of local-level posts, therefore, consists of the 272 candidates nominated by the BSP in its first assembly election in Uttar Pradesh. As the table indicates, the BSP organization in 1984 was dominated by Scheduled Castes,

[32] *Census of India 1981.*
[33] In these tables as well as in the survey data, I include the category "Kori" when counting Chamars. Koris are listed separately in the census. However, respondents themselves often did not distinguish between the two in their self-identifications.

Table 8.5. *Representation in the BSP in Uttar Pradesh, 1995–96*

	Total number of Posts	SC	Chamar	Pasi	Other SC	Non-SC	Total
National	1	100%	100%	0%	0%	0%	100%
State	10	85%	85%	0%	0%	15%	100%
Local	289	30%	23%	4%	3%	70%	100%

Source: For national and state posts, interviews (see Appendix A for details). For local posts, *Bahujan Sangathak*, November 11, 1996.

especially at the higher levels. Among Scheduled Castes, the most important posts in the party were captured by those professing to belong to the "Chamar" category. At the national level, the post of party president was occupied by Kanshi Ram, a Ramdassia Sikh. Ramdassia Sikhs are coded in Punjab as members of the "Chamar" category. In state-level posts, I include those appointed "in charge" of eastern and western UP as well as the eight individuals at the first training camp of the BSP in Delhi. Eighty percent of these posts were occupied by the members of the "Chamar" category. It is only at the lowest level of the party hierarchy that we see a broadening of the caste profile of the BSP. At this level, while Chamars were still the single largest category, they shared space with other Scheduled Castes as well as a sizable proportion of other ethnic categories.[34]

The Chamar domination of the top levels of the BSP in Uttar Pradesh remained relatively unchanged by 1996. Table 8.5 summarizes the representational profile of the BSP for the period 1995–96. As in Table 8.4, the national post refers to that of the party president. In state posts, I include ten of the eleven important cabinet portfolios. In local posts, I include the 289 candidates in the 1996 state assembly elections.

The table shows a significant turnover in the profile of the leadership at the lowest level, with an infusion of non–Scheduled Caste candidates. However, Chamars continued to dominate the higher levels of the party hierarchy. And at the local level, although there was a dilution in the number of Chamar candidates compared to 1984, Chamars continued to be the best-represented category among Scheduled Castes.

[34] The allotment of tickets to backward castes and Muslims was part of a strategy to supplement Scheduled Caste votes with the votes of other ethnic categories in order to produce a winning margin.

IV. The BSP in Punjab: Representational Blockage and Party Formation

The population of Punjab may be classified according to the cleavages of religion, language, region, and caste. Sixty-three percent of the population is Sikh and 34 percent Hindu. Eighty-five percent of the population professes to speak Punjabi and 15 percent Hindi.[35] The state is divided into at least three historical and cultural regions: Majha, Doaba, and Malwa. And both Hindus and Sikhs are also divided into hundreds of castes combined under different aggregate categories at different points in time. Scheduled Castes, both Hindu and Sikh, comprise 28.3 percent of Punjab's population. Among Scheduled Castes, the four largest census categories are Mazhabis (31 percent of the Scheduled Caste population), Chamars (including Ramdassia Sikhs) (27 percent), Adharmis (15 percent), and Balmikis (12 percent).[36] As in the case of Uttar Pradesh, each of these categories is itself composite. The census, for example, lists six caste names to be collectively coded as "Chamar": Chamar, Jatia Chamar, Rehgar, Raigar, Ramdasi, and Ravidasi. These smaller categories all differ from each other in social customs, religious practices, and traditional occupations. But there are also shared bases of identity that spill over census categories.

The BSP's first major electoral battle in Punjab was the 1985 election for the state legislative assembly. In Punjab, as in Uttar Pradesh, the BSP was quickly able to concentrate previously decentralized office-seeking activity under its own political label. R. L. Jassi, who joined the BSP as district convenor in 1984, was a college graduate who had contested assembly elections as an independent candidate before the BSP approached him.[37] Satnam Singh Kainth, a BSP MLA when I met him 1997, was studying for his master's degree when first approached by BAMCEF organizers. He had begun to participate in student union elections when the opportunity to join the BSP presented itself, and he contested the state assembly elections as a BSP candidate in 1985.[38] Darshan Singh Chumbar, a district activist in 1997, contested the state assembly elections as an independent in 1980.[39] When approached by BAMCEF organizers in 1981, he readily joined the new organization. The single most important force driving these elites

[35] *Twenty-Ninth Report of the Commissioner for Linguistic Minorities in India* (1991).
[36] *Census of India 1991.*
[37] Interview, February 20, 1997, Jalandhar (Punjab).
[38] Interview, February 16, 1997, Banga (Punjab).
[39] Interview, January 23, 1997, Hoshiarpur (Punjab).

190

toward the BSP was the representational blockage that they found in every other political party in Punjab. As one put it, in no uncertain terms:

Out of 100 tickets, it [Congress] gives 75 to upper castes and 25 to us. [He is referring here to the percentage of seats reserved for Scheduled Caste candidates.] Then, when the time comes to make the CM [chief minister], naturally the majority is against us. We will never be CM. With the BSP, even if we lose seats, even if we lose 48 and win 52 out of 100 seats, we are the ones who will be in power.[40]

This statement powerfully expresses the logic of the argument so far: The ethnic identity of those who occupy posts of power and prestige within a party's organization and previous governments is a signal of the ethnic identity of those who can expect to capture office if the party comes to power. Since positions of power in the Punjab Congress organization and governments were monopolized by upper and intermediate castes, emerging Scheduled Caste elites saw little chance of obtaining office themselves by joining the Congress party. The Akali Dal, the principal opposition party in Punjab, did not offer better prospects. Nor did the smaller parties in Punjab, including the BJP and the Communist Party. Since Scheduled Caste elites had little hope of rising up the ladder in Congress or any other party in Punjab, they turned instead to the Bahujan Samaj Party. In its first election in Punjab, the BSP found a critical mass of joiners comparable to that of Uttar Pradesh: It contested roughly 60 of the 117 seats in the Punjab legislative assembly (more than 50 percent); and although it was particularly strong in the Doaba region, it had party units across the state.[41]

However, uneven literacy rates among Scheduled Castes meant that the BSP in Punjab, as in the case of Uttar Pradesh, was overwhelmingly dominated by particular castes among the Scheduled Castes. The most literate in 1981 were the Adharmis, 40 percent of whom were literate, as compared to the general Scheduled Caste literacy rate of 24 percent. The second most literate category were Chamars (including Ramdassia Sikhs and others), with a literacy rate of 29 percent. Only 22 percent of Balmikis were literate, while Mazhabis, the most numerous among the Scheduled Castes in Punjab, had a literacy rate of 13 percent. The unevenness in literacy rates meant that the wave of office-seeking elites in 1981 consisted overwhelmingly of the Adharmi category, and to a lesser extent of the Chamar category.

---

[40] Interview, January 27, 1997, Hoshiarpur (Punjab).
[41] Interview with Tejinder Singh Jhalli, then the most important state leader of BAMCEF, February 27, 1997, Chandigarh (Punjab).

The early BSP organization in Punjab, therefore, was dominated by members of these two categories. The two state-level organizers of BAMCEF and then DS-4 were both Adharmis. And while data comparable in quality to the UP data on the caste profile of the BSP candidates in 1984 are not available for Punjab, BSP workers all acknowledge that Balmikis and Mazhabis were sparsely represented. The domination of the BSP organization in Punjab by Adharmis and Ramdassias had changed little by 1997. Of the twenty-four names I identified as holding positions of power formally or informally in the Punjab BSP in 1997, fourteen were Adharmis and Ramdassias, and only five belonged to Mazhabi Sikhs. And every member of Kanshi Ram's immediate coterie in Punjab belonged to either the Adharmi or the Ramdassia category.

V. The BSP in Karnataka: Representational "Openness" and Party Failure

The population of Karnataka can also be cut into several ethnic slices based on religion, language, region, and caste. The population is 85.4 percent Hindu and 11.6 percent Muslim. It is a linguistically diverse state, with 65.6 percent of the population speaking Kannada, 9.5 percent speaking Urdu, 8.1 percent speaking Telugu, and about 3 percent each speaking Marathi, Tamil, and Tulu.[42] As in the other states, the population is divided into hundreds of castes classified into different aggregate categories at different points in time. The Scheduled Castes constitute 16.4 percent of the state's population. The largest castes among Scheduled Castes in Karnataka, according to census categories, are Adi Karnataka (35.8 percent), Banjara (11.1 percent), Bhovi (11.1 percent), Adi Dravida (9.5 percent), Holaya (8 percent), and Madiga (5.53 percent). In Karnataka, even more than in the other states, census categories do not reflect the caste categories that are meaningful on the ground. The two principal categories currently meaningful among Scheduled Castes are the "Right Hand" castes (including Holayas and sections of the Adi Karnatakas and Adi Dravidas, among others) and "Left Hand" castes (including Madigas and also sections of the Adi Karnatakas and Adi Dravidas, among others).[43]

---

[42] *Twenty-Ninth Report of the Commissioner for Linguistic Minorities in India* (1991).
[43] See Charsley and Karanth, *Challenging Untouchability*, 13–17, for a discussion of these categories.

Table 8.6. *BSP candidates in Karnataka legislative assembly and parliamentary elections, 1989–98*

	Year of Election				
	1989	1991	1994	1996	1998
Total number of seats	224	28	224	28	28
Number of BSP candidates	5	1	77	3	6

Source: Election Commission of India, various years.

In 1984, when Kanshi Ram launched the BSP nationwide, he chose not to open a party unit in Karnataka or in any of the states in south India. The emerging class of literate Scheduled Castes in Karnataka were mobilized instead by the Dalit Sangharsh Samiti (DSS), an initially nonpolitical organization founded in 1973. The BSP launched the first significant effort to enter Karnataka in 1989, when Kanshi Ram inaugurated a state party unit and contested the legislative assembly elections in the state for the first time. However, the party failed to find a critical mass of joiners either in 1989 or in several repeated attempts in the decade that followed. Table 8.6 summarizes the number of candidates put up by the BSP in each election in Karnataka between 1989 and 1998.

In the 1989 assembly elections, the BSP was able to put up candidates in only 5 of the state's 224 constituencies. Nor was the BSP able to find activists to staff its organization. The party organization for the entire state at this time consisted of a state committee of five members, all located in the capital city of Bangalore. It had no district units outside Bangalore and was by the accounts of its own members an "ad hoc" party.[44] After 1989, the efforts intensified, but to no avail. As one party cadre put it: "We arranged so many seminars, called meetings, brought Dalit leaders together – but there was a poor response."[45] In the 1991 parliamentary elections, the BSP was able to contest only one out of Karnataka's twenty-eight seats. In the 1994 state assembly elections, it managed, through a merger with the Dalit Sangarsh Samiti, to put up candidates for 77 of the state's 224 seats. However, it was unable to retain even this small pool of candidates. Many of these candidates deserted the BSP soon after the 1994 elections, so that in the parliamentary elections two years later, the party was able to find only three candidates.

[44] Interviews with early cadres from the BSP in Karnataka, March 18–19, 1997, Bangalore (Karnataka).
[45] Interviews, March 18 and 19, 1997, Bangalore.

The emerging class of Scheduled Caste elites simply refused to knock on its doors. In 1989, only ten aspirants applied for a ticket from the BSP.[46] Subsequent years did not result in any appreciable increase in aspirants. Whereas in Uttar Pradesh and Punjab, BSP organizers reported finding "ready-made" cadres, BSP organizers in Karnataka reported considerable difficulty in finding anyone willing to run for election on a BSP ticket.[47]

Why was the BSP unable to find a pool of candidates and activists in Karnataka even after repeated attempts? Karnataka in 1981 was producing almost the same number of educated Scheduled Caste elites per village as Uttar Pradesh, and even more independent office seekers for each Scheduled Caste seat. Why did many of these elites come together under the BSP label in Uttar Pradesh but not in Karnataka? I argue here that the BSP's difficulty in finding a critical mass of joiners in Karnataka arose from the high degree of representation given to Scheduled Caste elites in the two major parties in the state. The presence of important Scheduled Caste leaders in both parties meant that these parties presented credible prospects for advancement for upwardly mobile Scheduled Caste elites. These elites, therefore, had no incentive to affiliate themselves with a new entrant. New parties have uncertain prospects, and the decision of upwardly mobile elites to affiliate themselves with a new entrant is essentially a risky investment in political office. In Uttar Pradesh and Punjab, Scheduled Caste elites had little choice but to take this risk.

BSP organizers acknowledged the presence of influential Scheduled Caste politicians in the major Karnataka parties as a major obstruction to party building. As one put it, the BSP could not flourish in Karnataka because "they [Scheduled Caste elites] got some benefit from other parties. Scheduled Castes in Karnataka have colluded with other parties for smaller benefits and are not in a position to come back."[48] The BSP cadre told the story scornfully, as one of the "selling out" of Scheduled Caste interests by self-interested elites. Whether or not their actions constituted a "sell-out," his assessment supports the general hypothesis advanced here: Presented with opportunities for advancement in the major parties in Karnataka, Scheduled Caste elites had no incentive to join the BSP. Had the BSP been able to present itself as a viable electoral option, Scheduled Caste voters in Karnataka would have had an incentive to defect to it over time. However,

---

[46] Interviews, March 18–19, 1997, Bangalore.
[47] Interviews, March 18–19 and March 25, 1997, Bangalore.
[48] Interviews, March 18–19, 1997, Bangalore.

to the extent that the emerging waves of Scheduled Caste office-seeking elites have been channeled toward other parties, Scheduled Caste voters in Karnataka have not so far been given the choice.

The case of Karnataka is a critical one for the argument presented here, since it establishes that Scheduled Caste elites are indifferent between ethnic and other types of parties in their search for a channel to office. Both Congress and the Janata Dal in Karnataka are multiethnic parties. Had upwardly mobile Scheduled Caste elites possessed a natural affinity for an ethnic party, we should have seen them gravitate toward the BSP in Karnataka regardless of the degree of representation given to Scheduled Castes in other parties. However, their dispersion across parties in Karnataka indicates otherwise. One imaginable condition under which the BSP, or any other party attempting to mobilize Scheduled Castes as a separate political force, might attract sufficient numbers of Scheduled Caste candidates and activists in Karnataka is if one of the major Karnataka parties were to disappear from the political arena. Such a disappearance is not an unlikely event: The history of Indian state politics is replete with instances of splits wiping out seemingly strong parties overnight. As long as these other parties exist, however, there is no space for the emergence of the BSP.

VI. Conclusion

I have argued in this chapter that upwardly mobile Scheduled Caste elites converged upon the BSP only in those states in which they did not find a channel in other parties. Where the competition offered such elites a space in party organizations and governments, such elites were equally content to join the competition. In the chapter that follows, I will show that the preferences of Scheduled Caste voters across parties correspond directly to their representational profiles. Once the BSP had established a monopoly on representation in Uttar Pradesh and Punjab, Scheduled Caste voters preferred the BSP to other political parties. However, even in these two states, voters from those Scheduled Caste categories whose elites were best represented in the BSP were more likely to prefer the BSP than voters from Scheduled Caste categories whose elites were less well represented in the BSP.

9

Why SC Voters Prefer the BSP

The previous chapter argued that a representational blockage in the competition was necessary in order to induce Scheduled Caste elites to join the BSP. In this chapter, I link representation with voter preferences. I show that Scheduled Caste voters in Uttar Pradesh and Punjab formulate preferences by counting heads across parties rather than by examining the issues that the parties stand on. Because the BSP had a monopoly on the representation of Scheduled Caste elites in these two states between 1984 and 1998, Scheduled Caste voters preferred the BSP to other parties. However, voters from the Scheduled Caste categories that were better represented in the BSP were more likely to prefer it than voters from underrepresented Scheduled Caste categories. The link between representation and voter preferences, furthermore, holds not just for Scheduled Caste voters but for voters from all other ethnic categories as well.

The data that I use to develop and test this proposition are drawn from across four elections in India, held between 1996 and 1998. For information about the ethnic profile of political parties, I rely on interviews with party personnel in each state conducted between 1996 and 1998. For party issue positions, I conduct a content analysis of campaign messages during the 1996 parliamentary election campaign. For data on perceptions of salient issues among Scheduled Caste voters, and on Scheduled Caste voter preferences independent of voting behaviour, I draw upon survey data from the Indian National Election Studies for the 1996 parliamentary election. Finally, for data on the voter preferences of other ethnic categories from other elections, I rely upon indirect evidence drawn from party and candidate strategies collected during four election campaigns.

The chapter is organized as follows: Section I predicts the preference distribution of Scheduled Caste voters across political parties in the states of Uttar Pradesh and Punjab if they formulate preferences by counting heads. (I exclude Karnataka from the analysis of Scheduled Caste voter preferences, since the sample of Scheduled Caste voters who expressed a preference is too small to be statistically reliable.) Section II predicts the preference distribution of Scheduled Caste voters across political parties if they formulate preferences by assessing party issue positions. Section III shows that the first prediction captures the distribution of Scheduled Caste voter preferences more accurately than the second. Section IV extends this proposition to voters from other ethnic categories in other states.

I. Head Counts and Scheduled Caste Voter Preferences

In order to ascertain how Scheduled Caste voter preferences might be distributed if they formulate preferences by counting heads, we must first establish the relevant level of the party organization that they are likely to consider. Should Scheduled Caste voters weight the ethnic identity of the candidate in their local constituency most heavily? Should they ignore the identity of that candidate and look instead at the ethnic identity of the state- or national-level party leaders? Or should they give some weight to party personnel at both levels? If the ethnic identities of party personnel had been identical at all levels, knowing the relative weights that Scheduled Caste voters assign to leaders across levels would have been irrelevant. However, because the ethnic identities of party personnel for all major parties differ across levels, knowing the relative weights is of critical importance, since the level at which voters choose to count heads will produce different hypothesized preference distributions.

At the *candidate level*, Scheduled Castes were represented in roughly the same proportion across parties in 1996, with the BSP slightly ahead of the others. Table 9.1 summarizes the degree of representation given to Scheduled Caste candidates in the candidate lists of all major parties or alliances in Uttar Pradesh and Punjab for the 1996 parliamentary elections. In Uttar Pradesh, the contest was between the Indian National Congress (INC); the Bharatiya Janata Party (BJP); the National Front/Left Front alliance (NF/LF), in which the Samajwadi Party (SP) was the dominant partner; and the BSP, fighting alone. In Punjab, the contest was among the INC, the BJP, the NF/LF, and an alliance between the BSP and the main regional party, the Shiromani Akali Dal (SAD).

The roughly equivalent representation of Scheduled Castes in the candidate lists of all parties is a consequence of the affirmative action policies

197

Table 9.1. *Percentage of SC candidates fielded by all major parties/alliances in 1996 parliamentary election*

	Party/Alliance			
State	INC	BJP	NF/LF	BSP/SAD
Uttar Pradesh	21.2	21.2	21.2	24.7
Punjab	23.1	23.1	23.1	38.5

Note: INC = Indian National Congress; BJP = Bharatiya Janata Party; NF/LF = National Front/Left Front, BSP = Bahujan Samaj Party; SAD = Shiromani Akali Dal.
Source: For INC, BJP, and NL/LF, based on candidates nominated in Scheduled Caste constituencies. For BSP, based on candidate list by ethnic identity provided by the BSP central office, April 1996.

Table 9.2. *Representational profile of major parties in Uttar Pradesh and Punjab at the state level, 1996*

	Party				
State	INC	BJP	NF/LF	SAD	BSP
Uttar Pradesh	Low	Low	Low	–	High
Punjab	Low	Low	Low	Low	High

Source: See Chapter 8.

mandated by the Constitution. Each party is constitutionally required to nominate only Scheduled Caste candidates in certain "reserved" constituencies in each state. All parties, therefore, nominate the constitutionally mandated percentage of Scheduled Caste candidates in these "reserved" constituencies but rarely nominate Scheduled Caste candidates in "general" constituencies. The BSP nominated Scheduled Caste candidates in both "reserved" and "general" constituencies. This accounts for the higher percentage of representation given to Scheduled Caste candidates by the BSP. However, in 1996 the BSP was attempting a diversification of its candidate base in order to secure a margin of votes from other ethnic categories. As a consequence, most BSP candidates in this election did not belong to Scheduled Caste categories.

The degree of representation given to Scheduled Castes by each party in the *state-level* leadership, however, diverges considerably across parties and across states. Table 9.2 summarizes the data on representation in state-level

198

leadership (presented more systematically in Figures 8.1 and 8.2 and Tables 8.4 and 8.5 in the previous chapter). As the table shows, Scheduled Caste elites were equally underrepresented at the state level in all parties except the BSP in Uttar Pradesh and Punjab.

While systematic data is not available for the ethnic profiles of all major parties at the *national level*, in 1996 only two of these parties had Scheduled Caste leaders who were nationally known and reported to play a prominent decision-making role: Ram Vilas Paswan, then in the NF/LF, and Meira Kumar, in the INC. We can safely conclude, therefore, that the degree of representation of Scheduled Caste elites at the national level was low for all parties except the BSP.

In Chapter 4, I proposed that in counting heads, voters should give greatest weight to party personnel at that level of the party organization where control over the distribution of patronage resources lies. In decentralized parties, where individual candidates have discretion over the distribution of such resources, voters will give greater weight to the ethnic identity of the candidate than to the ethnic identity of the party leadership. In centralized parties, the opposite is likely to be the case: Here the voter will ignore the ethnic identity of the candidate at the local level and concentrate mainly on the ethnic identity of the leadership. Each of the important parties in the states under study exhibit a centralized structure. The relevant level at which we should expect voters to count heads, therefore, is that of the party leadership. The ethnic identity of the candidate, then, may convey additional information, which may be useful in drawing further distinctions between two otherwise similar parties. For example, where the leadership of two competing parties is dominated by the "upper castes," the ethnic identity of the candidate might become an important distinguishing factor. However, consideration of the ethnic identity of the candidate at the constituency level should in all cases be subordinate to the ethnic identity of the party leadership.

Evidence from voter surveys in 1996 and 1998 substantiate this claim. Table 9.3 summarizes the relative percentage of voters in Uttar Pradesh and Punjab who reported giving weight to party, candidate, or both in making up their minds in the 1996 and 1998 parliamentary elections. As the table indicates, about half the voters in both states reported giving greater weight to the party in making their decision. Almost two-thirds of voters considered candidates along with parties. Only a minority of voters reported giving candidates more weight in their voting decisions than the parties from which they came.

199

Table 9.3. *Relative weight of party and candidate in voter decisions in Uttar Pradesh and Punjab (combined sample).* Question: When deciding whom to vote for, do you give greater importance to the party or the candidate?

	Party (%)	Both (%)	Candidate (%)	Don't Know (%)
1996 (N = 1,719)	50	11.8	26	12.2
1998 (N = 1,491)	44	20.9	18.6	16.5

Source: 1996 pre-poll survey; 1998 mid-poll survey.

Within the party, we should expect voters to give greater weight to the state than to the national party leadership, since, as I argued in Chapter 6, this is where control over patronage resources is concentrated. Control over the vast patronage resources at the disposal of the state government gives state-level leaders considerable independence from the national leadership. State party units in the Congress had come to enjoy significant autonomy from the national-level leadership by 1996. The NF/LF was a confederation of autonomous regional party units: the JD in Karnataka, Uttar Pradesh, and Orissa; the CPM in Kerala and West Bengal; and the SP in Uttar Pradesh. The parties in the NF/LF were practically independent of national-level coordination. Even the most hierarchically organized parties, the BJP and the BSP, in which we might have expected national-level leaders to hold the reins, have had to knuckle under to pressures from leaders of their state units.[1]

If Scheduled Caste voters in Uttar Pradesh and Punjab formulate preferences across parties by counting heads, and if they count heads at the state level, then they should prefer the BSP to all other parties in Uttar Pradesh and Punjab, regardless of any of the party issue positions.

II. Party Positions on Salient Issues and Voter Preferences

One simple test to determine whether voters consider party issue positions in formulating preferences is to see if there is a relationship between the parties that voters prefer and the parties that take a stand on the issues

---

[1] For a description of the relations between state and central units within Congress, see Paul Brass, *Factional Politics in an Indian State* (Berkeley: University of California Press, 1965); for relations within the BJP, see Christophe Jaffrelot, *The Hindu Nationalist Movement and Indian Politics* (New York: Viking, 1996). There are no secondary sources on the relationship between state and national party units for the BSP and the NF/LF, and the claims about the degree of autonomy of state units in these two formations are based on my own observation.

they believe to be salient. If voter preferences across parties are guided by party issue positions, then we should expect, at a minimum, voters to prefer a party that takes a position on the issues they believe to be important. If we find that voters prefer parties even if they do not take a position on the issues they believe to be important, this would be evidence that their preferences are guided by considerations other than party issue positions.

Note that this test probes for the minimal criteria that must be satisfied if voters formulate preferences based on issue positions. It does not require that voters be able to draw fine distinctions between the actual positions of parties on any given issue, or perform elaborate calculations about the distance between a party's position and their own on the issue they deem to be of greatest importance. It simply requires voters to prefer *a* party (any party) that takes *a* position (any position) on an issue that they believe to be important.

In order to obtain data on voter perceptions of issue salience, I rely upon a midcampaign survey conducted during the 1996 parliamentary election, in which voters were asked to identify the issues that they thought were most important in the election campaign. The same respondents were subsequently asked which parties they preferred, thus making it possible to compare their perceptions of issue salience with their preferences across parties. The question on issue salience was partly open-ended. Respondents could answer by choosing one of the several issue categories provided by the interviewer, by naming an issue not included in the interviewer's list, by naming "local issues" as important, by saying that "no issue" was important, or by refusing to answer. In order to identify which parties took positions on salient issues, I rely on a content analysis of the public pronouncements of all major parties or alliance formations in Uttar Pradesh and Punjab.

The sample used for the content analysis consists of a selection of the public statements of prominent party leaders, including campaign speeches, radio broadcasts, slogans, press conferences, and statements made during interviews. In contrast to previous studies of party issue positions, I explicitly exclude from the sample party manifestos, pamphlets, policy statements, and any other literature not intended for a mass audience.[2] Party manifestos

---

[2] See, for instance, Ian Budge, David Robertson, and Derek J. Hearl, eds., *Ideology, Strategy and Party Change: Spatial Analyses of Post-War Election Programmes in 19 Democracies* (Cambridge: Cambridge University Press, 1987).

in India, and probably elsewhere, are not an important channel of disseminating information to the electorate about party positions. They are printed in limited numbers[3] and, while circulated to journalists and researchers, are seldom found in the hands of voters. Any study that attempts to investigate the messages that parties send to the electorate, therefore, must focus on those promises within the manifesto (or outside it) that parties actually emphasize to the electorate. My focus here on public pronouncements is designed to do this, by looking only at those issues that politicians transmitted to a mass audience, and ignoring those that are simply spelt out on paper.

The sample of materials for the content analysis was selected in the following way. For the thirty-six days of the official campaign period, which lasted from April 7 until May 12, 1996, I randomly selected nine days. For each day selected, I obtained press clippings of all speeches and statements given by prominent party leaders, which are the principal means by which parties attempt to reach a mass audience. I excluded statements made by minor leaders and statements made at the constituency level, which are typically not intended for wide circulation. The clippings were obtained from two English-language newspapers published in different regions: the *Hindu* (published in Madras, in the south) and the *Indian Express* (published in New Delhi, in the north). I supplemented this sample with additional clippings that I had collected in a less systematic fashion during the campaign itself, which came from a wider selection of English newspapers; with tape recordings of speeches given at political rallies that I attended during the campaign period; and with posters and slogans that I collected during the campaign period.

There are three possible sources of bias in this sample. First, because newspaper reports are a journalist's selective account of what was actually said, they may reflect the journalist's personal biases in highlighting certain issues and ignoring others. The full text of a speech is always a better source than a report of the speech. Second, newspaper coverage biases the sample in favour of major parties and, especially, incumbents: The Congress and BJP, for example, were relatively well covered, while smaller parties, including the BSP and SP, received less press coverage. Third, the sample is chosen from English-language sources, which may not reflect the issues as they were actually transmitted in regional languages.

---

[3] This is based on interviews with members of the campaign committees of the BJP, the Congress party, and the Janata Dal.

I address the first problem by obtaining reports of the same rally or press conference from at least two sources, so that the bias in one source might be compensated for by others, and by supplementing them with tape recordings of speeches containing the entire text of a speech, where available. I address the second problem by relying more heavily on tape recordings of rallies for smaller parties that I attended than on the scarce news clippings. I find the third problem to be less important: Checks that I conducted comparing reports of the same speech in English and Hindi newspapers, for example, revealed little difference in the issues emphasized. Further, because the tape recordings of speeches were mainly in Hindi, supplementing the sample with these recordings goes some way toward ameliorating this source of bias.

For each sample of public pronouncements made by a given party or alliance formation, I counted every word or clause that described an "issue." I defined the term "issue" expansively as meaning any subject that a party identified as a point of collective concern. A party's articulation of an "issue," thus, took one of two forms: (1) the identification of a particular state of affairs as desirable (full employment, mass literacy) or undesirable (corruption, rising prices) and (2) the enumeration of specific policies (employment schemes, more jobs for teachers, the appointment of an anticorruption commission, price control policies) to address this set of affairs. I then grouped these individual issues under one of the seven broad categories included in the survey question: (1) good governance, (2) price rise, (3) corruption, (4) nationalism, (5) social justice, (6) local issues, (7) other. A list of the issues grouped under each broad issue category is contained in Appendix C.

The issue categories used in the survey did not always match the categories that parties used in their self-presentation. In several cases, the categories used in the survey coincided perfectly with the categories that parties used to present their messages. Here I followed the party's self-presentation in deciding how to categorize individual issues. In others, parties only occasionally packaged issues within these broad categories, but otherwise mentioned them individually. Here I also grouped the issues into the broad categories used by the parties themselves, even though these were not often used. In a third set of cases, parties did not use these broad categories at all. Here I relied upon my own judgment in deciding which issues went together under which category. This last, externally imposed categorization is justifiable to the extent that a voter, in answering the survey question, would have performed the same act of recategorization, mentally transferring issues from a party's self-presentation into

Table 9.4. *Party issue positions, 1996*

	Party				
Issue	Congress	BJP	NF/LF	Akali Dal	BSP
Good governance	**95.4**	**30.5**	**57.2**	**52.2**	0
Price rise	.92	1.5	3.0	0	0
Corruption	.92	**17.7**	**20.6**	**17.4**	4.2
Nationalism	**5.53**	**41.4**	0	0	0
Social justice	2.3	3.4	**10.7**	0	**91.6**
Local issues	0	0	0	0	0
Other	1.38	**5.4**	**8.4**	**30.4**	4.2

Source: Content analysis (see Appendix C).

the categories proposed by the interviewer. In some ambiguous cases, respondents may have placed the same issues differently than I have done, or differently from each other. These ambiguities apply mainly to the coding of some issues under the "good governance" category or under the category of "nationalism." As will be clear later on, however, the coding on these two categories does not affect the conclusions I draw from these data.

Once the individual issues had been placed into the broad issue categories, I calculated the number of times words or clauses in any broad issue category were mentioned as a percentage of all words or clauses mentioned in a party's campaign message. This told me whether or not a party took a position on any given issue category, and how much emphasis it placed on it. If an issue category was mentioned less than 5 percent of the time, I concluded that the party did not take a position on it. If an issue was mentioned at least 5 percent of the time, I concluded that the party took a position on it. The 5 percent threshold is chosen to be arbitrarily low in order to strengthen the disconfirmatory power of the test I employ here. By choosing a low threshold of emphasis, I increase the number of issue categories on which it is reasonable to assume that a party took a position. If voters prefer parties that mention the issue category they believe to be important less than 5 percent of the time, we can be fairly confident that party issue positions have no bearing on their preferences.

Table 9.4 summarizes the results of the content analysis. The numbers in each cell represent the percentage of times an issue category was mentioned. The bold numbers represent those issue categories on which the party concerned took a position. All other numbers represent those issue categories on which the party concerned did not take a position.

204

Note that this table does not yield any information about the content of party issue positions. Parties that take a position on "social justice," for example, might take very different positions on the issue. The issue of "social justice" refers to affirmative action for disadvantaged social groups in government employment, educational institutions, and representative institutions. Its lineage can be traced to the implementation of the Mandal Commission report in 1990, which recommended reserved positions for the "other backward classes" in government employment. The affirmative action policies recommended by the Mandal report were widely presented by pro-Mandal politicians as an issue of "social justice," and the term has since become a code word for all forms of affirmative action. The BSP took an extreme position on "social justice," recommending proportional representation for every ethnic category in India in every state institution on the basis of their strength in the population. The NF/LF took a less extreme position, recommending affirmative action for "weaker sections," without defining the percentage of the population involved or the extent of affirmative action benefits. The Congress party and the BJP said little on the issue. When confronted with the issue by the competition, Congress took a strictly limited position in favour of "social justice," recommending affirmative action within the existing framework for Christian Scheduled Castes, who were excluded from the list of affirmative action beneficiaries, but saying nothing about other ethnic categories or about the extension of the scope of affirmative action benefits. And the BJP, when it raised the issue, opposed affirmative action even for Christian Scheduled Castes. Table 9.4 does not capture these differences in the content of party positions.

As the incumbent party, Congress fought the 1996 election on practically a single-point platform, promising "good governance." Good governance, as presented by Congress, included law and order, sound economic policy, agricultural subsidies to farmers, full employment, mass literacy, and a host of rural development schemes. A second issue, faintly emphasized by Congress, was nationalism, invoked by references to the Pakistani threat and the Congress government's ability to respond to it effectively. Not surprisingly, Congress mentioned rising prices and corruption as little as possible. As the incumbent party, it bore responsibility for the price rise. And since many of its senior leaders had been implicated in a corruption scandal on the eve of the election, it was vulnerable to attacks from the opposition based on the corruption issue.

The BJP attacked Congress on the corruption issue. In addition, it promised good governance in terms indistinguishable from those used by Congress, promising sound economic policy, law and order, and rural development. Its principal distinguishing issue was nationalism. The BJP attempted to present itself as the party championing "cultural nationalism," in which it included many of its traditional Hindu nationalist promises, including the building of a temple in the north Indian town of Ayodhya, the introduction of a uniform civil code for all religious groups, a ban on cow slaughter, and developing a nuclear deterrent against Pakistan.

The National Front/Left Front and the Akali Dal both emphasized good governance, in terms indistinguishable from those used by the other two parties; and both attacked Congress on the issue of corruption. The NF/LF distinguished itself from other parties mainly by a position on social justice. The Akali Dal distinguished itself mainly by promises of greater regional autonomy for the state of Punjab, classified in the table as a set of issues belonging to the "other" category.

The BSP ran a single-point campaign in the 1996 election promising Scheduled Castes and all other minority groups a greater share in the government and administration. It described this promise most often using the Hindi term *bhagyadari*, meaning share or participation. However, it also referred to this promise as one of "social justice" or "social transformation."

If Scheduled Caste voters formulated preferences based on party issue positions, then we should see a correspondence between the percentage of Scheduled Castes who believed the issues emphasized by a particular party were important and the percentage who preferred that party. They should prefer those parties that take a position on issues they believe to be important, whether or not these parties have the "right" head count.

III. Head Counts, Issues, and Scheduled Caste Voter Preferences

If all parties had the "right" issue position, and the "right" head count, it would be impossible to distinguish whether voters formulate preferences by counting heads or by assessing the issues. This section shows, however, that at least for Scheduled Caste voters, the parties that have the "right" issue position are distinct from the parties that have the "right" head count, thus making it possible to tell which is a more important influence on voter preferences.

Table 9.5 summarizes the perceptions of Scheduled Caste respondents in Uttar Pradesh and Punjab about the most salient issues in the 1996

Table 9.5. *Scheduled Caste voter assessments of issue salience in Uttar
Pradesh and Punjab, 1996 (combined sample).* Question: What do you
think is the main issue around which the election is being contested
this time? (Read all except 0 and 8): 1 Good Governance, 2 Price
Rise, 3 Corruption, 4 Nationalism, 5 Social Justice, 6 Local Issues,
7 Any Other, 0 No Issue, 8 Don't Know.[a]

Issue	SC% (N = 102)
Don't know/no issue	12.7 (13)
Good governance	16.7 (17)
Price rise	29.4 (30)
Corruption	22.5 (23)
Nationalism	1.0 (1)
Social justice	**6.9 (7)**
Others	10.8 (11)

[a] Note that there is one important ambiguity in this question. The voter
might interpret this question as one asking for what *he* thinks is important,
or he might interpret the question as asking for *what he thinks that others
think* is important. How might this ambiguity affect the response? If
we assume that voters randomly select one or the other interpretation,
this should affect the number of voters who interpret the correction
"correctly" but not the distribution of responses. A smaller sample would
produce more imprecise results, but it would not produce bias.

Source: Midcampaign survey, 1996.

parliamentary election.[4] Each column summarizes the percentage of voters
who think that any given issue category is salient. The numbers in paren-
theses refer to the numbers of voters corresponding to the percentages.
The samples for Uttar Pradesh and Punjab, which represent identical cases
for the purpose of this test, have been combined in order to increase the
precision of the estimates. (The distribution of voter responses is identical
when the two samples are taken separately.)

Since only two parties took a position on "social justice," we can make a
clear prediction at least about the preferences of Scheduled Caste voters who
believed "social justice" to be the most important issue. In Uttar Pradesh
and Punjab, only 6.9 percent of the sample of Scheduled Caste respondents
believed that "social justice" was important. If Scheduled Caste voters in

---

[4] The sample here refers not to all Scheduled Caste respondents but only to those who
were interviewed in both waves of the survey, and only to those who reported a party
preference. For this reason, the sample size is significantly smaller than it might have been
otherwise.

Table 9.6. *Party preferences of Scheduled Caste voters in Uttar Pradesh and Punjab, 1996.* Question: Is there any political party that you consider to be close to you? (Yes/No) If yes, which party is it?

Party	% Who Prefer Party (N = 102)
BSP	67.6
BJP	11.8
NF/LF	10.8
INC	9.8

Source: 1996 post-poll survey.

Uttar Pradesh and Punjab formulated preferences based on an assessment of party issue positions, then only this 6.9 percent should prefer the BSP in these two states (and possibly less, assuming that some of these voters might prefer the NF/LF). Those who believed that "good governance," "price rise," and "corruption" were important issues should prefer one of the several non-BSP parties that took a position on these issues, although we may not be able to predict which of these specific parties they should support. However, if Scheduled Caste voters formulated preferences by counting heads, we should expect the majority to prefer the BSP in both states.

The data on Scheduled Caste voter preferences in Uttar Pradesh and Punjab reveal striking evidence in support of the proposition that the preferences of Scheduled Caste voters are not related to their assessments of party issue positions. Table 9.6 summarizes the preferences across parties of those Scheduled Caste respondents in Uttar Pradesh and Punjab who reported the perceptions of issue salience above. Although fewer SC voters thought the BSP's plank on social justice was more important than any other single issue, more Scheduled Caste voters (67.6 percent) preferred the BSP to any other party. And although the overwhelming majority of Scheduled Caste respondents thought that other issues, taken up by other parties, were more important, less than a third of Scheduled Caste voters expressed a preference for one of these other parties.

Figure 9.1 describes the preference distribution of Scheduled Caste respondents according to the issue category they believed was the most salient. As the figure indicates, the majority of those who thought that "good governance" was the most salient issue in the 1996 election, and who therefore

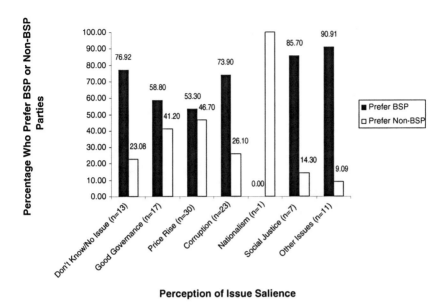

Figure 9.1. Preference distribution of Scheduled Caste respondents in UP and Punjab, 1996 parliamentary elections. *Source:* 1996 post-poll survey.

should have preferred any one of the non-BSP parties, preferred the BSP. Similarly, a majority of those who believed that "price rise" was the most important issue, and who therefore should have preferred one of the parties in the competition, preferred the BSP. The same is true of those who believed that any other issue category was salient (except for the one respondent who believed that "nationalism" was the most salient issue). Even those who had no opinion on issues or thought that no issue was important had a clear preference for the BSP. When most Scheduled Caste voters prefer a party that does not take a position on the issues they deem to be important over all parties that do, it seems relatively clear that their preferences are not based on a consideration of party issue positions. On the other hand, the distribution of preferences above is consistent with the hypothesis that voters formulate preferences based on head counts.

The failure of Scheduled Caste respondents to consider party issue positions in choosing among parties, it is important to point out, does not stem from a lack of information about these issue positions. An extraordinarily high percentage of Scheduled Caste respondents in UP and Punjab (60.5 percent) had direct contact with one or more campaign instruments

Table 9.7. *Party preferences of Chamar*
and non-Chamar voters in Uttar Pradesh
and Punjab, 1996 (combined sample)

Party	Chamars (%) (N = 30)	Non-Chamars (N = 15)
BSP	80	40
BJP	6.7	6.7
INC	0	6.7
JD/SP	13.3	40
Other	0	6.7

Source: 1996 post-poll survey.

(door-to-door canvassing, election rallies, radio, TV, or newspapers).[5] This is only slightly lower than the figure for the general population (72.2 percent). And if we consider also the indirect transmission of information about the campaign, the percentage of voters who may have heard of these issue positions is likely to be much higher. Although most Scheduled Caste voters can be expected to have had access to information about party issue positions, they chose to discount such information.

A further test of whether voters formulate preferences based on head counts comes from an examination of the difference in preference distributions among caste categories *within* the aggregate Scheduled Caste category. The preceding chapter pointed out that Chamars in both Uttar Pradesh and Punjab were much better represented at the upper levels of the BSP hierarchy than other Scheduled Castes. If Scheduled Caste voters formulate preferences based on head counts, then we should find that Chamars are more likely to prefer the BSP than other castes, independent of their position on issues. Table 9.7 summarizes the preferences of Chamars and non-Chamars across parties in Uttar Pradesh and Punjab. As the table indicates, Chamars are more likely than non-Chamars to prefer the BSP. Because the sample size of both subgroups is too small to permit reliable estimates, the data cannot be taken as an independent test of the proposition. It is illuminating, however, as a confirmation of patterns revealed in the broader sample of Scheduled Caste respondents.

[5] 1996 post-poll survey (N = 380 for combined sample of UP and Punjab).

IV. Head Counts and Voter Preferences across Ethnic Categories and across Elections

The evidence in the preceding section focused only on Scheduled Caste voters and only on the 1996 elections. Do voters from other ethnic categories formulate preferences in the same way, or is there something unique about Scheduled Caste voters? And does this hold true for other elections, or is there something unique about the 1996 election? Certainly, if we look at the previous elections in India, they appear to have an "issue-based" quality: Mrs. Gandhi's populist slogan *Garibi Hatao!* (Abolish Poverty!) is routinely given credit for her victory in the 1971 elections; the Janata Party's anti-Emergency platform is believed to be responsible for the rout of Congress in the 1977 elections; the anticorruption platform on which opposition parties fought the 1989 parliamentary election appears to have been at least partly responsible for their success; the BJP's promise to build a Ram temple at Ayodhya seems to have been responsible for the surge in its performance in the 1991 parliamentary elections, especially in the states of Uttar Pradesh and Gujarat; and the Telugu Desam's promise of a rice subsidy is generally seen to be the cause of the surge in voter support for that party in the 1994 assembly elections in Andhra Pradesh.

Survey data that would permit us to explore voter perceptions of issue salience and voter preferences across parties in India are not available for most elections before 1996.[6] Instead, I rely here on evidence from interviews with politicians conducted across four elections between 1996 and 1998 to show that the proposition that voters formulate preferences based on head counts applies not only to Scheduled Caste voters but to voters from all ethnic categories in India, and not only to the 1996 parliamentary elections but generally across Indian elections. Ideally, this proposition should be investigated across repeated elections over a longer time period. However, two features of these data should give us some confidence that they represent a typical pattern. First, these data cover four elections, both parliamentary and assembly elections (the 1996 parliamentary election, the 1996 assembly election in the state of Uttar Pradesh, the 1997 assembly election in the state of Punjab, and the 1998 parliamentary election). Second, the elite interviews, although conducted between 1996 and 1998, reflect

---

[6] The only comparable national election survey was conducted in 1971. However, the sample size for the 1971 survey does not permit a similar analysis of subgroup preferences across states.

accumulated learning over past elections about how voters formulate preferences. Because the data reflect the lessons of previous elections, and because
they yield the same results across four successive contemporary elections,
it is reasonable to expect that the patterns they reveal are typical.

Interviews with political entrepreneurs are an indirect but illuminating
way of ascertaining how voters formulate preferences across parties. Political entrepreneurs invest significantly in learning how voters formulate
preferences, since their own survival and advancement depend upon it. For
this reason, we should expect their perceptions to reflect reality accurately.
I found, in interviews with politicians across parties, across national and
local arenas of politics, across different types of elections, and across different types of constituencies, an overwhelming consensus that the identity
of party personnel was more important than the issues that the parties
stood on.

Let me start with those responsible for coordinating the national-level
campaigns of the major parties in the 1996 parliamentary campaign. According to a member of the BJP's central election management committee
in 1996: "People do not vote on issues they say they care the most about."[7]
According to a member of the party's manifesto committee and publicity
committee: "In India, people do not cast their vote, they vote their caste."[8]
A senior leader of the Janata Dal concurred. "Politics," in his words, consists, not in discovering the "right" *issue* dimensions, but in "constructing
the 'right' *alliances*" between parties with different head counts.[9] The actions of Kanshi Ram, the leader of the BSP, reflect this consensus better
than words. Although he stated the party's "official" position on a range of
issues when questioned by journalists, the BSP did not even bother to print
an election manifesto during the period under study. The most striking aspect of these admissions is that they come from precisely those individuals
responsible for defining the issues that their parties stand for and trans-
mitting them to the electorate. At the end of this section, I address the
obvious puzzle of why, if politicians believe their issue positions do not
matter, they take issue positions at all. Why not simply turn the election
campaign into a description of the identity of party personnel? Here, however, it is sufficient to note that it is because these admissions are made by

---

[7] Interview, Pramod Mahajan, June 11, 1996, New Delhi.
[8] Interview, V. N. Gadgil, April 7, 1996, New Delhi.
[9] Interview, V. P. Singh, April 15, 1996.

those charged with publicizing their parties' issue positions that we should give them considerable weight as evidence.

What about politicians at the constituency level, where votes are actually won and lost? If candidates believe that voters formulate preferences based on their issue positions, then they should present themselves as the champions of the most advantageous issues in their election campaigns. On the other hand, if candidates believe that voters formulate preferences by matching their own identities with those of the party that they represent, then they should deemphasize issues but emphasize the match between the ethnic identity of the voter and that of the party.

Interviews with candidates and campaign workers in twenty constituencies conducted during the four election campaigns support the latter prediction. The list of constituencies in which interviews were conducted is described in Appendix B. The constituencies differ from each other on every significant dimension: region (the list includes constituencies from eight states in northern, eastern, western, and southern India), degree of urbanization (the list includes constituencies located in India's main urban centers, including Bombay, Calcutta, and Bangalore, as well as constituencies in districts with some of the smallest urban populations in the country, including Gonda, Mainpuri, and Hoshiarpur), socioeconomic profile, competitive configuration, political history, and ethnic demography. It is precisely this wide range of variation that makes the findings more convincing. Despite the important differences between them, I found in almost every case that party workers from all parties – ethnic, nonethnic, and multiethnic – believed that the ethnic identity of their party and candidate was more important than the issues that they stood on.

The following extract from an interview at the party office in Mainpuri parliamentary constituency in western Uttar Pradesh is typical of the Congress party strategy across constituencies:[10]

KC: Can you tell me about the issues you are emphasizing in this election campaign?

Congress worker: There are two types of Yadavs in this constituency: Ghosi Yadavs and Kamaria Yadavs. Our candidate is Ghosi and Mulayam Singh Yadav [the SP candidate] is Kamaria.

KC: And what issues will your candidate emphasize?

Congress worker: Caste is our only issue.

---

[10] Interview, April 11, 1996, Mainpuri.

The leading candidate in Mainpuri was Mulayam Singh Yadav, the leader of the Samajwadi Party, which belonged to the NF/LF alliance in Uttar Pradesh. Had the Congress party campaign in Mainpuri wanted to undercut Yadav's support by activating new issue dimensions, there were plenty of issues that they might have emphasized. Yadav had been the former chief minister of Uttar Pradesh and might have been attacked by Congress on a range of controversial policies that he had enacted as an incumbent.[11] Instead, however, Congress chose to attack Yadav by activating a latent subdivision within the Yadav category. Yadavs were the single largest ethnic category in Mainpuri parliamentary constituency and were believed to be strong supporters of Mulayam Singh Yadav. The Samajwadi Party gave more positions to Yadav leaders in Uttar Pradesh than any other political party in UP, and certainly more than the Congress party. A head count based on the Yadav category would clearly have given Mulayam Singh an edge. The Congress party, therefore, attempted to maneuver itself into an advantageous position by activating fissures between "Ghosi Yadavs" and "Kamaria Yadavs," which would show Congress to be more "representative" than the SP.

Note that the line of questioning in this interview, as in the other interviews, reflects a bias in favour of issues. My first question encouraged the respondent simply to list the issue positions emphasized in the Congress campaign, whether or not he thought these issue positions were important to voters. When the respondent answered with a statement about the ethnic identity of the Congress candidate, my second question led him back to the identification of issue positions. Despite questions that were biased toward finding the opposite result, the ethnic identity of the candidate emerged as the most important component of the local election campaign.

The Congress worker in Mainpuri is typical of workers from other parties in other constituencies. In Dausa constituency in Rajasthan, the Congress candidate was Rajesh Pilot, a former Congress minister who had forged a reputation for himself for, among other things, his handling of the Kashmir issue, his position on "secularism," and his criticism of corruption in the Congress party. Had he chosen to, he might have marketed himself in this constituency on any of these issues. Instead, his campaign emphasised his identity as a Gujjar in a constituency where Gujjars constituted a sizable proportion of the electorate. According to one of his campaign

[11] These include the affirmative action policies adopted in local body elections and the repeal of the anticopying act.

214

workers: "Caste is our silent appeal here."[12] In Katra Bazaar assembly constituency in eastern Uttar Pradesh, the defeated Congress candidate attributed his defeat not to his taking the "wrong" issue positions but to his being from the "wrong" caste category: "We are very few, at most 500 in Katra. This was my biggest minus point. In an election where caste and community is everything, people from my community were simply not numerous enough."[13] Even Manmohan Singh, the former Congress finance minister, who was credited with the introduction of India's economic liberalization programme, found his policy credentials irrelevant to his campaign in the 1999 parliamentary elections. His BJP opponent criticized him "because his daughters had married Hindus and suggested that Mr. Singh's turban be removed to see if he really had unshorn hair like a true Sikh." The rejoinder of a Congress party campaigner to this charge was to cast similar aspersions on the BJP candidate: "Why doesn't the BJP man drop his trousers so we can see if he's a Hindu or a Muslim?"[14] Issues clearly had little to do with this debate. The only constituency in my sample where the primacy of head counts over issues in the Congress campaign did not clearly appear was the city of Bombay, where the Congress candidate devoted considerable time to spelling out his party's position on economic policy. Bombay was a prominent exception. In all other constituencies, including constituencies situated in the cities of Bangalore and Calcutta, the party's ethnic identity was clearly more important to voters than what the party stood for.

The BJP, like the Congress party, attempted to publicize the match between its party personnel and its target ethnic categories. The only difference between the strategies of the BJP and Congress was the BJP's uniform exclusion of Muslims. While Congress targeted different ethnic categories across constituencies, including in some constituencies those it excluded in others, the BJP targeted only Hindus. However, since all political parties in each of the states studied here were dominated by Hindus, the BJP attempted to distinguish itself by emphasizing the caste or linguistic identity of its candidates. In Dharwad constituency, in Karnataka, for example, a BJP campaign worker was forthright: "We are collecting Hindus and that is all."[15] Among Hindus, he emphasized that the BJP had nominated a Lingayat candidate in order to court the support of the numerous Lingayats

---

[12] Interview, Dausa, April 3, 1996.
[13] Interview, Katra Bazaar, October 9, 1996.
[14] *New York Times*, September 15, 1999.
[15] Interview, April 19, 1996, Hubli.

in the constituency. In Dhandukabad, in Gujarat, similarly, BJP campaigners sought the support of "every one apart from Muslims."[16] And among
Hindus, it sought the support particularly of the Kohli Patels, the most
numerous category in that constituency, by emphasizing that a Kohli Patel
candidate had recently been elected to the district *panchayat* (village council)
on a BJP ticket. In Latur constituency, in Maharashtra, BJP workers also
sought to emphasize the match between their candidate and the Maratha
ethnic category, which they estimated to be one of the two most numerous
categories in Latur constituency. When asked why voters should vote for
the BJP candidate rather than for the Janata Dal candidate, who was also a
Maratha, they emphasized not issue-based differences, but further divisions
within the Maratha category. According to them, "the Janata Dal candidate
is not native." As a Maratha from outside the constituency, they believed
that he would have less appeal among Marathas in Latur looking for their
"own" man.[17]

The BSP is perhaps the most open of all parties about courting voter
support directly by matching the ethnic identity of its party personnel with
the ethnic identity of its target voters. Before each election, the BSP party
office routinely released an ethnic profile of its party organization and candidates to the press and to its campaign workers, in lieu of a manifesto.
And these lists were then used as the centrepiece of the party's election
campaign. The following extract from a speech by BSP leader Mayawati
illustrates the BSP's use of this strategy during the 1998 elections:[18]

There are eighteen seats in this state reserved for Scheduled Caste candidates. But
the BSP has given 21 seats to Scheduled Castes, 3 more than the 18 seats reserved
for them by the constitution. Among these 21 seats, we have given 5 to the Pasi
community, 1 to the Dhobi community, 1 to the Kori community, 1 to the Khatik
community and 13 seats to the Chamar community.

I want to tell my Muslim brothers also that this time, the BSP has given the single
largest number of seats in Uttar Pradesh to Muslim candidates. We allotted these
seats to Muslims where the Muslim *Samaj* [community] had at least two lakh votes.
In all these constituencies, the votes of the Dalit Shoshit Samaj [literally translated
as the "oppressed people," this is in practice a term synonymous with Scheduled
Castes in Uttar Pradesh] will be cast for these candidates in any case. If in all these
constituencies the two lakh Muslim votes come to us as well, then I can assure

[16] Interview, April 24, 1996, Dhandukabad.
[17] Interview, April 21, 1996, Latur.
[18] BSP election rally, Sahranpur, February 14, 1998.

216

you that all of the fourteen candidates from the Muslim community will become members of parliament.

...I want to tell my Backward Caste brothers that your population in Uttar Pradesh is also very large. The Bahujan Samaj party has given the slogan: *"Jiski Jitni Sankhya Bhaari, Uski Utni Bhagyadari"* [Each group will get a share in power equal to its proportion in the population]. Keeping this in mind, since the population of the backward castes is greater than all other castes in Uttar Pradesh, we have given them 35 seats. My Saini brothers will be happy to hear that in the neighbouring seat of Muzaffarnagar, we have given the seat to Rajaram Saini....In addition, we have also given opportunities to other communities related to the Sainis: the Maurya community, the Shakya community, the Kashyap community, and the Kushwaha community in other parts of Uttar Pradesh.

As the speech indicates, the BSP sought the support of Scheduled Caste voters by allotting tickets to Scheduled Caste candidates. However, because this speech was made in a constituency in which the majority of Scheduled Castes had already massed behind the BSP, while the support of others was more uncertain, the BSP underplayed the level of Scheduled Caste representation at higher levels in the party and concentrated on matching candidates and voters from other ethnic categories. The BSP's method of campaigning, furthermore, relied on highly segmented methods of building support, so that members of each ethnic category were encouraged to approach others of their "own" kind but not to build cross-ethnic support. As a BSP candidate put it: "Our strategy is that our SC brothers are here to convince SCs, Yadavs to convince Yadavs, and Kurmis to convince Kurmis."[19]

The components of the NF/LF followed the same strategy. When asked how the JD was appealing to its target voters, a JD campaign worker in Bangalore North constituency focused mainly on the identity of his party and candidates.[20] The JD targeted Muslim voters by emphasizing that C. M. Ibrahim, the recently appointed state JD president, was the first Muslim to be appointed state president of any party unit in Karnataka. The party also emphasized that Jaffer Shareif, a prominent Muslim congressman denied a ticket for this election, was supporting the JD indirectly. The votes of at least a portion of the backward castes, he expected, would come to the JD because of the local candidate, who was a Vokkaliga. It is not that the JD did not mention issues to its target voters. When asked what issues his party was emphasizing, he noted that "secularism" was the most important plank

[19] Interview, February 1998 parliamentary elections.
[20] Interview, April 18, 1996, Bangalore.

of his party. The *credibility* of the promise to promote secularism, however, was underlined by pointing to the prominent positions given to Muslims in the state leadership.

The sample of constituencies examined here includes only a sprinkling of communist candidates. Data from secondary sources, however, suggests that even the communists, whom we might have expected to target class categories on the basis of economic issues, construct their strategy based on the perception that voters formulate preferences based on head counts rather than issues. In a 1956 study, Selig Harrison argued that the Communist Party built its base in Andhra Pradesh by successfully manipulating tensions between the two dominant castes in Andhra Pradesh, which were then the Kammas and the Reddis. The Reddis in Andhra, according to Harrison, gravitated toward Congress. The Kammas, meanwhile, found a home in the Communist Party. According to Harrison, "since the founding of the Andhra Communist party in 1934, the party leadership has been the property of a single subcaste, the Kamma landlords, who dominate the Krishna-Godavari delta."[21] Kamma voter support followed, and "a significant section of the Kammas plainly put their funds, influence, and votes behind the Communist Kamma candidates."[22] In Kerala, the communist parties, although initially dominated by high-caste Nairs, broadened their leadership to include members particularly of the Ezhava caste. By 1967, according to Hardgrave, six of the eleven top party leaders of the CPM (Communist Party of India [Marxist]) "came from the depressed castes (5 Ezhavas and 1 Harijan).... At the district and local levels, CPM leadership resides predominantly within the hands of the lower-caste cadres."[23] The CPM in Kerala had recognized the importance of caste early in its electoral strategy, and the incorporation of Ezhava and other low-caste leaders was

---

[21] Selig Harrison, "Caste and the Andhra Communists," *American Political Science Review*, Vol. 50, No. 2 (1956): 381. Myron Weiner, in *Party Building in a New Nation: The Indian National Congress* (Chicago: University of Chicago Press, 1991), subsequently argued that Kammas were not concentrated solely among the communists but also in Congress. This does not undercut the main point here, however, which is that Kammas should prefer the Communist Party because it represented their category, rather than because of the issues it stood on. If we find later that Kammas were distributed between the Communist and Congress parties, then it follows that Kamma support should be distributed between them, even though their policies might be radically different.

[22] Harrison, "Caste and the Andhra Communists," 395.

[23] Robert Hardgrave, "The Kerala Communists: Contradictions of Power," in Paul R. Brass and Marcus F. Franda, eds., *Radical Politics in South Asia* (Cambridge, MA: MIT Press, 1973), 133.

a deliberate attempt to recruit support from voters who belonged to these categories.[24] In West Bengal's parliamentary elections in the 1996 parliamentary election, a CPM politburo member highlighted his party's effort to court Scheduled Caste support by fielding seven Scheduled Caste candidates in "general" constituencies.[25] Similarly, in the Punjab assembly elections in 1997, a CPM politburo member argued that in order for the CPM to expand its base among Scheduled Castes and Backward Castes, the CPM leadership needed to incorporate individuals from these categories into leadership positions.[26]

Let me address, finally, the puzzle that this consensus in party strategies raises: If voters choose between parties based on a head count, and political entrepreneurs know this, then why do they devote time and resources to staking out irrelevant positions on issue dimensions? In Mainpuri constituency, the Congress worker was blunt: The caste of the Congress candidate was his party's only issue at the constituency level. Why would politicians in all parties not follow suit at higher levels and simply dispense with campaign committees, manifestos, and policy statements devoted to publicizing issue dimensions?

In part, the answer lies in legal and normative constraints. The Election Commission of India forbids the overt use of caste or communal rhetoric to court votes. According to the code of conduct issued by the Election Commission: "No party or candidate shall indulge in any activity which may aggravate existing differences or create mutual hatred or cause tension between different castes and communities, religious or linguistic. . . . There shall be no appeal to caste or communal feelings for securing votes."[27] Since the speeches of national leaders and other overt methods of campaigning are easily policed, political parties are compelled to raise issues through these overt channels. The message about the ethnic identity of party personnel is then transmitted only at the constituency level, which is more difficult to police.

Legal and normative constraints, however, are not the entire answer. Why would parties comply with legal and normative constraints that

---

[24] For Ezhava support for the communists, see T. J. Nossiter, *Communism in Kerala* (Berkeley: University of California Press, 1982); and Lloyd I. Rudolph and Susanne H. Rudolph, *The Modernity of Tradition* (Chicago: University of Chicago Press, 1967).

[25] Interview, May 5, 1996, Calcutta.

[26] Interview, February 11, 1997, Chandigarh.

[27] Election Commission of India, *Model Code of Conduct for the Guidance of Political Parties and Candidates* (Delhi: Election Commission of India, 1998), 1.

damage their interests by forcing them to blunt their electoral strategies? The explanation for their compliance, and for the variation in their degree of compliance, I argue here, lies in strategic considerations. Parties that seek to build differentiated ethnic coalitions, with different in-groups and out-groups in different constituencies and states, have an incentive to stake out issue positions at the more visible levels of politics, which they can then guarantee at the local level by emphasizing the ethnic identity of the party personnel. For such parties, an issue position serves as a "cover" under which to send out targeted messages about party personnel at the constituency level. Congress, which relies on an aggregation of various coalitions, normally adopts this strategy, as do the parties in the NF/LF alliance. Congress, therefore, does not have an incentive to challenge these norms.

For ethnic parties, however, which seek to build uniform ethnic coalitions with the same in-group and the same out-group in all constituencies, announcing their ethnic identity clearly is a viable strategy. We should expect such parties to challenge the legal and normative constraints described here. The BJP, for example, complied with these norms in the early 1980s, only to jettison them in the latter part of the decade. The BSP also used the rhetoric of ethnic identity overtly in its campaigns between 1984 and 1998. It is only as the BJP and the BSP began to broaden their initial support base, and to transform themselves slowly from ethnic to multiethnic parties, that they resorted to the strategy of abandoning overt ethnic messages.

V. Conclusion

If the argument proposed here is correct, then two implications follow for those concerned with studies of elections and voting in India and cross-nationally. In the past, studies of parties and elections in India have interpreted electoral victories and defeats as evidence of voter response to party issue positions. The argument here suggests that we should reinterpret these victories and defeats as resulting from a change in the representational profile of political parties and alliances, or from a change in the categories with which voters identify, rather than from a change in party issue positions. It suggests, for instance, that in explaining Mrs. Gandhi's electoral success in 1971, we should look beyond the *Garibi Hatao!* (Abolish poverty!) issue – which in any case is no different from the standard promises of every political party in India in every election – to changes in the representational profile of Congress prior to the election campaign. Preliminary evidence points to major changes in the ethnic profile of the Congress party organization, including the rise of Backward Castes and Scheduled Castes in Karnataka (described in Chapter 11) and the elevation of backward caste leaders in Punjab (including Zail Singh, who was made chief minister in 1972) and Gujarat. Similarly, it suggests that the reasons for the success of the Janata Party in the 1977 elections, the success of the BJP in 1991, and the success of the Telugu Desam in 1994 lie not in the issues that each party or alliance represented, but in changes in the ethnic categories that each party or alliance attempted to represent prior to the election. Further, it suggests that cross-national research on party politics and voting behaviour should be sensitive to the importance of ethnic categorizations rather than issue dimensions in guiding party strategy and voter choice in India and other patronage-democracies.[28]

---

[28] For examples of research that include India in cross-national investigations of party issue positions, see John Huber and Ronald Inglehart, "Expert Interpretations of Party Space and Party Locations in 42 Societies," *Party Politics*, Vol. 1, No. 1 (1995): 73–111; and Ian Budge and Dennis Farlie, *Voting and Party Competition* (London: Wiley, 1977).

10

Why SC Voter Preferences Translate into BSP Votes

Where we are strong, people will vote for us: there is a wave effect.[1]

First we were very resistant to the BSP people – we said Ambedkar [the Scheduled Caste leader from whom the BSP derives its ideology] is not a God so why should we believe in him. Most people here supported the Congress. Then later we shifted – there was no benefit from Congress for this village, and then, Congress was also getting weak.[2]

The previous chapter showed that the preferences of Scheduled Caste voters across parties correspond directly to their representational profile. In this chapter, I argue that for substantial numbers of Scheduled Caste voters, preferences do not automatically translate into votes. Even though they prefer the BSP, these voters are likely to vote for the BSP only when they expect their vote to install the BSP in government, or to affect the victory or defeat of one of its competitors. Where they do not expect to be able to affect the outcome in one of these two ways, they are unlikely to vote for the BSP. These Scheduled Caste voters, in other words, are strategic rather than expressive actors: They treat the vote as an instrument through which to obtain the best possible outcome rather than as an opportunity to declare their preferences. This chapter does not offer a precise estimate of the proportion of strategic voters among Scheduled Castes. However, it does provide evidence to indicate that this proportion is substantial, and that without the support of such voters, the BSP could not obtain majority support among Scheduled Castes.

---

[1] Interview with BSP state-level leader in Delhi, March 6, 1998.
[2] Interview with Scheduled Caste respondent in Uttar Pradesh, December 1, 1997.

Expectations of efficacy, in turn, depend upon the distance between the numerical strength of the Scheduled Castes in the electorate and the threshold of winning or leverage imposed by the competitive configuration. Scheduled Castes know that others from their category also prefer the BSP to other parties. They also know that those groups not represented by the BSP (or its partner, where it contests elections in alliance) are not likely to prefer the BSP. Simply by counting heads in their constituency and in their state as a whole, therefore, they have the capacity to make some prediction about the efficacy of their vote. If the proportion of Scheduled Castes in the electorate is large enough to carry the BSP past the threshold of winning or leverage, then Scheduled Caste voters know that coordinated action on their part will give their vote efficacy. Consequently, they should coordinate successfully in voting for the BSP. However, where Scheduled Castes are too few to enable the BSP to cross the threshold either of winning or of leverage, they know that their vote will be ineffectual. In this scenario, strategic voters fail to coordinate in voting for the BSP.

I test the hypothesis that substantial numbers of Scheduled Castes vote strategically using multiple sources of data drawn mainly from Uttar Pradesh and secondarily from Punjab. The chapter relies more heavily on Uttar Pradesh because of the superior availability of data on Scheduled Caste voting patterns over time in this state. Elections in Punjab were postponed in 1989, and boycotted by the Akali Dal, the main opposition party, in 1992. As a result, there are fewer data points for this state. Finally, because the BSP was not a viable electoral competitor in Karnataka, it is excluded entirely from the analysis.

The principal alternative to the strategic voting hypothesis is proposed by Donald Horowitz, who describes ethnic voting as an expressive act, driven by strong psychological attachments and not subject to cost-benefit calculations.[3] According to him, "irresistible" pressures from such expressive voters force political entrepreneurs to form ethnic parties even when such parties have little prospect of electoral success and therefore little chance of giving their target ethnic group control of the state.[4] Perhaps because of the relative lack of systematic micro-level data on ethnic voting patterns, little empirical research so far has actually tested this

---

[3] Donald Horowitz, *Ethnic Groups in Conflict* (Berkeley: University of California Press, 1985).
[4] Horowitz, *Ethnic Groups in Conflict*, 307. See also pp. 306–311 on the growth of ethnic party systems.

proposition.[5] EI, the method of ecological inference developed by Gary King, opens up new possibilities for obtaining data on ethnic voting across time and space (elaborated in Appendix E).[6] This chapter, therefore, takes advantage of EI to generate constituency-level data on ethnic voting in order to test the hypotheses of expressive and strategic voting against each other.[7]

The chapter is organized as follows. Section I lays out the rationale for expecting substantial sections of Scheduled Castes to be strategic rather than expressive voters. Section II tests the hypothesis that Scheduled Castes are more likely to vote for the BSP in those constituencies where they expect to exercise "leverage" than where they do not, based on an EI analysis of constituency-level data on Scheduled Caste voting patterns in Uttar Pradesh. Section III tests the observable implications of both hypotheses further, using ethnographic data from election campaigns and survey data from the Indian National Election Studies. Although none of these tests permit a precise estimate of the volume of strategic voting, each independently supports the hypothesis that significant numbers of Scheduled Caste voters vote strategically. Section IV, the conclusion, outlines the implications of the argument presented here for the literature on ethnic mobilization and strategic voting. By "strategic voting," I mean voting for one's preferred party only when such a vote has a probability of producing a desired outcome, and for some other party when it does not.[8] By "expressive voting," I mean voting without regard to the expected outcome.

I. Why We Should Expect Strategic Voting among Scheduled Caste Voters in Uttar Pradesh

In Uttar Pradesh, prior to 1984, members of Scheduled Caste categories were underrepresented in positions of power in all political parties,

---

[5] For work in progress, see Karen Ferree, "Ethnicity and Strategic Behaviour: Split Ticket Voting in Durban 1994," paper presented at the Laboratory in Comparative Ethnic Processes, Duke University, March 23, 2000.

[6] Gary King, *A Solution to the Ecological Inference Problem* (Princeton, NJ: Princeton University Press, 1997).

[7] See Appendix E for a description of data problems in studying strategic voting, and for a discussion of the possibilities of solving at least some of these problems using EI.

[8] This definition is adapted from John W. Galbraith and Nicol C. Rae, "A Test of the Importance of Tactical Voting: Great Britain 1987," *British Journal of Political Science*, Vol. 19 (1989): 126.

notwithstanding the presence of Scheduled Caste legislators from "reserved constituencies." Faced with a choice between parties in which they were equally underrepresented, Scheduled Caste voters in Uttar Pradesh voted for the ruling Congress party. Once the BSP presented itself as a viable option on the electoral market in Uttar Pradesh, Scheduled Caste voters had two possible choices: to defect to the BSP or to remain with Congress. Since the BSP was staffed mostly by co-ethnics, especially at the higher echelons of the party organization, SC voters preferred the BSP to the Congress party, which was dominated by Hindu upper castes.

If Scheduled Caste voters in UP vote strategically according to the model outlined in Chapter 4, they should defect to the BSP based on the magnitude of the difference between the benefits given to them by Congress, if it wins or obtains influence (b_2); the benefits given to them by the BSP, if it wins or obtains influence (b_1); and the BSP's probability of winning or obtaining influence (p).

The Value of b_1 and b_2 for Scheduled Caste Voters

As I argued in Chapter 6, Scheduled Castes in Uttar Pradesh, and in India more generally, are among the social groups most dependent upon the discretion of the elected officials who control the state. There is some variation, however, in the degree of dependence upon the state among Scheduled Castes. Eighty-eight percent of the Scheduled Caste population in Uttar Pradesh reside in rural areas;[9] 79 percent are illiterate;[10] and 58 percent live below the poverty line and have no access to land.[11] This poor, landless, rural, and illiterate majority among Scheduled Castes is most dependent upon the state. Forty-two percent of Scheduled Castes in Uttar Pradesh have access to land as independent cultivators, sharecroppers, or tenants.[12] Twenty-one percent of Scheduled Castes in Uttar Pradesh are literate.[13] A small middle class among Scheduled Castes either is self-employed or, through affirmative action policies, has obtained government employment. This minority of "better-off" Scheduled Castes and

[9] *Census of India 1991.*
[10] Ibid.
[11] *Basic Rural Statistics 1996; Census of India 1991.*
[12] *Census of India 1991.*
[13] Ibid.

their dependents rely to a lesser degree upon the discretionary power of elected officials.

Congress party rule in Uttar Pradesh favoured the upper castes who dominated the Congress party organization.[14] However, it also gave Scheduled Castes limited access to the numerous political favours they required from those in control of the state (b_2). Further, the election of Scheduled Caste legislators from the Congress party from "reserved" constituencies accorded Scheduled Caste voters a small degree of psychic satisfaction, even though these legislators were largely excluded from positions of power in the Congress party organization and governments.

The benefits (b_1) that Scheduled Castes might expect from voting for the BSP if it is in a winning position or influential position are larger. The BSP has consistently promised to give first priority to Scheduled Castes in its governing agenda. As Mayawati put it: "My single aim is to ensure that work meant for Dalits [Scheduled Castes] gets done. Everything else is towards that goal."[15] Even as a member of a coalition government, the BSP has acted aggressively to protect Scheduled Caste interests, enacting laws giving Scheduled Castes greater access to land, implementing existing provisions protecting Scheduled Castes from discrimination and violence, penalizing bureaucrats for not being sufficiently responsive to Scheduled Caste voters, and earmarking development funds primarily for Scheduled Castes. For many Scheduled Castes, furthermore, the installation of a Scheduled Caste chief minister in the state for the first time also conferred the psychological benefits that come from having control over the lives of individuals from upper-caste categories.

When the BSP does not win but exercises "leverage" over someone else's winning or losing, voting for the BSP is also likely to bring with it benefits larger than b_2. By voting for the BSP in close races, Scheduled Caste voters indirectly put one candidate in a winning position or deny victory to another. As a broker for Scheduled Caste votes, the BSP leadership can then extract concessions from the winning candidate as a reward, or bargain with the losing candidate by holding out the possibility of the reversal of the verdict in the next election. Scheduled Caste voters here exercise their influence *indirectly*, by voting for the BSP and affecting a third party's

---

[14] Paul Brass, *Factional Politics in an Indian State* (Berkeley: University of California Press, 1965); Zoya Hasan, *Quest for Power: Oppositional Movements and Post-Congress Politics in Uttar Pradesh* (Delhi: Oxford University Press, 1998).

[15] *India Today*, September 22, 1997.

electoral outcome. As a collection of individuals or small groups, they have little to offer either candidate, and little capacity to enforce the delivery of benefits in return. But by throwing their combined strength behind the BSP and delegating to it the power to act as a "broker" for their consolidated interests, Scheduled Caste voters have greater influence over the electoral outcome, and greater power to extract and enforce the delivery of patronage benefits. At the same time, by reversing the customary roles of overlord and suppliant between the Scheduled Caste voter and the upper-caste candidate whose political fate he controls, such influence also provides enhanced self-esteem.

So far, I have not discussed the possibility of obtaining psychic benefits simply through the *act* of voting for the BSP, even if the BSP is a clear loser. Does the act of voting for the BSP not provide Scheduled Caste voters with at least *some* psychic satisfaction? They are engaging, after all, in an act of self-affirmation by openly rejecting the authority of those who belong to the dominant castes. For most Scheduled Caste voters, however, the act of voting is simply one episode in a series of interactions with the authority of the dominant group in which they continue to play a subordinate role. Their subordination in these other arenas is a powerful force in creating and maintaining low self-esteem. According to Clark, individuals "whose daily experience tells them that almost nowhere in society are they respected and granted the ordinary dignity and courtesy accorded to others will, as a matter of course, begin to doubt their own worth."[16] As a one-day interruption in this broader set of interactions, an act of rebellion at the polling booth is an insignificant source of self-esteem. An ineffectual vote, rather, is likely to compound feelings of inferiority further by underlining not just the material and social subordination of Scheduled Castes, but also their political impotence. As a statement from one Scheduled Caste attests, there is little capacity for self-assertion without political power: "If we send our man to parliament, whether he becomes the PM or sits in the opposition, he can speak up for us. But if we don't get a seat there, how will we be heard?"[17]

I have argued that Scheduled Castes can reasonably expect to gain greater material and psychic benefits when the BSP is in a winning or influential position (b_1) than otherwise (b_2). The magnitude of the difference

[16] Cited in Henri Tajfel, *The Social Psychology of Minorities* (London: Minority Rights Group, 1971), 10.

[17] *Economic and Political Weekly*, October 9, 1999.

between b_1 and b_2, however, is likely to vary with the degree of economic subordination of individual Scheduled Castes. The poorer and more vulnerable among the Scheduled Castes risk economic and social retaliation by upper-caste landlords for their defiance in voting for the BSP. In one district in Uttar Pradesh, for example, Scheduled Caste labourers who voted for the BSP were prevented by Brahmin landowners from entering their farms. "There is no need for you to come to our farms anymore," they were told. "Why don't you go and work in Mayawati's farms?[18] For an economically vulnerable population, the economic losses sustained in everyday life by voting for the BSP may reduce the net benefit b_1 and therefore the magnitude of the difference between b_2 and b_1. For better-off Scheduled Castes, however, who are less vulnerable to economic retaliation by upper-caste employers, the magnitude of the difference between b_2 and b_1 is likely to be greater. The value of p that is high enough to induce strategic Scheduled Caste voters to vote for the BSP, therefore, is likely to vary. The greater the economic subordination of Scheduled Caste voters, the smaller the magnitude of the difference between b_2 and b_1 is likely to be. Such voters should defect to the BSP at higher levels of p than the Scheduled Caste middle class, for whom the magnitude of the difference between b_2 and b_1 is likely to be large.

Estimating p

How might Scheduled Caste voters formulate expectations about whether the BSP is likely to win power and about whether voting for the BSP is likely to give them leverage, or whether their vote is likely to be wasted? Few Scheduled Caste voters in Uttar Pradesh have access to opinion polls. According to a postelection survey conducted by the Center for the Study of Developing Societies in India, 82 percent of Scheduled Castes do not read the newspaper; 52.4 percent profess that they do not listen to the radio; 63.4 percent report that they do not watch TV; and 76 percent claim not to have seen or heard of the opinion polls predicting the election outcome.[19] It

---

[18] Interview, November 30, 1997. Because this respondent belonged to the Congress party and had no stake in misreporting, his account is more credible than it might have been had it come from a BSP voter, who might have wanted to exaggerate the retaliation.

[19] CSDS post-poll survey 1996 (N = 380). These figures are slightly lower than those for the general population in Uttar Pradesh and Punjab, of which 66.7 percent do not read the newspaper, 45 percent do not listen to the radio, 48.9 percent do not watch TV, and 69.5 have not heard of the polls (N = 1,627).

would be a mistake to conclude from this lack of access to the mass media, however, that these voters lack information about the preferences of others and so lack the means to engage in strategic behaviour. If voters formulate preferences across parties by counting heads belonging to their ethnic group across parties, then sufficient information is available about other voters' preferences and probable voting behaviour independent of opinion polls and election surveys. Here, the Scheduled Caste voter attempting to figure out how others' preferences are distributed needs simply to count heads belonging to each ethnic category in the general population and then to identify the party that members of each ethnic category are likely to prefer by counting heads in the party apparatus. He can then infer the probable electoral outcome if all voters vote sincerely, and formulate his own strategy accordingly. Polls and surveys certainly increase the available information about ethnic demography and voting patterns. However, voters have a great deal of knowledge even in their absence. Scheduled Caste voters could make a similar assessment of the likely electoral outcome at the level of their individual constituency, based on the ethnic demography of the constituency and the ethnic profile of parties competing in that constituency.

II. "Leverage" and Scheduled Caste Voting Behaviour

This section presents a test of the model of strategic voting based on constituency-level voting patterns among Scheduled Castes in three consecutive elections for the state legislative assembly in Uttar Pradesh between 1984 and 1991. The BSP contested each of these three elections without an alliance partner. In most constituencies, the Scheduled Caste population was not numerous enough to take the BSP to a winning position and therefore to permit it to be a viable contender for control of the state government. However, in several constituencies the Scheduled Caste population was large enough to exercise leverage over the victory or defeat of another party's candidate. If the majority of Scheduled Caste voters vote strategically, then we should see a substantially larger proportion of Scheduled Castes voting for the BSP in constituencies where they believe the probability of exercising leverage is high than in constituencies where they believe it is low. If the majority is voting expressively, on the other hand, there should be no difference in the level of Scheduled Caste support for the BSP between these two categories of constituencies.

The estimates of constituency-level voting behaviour used here are generated using EI, which estimates the voting behaviour of individuals in each constituency by borrowing strength from aggregate data on demography and voter behaviour for all constituencies taken together.[20] Appendix E provides information about how to evaluate my use of the EI method.

The data set I use here is comprised of electoral variables, variables coding the ethnic identity of BSP candidates, and demographic variables for the 425 legislative assembly constituencies in the state of Uttar Pradesh for the 1984, 1989, and 1991 legislative assembly elections. The BSP also contested legislative assembly elections in the state in the years 1993 and 1996. However, because it contested these elections in alliance with other parties, it is difficult to obtain accurate estimates of the percentage of Scheduled Castes who voted for the party in these elections.

The electoral data were compiled from official reports published by the Election Commission of India and also from BSP official publications.[21] Data on the ethnic identity of BSP candidates for each election were compiled through interviews. Data on demographic variables at the constituency level in India are normally unavailable, with one important exception: Following the delimitation of constituencies in 1976, the Election Commission of India published figures on the percentage of Scheduled Castes in each constituency. The data set also includes, therefore, constituency-level demographic data on the percentage of Scheduled Castes.[22] Data on all other demographic variables are available only for the "district," which in India is a census unit that does not coincide with electoral constituencies. Each district, however, perfectly contains between one and fourteen assembly constituencies. For each constituency, therefore, I use data on demographic variables from the district to which it belongs as a rough indicator of the demographic profile of the constituency. These data can disguise significant variation in the demographic profiles of constituencies within a district. However, they are the best available source of information.

In order to test this hypothesis, I first categorize each constituency in each election according to whether or not Scheduled Castes can reasonably expect that voting for the BSP would give them a high probability of

---

[20] King, *A Solution to the Ecological Inference Problem*.

[21] Since the BSP was not officially registered in 1984, BSP candidates are listed as "independents" in the official results. I used the March 1986 issue of *Oppressed Indian*, an internal party publication, to match the identity of "independents" with BSP candidates.

[22] Obtained from the data archive of the National Election Studies Project, Centre for the Study of Developing Societies, New Delhi, India.

exercising leverage. The measure of leverage, L_{it}, that Scheduled Castes have in constituency (i) for an election at time (t) is constructed as follows:

$$L_{it} = X_i - M_{i(t-1)}$$

where X_i is the percentage of Scheduled Castes in the electorate of constituency (i) (which remains constant across elections), and $M_{i(t-1)}$ is the margin of victory in constituency (i) in the previous election (i.e., winner's vote share − runner-up's vote share in constituency (i) in the election at time $(t-1)$). I treat the margin of victory in the previous election as an indicator of the likely distance between the winner and the runner-up in the current election. This assumes that the structure of party competition and the relative strength of each party in each constituency is roughly constant across these elections. While this assumption may not always hold in practice, it is the analyst's best guess about how close the current race is likely to be in the absence of detailed information on a constituency-by-constituency basis. Where the percentage of Scheduled Castes in the constituency equals or exceeds this margin ($L_{it} >= 0$), they can reasonably expect to have a high probability of affecting the electoral outcome through coordinated action. Where the percentage of Scheduled Castes in the constituency is below this margin ($L_{it} < 0$), they can expect to have a low probability of affecting the outcome, even through coordinated action.

I pool the data across elections in order to increase the number of observations. In order to control for other variables that might affect support for the BSP among Scheduled Castes, I then restrict this pooled sample in three ways.

First, I select only those constituencies in which the BSP is contesting at least its second election. In the first election in any constituency, the BSP is likely to be organizationally weak, and may not have had sufficient time to transmit information about itself to Scheduled Caste voters. By the second election, however, the BSP would have acquired an electoral history in the constituency as well as a minimum of at least five years to build its local party unit and to organize voters. This selection criterion, therefore, allows us to control for variation in the organizational strength of the BSP.

Second, I select only those constituencies in which Chamars, the Scheduled Caste category best represented in the BSP, are in a majority. In an unrestricted sample, evidence of strategic voting would be less convincing, since it could be attributed to the behaviour of underrepresented Scheduled Castes who in any case have less reason to behave expressively. Restricting the sample to Chamar-majority constituencies, however, allows us

Table 10.1. *Demographic profile of Scheduled Castes across samples (district-level data)*

	Literate (%)	Urban (%)	Cultivators (%)	Labourers (%)	In Trade or Commerce (%)
Sample 1 $L_{it} < 0$	24.24	16.42	10.37	12.45	.82
Sample 2 $L_{it} >= 0$	22.51	13.81	11.35	13.34	.71

Source: Census of India 1991.

to conduct a stronger test of strategic voting by determining whether or not substantial numbers of even the best-represented caste categories vote strategically rather than expressively.[23]

Third, I restrict the sample to those constituencies in which the BSP fields a Scheduled Caste candidate. This restriction allows us to control for possible effects on the Scheduled Caste vote introduced by fielding local candidates from a different caste category. It also permits more reliable estimates of Scheduled Caste voting patterns (see Appendix E for details).

The restricted sample is then split in two. Sample 1 consists of constituencies where Scheduled Caste voters have a low probability of exercising leverage by voting for the BSP (i.e., $L_{it} < 0$). Sample 2 consists of constituencies where Scheduled Caste voters have a high probability of exercising leverage by voting for the BSP (i.e., $L_{it} >= 0$). Scheduled Caste voters across the two samples, viewed as an aggregate, do not differ in any other significant way. Had reliable demographic data been available at the constituency level, we could have controlled directly for the influence of these demographic variables through regression analysis using constituency-level data. However, in the absence of such data, we can ascertain whether or not Scheduled Castes in the two samples differ by looking at the demographic profiles of Scheduled Castes in the districts (the census units) from which the constituencies are drawn. Table 10.1 summarizes the demographic profile of Scheduled Castes across districts included in the two samples. As the table indicates, there is no substantive difference between the demographic profiles of Scheduled Castes in the two samples. Nor is there any geographical variation between the two samples. Constituencies that belong to the same districts and the same geographical regions are found in both samples.

If substantial numbers of Scheduled Castes are voting strategically, then the mean vote for the BSP in Sample 2 ($L_{it} >= 0$) should be substantially higher than in Sample 1 ($L_{it} < 0$). In addition, the percentage of

[23] The results are the same for the unrestricted sample.

Table 10.2. *Leverage and Scheduled Caste voting behaviour*

	N	Mean Percentage of Scheduled Castes Voting for the BSP	% of Constituencies in which a Majority of SCs Vote for the BSP
Sample 1 (BSP has no leverage)	34	40.4%	35%
Sample 2 (BSP has leverage)	87	51.1%	46%
Difference in means		10.72%	11%
Level of significance (one-tailed test)		.05	.05

constituencies in which the BSP wins majority support among Scheduled Castes in Sample 2 ($L_{it} >= 0$) should also be substantially higher than in Sample 1 ($L_{it} < 0$). On the other hand, if Scheduled Castes are voting expressively, then there should be no significant difference in either quantity across samples. Note, however, that we might certainly expect some Scheduled Castes to vote for the BSP even in Sample 1, which is composed of those constituencies with a low probability of exercising leverage. These votes could come from better-off Scheduled Caste voters who were willing to defect to the BSP at low values of **p**. Further, we might expect some strategic voters to simply miscalculate, given the prevailing uncertainty about electoral outcomes.

Table 10.2 summarizes the differences in the two quantities of interest across samples, based on EI estimates. The data show that the percentage of Scheduled Castes voting for the BSP in those constituencies in which it has a high probability of exercising leverage is higher by 10 percent than in those constituencies where it has a low probability. The percentage of constituencies in which the BSP obtains the support of a majority of Scheduled Castes is higher by 11 percent in those constituencies in which Scheduled Caste voters have a high probability of exercising leverage than where they do not. In both cases, the differences are significant, substantively and statistically (at the .05 level). The data therefore indicate that at least 10 percent of Scheduled Caste voters are voting strategically.

Note, however, that even in those constituencies in which Scheduled Caste voters have a low probability of exercising leverage, 40 percent, on average, vote for the BSP. Without individual or at least constituency-level data on the economic characteristics of these voters, we cannot identify whether these voters are (1) expressive voters who vote for the BSP regardless of its probability of winning or exercising leverage or (2) strategic voters from "better-off" groups among the Scheduled Castes within these districts who are simply willing to defect to the BSP at lower probabilities than others, based on a higher estimated difference between b_1 and b_2. Thus, while we can ascertain that significant strategic voting is occurring based on these data, we cannot ascertain its volume more precisely.

III. Testing Additional Observable Implications

This section derives additional observable implications from the strategic and expressive voting hypotheses and tests them using ethnographic and survey data from the states of Uttar Pradesh and Punjab for the period 1996–98. The ethnographic data are drawn from tape recordings of speeches made by BSP leaders during election campaigns in the states of Uttar Pradesh and Punjab. The survey data are drawn from four consecutive election surveys conducted in these states between 1996 and 1998. Survey data that coincide exactly with the 1984–91 period for the state of Uttar Pradesh would have been valuable but unfortunately are not available.

BSP Election Campaign

If the majority of Scheduled Castes vote strategically, then we should find further evidence for the argument presented here in the election strategy of the BSP. Kanshi Ram has been the BSP's principal spokesperson and strategist in each election throughout the period 1984–98. We might expect him, therefore, to adjust his election strategy to respond to the voting behaviour of his target constituency. If large numbers of Scheduled Caste voters vote strategically in the manner predicted by the argument made here, then he should attempt to convince voters that the probability of winning or obtaining influence is high by constructing an advantageous ethnic demography and encouraging voters to believe that others will vote in the BSP's favour. On the other hand, if Scheduled Caste voters are predominantly expressive in their behaviour, then he should exhort them to vote for the BSP mainly on the basis of ethnic solidarity or emotion or ideological conviction rather than efficacy. Especially because the population of Scheduled Castes is typically not large enough for the party to win an election on its own, and often not large enough even to influence the electoral verdict in a single

234

constituency, we should expect Kanshi Ram and other BSP campaigners to sidestep the issue of winning and influence altogether.

The BSP's election campaigns across time and space are more consistent with the first argument than the second. During each election, Kanshi Ram presents Scheduled Caste voters with a precise goal for the election and offers a clear road map showing how this goal might be reached. When the degree of influence of Scheduled Caste voters varies across constituencies, regions, and states, he is meticulous about identifying where they have greater leverage. Consider, for instance, the following verbatim extract from Kanshi Ram's speech in the parliamentary seat of Sahranpur in Western Uttar Pradesh, where he stood for election in 1998.[24]

What is our goal for this election? The BJP and its allies had 193 seats in parliament. From 193, they tried to buy MPs and form the government. So why are we fighting the election from all 85 seats in Uttar Pradesh? Because our goal is that in Uttar Pradesh we can reduce the BJP's seats by 25. On its own, the BSP can reduce the BJP's seats by 25–30. In this way, in Madhya Pradesh, we can reduce the BJP's seats by 15. In Bihar, we have left the field open for Laloo Prasad Yadav because he can reduce the 20–25 seats the BJP has there. In Punjab, we have allied with Congress to get the BJP's seats reduced, and not to permit it to form the government. In this way, we have decided to fight the elections jointly with Chaudhury Devi Lal in Haryana. In Karnataka, we have joined hands with Bangarappa in order to ruin the BJP. And in Gujarat, we are giving Waghela unconditional support, so that he can continue to do his work and defeat the BJP in Gujarat. In Uttar Pradesh, we have given our workers the responsibility to get the BJP trounced in all 85 seats.... Here in Sahranpur, you are in the position to destroy the BJP. We have made arrangements that the BJP should not be in a position to win more than 100 seats so that after the election when they have less than a hundred MPs, they will not be in a position to form the government by buying MPs.

It is especially significant that Kanshi Ram sent this message from his own parliamentary platform in Sahranpur. The parliamentary contests in which national political leaders are candidates attract nationwide media attention. National political leaders typically use their own platforms to make lofty symbolic statements, leaving the nitty-gritty of voter arithmetic to other speakers in less conspicuous contexts. Kanshi Ram's decision to send a nationwide message outlining the precise numbers of seats in which the BSP had leverage in each state suggests that he believed such information to be useful to Scheduled Caste voters.

---

[24] Transcript of speech from a BSP election rally in Sahranpur, February 14, 1998.

As another example, consider Kanshi Ram's address to Scheduled Caste crowds in Hoshiarpur district in the state of Punjab, inaugurating the BSP's election campaign for the state legislative assembly. To form a government in Punjab, he informed voters, any single party needed approximately 60 of the 117 seats in the state's legislative assembly. "We cannot win all these seats," he said candidly. "However, our goal is not to let anyone else win 60 seats."[25] He exhorted voters to aim to win twenty to thirty seats in Punjab and to "spoil" enough election victories in other constituencies to ensure that these twenty to thirty seats gave it influence in the coalition government that he predicted was certain to result.

These examples are typical of the BSP's election campaign for the entire period under study. Since its first elections in 1984, Kanshi Ram has repeatedly portrayed the party as a party with the strength to make others lose. The BSP newspaper wrote, interpreting its first election results in the states of Uttar Pradesh and Punjab in 1985: "Even though the BSP's own candidates did not win anywhere in the legislative assembly election, the 2.44% of votes that it received were important in getting Congress to lose in the districts of Western Uttar Pradesh. . . . Congress was forced to relinquish many seats in Punjab because the votes of Scheduled Castes and backward castes went to the BSP in Punjab."[26] The frequent repetition of messages like these, whether or not they are true, creates a perception among both Scheduled Castes and candidates from other parties that their votes are efficacious.

It is typical, furthermore, to find attempts in Kanshi Ram's speeches to construct a favourable ethnic demography and to present Scheduled Caste voters with scenarios based on this demography that suggest that the probability of obtaining his stated goal through coordinated action is high. In a speech delivered in the state of Uttar Pradesh in July 1996, for instance, he noted: "Realistically, we can aim for about 41 percent of the vote in UP. We have 50 percent of all the SC [Scheduled Caste] votes. If all the SCs vote for us, our target will be fulfilled . . ." (speech at Lucknow, July 30, 1996). Similarly, he noted in Hoshiarpur that if all the caste categories listed under the "Scheduled Caste" category voted together, "we will win all seats in Hoshiarpur, we would get more than 50 percent of the votes" (speech at Hoshiarpur, January 25, 1997). In both cases, Kanshi Ram presented an optimistic picture of the efficacy of Scheduled Caste votes. The Scheduled

---

[25] Transcript of speech from a BSP election rally in Hoshiarpur, January 25, 1997.
[26] *Bahujan Sangathak*, January 12, 1987 (translation mine).

Castes constituted 21 percent of the population of the State of Uttar Pradesh and 33 percent of the population of the district of Hoshiarpur. If Scheduled Castes were guessing about the efficacy of their votes based on percentages in the population, they would probably have guessed lower. However, Kanshi Ram chose to manipulate the uncertainty between "true" population figures and turnout rates in order to inflate the percentage of Scheduled Caste voters, thus making his optimistic assessment credible.

Throughout these and other election speeches, Kanshi Ram presents himself as a self-described "scientist" making a careful assessment of the likely outcome of the election and the Scheduled Castes' efficacy in bringing about this outcome. If most Scheduled Castes voted expressively, such painstaking attention to electoral arithmetic and election forecasts would be difficult to explain. Expressive voters should vote for the BSP based on its identity as a Scheduled Caste party, and should be indifferent to whether or not their vote makes any difference to the outcome. Indeed, we should expect a leader addressing expressive voters to present himself as an ideologue rather than as a scientist. Kanshi Ram's demeanor and the content of his speeches, however, are consistent with the view that Scheduled Caste voters vote strategically. It makes sense for a leader addressing strategic voters to dwell at length on the mathematics of obtaining influence or victory. In the world of strategic voting, a forecast of the election result can be self-fulfilling if voters believe that the forecast is reasonable and adjust their voting behaviour accordingly.

Timing of Decision

The election campaign typically transmits information to voters about the competitiveness of different parties at the constituency and state levels. If Scheduled Caste voters formulate expectations about the election results by counting heads, they are likely to have significant information about the preferences of other voters prior to the campaign. However, as already noted, this process still generates considerable uncertainty. Which categories should voters use to make the head count? Which way will the underrepresented voters vote? Where voters from the same ethnic category are represented in more than one party, which way are they likely to lean? Election campaigns transmit precisely such information. For those voters who are strategic, the information transmitted during the campaign is valuable. It permits them to update their expectations about the competitive configuration and, if necessary, to adjust their voting decisions accordingly.

Table 10.3. *Timing of decision: Scheduled Castes in Uttar Pradesh and Punjab.*
Question: When did you make up your mind about whom to vote for?

	Average (%)[a]	1996 Parliamentary, UP and Punjab (%)	1996 Assembly, UP (%)	1997 Assembly, Punjab (%)	1998 Parliamentary, UP and Punjab (%)
Sample Size	NA	N = 380	N = 1,224	N = 1,180	N = 313
During campaign	37.6	57.4	32.4	30.3	57.1
Before campaign	53.52	21.8	57.6	64.6	32.3
Can't say/NA	9.52	20.8	10	5.1	10.6
TOTAL	100	100	100	100	100

[a] Weighted by sample size.

Source: 1996 post-poll survey; 1996 exit poll (Uttar Pradesh); 1997 exit poll (Punjab); 1998 post-poll survey.

For those voters who are expressive, however, such information is irrelevant, since their voting decisions are independent of the competitive configuration. One test of whether significant percentages of Scheduled Caste voters are voting strategically, therefore, is to look at when Scheduled Caste voters arrive at their voting decisions. The higher the percentage of voters who decide during the campaign, the higher the percentage of strategic voters is likely to be. Conversely, the higher the percentage of voters who decide before the election, the higher the likely percentage of expressive voters.

The second column in Table 10.3 describes the average percentage of Scheduled Caste voters who made up their minds during and before the campaign across four elections, the April 1996 parliamentary elections, the October 1996 legislative assembly elections in Uttar Pradesh, the 1997 legislative assembly elections in Punjab, and the 1998 parliamentary elections. The remaining columns report the figures for each election individually. For the parliamentary elections, I use a combined sample of Scheduled Castes in both Uttar Pradesh and Punjab. For assembly elections, the sample consists only of Scheduled Caste voters in the state where the election was conducted. I supplement the data on UP here with data from Punjab, where available, in order to increase the size of the sample sufficiently to permit estimates for subgroups such as Chamars. The voting patterns of Scheduled Castes in both states, viewed separately, are similar.

The second column shows that an average of 37.6 percent of Scheduled Caste voters in all elections made up their minds about whom to vote for during the campaign period. This indicates that *at least* 37.6 percent

238

of Scheduled Caste voters are voting strategically rather than expressively. Given the presumption in favour of expressive voting, this is in itself an important finding, since it suggests that the percentage of strategic voters is far higher than theories of ethnic voting would lead us to expect. On average, 53.32% of voters made up their minds before the election campaign. A close look at the figures for individual elections suggests that this may indicate the *upper bound* on the percentage of expressive voters rather than their actual strength. There is a puzzling fluctuation in the percentage of voters who decide during the campaign according to the type of election: In both parliamentary elections, only between 20 and 30 percent report knowing their minds before the election campaign, while in assembly elections, almost two-thirds of Scheduled Caste voters know their minds before the campaign begins. Expressive voters should have known their minds before the campaign in each case. Why do we see greater indecision in the parliamentary elections and less in the assembly elections? One plausible answer may be that voters take more interest in gathering information about assembly elections as a consequence of the greater stake they have in who controls the state government. Consequently, in assembly elections they are likely to be better informed about the competitiveness of parties before the campaign begins. If this interpretation is correct, then the large percentage of voters who know their minds before the campaign in assembly elections may include a large number of better-informed strategic voters, in addition to purely expressive voters. If so, then we can conclude from Table 10.3 that *at least* 37 percent of Scheduled Castes voters, but possibly more, vote strategically.

Table 10.4 replicates Table 10.3 for Chamar voters. If substantial numbers of even the best-represented category exhibit evidence of indecision before the campaign period, this should give us more confidence in the strategic voting hypothesis. The sample for Chamars, I should point out, is considerably smaller than the sample for all Scheduled Castes, and the estimates are correspondingly more uncertain. The table indicates that approximately the same percentage of Chamars, on average, are undecided before the election campaign than the rest of the Scheduled Caste population.

The interpretation of these data assumes that all respondents answered truthfully. In order to assess the reliability of the data, it is important to ask whether this assumption is justified. How do we know that Scheduled Caste voters were not misreporting the time at which they decided to vote? If, as I argue, the vote is an instrument through which voters secure (or lose) benefits, then even those voters who have made up their minds might report

Table 10.4. *Timing of decision: Chamars in Uttar Pradesh and Punjab.*
Question: When did you make up your mind about whom to vote for?

	Average[a] (%)	1996 Parliamentary, UP and Punjab (%)	1996 Assembly, UP (%)	1997 Assembly, Punjab (%)	1998 Parliamentary, UP and Punjab (%)
Sample size	NA	N = 95	N = 449	N = 426	N = 88
During campaign	37.9	58.9	31.6	33.3	69.3
Before campaign	54.4	23.2	60.1	62	22.7
Can't say/NA	7.7	17.9	8.3	4.7	8
TOTAL	100	100	100	100	100

[a] Weighted by sample size.

Source: 1996 post-poll survey; 1996 exit poll (Uttar Pradesh); 1997 exit poll (Punjab); 1998 post-poll survey.

being undecided, out of fear of disclosure. If their decision were revealed, it might encourage candidates to give up on them instead of bidding for their support.

The data I rely on here were purposefully chosen to minimize such incentives to misreport. In each case, I use data from the surveys administered *after* the election rather than before. Had the data reflected information gathered during the campaign, we might have expected voters to pretend to be undecided even if they were not, and so to encourage bids for their support. However, once the election campaign is over, voters have no such incentive to misreport. Furthermore, voters were not asked to tell the interviewer which party they voted for. They were simply asked to mark a ballot paper that resembled the ballot paper for the actual elections and deposit it in a box, without naming the party directly. Since they were only required to tell the interviewer when they had made up their minds but not whom they had voted for, we can be more confident that they would have had few incentives to lie.

Vote Switching in Different Competitive Configurations

A third test of strategic and expressive voting comes from studying the impact of the different competitive configurations introduced by alliance formation on Scheduled Caste voting behaviour. Forming an alliance affects the BSP's prospects of winning control of the state government, and this is also true of other parties. At the same time, alliances formed between other parties in the electoral arena affect the electoral prospects of the BSP. If Scheduled Caste voters are voting expressively for the BSP, then such changes in the competitive configuration should have no effect on their voting behaviour. The same proportion of Scheduled Caste voters who vote for the BSP when it stands alone should vote for it when it is in alliance. Similarly, the same proportion of Scheduled Caste voters who vote for the BSP when the competition stands alone should continue to vote for the BSP when the competition forms an alliance. However, if Scheduled Caste voters are voting strategically, then we should see Scheduled Caste voters switch into the BSP alliance from other parties when it appears to be a likely winner, or to switch away from the BSP to other alliances if these alliances appear to be more viable winners, or both, if the electoral prospects of both are equally uncertain.

In this section, I test whether or not Scheduled Castes switch their votes in different competitive configurations, using data on voting behavior in the April 1996 and October 1996 assembly elections in Uttar Pradesh. The BSP has also repeatedly formed alliances in Punjab, and Scheduled Caste voting behaviour there should be subject to the same logic. However, the question that would allow us to explore the extent of vote switching in Uttar Pradesh was not included in the election survey on Punjab, making it impossible to test the hypothesis using data from that state.

In the October 1996 assembly elections in Uttar Pradesh, the BSP formed an alliance with the Congress party. The BSP-Congress alliance was not the only one in Uttar Pradesh in these elections. The Samajwadi Party was part of the United Front, a broad front of opposition parties. The United Front had also contested the previous parliamentary elections as an alliance. However, it had now been enlarged to include two other parties, the Congress (T) and the Bharatiya Kisan Kamgar Party (BKKP), which had not been part of the alliance in the previous elections. In the unstable electoral atmosphere of Uttar Pradesh, the alliances enhanced the electoral prospects of both formations, although it was not clear by how much. At the same time, the coalescence of the BSP and Congress, on the one hand, and the United Front, on the other, had an uncertain impact on the BJP, which was the only party contesting alone. In some regions, the division of votes between the two alliance formations might improve the electoral prospects of the BJP. However, in others this electoral consolidation might push down the vote share of the BJP. If Scheduled Castes were voting expressively for the BSP, these changes in the competitive arena should have had no impact on support for the BSP among

Table 10.5. *Vote switching between Uttar Pradesh parliamentary and assembly elections, 1996*

	All SCs	Chamars
Percentage who voted for other parties in the parliamentary election but switched into the BSP-Congress alliance in the assembly election	22.7 (N = 203)	28.8 (N = 59)
Percentage who voted for the BSP or Congress in the parliamentary election but for some other party in the assembly election	8.7 (N = 679)	5.4 (N = 294)

Source: 1996 post-poll survey; 1996 exit poll (Uttar Pradesh).

Scheduled Castes. But if Scheduled Castes were voting strategically, then we should see considerable volatility in the BSP support base across the two elections.

A glance at the total percentage of Scheduled Castes voting for the BSP and Congress presents a misleading picture of stability. In the parliamentary elections, the two parties, contesting individually, captured a total of 71.4 percent of the Scheduled Caste vote. In the assembly elections, the alliance captured 73 percent of the Scheduled Caste vote. These totals appear to amount to a simple aggregation of the individual vote bases of both parties. However, this stability in the aggregate figures masks considerable volatility in individual voting among Scheduled Castes. In the exit poll conducted after the 1996 assembly elections, voters were asked which party they had voted for in the assembly elections and which party they had voted for in the parliamentary elections. Table 10.5 summarizes these responses for Scheduled Castes generally, and for Chamars in particular.

As the table indicates, a significant number of those who voted for other parties in the parliamentary election switched to the BSP-Congress alliance in the assembly election, and a smaller number of those who voted for the BSP or Congress in the parliamentary elections switched to other parties in the assembly election. This is true both for Scheduled Castes generally and for Chamars in particular (although, as before, the sample size for Chamars is considerably smaller and the estimates correspondingly more uncertain). This test does not permit us to estimate the percentage of voters voting strategically, since we do not know whether those who continued to vote for the same party remained loyal out of strategic or expressive considerations. However, it does permit us to establish that a significant amount of strategic voting took place in these two elections.

242

How do we know that the responses to the question are reliable? There may be a bias in the responses in favour of consistency. Respondents who have just come out of the polling booth having voted for one party may have an incentive to report that they voted for the same party in the previous elections even when they did not, and thereby to impose a false consistency on their choices. As before, the procedure that interviewers followed in asking respondents about their voting decisions minimizes these incentives to misreport. Voters emerging from the polling booth were first asked to indicate whom they just voted for by marking a ballot paper and placing it into a ballot box carried by the interviewer. The question about whom they had voted for in the previous election was then asked some questions later. Because the two questions were separated, and because the respondent did not have to openly declare an answer to the first before answering the second, we can be fairly confident that the two questions were independently answered. More importantly, however, if the tendency to misreport is caused by a desire to appear consistent, then this should give us even greater confidence in the finding that substantial numbers of Scheduled Caste voters are voting strategically. In the absence of such a bias, we should see more rather than less vote switching.

IV. Conclusion

This chapter has shown, through multiple tests using multiple sources of data, that significant numbers of Scheduled Castes do not vote for their preferred ethnic party unless it is likely to cross the threshold of winning or influence. The estimates of the percentage of Scheduled Castes who vote strategically range from at least 10 percent, based on the EI analysis, to at least 37 percent, based on the survey data presented in Table 10.3. A more precise estimate of the volume of strategic voting in favour of the BSP would require election surveys designed specifically to obtain information on the expected benefits that different groups of voters might expect to receive from across parties. So far, the dominant assumption of expressive voting in the work on ethnic parties has meant that such questions have rarely been asked. The purpose of this chapter has been to show that asking such questions is important to understanding the degree of support for ethnic parties, in India and outside.

The argument here also outlines new areas of inquiry for the literature on strategic voting. This literature has been confined mainly to postindustrial societies, both in its development of models of strategic voting and in their empirical application. By extending this literature to patronage-based democracies, this chapter highlights three important areas of theoretical and empirical investigation.

First, it suggests that in patronage-democracies, the levels of strategic voting may be higher than in postindustrial democracies. The extensive literature on strategic voting in Britain, for example, indicates that the percentage of voters who vote strategically may in fact be quite low. Estimates of the percentage of strategic voters in these studies range from 5 to 23 percent.[27] While the volume of strategic voting in patronage-based societies remains to be established empirically, the logic I outline in this book suggests that the number of voters voting strategically in patronage-based democracies should be significantly higher, since the stakes attached to the vote for large numbers of voters in such democracies are significantly higher.

Second, it suggests that the *type* of strategic voting is likely to differ between patronage-based and postindustrial societies. Cox notes, for example, that strategic voters have no incentive to vote for a locally hopeless party that is nationally competitive.[28] By a locally "hopeless" party, Cox means a party that has no chance of winning. The reasoning is that voters concerned about the efficacy of the vote have no incentive to vote for a locally hopeless party, since such a vote will not change the overall outcome. If voters are primarily motivated by the desire to change the overall outcome, then this reasoning is justified. However, if voters are primarily motivated by the desire to obtain benefits, then they have strong incentives to vote for a party that is competitive at the state or national level even when it is locally hopeless in order to signal the loyalties that would allow them to reap rewards in the form of benefits later. Further, as I have argued, benefit-seeking voters have strong incentives to vote for their preferred party if it promises them leverage at the local level, even if such a party is unlikely to be a local winner.

Finally, the argument here highlights the importance of ethnic demography and the ethnic profiles of political parties as an important variable structuring expectations about probable electoral outcomes. The ability of voters to vote strategically, as Cox points out, depends upon "the availability and clarity of free information regarding the relative standing of

[27] Gary Cox, *Making Votes Count* (Cambridge: Cambridge University Press, 1997), 83–84.
[28] Ibid., 183.

244

candidates."[29] The presumption in the literature on strategic voting is that opinion polls are the principal sources of such information. If this is true, then we should expect the phenomenon of strategic voting to be limited in both space and time: We should observe this phenomenon only *after* the advent of universal literacy and the introduction of election polling in the mass media, and it should be limited mainly to those societies with high levels of literacy and access to such media. However, if ethnic demography and the ethnic profiles of political parties are important sources of information about probable electoral outcomes, then we should expect to find strategic voting to be a more widespread phenomenon, historically and spatially.

[29] Ibid., 79. See also Stephen Levine and Nigel S. Roberts, "Electrons and Expectations: Evidence from Electoral Surveys in New Zealand," *Journal of Commonwealth and Comparative Politics*, Vol. 29, No. 2 (1991): 129–152, and Mark Fey, "Stability and Coordination in Doverger's Law: A Formal Model of Preelection Polls and Strategic Voting," *American Political Science Review*, Vol. 91, No. 1 (1997): 135–147.

11

Explaining Different Head Counts in the BSP and Congress

Previous chapters demonstrated that the success of the BSP among Scheduled Caste voters was contingent upon the representational profile of the BSP and its main competition, the Congress party. This chapter addresses the underlying question: What explains the relative ability of Congress and the BSP to incorporate Scheduled Caste elites across states and across time? Why did Congress incorporate Scheduled Caste elites into its organization and governments to a greater degree in Karnataka than in Uttar Pradesh and Punjab? And in Uttar Pradesh and Punjab, why did it not incorporate these elites even after the emergence of the BSP as a competitive threat? Why did the BSP, avowedly a Scheduled Caste party, not incorporate Scheduled Caste elites from a wider spectrum of caste categories in any of the three states at its point of entry? And why did it not subsequently move to incorporate these elites in order to improve its electoral performance?

In this chapter, I apply the model of elite incorporation developed in Part I to explain the differential ability of both parties to incorporate Scheduled Caste elites across Indian states. The incorporation of Scheduled Caste elites by the Congress party in Karnataka took place during a period when it had a competitive organizational structure. Its switch to a centralized structure following 1972, however, rendered it closed to rising Scheduled Caste elites in other states. The BSP, meanwhile, had a centralized organizational structure since its inception. In each state, therefore, it found it extraordinarily difficult to open itself to new entrants once it acquired an initial core of activists. In Uttar Pradesh, its high probability of winning since 1993 allowed it to compensate for the low probability of ascent and temporarily house elites from different Scheduled Caste categories under the same roof. In Punjab and Karnataka, however, its low prospects of

246

winning, combined with its centralized organizational structure, rendered it closed to new elites.

I. Explaining Differential Incorporation in the Congress Party

Founded in 1885, the Indian National Congress exhibits significant temporal variation in its rules for intraparty advancement. The two defining rules of competitive party organizations (open membership and intraparty elections through majority rule) were introduced into Congress in 1920. This section describes the evolution of these rules and their impact on elite incorporation in the party.

Between 1885 and 1899, Congress was an amorphous "movement" rather than a political party. The first attempt at institutionalization came in 1899, with its first constitution. Between 1899 and 1907, de facto restrictions on membership and the narrow scope of intraparty elections gave Congress the character of a "closed" organization. Congress "membership" during this period consisted of the delegates to the annual sessions. These delegates were to be indirectly elected by "political associations or other bodies and by public meetings."[1] This effectively restricted membership to the wealthy, educated, and high-caste, since during this period it was only individuals with these attributes who were active in associational life or enjoyed public prominence. Limited intraparty elections were introduced for delegates to the National Congress Committee, the apex body of Congress at the time. However, the elected positions were limited to forty of the forty-five members of the National Committee, and no attempt was made to extend the principle of intraparty elections to the provincial congress committees. Except for the forty positions at the apex of the party organization, therefore, success in intraelite competition at higher levels within the party did not require the building of coalitions of support with those at lower levels. And even in cases where faction leaders attempted to build support from below, the de facto restrictions on membership meant that while they enlisted lower-level functionaries within the party in their cause, there was no incentive to recruit new elites from outside the party.

The constitution of 1908 introduced a permanent organizational structure, with a ninety-seven-member All India Congress Committee (AICC) at the apex, followed by the provincial congress committees, district congress

---

[1] Congress constitution of 1899, in N. V. Rajkumar, *Development of the Congress Constitution* (Delhi: All India Congress Committee, 1949), 6–10.

All India Congress Committee (AICC)

Provincial Congress Committee (PCC)

District Congress Committee (DCC)

Other, lower-level bodies

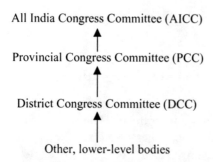

Figure 11.1. The Congress party organization.

committees (DCCs), and then other, lower-level bodies. This structure is illustrated in Figure 11.1.

"Membership" in Congress following 1908, consisted of membership in one or more of these permanent bodies. The membership criteria laid out in the 1908 constitution were open: An individual had only to be twenty-one years of age and to accept in writing the rules and constitution of the Congress in order to be made a member. The principle of intraparty elections was also broadened. With the 1908 constitution, the provincial congress committees were to be elected in part by the district congress committees. In turn, members of the PCCs elected representatives to the AICC from among their members. The provision for election of members of an expanded AICC and the PCCs meant that the principle of intraparty elections had been significantly broadened as compared to 1899. In an important departure from the principle of elections for all party posts, however, the membership of the PCCs consisted not only of those elected by the DCCs, but also of as many delegates to the Congress sessions and as many representatives of Congress-recognized public associations or political bodies as "each Provincial Committee may think fit to determine."[2] This meant, in effect, that factional leaders within the PCCs could bolster their own positions simply by nominating new members from these additional bodies, without having to recruit support from below. As a result, although an open membership rule was introduced, the departure from the principle of intraparty elections meant that an incentive structure that linked factional competition within the party to the incorporation of new elites from the outside was still missing.

[2] Article VII, 1908 constitution in Rajkumar, ibid., 14–34.

The 1920 constitution made intraparty elections the sole method of obtaining influential positions within the party. According to this constitution: "Each Provincial Congress Committee shall consist of representatives elected annually by the members of the District and other Committees in accordance with the rules made by the Provincial Congress Committee."[3] The size of the AICC, furthermore, was now expanded to 350 members, all of whom were elected. References to additional members drawn from public associations or political bodies or delegates were conspicuous by their absence. The only way to obtain and maintain a seat on the PCC, or on the AICC, was through election by the lower levels in the party. The principle of open membership had already been established in 1908. By making intraparty elections the sole channel of advancement within the organization, the 1920 constitution transformed the Congress organization from a closed to an incorporative body.[4] Competitive rules were in effect until 1972, when they were abolished by Indira Gandhi.

In 1920, the Hindu upper castes constituted 73 percent of the All India Congress Committee.[5] The dominance of Hindu upper castes in the national organization was duplicated in the Congress party units at the state level as well. Hindu upper castes, therefore, correspond to ethnic category A in Figure 5.1 for party units in all states. Category B differed from state to state. In Karnataka, as in most of the South, category B was comprised of "non-Brahmins."[6] In Punjab, category B was comprised of

---

[3] Article VI (c), 1920 constitution of Rajkumar (1949), ibid., 47–59.

[4] The 1920 constitution has been widely acknowledged as a major turning point in the history of the Congress party because it introduced measures that significantly affected the subsequent course of the nationalist movement and post-independence politics: the introduction of the "four *anna*" membership rule, which allowed Congress to raise funds through nominal contributions by members; the institution of the Congress Working Committee (CWC), which became the nucleus of power within the organization; and the principle of the linguistic organization of Congress units, which culminated in the linguistic reorganization of the Indian states. The extension of the principle of intraparty elections in 1920, however, has been given less attention than it deserves among this plethora of changes, considering the major impact that it had on the incorporative capacity of Congress and therefore on the character of party competition in India.

[5] Gopal Krishna, "The Development of the Indian National Congress as a Mass Organization 1918-1923," *Journal of Asian Studies*, Vol. 25, No. 3 (1966): 413–430. Estimated with unknowns removed.

[6] James Manor, *Political Change in an Indian State* (Delhi: Manohar, 1977); Eugene F. Irschick, *Politics and Social Conflict in South India* (Bombay: Oxford University Press, 1969); Myron Weiner, *Party Building in a New Nation* (Chicago: University of Chicago Press, 1967).

Sikhs.[7] In Uttar Pradesh, category B was comprised of a collection of cultivating castes alternately labeled *"kisans"* (farmers) and "other backward castes."[8] In each case, the label served to capture a larger coalition than other available labels and so increased the bargaining power of elites vis-à-vis faction leaders in the Congress party. The "non-Brahmin" label in Karnataka included, in its broadest interpretation, the majority of Hindu castes, the untouchables, Muslims, and Christians. In practice, elites mobilizing as non-Brahmins, came principally from elite subcastes within the Vokkaliga and Lingayat caste categories, which constituted a much narrower slice of the population. But by labeling themselves as non-Brahmins, they were able to portray themselves as brokers for the majority of the population. Similarly, Sikhs in Punjab came mainly from the Jat caste. By choosing the label "Sikh" rather than "Jat," however, they identified themselves as representatives of a broader set of interests. By the same logic, "backward caste" elites in Uttar Pradesh came mainly from the Jat and Bhumihar castes, which constituted less than 2 percent of the population. But the use of the broader label allowed them to present themselves as representatives of the interests of more than half the population of Uttar Pradesh.

Between 1920 and 1972, when competitive rules were in effect, the Congress party demonstrated a remarkable capacity to absorb elites from rising ethnic groups while keeping dominant elites acquiescent. Throughout this period, party elections were hotly contested. Evidence of the link between competitive elections and elite incorporation is contained in the fact that each intraparty election was accompanied by a surge in the party membership rolls.[9] In Karnataka, non-Brahmin elites initially organized separately through the Non-Brahmin Federation, a separate political party. By the late 1930s, however, the Non-Brahmin Federation had merged into the Congress party.[10] In Punjab, Sikhs initially organized separately in the Akali Dal. By 1937, however, there was a one-way exodus of Sikhs from the

---

[7] Baldev Raj Nayar, *Minority Politics in the Punjab* (Princeton, NJ: Princeton University Press, 1966).

[8] For a description of the use of the two alternative labels by Charan Singh and the Socialist Party in the 1950s, see Christophe Jaffrelot, "The Rise of the Other Backward Classes in the Hindi Belt," *Journal of Asian Studies*, Vol. 59, No. 1 (February 2000): 86–108.

[9] Susanne Rudolph, *The Action Arm of the Indian National Congress: The Pradesh Congress Committee* (Cambridge: Center for International Studies, 1955); Paul Brass, *Factional Politics in an Indian State* (Berkeley: University of California Press, 1965).

[10] Manor, *Political Change in an Indian State*, 99–104.

Akali Dal to the Congress party. In Uttar Pradesh, cultivating castes initially did not organize separately and were incorporated into the Congress party in the early 1920s.[11]

The degree to which the new entrants displaced old factional leaders within the Congress party differed across the three states depending upon the size of the modernizing pool in each of the three categories. In Karnataka, non-Brahmins effectively eclipsed the Brahmin leadership of the Congress party within a brief period. As Manor describes it:

Some tensions were bound to develop and a few men on both sides withdrew from the organization. But in the light of past antipathies, it is surprising how few deserters there were. When non-Brahmins took control of most district level units of the Congress and used their power in the district committees to achieve dominance over the Working Committee, most Brahmins accepted this.[12]

In Punjab, Jat Sikhs did not displace Hindu leaders entirely, but they gained the upper hand over the course of two decades. In Uttar Pradesh, however, the Jat leader Charan Singh could not similarly displace the upper-caste leadership of the Congress party, since individuals from his target category simply did not have enough educated elites in the party. Even as late as 1962, the cultivating castes constituted only 11 percent of all Congress candidates and only 9 percent of Congress assembly members.[13]

Scheduled Castes were last in line to be incorporated through the process of intraparty competition. This is because the movement of any ethnic category into the party and then up the party hierarchy depends on the size of its educated middle class. The larger this middle class, the greater the ability of elites from this category to displace elites from other ethnic categories higher in the party hierarchy. The emergence of such a middle class among Scheduled Castes, however, was guaranteed to be a slow process. At independence, Scheduled Castes had the lowest literacy rates of all ethnic categories. In addition, the majority of Scheduled Castes were in labour and service occupations, dependent upon upper castes for a living. A large middle class could be expected to emerge among Scheduled Castes only after the government's affirmative action policies in higher education and government employment, introduced in 1950, had had time to take effect.

---

[11] Brass, *Factional Politics in an Indian State.* However, backward caste elites exited the party in 1967 with the defection of Charan Singh.

[12] Manor, *Political Change in an Indian State*, 115.

[13] Ralph Christian Meyer, "The Political Elite in an Underdeveloped Society" (Ph.D. dissertation, University of Pennsylvania, 1969), Table V-5, p. 190.

Assuming that the first wave of beneficiaries of the affirmative action policies would consist of those who entered the educational system after 1950, we should expect the first push for entry into the political system to emerge slowly as this generation came of age. And the displacement of upper-caste elites in the Congress party should have occurred only subsequently, when this first wave of elites had amassed a sufficient following to pull themselves up the factional ladders.

In Karnataka, however, Scheduled Caste elites obtained a head start in the race to the top of the party organization. Recall the data presented in Figures 8.1 and 8.2 (p. 179) on the degree of representation given to Scheduled Caste elites across the three states under study. As those figures indicate, Scheduled Caste elites were equally underrepresented in the Congress party organizations and governments in all three states until 1972. Following 1972, however, we see a divergence in the patterns of representation across states: The posts given to Scheduled Caste elites in Karnataka rose in both number and importance, while the posts given to Scheduled Caste elites in Punjab and Uttar Pradesh remained relatively unimportant.

For most observers of Indian politics, the first explanation that leaps to mind for the earlier ascent of Scheduled Castes in Karnataka than in the other two states is the history of caste-based mobilization during the colonial period. According to this argument, a longer history of caste-based mobilization pushed elites from subordinate caste categories in the South into politics earlier than their counterparts in the North, giving them a head start in their ascent up the Congress party organization and governments. I found this view to be commonly held not only among scholars but also among politicians from these caste categories.[14] It was also my own working hypothesis. But the *timing* of Scheduled Caste ascent within the Congress party organization in Karnataka revealed it to be a mistaken one. If caste mobilization during the colonial period had been the driving force behind the greater representation given to Scheduled Caste elites in Karnataka, we should have seen a divergence in the patterns of representation in the three states from the beginning of the postcolonial period. However, as the two figures indicate, the surge in representation of Scheduled Castes in Karnataka began only in 1972. The explanation for this surge, therefore, cannot be located in the distant colonial past but must be found in postcolonial developments.

---

[14] Interviews in Karnataka, March–April 1997.

I argue here that the head start enjoyed by Scheduled Caste elites in Karnataka was a consequence of the Congress party split in 1969 into Congress (I), led by Mrs. Gandhi, and Congress (O), led by the "Syndicate" (a coalition of regional bosses).[15] The split manifested itself differently across the three states. The leader of the Syndicate, S. Nijalingappa, was from Karnataka and had obtained the support of the majority of party MLAs, MPs, and party office bearers in the state.[16] Consequently, the split resulted in the en bloc defection of the entire front line of the Congress party leadership in Karnataka to Congress (O). In Uttar Pradesh and Punjab, however, the state party units were firm backers of Mrs. Gandhi.[17] A minority faction in Uttar Pradesh, led by Chandra Bhanu Gupta, left Congress (I) after the split. However, in both Uttar Pradesh and Punjab, the split left the party units in these states relatively intact.

The differential impact of the split had a critical impact on patterns of representation of Scheduled Castes in the state Congress party units in each of the states. In Karnataka, the en bloc defection of the Congress leadership to Congress (O) left a yawning leadership vacuum in Congress (I), which sucked Scheduled Caste elites upward before they had acquired the strength to mount an effective leadership challenge themselves. When elections were held in Karnataka in 1972, they were in a position to capture some of the plum portfolios. In Uttar Pradesh and Punjab, however, the split left no such leadership vacuum, and Scheduled Caste elites, not yet strong enough to displace dominant elites from within, remained in a subordinate position. I should emphasize that even in Karnataka, the Scheduled Castes were not the main beneficiaries of the Congress split. Rather, it was sections of the backward castes, placed higher in the Congress hierarchy at the time of the split, who benefited most. However, Scheduled Caste elites were able to capture for themselves a second place in the organization, which they then used to pull themselves and their followers up further.

It is important to note that the split resulted in the ascent of Scheduled Caste elites in the organization *only because it took place in a competitive organization*. The competitive organizational structure in place during the period predating the split had raised Scheduled Caste elites to second and third rungs of leadership within the Congress party organization

---

[15] For reporting on the split, see *Times of India*, November 12 and 23, 1969.

[16] For multiple assessments of the strength of "Syndicate" support in Karnataka (then known as Mysore), see *Times of India*, October 10, 11, 16, 25 and November 23 and 28, 1969.

[17] For assessments of the strength of support for Mrs. Gandhi in these states, see also ibid.

and so positioned them to benefit from the split once it took place. In a centralized system, they would not have risen up the leadership ladder and so would not have been in a position to benefit from the split. Splits within a centralized party, in general, should reproduce the existing leadership profile. The frequent splits in the centralized Lok Dal in Uttar Pradesh are a case in point. A centralized party led initially by a charismatic leader (Charan Singh), the Lok Dal lacked the mechanism to raise new elites within the ranks of the party organization. As a consequence, the ethnic composition of the leadership in the political parties that have emerged from the Lok Dal has been relatively stagnant. Although the party has repeatedly split, recombined, and split again since 1980, the intermediate and backward castes have continued to dominate the leadership each new party fragment. We simply do not see the rise of Scheduled Caste elites in either the Janata Dal or the Samajwadi Party, the two significant parties in Uttar Pradesh that trace their lineage to the Lok Dal.

The 1969 split gave Scheduled Caste elites in Karnataka only a head start in the race for power within the Congress organization over those in Punjab and Uttar Pradesh. Had the process of intraparty competition within Congress continued, we should have expected Scheduled Caste elites in Uttar Pradesh and Punjab to catch up with those in Karnataka over time. In particular, we should have expected Scheduled Castes in Punjab, with the largest numbers and the fastest-rising literacy rates among Scheduled Castes in the country, to have soon produced elites capable of mounting a challenge to the factional leadership from within.

However, the cancellation of intraparty elections in 1972 arrested the process of continuous elite incorporation and froze the leadership in each of the three states. At the point at which the elections were cancelled, Scheduled Caste elites in Karnataka, pulled up during the Congress party split, had already come to occupy important positions in the Congress government and organization. This presented the BSP with a high threshold to cross when it emerged a decade later. In Uttar Pradesh and Punjab, by the time a Scheduled Caste middle class large enough to challenge the ethnic categories in control of the Congress party had emerged, the gates of the Congress party leadership had been closed. Consequently, the Scheduled Caste middle class in these states turned to the BSP instead.

So far, I have explained why Congress incorporated Scheduled Caste elites to a greater degree in Karnataka than in Punjab and Uttar Pradesh prior to the emergence of the BSP. Why, however, did it not react to the competitive threat posed by the BSP by incorporating Scheduled Caste elites subsequently? The answer becomes clear given the framework proposed so far. As I argued earlier, the incorporation of new elites into the party poses a collective action problem that Congress was able to solve only through the introduction of competitive rules. These rules worked to bring about elite incorporation into the Congress party independent of electoral incentives. As long as they were in existence, Congress absorbed new elites regardless of whether or not such absorption was electorally profitable. But in the absence of these rules, elite incorporation did not take place, notwithstanding the electoral incentives. While Congress men in Punjab and Uttar Pradesh saw the advantage of incorporating Scheduled Caste elites into the organization as a whole, each had an incentive individually to resist the entry of these elites into his own party unit in the hope that some other elite would pay the price of such incorporation. Had Congress been in a winning position, it is conceivable that a centralized leadership could have solved the collective action problem at any one point in time by offering selective benefits to Congress men who were most threatened by the incorporation of new elites. As a losing party at both the state and the central level, however, Congress did not possess the resources to offer these benefits. It was thus embroiled in a catch-22 situation: It needed to incorporate Scheduled Caste elites in order to win the election, but unless it won the election, it did not have the capacity to incorporate these elites.

Furthermore, it was not only old elites who were resistant. New Scheduled Caste elites were also reluctant to enter the Congress party. Recalling the equation on p. 101, it is clear that once the Congress organization became centralized, the expected probability of obtaining office through the Congress party was close to zero for these elites. As a result, they remained indifferent toward politics as long as there was no alternative to the Congress party. Once a rival party emerged in the form of the BSP, the threshold that it needed to cross in order to attract these elites was extremely low.

In the following section, I explain why the BSP was itself constrained in its ability to incorporate those elites excluded by the Congress party. Before moving to the BSP, however, one important objection to the argument presented here remains to be addressed. In a recent study of India's party system, Pradeep Chhibber argues that "contrary to most perceptions, there is little evidence that the Congress party had a well developed organization, especially beyond the state level."[18] If he is right, then the explanation for successful elite incorporation obviously must lie elsewhere.

Chhibber's argument challenges the reigning consensus in the scholarship on the Congress party: Every major study describes a well-established party organization before 1972 and an organization in decline thereafter.[19] But the weight of the evidence is insufficient to displace this consensus. Chhibber bases his counterargument upon two separate pieces of evidence: (1) survey data on the views of party activists in 1967 and 1993, where Congress elites at both time periods described their organization as "weak," cited a lack of communication between various levels of the organization, and exhibited lower levels of party identification; and (2) quotations from intraparty documents, which indicate that the Congress party was not well established in princely India (i.e., the areas of India ruled indirectly by the British through their princely rulers), in 1936 and that even in the provinces of British India (i.e., areas administered directly by the British), many districts were without a Congress organization in 1955.[20]

However, the survey data provide at best a measure of elite perceptions of *effectiveness* of the Congress organization in performing unnamed functions. It provides no information about the *extent* of organization across Indian states. Further, the evidence from intraparty documents about the weakness of the Congress organization in princely India in the 1930s does not preclude the subsequent spread of the Congress organization. Manor's study of Mysore state, for example, describes the setting up of a Congress organization in Mysore in 1937.[21] Finally, even in British India, studies of the Congress organization accept that the Congress party orgnization was absent or weak in some districts. They argue simply that the majority of districts across India had functioning Congress organizations, an argument that Chhibber's evidence does not contradict. Macro-level evidence for this claim comes from aggregate data collected by Gopal Krishna in 1921 and 1922, showing that district Congress committees existed in 213 of the

---

[18] Pradeep Chhibber, *Democracy without Associations* (Ann Arbor: University of Michigan Press, 1999), 51.

[19] Rudolph, *Action Arm of the Indian National Congress*; Weiner, *Party Building in a New Nation*; Rajni Kothari, "The Congress System in India," *Asian Survey*, Vol. 4, No. 12 (1964): 1161–1173; James Manor, "Parties and the Party System," Atul Kohli, ed., *India's Democracy* (Princeton, NJ: Princeton University Press, 1988); Brass, *Factional Politics in an Indian State*.

[20] Chhibber, *Democracy without Associations*, 72–78.

[21] Manor, *Political Change in an Indian State*.

220 districts of British India (Krishna makes no such claims about princely India).[22] Micro-level evidence comes from district-level studies conducted by Weiner and Brass, among others, in Gujarat, West Bengal, Uttar Pradesh, Andhra Pradesh, Tamil Nadu, and Karnataka, stretching across eastern, western, and southern India, which describe functioning Congress units.[23] In the absence of convincing evidence to the contrary, therefore, there is no reason to reject the consensus that the Congress party established an organizational structure in most districts from the 1920s onward, although the pace at which this organization developed, and its effectiveness in performing certain functions, may have differed across districts.

II. Explaining the Incorporation of Scheduled Castes in the BSP

Since it is a political party that targets Scheduled Castes, we would have expected that the doors of the BSP's organization would be wide open to Scheduled Caste elites. Furthermore, because the BSP leadership deliberately attempts to mobilize voters by promising representation to each caste from among the Scheduled Castes, we would have expected the BSP's own leadership profile to be representative of elites from across the spectrum of Scheduled Castes. Contrary to expectations, however, the BSP's organizational structure renders it deeply resistant to the incorporation of new entrants.

The BSP had a centralized organizational structure during the 1984–1998 period, which made elite incorporation a zero sum game. The induction of new entrants took place only through the displacement of old ones. Displacement within the BSP's organizational structure, furthermore, carried with it the high risk of being permanent. The incentive structure for elites within the party, therefore, ran directly counter to the electoral incentives facing the party as a whole. Even though the BSP would have benefited from incorporating new elites, any individual elite within the BSP saw the induction of new entrants as a life-and-death struggle and had a strong incentive to resist such entry.

The initial core of the BSP in every state came from Scheduled Caste government employees. Because government employment was typically captured by the most literate castes among the Scheduled Castes, this meant that the BSP, like the Congress, was dominated initially by the early

[22] Krishna, "The Development of the Indian National Congress," 415–417.
[23] Weiner, *Party Building in a New Nation*; Brass, *Factional Politics in an Indian State*.

modernizers among its target ethnic categories. Recall Figure 5.4 which describes the initial composition of a centralized party. For the BSP in the state of Karnataka, category A corresponded to the Holeyas; in Punjab, category A corresponded to the Chamars, where the label "Chamar" includes Adharmis and Ramdassias; and in Uttar Pradesh, category A also corresponded to Chamars, where the label "Chamar" includes the Jatav, Kureel, Dhusia, Jhusia, and Kori caste categories.[24]

Party posts in the BSP were allotted by the party leader, Kanshi Ram, and his close associates by using a combination of predictable and arbitrary criteria. The predictable criterion consisted of allotting posts on the basis of a system of proportional representation. Kanshi Ram awarded posts to "representatives" of each caste category by taking the numerical strength of the caste category into account, paying special attention to those from numerically weak castes.[25] In choosing between aspirants from the same category, he favoured individuals who mobilized greater support *within* their own ethnic category.

The experience of Ram Prakash,[26] one aspirant for a ticket from the BSP, is typical. Ram Prakash's first step was to obtain access to Kanshi Ram. Kanshi Ram asked Prakash to contact him again after "building his base" – i.e., demonstrating support among members of his own Scheduled Caste category, the Dhobis. Prakash consequently began attempting to construct caste networks, visiting areas where members of the Dhobi caste lived, contacting representatives of caste associations, and calling public meetings for his caste men. At the same time, however, Kanshi Ram did not encourage aspirants to mobilize cross-ethnic support. Ram Prakash, therefore, had no incentive to seek out Scheduled Castes other than Dhobis. In fact, to the extent that elites from other caste blocks were similarly mobilizing their own caste men, his own chances of obtaining a ticket were jeopardized.

Whereas a competitive system incorporates new elites by expanding vertical linkages within existing factions, the BSP relied on lateral expansion through the multiplication of monoethnic factions. This is represented in Figure 11.2. The integration of new elites through vertical linkages in a competitive system effectively assigns each new elite a place in a queue

---

[24] The census groups all of these categories, except Kori, together under the same label.

[25] Interview with BSP activist, New Delhi, December 1996.

[26] The name and caste of the respondent have been changed. Based on repeated interviews with the respondent, as well as attendance at events organized to activate these networks, between 1996 and 1998.

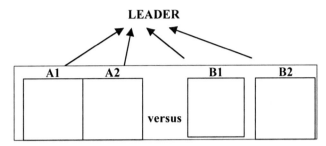

Figure 11.2. Incorporation of new elites through the multiplication of mono-ethnic factions.

for leadership within each faction. In this system, new elites are accommodated by distributing and subdividing *probabilities* of obtaining posts, rather than by expanding the number of posts itself. The BSP organization, however, had no means of assigning probabilities to new elites. New elites were brought in either through the actual provision of new posts or not at all.

The limitations of this strategy quickly become apparent. In the early stages of party building, new elites could be brought in without displacing old ones by the creation of new posts. In one district, for example, the district and block presidents of the BSP came mostly from the Chamar caste. Kanshi Ram inducted a new entrant, from the Saini (backward) caste, not by displacing his Chamar party men from their positions but by creating a new post, "Youth President of the BSP," for the new entrant. Older elites in the party comforted themselves by pointing out that the post of "Youth President" existed only on paper and did not carry any real power within the party. The new entrant, however, saw his post as a sign of recognition from the party president and a foundation on which to build a following. Kanshi Ram employed similar devices at the state level in Uttar Pradesh, through the creation of multiple posts – "State President," "State Convenor," "State Coordinator" – that avoided a power struggle by giving roughly equivalent positions to a number of elites simultaneously. Because the number of offices within a party organization cannot expand infinitely, however, sooner or later this method of incorporation runs into a zero-sum situation, where the induction of any new elites into positions of influence within the party organization necessarily entails the displacement of old ones.

A second mechanism exacerbated the problem of elite incorporation into the BSP. Because Kanshi Ram promised representation to elites on the basis of demonstrated support among their "own" ethnic categories, each of these elites had an incentive to beat the competition by further subdividing the category itself. Imagine two competing elites from group A: A1, who commands the support of 60 percent of the As, and A2, who commands the support of 40 percent. As the leader of 40 percent of the As, A2 would lose out to A1. However, if he is able to successfully redefine his 40 percent as an ethnic category in itself, he then redefines himself as the leader of his own ethnic category rather than of a faction within a larger category, and thereby becomes a viable candidate for induction into the party leadership. The pressure for posts within the BSP, therefore, came not only from the induction of new monoethnic factions, but also from the incentives for the repeated "involution" of existing factions through the activation of subethnic differences by losing elites.

The system of centralized allotment of at least one post for each category, even if consistently applied, would have resulted in a closed party organization once the space for new posts was exhausted. However, an additional difficulty was introduced by the fact that it was mixed with a set of unpredictable criteria. Kanshi Ram also allotted posts based on considerations of personal loyalty, as a way to undercut rivals, and as a way to reward individuals for services rendered in other areas. The mixing of this criterion with arbitrary elements meant that dominant elites in the BSP faced a high degree of uncertainty in relinquishing their posts. As a result, they resisted the incorporation of new elites with even greater tenacity.

In order for the BSP to incorporate new elites, therefore, it needed to promise an abnormally high probability of winning the election. A high probability of winning enabled it to induct new entrants in two ways: First, it increased the expected probability of obtaining office through the BSP by offsetting the low probability of ascent up the party ranks for new elites. Second, it enabled the BSP leadership to incorporate new elites through the expansion of available posts. Throughout 1984–98, therefore, the BSP was in the catch-22 situation faced by Congress after 1972: It needed to incorporate new Scheduled Caste elites in order to win, but it could not incorporate these elites unless it won.

In the state of Uttar Pradesh, the BSP was able to break out of this situation through a series of alliances. In 1984, the majority of positions in the BSP party organization and candidate lists were occupied by Chamars. The support of Chamars is not sufficient to take a party to a winning position in Uttar Pradesh. In 1993, the BSP formed an alliance with the Samajwadi Party. The alliance, taking advantage of the winner-take-all electoral system, "magnified" the support bases of each of the two parties, catapulting them into control of government. Once in control of

260

government, the party had an expanded pool of offices to distribute and so could attract new elites while keeping older ones acquiescent despite its centralized roles. Between 1993 and 1997, the BSP leveraged itself into a governing position three times – as a coalition partner in the 1993 government with the Samajwadi Party, as a minority government supported from the outside by the BJP in 1995, and as a coalition government with the BJP in 1997. Each term in government gave it new resources with which to maintain the allegiance of elites in fierce competition for offices.

Even with control of government, however, the BSP's hold on these elites was tenuous. In the absence of an organizational structure that permitted elites from different ethnic categories to coexist and alternate, the BSP was in imminent danger of disintegration even when it won and especially when it lost. As a party in government, the BSP was ridden with frequent defections in Uttar Pradesh, as monoethnic factions were periodically elbowed out. Between 1993 and 1996, we witnessed the exit from the BSP of at least four significant factions: a Muslim faction, a Kurmi faction, a Pasi faction, and even a Chamar faction. The 1996 assembly elections, in which all parties attempted, by orchestrating alliances or inducing defections, to cobble together the numbers to form a government, produced a highly uncertain verdict. During the period of uncertainty, the threat of defections to other parties among its elites was so high that the BSP locked up its elites and placed them under armed guard for the duration of coalition negotiations.

In Punjab and Karnataka, meanwhile, the competitive configuration did not afford the BSP an opportunity to build alliances and so break out of its catch-22 position. As a consequence, it was not able to incorporate new elites into the party even temporarily. Given that the BSP targeted Scheduled Castes specifically, and itself drew a link between elite incorporation and electoral success, its inability to incorporate elites from across the spectrum of Scheduled Castes is a deeply paradoxical result.[27]

---

[27] A directive from the Indian Election Commission has forced both the BSP and Congress to introduce intraparty elections. If implemented, this directive should have the effect of making both party organizations more incorporative and therefore more successful.

12

Extending the Argument to Other Ethnic Parties in India

THE BJP, THE DMK, AND THE JMM

This chapter applies the hypothesis developed through the study of the BSP to three other ethnic parties in India: the pro-Hindu Bharatiya Janata Party (BJP) in India's 1991 parliamentary elections (section I); the pro-Tamil Dravida Munnetra Kazagham (DMK) in the state of Tamil Nadu in the 1967 legislative assembly elections (section II); and the pro-Jharkhand Jharkhand Mukti Morcha (JMM), a regionalist party that called for the creation of a new state of Jharkhand out of the state of Bihar and its neighbours, in the 2000 legislative assembly elections in Bihar (section III). I rely for these analyses mainly on several excellent secondary studies of these parties and their vote bases. The data available from these studies are not sufficiently precise to permit a systematic evaluation of the argument. Instead, I hope to show only that in each case, the hypothesis proposed in this book generates a more plausible explanation than the alternatives for an otherwise puzzling outcome.

I select these three parties in order to maximize the range of variation in the data, keeping the condition of patronage-democracy constant. The three parties differ, first, in the *type of category* that they sought to mobilize. The BJP in 1991 targeted the religion-based category "Hindu." The DMK defined its target ethnic category in 1967 as a linguistic/regional category of Tamil speakers in Tamil Nadu. The Jharkhand Mukti Morcha defined its target ethnic category in 2000 as "Jharkhandis," by which it meant all inhabitants of the Jharkhand region. Second, they differ in the relative *size* of their target ethnic categories: Hindus in India and Tamil speakers in Tamil Nadu are both majority categories, while Jharkhandis constituted a regionally concentrated minority within Bihar. Third, they differ in the size of the *political arena* in which they operated: The BJP in 1991 was a nationwide party; the DMK in 1967 concentrated its efforts in the southern

262

state of Tamil Nadu; and the Jharkhand Mukti Morcha in 2000 contested in the state of Bihar. Finally, the three parties differ in the type of elections and the time period chosen for analysis.

I. The Bharatiya Janata Party (BJP)

The Bharatiya Janata Party (BJP), officially founded in 1980, is the direct descendant of the Bharatiya Jana Sangh (BJS), founded in 1951. The Jana Sangh was created as the political wing of the Rashtriya Swayamsevak Sangh (RSS), an ostensibly nonpolitical, cadre-based Hindu nationalist organization. In 1977, the Jana Sangh merged with several non-Congress parties to form the Janata Party. Three years later, Jana Sangh members left the Janata Party en masse and created the BJP. Like its predecessor, the BJP maintains close ties with the RSS and its affiliated organizations. Most influential leaders of the BJP at the national and state levels are alumni of the RSS, and many key organizational posts within the BJP are held by cadres (*pracharaks*) on deputation from the RSS.

I select 1991 as the year for analysis since this is the principal parliamentary election that the BJP contested on an openly pro-Hindu platform.[1] From 1980 to 1986, the BJP had dissociated itself from a pro-Hindu appeal, attempting to present itself as a "catchall" party, indistinguishable from Congress. But following 1986, it changed tack. It aligned itself with the Ramjanmabhoomi movement, initiated by the Vishwa Hindu Parishad (VHP), a religious revivalist organization also affiliated with the RSS, which called for the demolition of a mosque in the north Indian town of Ayodhya and its replacement with a temple. The BJP made the temple mosque controversy central to its election campaign in 1991, framing the election as a referendum on the rights of India's Hindu "majority." The mosque was unlawfully demolished by activists from the BJP and other RSS affiliates in 1992. Since the demolition, the BJP has progressively moderated its platform, giving up several of the planks that established its distinct identity as a "pro-Hindu" party.

The BJP obtained only 20 percent of the national vote in 1991, which translated into the support of at most one-fourth of its target Hindu "majority." (For the method of estimating the degree of support among

---

[1] I trace changes in the BJP platform between 1951 and 1991 through a study of the election manifestos of the BJP in Kanchan Chandra, "Inside the BJP: Political Actors and Ideological Choices," paper presented at the 1994 meeting of the Association of Asian Studies, Boston, March 1994.

Hindus, see Appendix F).[2] This was the highest level of support that the BJP and its predecessor party, the BJS, had ever obtained from Hindus: Between 1952 and 1989, the votes of Jana Sangh and then the BJP had ranged from 3.1 percent in 1952 to 11.5 percent in 1989, which translated into an estimated level of support of between 4 and 14 percent of India's Hindu majority.[3] But at the same time, the response can be judged to be lukewarm. The BJP was the principal party that openly aligned itself with India's Hindu "majority." The other significant party to champion the so-called Hindu cause was the Shiv Sena in the state of Maharashtra, with which the BJP formed an electoral alliance. Yet most Hindus did not vote for the BJP.

There was, furthermore, significant variation in the degree of support the BJP received from among Hindus across states. Most states in India, as Map 1.3 (p. 24) shows, have a Hindu majority. But, as Map 1.4 (p. 25) shows, the BJP obtained the support of a majority of Hindus only in the western state of Gujarat. In a swathe of states extending diagonally across India, it obtained moderate levels of support from Hindus, ranging from 24 percent in Goa to 48 percent in Delhi. [4] And in a third belt of states, extending mainly along India's southern and eastern peripheries, it obtained negligible levels of support among Hindus. Why did only one-fourth of Hindus vote for the BJP in 1991, and why did more Hindus vote for the BJP in some states than in others?

Most analyses of the BJP's performance in 1991 focus on explaining why the BJP succeeded in obtaining greater support among Hindus in 1991 than it had in previous elections, rather than on posing the question of why it failed to obtain more support among Hindus, or why it did better among Hindus in some states than in others. But these questions are all variations on the same theme, and the answer to one should also provide the answer to the others.

One common explanation attributes the rise of the BJP to an increased perception of threat on the part of the Hindu "majority." The origins of

---

[2] A survey conducted by the Indian National Election Studies Project in 1996 that probed past voting patterns of respondents (N = 918) puts this estimate even lower, at 18 percent.

[3] David Butler, Ashok Lahiri, and Prannoy Roy, *India Decides: Elections 1952–1995* (New Delhi: Living Media, 1995).

[4] In Maharashtra, although only an estimated 24.9 percent of Hindus voted for the BJP, taking into account the votes won by its alliance partner drives this percentage higher. The Shiv Sena in Maharashtra obtained the support of an estimated 11.7 percent of Hindus in these elections. Thus, the BJP and Shiv Sena taken together obtained 36.6 percent of the Hindu vote in these elections.

this perception, according to this argument, lay in a highly publicized conversion of Scheduled Castes to Islam in Meenakshipuram in Tamil Nadu in 1981, which stoked fears of a change in the numerical balance between Hindus and Muslims. This incident was followed by the rise of insurgent movements in the Muslim-majority state of Kashmir and in the Sikh-majority state of Punjab; the assassination of Indira Gandhi by her Sikh bodyguards in 1984; and a controversial bill passed by the Rajiv Gandhi government in 1986 extending religious autonomy in matters of civil law, which was widely interpreted as "pandering" to sections of the Muslim clergy. This chain of incidents, the argument runs, created a "minority complex" among the Hindu majority, which reacted by voting for the BJP in the 1991 parliamentary elections in larger numbers than before.[5]

This argument, however, is belied by the pattern of support for the BJP. If anti-minority backlash feeds support for a pro-Hindu party, then pro-Hindu parties should have historically fared best in those states in which non-Hindus have been most assertive. But the BJS and then the BJP traditionally fared poorly among Hindus in Jammu and Kashmir and Punjab, the two states in which Hindu minorities were most threatened by political mobilization on the part of non-Hindu majorities.[6] Map 1.3 does not report the BJP's vote in these two states in 1991, since parliamentary elections were postponed in both during that year. But when parliamentary elections were held in Punjab a year later, the Congress party rather than the BJP was the main recipient of Hindu votes.[7] The argument also leaves unexplained the variation in the performance of the BJP across north and south India. Hindus in the southern state of Kerala during the same period, for instance, were also reportedly "gripped by Hindu insecurity because of the perception that Muslims and Christians are rising in numbers."[8] Meenakshipuram, the site of the conversion of Scheduled Castes to Islam that is believed to have set off the Hindu backlash, is located in the southern

---

[5] Shekhar Gupta, "The Gathering Storm," in Marshall Bouton and Philip Oldenburg, eds., *India Briefing* (Boulder, CO: Westview Press, 1990), 25–51.

[6] Butler, Lahiri, and Roy, *India Decides*.

[7] The Congress party received 49.27 percent of the aggregate vote in Punjab, while the BJP received 16.5 percent. I do not attempt here to estimate the percentage of Hindu support received by each party. These estimates would be unreliable for this election, which was boycotted by one of the main parties in Punjab, the Shiromani Akali Dal, and which was characterized by abnormally low turnout rates. But since both Congress and BJP votes in Punjab come predominantly from Hindus, these aggregate figures are sufficient to show that Congress received substantially greater support from Hindus than the BJP did.

[8] *India Today*, May 31, 1986.

state of Tamil Nadu. Yet the degree of Hindu support for the BJP was negligible in both these states.

A second explanation places the explanatory burden for the rise of the BJP in part on the organizational decay of the Congress party.[9] But this explanation is incomplete to the extent that it does not explain the *timing* of the shift in support for the BJP. The 1969 split in the Congress party was an instance of a serious organizational crisis. But this did not result in a surge in support for the BJP's predecessor, the BJS. Instead, it led to a regeneration of the Congress party under Indira Gandhi. Further, the Congress can be said to have been in decay throughout the 1980s. However, this decay was not reflected in its electoral performance. Finally, even allowing for an intensification of the organizational decay in the Congress in the years prior to 1991, the question remains of why the BJP, in particular, filled the vacuum, instead of another party or a collection of parties.

In a more fully developed argument, Pradeep Chhibber explains the rise of the BJP as a consequence of a shift in voter preferences caused by three key shifts in the policy positions of political parties.[10] The first such shift was the announcement by the Janata Dal–led government in 1990 that it would implement the Mandal Commission report, which recommended the reservation of 27 percent of central government jobs for the "Other Backward Classes," which it defined to mean Other Backward *Castes*. The result, according to Chhibber, was a polarization of the electorate on caste lines that shifted the votes of the upper castes to the BJP.[11] The second policy shift was the BJP's call for a reduced role for the state in the economy which, Chhibber maintains, led middle class voters who sought reduced state intervention to switch their preferences from the Congress party to the BJP.[12] And the third policy shift was "Congress's explicit linkage of central government policy to electoral considerations,"[13] which led voters to develop preferences on national policy, but at the same time switch to the BJP out of a dissatisfaction with Congress.[14]

[9] See, for instance, Ashutosh Varshney, "Contested Meanings: India's National Identity, Hindu Nationalism and the Politics of Anxiety," *Daedalus*, Summer 1993, pp. 227–261.

[10] Pradeep Chhibber, *Democracy without Associations* (Ann Arbor: University of Michigan Press, 1999).

[11] Ibid., 150.

[12] Ibid., 159.

[13] Ibid.

[14] Ibid.

This argument is supported by separate analyses of the characteristics of BJP elites and BJP voters. BJP activists, the data show, are more likely to be upper-caste, to have distinct views on state intervention, and to believe that national issues are important. And among voters, the data show that caste, occupation, and preferences on national policy are correlated with the vote for the BJP. These data, however, tell us only that the socioeconomic background and views of BJP activists and voters are similar, but not that the policy positions articulated by the activists are responsible for a shift in the allegiance of the voters. Further, Chhibber does not provide an estimate of the numerical strength of the overlapping categories of upper-caste voters, middle-class voters, and voters with preferences on national policy. Even if all three categories voted for the BJP in large numbers, therefore, it is not clear that their combined strength would be sufficient to account for the increase in the BJP's vote share.

Indeed, survey data from the Indian National Election studies show that a significant and increasing proportion of the BJP's votes in the 1990s came from *backward castes*, belying the prediction that it is the upper castes who are responsible for its improved performance. Table 12.1 breaks down the BJP's vote by caste for the three elections between 1991 and 1998 for which data are available. As the table indicates, while the single largest proportion of the BJP's votes in 1991 came from upper and intermediate castes, backward castes were a close second, contributing 37 percent of the BJP's vote. And by 1998, backward castes had *exceeded* the contribution of upper castes to the BJP's votes.

The organizations of both the Bharatiya Jana Sangh and the BJP in its early years were dominated by upper castes. In 1991, however, both upper castes and backward castes voted for the BJP in greater proportions than before. If the BJP obtained increased support among Hindus from these

Table 12.1. *Profile of BJP Vote, 1991–98*

	1991 (N = 902)	1996 (N = 1,912)	1998 (N = 1,742)
Upper and intermediate caste	46.9%	43.72%	40.41%
Backward caste	37.03%	35.72%	42.65%
Scheduled Caste	9.76%	12.29%	9.82%
Scheduled Tribe	6.32%	8.26%	7.12%

Source: For 1991, 1996 pre-poll survey that questioned voters about past voting patterns; for 1996, 1996 post-poll survey; for 1998, 1998 post-poll survey.

caste categories in 1991, then, the argument of this book suggests that the explanation for the BJP's performance must lie, *not in a change in its policy positions, but in a change in its ability to represent elites from caste-based subdivisions among the "Hindu" category, and/or a change in the degree of efficacy of those voters whose elites are best represented in the BJP.* I now offer some suggestive evidence in support of this hypothesis from the two states of Gujarat and Bihar.

Gujarat

The western state of Gujarat was the site of the BJP's best performance among Hindus in 1991. As Map 1.4 (p. 25) shows, the party won the support of 56 percent of Hindus in this state.

In the 1991 elections, the main parties competing for power in Gujarat were the Congress; the BJP; and three splinters parties born of the Janata Dal, of which the largest was the Janata Dal (Gujarat), or the JD(G). The Congress formed an electoral alliance with the JD(G), while the BJP contested alone.

The Congress party in Gujarat represented elites principally from the Kshatriya caste category, who constituted roughly 29 percent of the population of Gujarat. The Kshatriya caste category included both "upper-caste" Kshatriyas, who constituted roughly 5 percent, and "backward caste" Kshatriyas, who constituted roughly 24 percent of the population of Gujarat.[15] To a lesser extent, Congress also represented elites from the Scheduled Castes (7 percent of Gujarat's population), Scheduled Tribes (14 percent), and Muslims (8 percent).[16] The Janata Dal gave representation principally to elites from three upper- and middle-caste categories: the Banias (approximately 3 percent), the Brahmins (approximately 4 percent), and the Patidars (approximately 12 percent).

The Bharatiya Janata Party in Gujarat initially shared the ethnic profile of the Janata Dal, representing the upper and middle castes.[17] But it had

[15] The data on the caste profile of the population in this paragraph, based on the 1931 census, are from Atul Kohli, *Democracy and Discontent* (Cambridge: Cambridge University Press, 1990), 241. The assessment of the caste profile of the Congress and Janata Dal in Gujarat are also from Kohli, p. 257.

[16] *Census of India 1991.*

[17] Ghanshyam Shah, "The BJP's Riddle in Gujarat: Caste, Factionalism and Hindutva," in Thomas Blom Hansen and Christophe Jaffrelot, eds., *The BJP and the Compulsions of Politics in India* (Delhi: Oxford University Press, 1998), 243–266.

broader aspirations. It began to open its doors to the roughly 23 percent of the population in Gujarat, made up mainly of voters from the backward castes, that remained unincorporated in any party. Although it preserved the dominance of upper castes within the party, the BJP brought in elites from these castes as "junior" partners: 30 percent of its district-level leaders in Gujarat, as well the state president of the BJP, came from the backward castes by 1991.[18] At the same time, it also began to offer representation to Scheduled Castes and Tribes and so to wean them away from the Congress party. Elites from these groups, seeking office but indifferent to the party that gave them a channel to office, responded to these widened opportunities. As Shah notes:

There are a number of such individuals from the Dalit, tribal and OBC communities who did not support the party's ideology of Hindu unity, except its anti-Muslim component, and who were not comfortable with the attitude of the upper-caste party bosses. Nonetheless, they remained in the party because they got positions which satisfied their desire for gaining some importance and acceptance in the organization.[19]

These changes in the BJP's elite profile, combined with the splintering of the Janata Dal, according to the argument of this book, should have transformed the preference distribution of voters in Gujarat by 1991. Given the subordination of the JD(G) to the Kshatriya-dominated Congress and the weakness of the other JD splinters, it was reasonable for upper-caste voters to prefer the BJP, since this was the principal party in which elites from their category were dominant. At the same time, non-Kshatriya backward castes should also have preferred the BJP, since their elites were represented to a greater degree in the BJP than in the competition. The preferences of voters from Scheduled Castes and Scheduled Tribes should have been distributed between the Congress-led alliance and the BJP, since they were given representation in both. Taken together, voters from those caste categories that found representation in the BJP were sufficiently numerous to affect the electoral outcome through coordinated action. This combination of representation for a broad range of groups with efficacy, I suggest, accounts for the BJP's capture of large sections of the vote in this election in Gujarat.

---

[18] Ghanshyam Shah, "The BJP and Backward Castes in Gujarat," *South Asia Bulletin*, Vol. 14, No. 4 (1994), 63.

[19] Shah, "The BJP's Riddle in Gujarat," 256.

Bihar

In Bihar, the BJP did not do as well, obtaining only 19 percent of the Hindu vote. The main parties that the BJP faced in the 1991 elections were the Congress, the Janata Dal, and the Samajwadi Janata Party (a splinter party from the Janata Dal), all of which contested a majority of seats in the state. Other, smaller parties also entered the fray, but they contested only a small number of seats.

Congress and the BJP in Bihar were dominated by the upper castes, who constitute approximately 15 percent of the state's population.[20] As in the case of Gujarat, the BJP had begun to incorporate backward castes, who constituted an estimated 48 percent of Bihar's population, to a limited degree. In the 1991 elections, for instance, the BJP gave 31 percent of its tickets to backward caste candidates, compared to 44 percent to the upper castes.[21] (This does not tell us about the extent to which backward castes were being elevated to positions of power in the party organization, but it represents the best available data on the incorporation of backward castes in the outer peripheries of the organization.) But unlike the situation in Gujarat, where a large section of the backward castes were unincorporated into the party system, backward castes were well represented in the party system in Bihar, dominating both the Janata Dal and the Samajwadi Janata Party. Laloo Prasad Yadav, the leader of the Janata Dal and the former chief minister of Bihar, was from the backward castes. And, although detailed studies of the ethnic profile of party organizations and cabinets of Janata Dal and the SJP have yet to be undertaken, available data on their candidate lists show that they gave greater representation to backward castes than other parties in the competition.[22] Muslims, who constitute 15 percent of Bihar's population, were also given greatest representation in the candidate lists of the Janata Dal, followed by the SJP and the Congress. The Scheduled Castes

[20] The data on the caste profile of Bihar's population, based on the 1931 census, are from Kohli, *Democracy and Discontent*, 208; the assessment of the caste profile of the Congress and BJP is based, apart from Kohli, on Christophe Jaffrelot, "The Sangh Parivar between Sanskritization and Social Engineering," in Thomas Blom Hansen and Christophe Jaffrelot, eds., *The BJP and the Compulsions of Politics in India* (Delhi: Oxford University Press, 1998), 22–71; and Francine Frankel, "Caste, Land and Dominance in Bihar: Breakdown of the Brahmanical Social Order," in Francine Frankel and M. S. A. Rao, eds., *Dominance and State Power in Modern India*, Vol. I (Delhi: Oxford University Press, 1989).

[21] Ravindra Kumar Verma, "Caste and Candidate Selection: Lok Sabha Poll in Bihar," *Economic and Political Weekly*, June 1–8, 1991; Ravinder Kumar Verma, "Caste and Bihar Politics," *Economic and Political Weekly*, May 4, 1991.

[22] Ibid.

and Scheduled Tribes, who form 15 percent and 8 percent, respectively, were given more or less equivalent representation across parties.[23]

According to the hypothesis proposed in this book, the upper castes in Bihar should have preferred the BJP and Congress in 1991. But the Backward Castes should have preferred the JD or the SJP. In this, Bihar differed from Gujarat. There, the limited representation that the BJP gave to backward castes was sufficient to give it a comparative advantage. But in Bihar, the domination of backward castes in competing parties meant that the BJP had to cross a considerably higher threshold of representation for backward caste elites in order to obtain this advantage. Muslims should also have preferred the JD or the SJP, while the preferences of Scheduled Castes and Scheduled Tribes should have been dispersed across parties.

Given this distribution of preferences, the BJP had a low probability of winning. Even an en masse vote for the BJP among upper castes would not have been sufficient to take it to a winning position. The more likely winners in this state were the Janata Dal and the Samajwadi Janata Party, which incorporated elites from categories comprising a majority of categories in the state. This combination of a lack of comparative advantage in representation and a low level of efficacy accounts, I suggest, for the BJP's failure to obtain the support of a majority of Hindus in this state.

Primary research on the caste profile of the BJP and its competition, and on the precise contours of the competitive configuration in each state, is required to investigate this suggestion more systematically. But a broad survey of the pattern of variation in the BJP's support among Hindus across Indian states, based on the data that are available, suggests that this argument is plausible. The BJP did particularly well in northern states in which Congress and other political parties were slow to incorporate backward caste elites.[24] Conversely, the BJP did badly in southern states where the limited positions given by the BJP to backward caste elites were surpassed by the already high levels of representation given to them in other parties. BJP leaders themselves acknowledge the link between representation and success. A party "committee for broadening the base of the party" in

---

[23] Ibid. The data on the population of Muslims, Scheduled Castes, and Scheduled Tribes in Bihar are from the *Census of India 1991*.

[24] Christophe Jaffrelot, on whose work this section draws, has collected perhaps the most exhaustive data on the caste profile of the BJP in north India. A similar exploration of south India remains to be undertaken.

Madhya Pradesh, for instance, recommended the promotion of elites from the backward castes and other subordinate groups within the party, and advocated that "data concerning the social composition of each constituency be collected, computerized and taken into account before the distribution of tickets."[25]

Why was the BJP able to induct backward caste elites to a greater degree than its predecessor, the BJS? At the same time, why was the incorporation of backward caste elites within the BJP limited, especially when BJP leaders were aware that their electoral progress depended upon such incorporation? The argument here suggests that the answer should lie in the BJP's organizational structure. The BJP's constitution allows for a greater degree of intraparty competition than that of its predecessor, the BJS. Unlike most of its competitors, the BJP has been meticulous about holding periodic intraparty elections for all key posts since 1980. But the rules for election become less competitive as we move from lower to higher levels of the party hierarchy. As a consequence, although backward castes and other elites have begun to be inducted at lower levels in the party hierarchy, their ascent up the ladder of power has been slow and sometimes aborted. The remainder of this section develops this argument.

The BJP's internal organization prior to the 1991 election was structured as follows:[26] At the apex was the national president, the National Executive, and the National Council. The National Executive, appointed by the president, was the principal policy-making body of the party. The principal function of the National Council was to participate in the electoral college, which elects the president. This structure was replicated at the state level, with a state president, a State Executive appointed by the president, and a State Council. The State Council participated in the election of both the state president and the national president. At lower levels were the district committees, *mandal* committees, and local committees, each headed by an elected president and office-bearers nominated by the president. The most important elected post at each level was that of president. The president had the power to nominate office-bearers at each level.

The rules for advancement at the *lower* levels of the party were competitive. Membership in the party was relatively unrestricted: Any individual

[25] Jaffrelot, "The Sangh Parivar between Sanskritization and Social Engineering," 65.
[26] Bharatiya Janata Party, *Constitution and Rules (As Amended by the National Council up to 23rd July, 1989)* (New Delhi: Bharatiya Janata Party, n.d.). The organizational structure is broadly similar today.

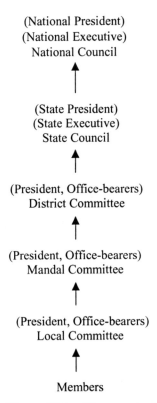

(National President)
(National Executive)
National Council

(State President)
(State Executive)
State Council

(President, Office-bearers)
District Committee

(President, Office-bearers)
Mandal Committee

(President, Office-bearers)
Local Committee

Members

Figure 12.1.   The organization of the Bharatiya Janata Party.

over eighteen years old could join the party by paying a nominal subscription and professing acceptance of the party constitution. All members at the local level, in turn, participated in the election of the local committee and its president. The elected local committees then elected the *mandal* committee and its president. And the elected *mandal* committees elected the district committee and its president.

At the levels of party organization *above* the district, however, the rules for intraparty advancement became more centralized. The electorate for state president, for instance, consisted not only of the members elected at lower levels, but also of a large contingent of members appointed from above by the National Executive. The electorate for a new national president, similarly, consisted not only of elected members from lower-level bodies but also of members appointed by the outgoing president. While the outgoing national president had formal control over these appointments, they were typically made in consultation with a cabal of senior RSS and BJP leaders. Secondly, although the process for nomination of candidates was nominally unrestricted (any ten members of the electoral college could propose the name of a member for the post of president), the RSS-BJP cabal controlled the process for candidate selection in practice, with the result that elections for the post of national or state president were rarely contested.

There was, furthermore, a parallel structure of nonelected authority in the BJP from the district level onward. At the lowest levels of the party hierarchy (local and *mandal* units), all office-bearers were appointed from among the elected members. But at the district level, the constitution made provision for the appointment of a "General Secretary (Organization)" "from outside the elected members of his committee."[27] At the state and national levels, similarly, the general secretary (organization) was appointed by the state and national presidents, respectively, and need not have been elected by a lower-level body. The post of organizational secretary was of great importance within the party hierarchy. It was usually filled by an RSS cadre on "deputation" to the BJP. The organizing secretary typically had direct access to senior RSS and BJP leaders at higher levels and was at least as important as the state president.

In order to rise through *lower* levels in the party hierarchy of the BJP, then, aspiring elites needed only to court support from below. But in order to win elections beyond the district level, aspiring elites needed not only to cultivate support from below, but also to curry favour with the outgoing president and the RSS-BJP selectorate, who controlled the outcome. Alternatively, they did not need to go through the process of elections at all. A second, and perhaps superior, route to the higher levels of the party organization was ascent through the ranks of the RSS and its affiliates to the position of organizing secretary in the BJP.

The "semicompetitive" system of the BJP explains its limited incorporation of backward caste elites. On the one hand, the open elections up to the district level attracted newly mobilizing elites to lower levels of the party organization. Beyond the district level, however, the increasing centralization of the system blocked the further ascent of these newly modernizing elites up the party organization. Upper-caste elites, already in control of the party organization, did not need the support of these new entrants in order to retain their power. In fact, in a party system in which decisions were

---

[27] BJP *Constitution and Rules*, 8.

made by a small group of leaders at the top, they could not be confident of return if they were displaced.

As a result, the BJP was unable to incorporate backward caste elites at higher levels of the party. The RSS-BJP leadership, with an eye to the elections, repeatedly attempted to appoint backward caste leaders to prominent positions. But it was frequently forced to back down in response to the threat of revolt from its upper-caste personnel. In Uttar Pradesh in 1991, for instance, the selectorate appointed Kalyan Singh, from the backward Lodh caste, chief minister. Following intense rivalry between Kalyan Singh and upper-caste aspirants for the post, however, Kalyan Singh was expelled from the party. The expulsion of Kalyan Singh marked the ascendancy of upper castes within the party, with the posts of both the chief minister and the state president in Uttar Pradesh going to upper-caste aspirants. In Gujarat, similarly, the struggle between upper-caste and backward caste aspirants resulted in a vertical split in the BJP following the 1991 elections.

Given the difficulty of incorporating backward caste leaders into the party organization, despite the knowledge that such incorporation would improve the party's electoral prospects, the BJP has chosen to improve its electoral prospects since 1991 by seeking alliance partners in parties dominated by backward castes, rather than by attempting further elevation of backward castes within its party organization.[28] As a result, even though it has obtained enough seats through its alliance partners to become the leader of coalition governments since 1998, its vote share at the national level has increased much more slowly, from 20 percent of the national vote in 1991 to only 24 percent in 1999.

II. The Dravida Munnetra Kazagham (DMK)

The DMK was founded in 1949, in the southern state of Tamil Nadu (then Madras). I analyze the DMK's performance in the 1967 legislative assembly elections, since these are the first elections in which it both had the organizational resources to be a viable contender and in which it made an open pro-Tamil appeal. In the first legislative assembly elections that it contested in Tamil Nadu, in 1957, the DMK fought the elections on a secessionist platform but had not yet established an organizational base throughout the

[28] Jaffrelot, "The Sangh Parivar between Sanskritization and Social Engineering."

state.[29] In the next elections, in 1962, although it had expanded its organizational base, it contested the elections mainly on economic issues.[30] In 1967, however, the party both had an organizational base and also made the issue of language central to the election campaign.

The DMK's target category of Tamil speakers constituted a majority of 83 percent in the state of Tamil Nadu.[31] Map 1.5 in Chapter 1 (p. 26) describes the distribution of Tamil speakers across Tamil Nadu. As the map indicates, Tamil speakers constituted a majority in every district in Tamil Nadu except the western district of the Nilgiris. The principal linguistic minorities in Tamil Nadu consisted of speakers of Kannada, Malayalam, Telugu, and Urdu. The speakers of the first three languages were concentrated mainly on the peripheries of Tamil Nadu, in the districts adjoining the states of Karnataka, Kerala, and Andhra Pradesh, respectively. Urdu speakers were more dispersed, mainly across districts in the north.[32]

In the 1967 elections, there were two principal forces struggling for control of the Tamil Nadu government: the Congress, which was the dominant party in Tamil Nadu and contested alone, and the DMK-led opposition front, comprising also the Swatantra Party, the Communist Party of India (Marxist) (CPM), the Praja Socialist Party (PSP), and the Samyukta Socialist Party (SSP).[33] The other four parties that contested the election were not contenders for power, contesting in only a handful of Tamil Nadu's 234 constituencies.[34]

The issues dominating the 1967 elections were the status of Tamil relative to Hindi and the relations between Tamil Nadu and the centre.[35] In the years preceding this election, the central government, led by the Congress party, had implemented an act replacing English with Hindi as the official language of India. While English had been retained as an "associate, additional language," the central government had also asked non-Hindi-speaking states, including Tamil Nadu, to report on the steps they proposed

[29] Marguerite Ross Barnett, *The Politics of Cultural Nationalism in South India* (Princeton, NJ: Princeton University Press, 1976), 93.
[30] Robert Hardgrave, "The DMK and the Politics of Tamil Nationalism," *Pacific Affairs*, Vol. 37, No. 4 (1964–5): 396–411.
[31] *Census of India 1961*.
[32] Ibid.
[33] Barnett, *The Politics of Cultural Nationalism*, 147.
[34] Craig Baxter, *District Voting Trends in India* (New York: Columbia University Press, 1969).
[35] Barnett, *The Politics of Cultural Nationalism*, 136.

to take to use Hindi.[36] In protest, the DMK launched a series of anti-Hindi agitations that erupted in widespread violence. The elections were held in the aftermath of that violence.

The result was a surge in support for the DMK. From 27.1 percent of the vote in 1962, the party increased its vote share in Tamil Nadu to 40.6 percent.[37] This indicates an increase in support for the DMK from one-third to almost one-half of Tamil speakers in Tamil Nadu. (See appendix F for the method informing this estimate.) The DMK also won the majority of seats in the legislative assembly and replaced Congress as Tamil Nadu's governing party.

The surge in support for the DMK is conventionally interpreted as a consequence of its pro-Tamil platform. But this interpretation overlooks the extent to which the Congress party *retained* the support of Tamils. Although the Congress's share of seats in the Tamil Nadu Legislative Assembly was small (50 compared to the DMK's 138), its share of the overall vote, at 41.4 percent, was actually *greater* than that of the DMK. While some of these votes came from linguistic minorities in Tamil Nadu, substantial numbers of Tamils continued to vote for the Congress in these elections. Indeed, the performance of Congress in 1967 compares favourably to its performance in the previous elections, held before the emergence of the language issue. In those elections, Congress did only slightly better, with 46 percent of the vote (although it won a larger proportion of seats).

Why did more voters not defect to the DMK from Congress, despite the polarization over the language issue? The puzzle is intensified when we look at the variation in support for the DMK among Tamil speakers across districts in Tamil Nadu. Map 1.6 in Chapter 1 (p. 27) describes this variation. As we move from north to south, the level of support for the DMK among Tamil speakers declines.[38] The principal recipient of Tamil votes in southern districts was the Congress party. Why did more Tamils not respond to the DMK's call, and why did more Tamils respond in northern Tamil Nadu than in the South?

The argument of this book suggests that the explanation for both the degree of Tamil support for the DMK and the variation in this degree of

---

[36] Paul Brass, *The Politics of India since Independence* (Delhi: Cambridge University Press, 1990), 166.

[37] Baxter, *District Voting Trends in India*.

[38] The lower levels of support here are not simply an artifact of the seats that the DMK did not contest. The front as a whole performed worse in the South than in the North.

Table 12.2. *Representational profile of the DMK and Congress, 1968*

	DMK (%) (N = 38)	Congress (%) (N = 120)
Brahmins	0	8.3
Non-Brahmins	71	75
Scheduled Castes	0	4.2
Muslims	5.3	1.7
Unclassified Hindus	13.2	2.5
North Indian	0	1.7
Christian	0	.8
No response	10.5	5.8
Total	100	100

Source: Adapted from Barnett, *The Politics of Cultural Nationalism*, pp. 200–1.

support across districts in Tamil Nadu must lie, not in the different electoral platforms of the two parties, but in the representational opportunities that each gave to subdivisions among Tamil speakers, and in the degree of efficacy that members of these categories possessed in a bipolar contest.

Available data on the ethnic profiles of the party organizations and governments of the Congress and the DMK in Tamil Nadu support this argument. The principal divisions among Tamils in Tamil Nadu for the period under analysis were based on caste. Prior to the emergence of the DMK, the principal cleavage within Tamils had been between "Brahmins" and "non-Brahmins," a blanket category used to describe all caste categories other than the Brahmins.[39]

Table 12.2 describes the caste profile of the apex decision-making bodies of both parties in Tamil Nadu: the DMK's "General Council" and the Tamil Nadu Pradesh Congress Committee. These data are based on a survey conducted by Barnett in 1968.[40] Although the data were collected immediately *after* the election, they are by all accounts an accurate representation of the ethnic profiles of the two parties beforehand. Seventy-six percent of the members of the DMK General Council, according to Barnett, were founders of the party, recruited into the DMK in 1949, and therefore likely to have occupied senior positions in the party prior to 1967.

Table 12.2 indicates that the DMK and the Congress had comparable profiles in 1967. Non-Brahmins were the best-represented category in the

[39] Narendra Subramanian, *Ethnicity and Populist Mobilization* (Delhi: Oxford University Press, 1999), 136.
[40] Barnett, *The Politics of Cultural Nationalism*, 200–1.

Table 12.3. *Caste composition of Congress and DMK cabinets, 1957–67*

Year	Chief Minister	UC	BC	SC	Other
1957	Kamaraj (INC)	2	3	1	2
1967	Annadurai (DMK)	2	3	1	2

Source: Subramanian, *Ethnicity and Populist Mobilization*, 219.

organizations of both parties, although the Congress gave greater representation to Brahmins than the DMK did. These data are further supported by data on the cabinets of the two parties, summarized in Table 12.3. Although a DMK cabinet replaced a Congress cabinet in 1967, the ethnic profile of the cabinet remained the same.

In a bipolar competition with virtually identical representational profiles, the two parties had an equal chance of winning the election. As a result, voters should have voted according to their preferences. This is consistent with the roughly evenly balanced vote shares that we see for Congress and the DMK in 1967.

At the same time, this also suggests an explanation for the otherwise puzzling regional variation in support for Congress and the DMK. Although both parties gave comparable representation to members of the "Non-Brahmin" caste category, there was some variation in the degree of representation that each party gave to caste categories among the non-Brahmins. The DMK gave greater representation to "forward non-Brahmins" (42 percent in its General Council), while the Congress gave greater representation to "backward non-Brahmins" (42.5 percent in the Tamil Nadu Congress Committee).[41] Annadurai, the DMK chief minister and the founder of the DMK, was from a forward caste among non-Brahmins (Mudaliar),[42] while Kamraj, the Congress chief minister and president of the Tamil Nadu Congress Committee, was from the Nadar caste, a backward caste among non-Brahmins. The DMK's stronger performance in the North and its weaker performance in the South appears to be the product of these differences in caste profiles. The southern and the northern districts have a distinct distribution of castes.[43] Indeed, Nadars, best represented in the

---

[41] Ibid.

[42] Robert Hardgrave, *The Dravidian Movement* (Bombay: Popular Prakashan, 1965), 35.

[43] Robert Hardgrave, *The Nadars of Tamil Nadu* (Berkeley: University of California Press, 1969), 218–219; David Washbrook, "Caste, Class and Dominance in Modern Tamil Nadu," in Frankel and Rao, eds., *Dominance and State Power in Modern India*, 223.

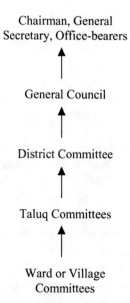

Chairman, General
Secretary, Office-bearers

↑

General Council

↑

District Committee

↑

Taluq Committees

↑

Ward or Village
Committees

Figure 12.2.   The organization of the DMK.

Congress party, are concentrated in the southern districts of Tamil Nadu.[44] This regional variation in the distribution of castes represented in both parties, I suggest, accounts for the regional variation in the number of votes they were able to obtain from Tamil voters.

What explains the relative success of both the DMK and the Congress party in incorporating elites from non-Brahmin castes? The argument of this book predicts that both parties must have had competitive rules for intraparty advancement. Congress, as I showed in the previous chapter, was in fact competitive during this period. The DMK's organization was equally so. Figure 12.2 describes the DMK's structure.[45] All party posts in the DMK were filled through open elections.[46] The ward or village committees elected secretaries, who then became members of the *taluq* committee. The *taluq* committee then elected a secretary as well as five other delegates to the district committee. The district committee in each

---

[44] Hardgrave, *The Nadars of Tamil Nadu*, Appendix I, 269–72; Washbrook, "Caste, Class and Dominance," 223.

[45] Hardgrave, *The Dravidian Movement*, 33.

[46] Subramanian, *Ethnicity and Populist Mobilization*, 145, 234–5; Hardgrave, *The Dravidian Movement*, 33.

district elected ten of its members to the General Council. And the General Council elected not only the chairman, general secretary, and treasurer of the party, but also influential committees, including the parliamentary board and an audit committee.[47] The party's internal organizational elections at both the district and more senior levels were hotly contested affairs.[48] With two internally competitive parties in Tamil Nadu, upwardly mobile elites from across subdivisions within the "Tamil" category were snapped up as soon as they arose, translating into a high level of support for both parties among Tamils in 1967, despite their distinct platforms.

III. Jharkhand Mukti Morcha (JMM)

The Jharkhand Mukti Morcha (JMM), founded in the state of Bihar in 1972, is a regionalist party whose principal demand was the creation of a separate state of "Jharkhand," comprising areas of Bihar and its neighbouring states. The demand for Jharkhand, voiced first during the colonial period, was initially intended to champion the cause of the Scheduled Tribes who resided in the region against "*dikus*," or outsiders, who were believed to have migrated to Jharkhand subsequently.[49] Scheduled Tribes were not a majority in the Jharkhand region, comprising only 28 percent of its population.[50] The demand for a tribal homeland in Jharkhand had been justified, therefore, not on the grounds of majority status, but on the grounds that the Scheduled Tribes were the original inhabitants of the region. The Jharkhand Mukti Morcha broadened the definition of Jharkhandis beyond the Scheduled Tribes. It defined the "people of Jharkhand" as including all those who resided in Jharkhand, including "tribals, Harijans, Kudmis, [and] Backward communities," whom it described as belonging to a common "subnationality."[51]

In the 2000 elections for the legislative assembly in Bihar, there were four principal alliances or parties in the fray, apart from the JMM. The first

---

[47] Hardgrave, *The Dravidian Movement*, 34.

[48] Subramanian, *Ethnicity and Populist Mobilization*, 235.

[49] Myron Weiner, *Sons of the Soil* (Princeton, NJ: Princeton University Press, 1978); Stuart Corbridge, "The Ideology of Tribal Economy and Society: Politics in the Jharkhand, 1950–1980," *Modern Asian Studies*, Vol. 22, No. 1 (1988): 1–42.

[50] *Census of India 1991*.

[51] "Memorandum for the Formation of Jharkhand State" submitted to the president of India by the Jharkhand Mukti Morcha, August 11, 1989. Text contained in Sajal Basu, *Jharkhand Movement: Ethnicity and Culture of Silence* (Shimla: Indian Institute of Advanced Study, 1994), 116.

was the BJP-led National Democratic Alliance (NDA), including the BJP, the Samata Party, the Janata Dal (United) or JD(U), and the Bihar People's Party (BPP). The NDA was the ruling alliance in the central government and the opposition alliance in the legislative assembly of Bihar. The second was the front led by the Rashtriya Janta Dal (RJD), the ruling party in the legislative assembly of Bihar. The other parties in the RJD-led front included the Communist Party of India–Marxist (CPM) and the Samajwadi Janata Party (SJP). The third was the left front, which included the Communist Party of India (CPI) and the Communist Party of India–Marxist-Leninist (CPI-ML). The Indian National Congress, which contested alone, was the fourth force.

The central election issue was the creation of the state of Jharkhand. All four alliances in these elections supported the demand for the creation of Jharkhand. The disagreements were mainly over the boundaries of the new state, its name, and the time frame in which it was to be created. The JMM, however, was the principal party in this election that had a long-term commitment to the cause of Jharkhand. The others were more recent converts to the cause. In the case of the RJD, whose leader had declared only a short while before that the state of Jharkhand would be formed over his "dead body," the conversion occurred literally on the eve of the election.[52]

Surprisingly, however, the JMM fared poorly in the 2000 elections. It obtained only 16 percent of the vote in the Jharkhand region (see Table F.4, p. 316).[53] Smaller pro-Jharkhand parties fared much worse. As one commentator noted of this election: "The biggest paradox... is that the Jharkhand parties, which had spearheaded the movement, find themselves marginalised."[54] The BJP emerged as the party with the largest vote share (25 percent). The Congress party ran second, with 20 percent of the vote. The JMM came third, followed by the RJD, with 11 percent of the vote.

Further, there was significant variation in the degree of support for the JMM among Jharkhandis. As Map 1.7 (p. 28) shows, the JMM's base of support extended mainly along the eastern belt of the Jharkhand region. And within this region, it obtained a majority of the votes in only

---

[52] *The Hindu*, February 10, 2000.
[53] All vote shares here are from Election Commission of India, *Statistical Report on the General Election, 2000 to the Legislative Assembly of Bihar*.
[54] *The Hindu*, February 11, 2000.

three constituencies. In others, the JMM obtained only a negligible share of the vote.

Why did the JMM fail to obtain the support of Jharkhandis across the state? One obvious answer is the "hijacking" of the JMM's traditional platform by all other parties in the 2000 elections. Indeed, the BJP made good on its campaign promise a few months after the elections, carving out the new state of "Vananchal" from the Jharkhand region. This argument, however, raises two further questions: First, what made their promises credible? Not only were these other parties recent converts to the Jharkhand cause, they were also responsive to constituencies outside Jharkhand, against whose interests they were bound to balance the creation of a new state. Why then did voters choose these parties over the JMM, which had a consistent history of support for Jharkhand and could champion the exclusive cause of "Jharkhandis"?

Further, what explains the variation in the pattern of support for the JMM among Jharkhandis in different parts of the region? Given that all political parties supported the cause of Jharkhand, we should have found an even dispersion of support for the JMM and other parties. Instead, the support base of the JMM was heavily concentrated in the East. Why were Jharkhandis in the other parts of the state less supportive of the JMM?

A second explanation, given the history of the pro-Jharkhand movement as a tribal movement, might be that only the Scheduled Tribes voted for the JMM, while members of other categories, included only recently in the definition of "Jharkhandi," voted for other parties instead. However, the distribution of support suggests that the JMM's support was limited even among Scheduled Tribes. The Scheduled Tribe population in Jharkhand is heavily concentrated in a small number of constituencies. Twenty-seven of the legislative assembly seats in this region have a majority of Scheduled Tribe voters, ranging from 51 percent to 70 percent.[55] One way to ascertain the degree to which a political party obtains the votes of the Scheduled Tribes in the absence of survey data, then, is to study the percentage of the vote that it obtains in Scheduled Tribe–majority constituencies. The JMM obtained a majority of the vote in only one of these twenty-seven constituencies. It obtained a respectable share of the vote (between 15 and 50 percent) in twelve others, concentrated largely in the eastern region of Jharkhand. But in fourteen of these twenty-seven constituencies, the JMM

---

[55] Data on the percentage of Scheduled Tribes across constituencies, based on Election Commission publications, were obtained from the CSDS data archive.

obtained less than 15 percent of the vote. These data make it clear that substantial sections of the Scheduled Tribes did not vote for the JMM in 2000.

A third explanation points to the high degree of fragmentation among Scheduled Tribes. The Scheduled Tribes in Jharkhand include four main categories: the Santals, who make up 35 percent of the Scheduled Tribe population, followed by the Oraon (18 percent), the Munda (15 percent), and the Ho (9 percent). The remaining 23 percent of the Scheduled Tribe population in Jharkhand is made up of twenty-six tribes, none of which comprises more than 2 percent of the population.[56] These categories differ from each other on the basis of language and religion. The degree of fragmentation among Scheduled Tribes, according to a common assessment, is reflected directly in the high degree of infighting among tribal leaders, to the detriment of the JMM and other pro-Jharkhand parties. One commentator explained the verdict of the 2000 election thus:

The history of the Jharkhand movement, based on ethnic and regional demands, has been a story of splits and divisions in it, on ethnic and religious lines. . . . It is clear that the tribal leaders concentrated more on infighting than on mobilizing support for the cause. The leaders are accused of getting influenced by electoral politics. This has been the reason for the Jharkhand parties losing their support base and the BJP building its political network throughout Bihar.[57]

But the political fragmentation of the Scheduled Tribes in Jharkhand is itself a puzzle in need of explanation. Fragmentation, I have argued, is typical of all ethnic categories. The key question in the case of the JMM, then, is why it was not able to create a cohesive political category out of these fragments, as other ethnic parties have done more successfully.

According to the hypothesis outlined earlier, the variation in the support for the JMM among Jharkhandis should depend on a difference in the relative representational opportunities provided by the JMM to elites from different ethnic categories in Jharkhand and/or the efficacy of those voters whose elites are best represented in the JMM organization. The ethnic categories given greatest representation in the JMM are Santals and, to a lesser extent, Kurmis (a caste rather than a tribal category). The leader of the JMM, Shibhu Soren, is from the Santal category. Of the five (out of

---

[56] *Census of India 1981*; Susana Devalle, *Discourses of Ethnicity: Culture and Protest in Jharkhand* (New Delhi: Sage Publications, 1992).
[57] Kalyan Chaudhuri, "The Day of Jharkhand," *Frontline*, Vol. 17, No. 24 (November 25–December 8, 2000).

six) principal office bearers of the JMM in 1989 about whom information is available, two were Santal (including Soren), two Kurmi, and one Muslim. While more detailed data await collection, secondary sources on the JMM concur that "in the Jharkhand Mukti Morcha, leadership is in the hands of the Santal."[58]

Santals, as noted above, constitute 35 percent of the Scheduled Tribe population of Jharkhand and approximately 10 percent of the population of Jharkhand as a whole.[59] They are territorially concentrated in eastern Jharkhand. This concentration makes them efficacious in taking their preferred party to a winning or influential position in constituencies in this region. In the multipolar contest of 2000, even a small number of seats could potentially have given a political party a king-making position. As a result, Santal voters in eastern Jharkhand could afford to vote consistently with their preferences. At the same time, voters from other ethnic categories in the eastern region also had an incentive to vote with the Santals, since it was unlikely that non-Santal candidates would obtain a winning or influential position in these areas.

But voters from outside the eastern region had less incentive to vote for the JMM. Since the JMM did not offer representation to elites from their categories, they had no reason to prefer it. And since other voters from their region did not prefer the JMM, they had no reason to expect that it would acquire a winning or influential position in their region. The restriction of the representational profile of the JMM to the Santal, and the concentration of these voters in the eastern belt of Jharkhand, then, explains both the relatively poor performance of the JMM among Jharkhandis and the pattern of variation in its support base better than the alternatives.

Why, in turn, was the JMM not able to broaden its representational profile? This book suggests that the answer lies, not in the inherent problems posed by the fragmentation of Scheduled Tribes but in the absence of a competitive organization. Of all the parties studied here, the quality of secondary data on the JMM is unfortunately the poorest. As a relatively small party, the JMM has not attracted the scholarly attention awarded to the DMK and the BJP. However, the accounts of the organizational structure of the party that do exist describe it as a centralized party held together

---

[58] Sachchidananda, "Pattern of Politico-Economic Change among Tribals in Middle India," in Francine Frankel and M. S. A. Rao, eds., *Dominance and State Power in Modern India*, Vol. II (Delhi: Oxford University Press, 1990), 313; Upjit Singh Rekhi, *Jharkhand Movement in Bihar* (New Delhi: Nunes Publishers, 1988), 226.

[59] *Census of India 1981; Census of India 1991.*

by the charismatic leadership of Shibhu Soren.[60] If this description of the JMM organization is supported by research based on primary sources, it explains why, despite its aspirations, the party has been unable to unite elites from across subdivisions among Scheduled Tribes and Jharkhandis more generally under a single political umbrella and, consequently, why it has failed to obtain the support of voters from these categories.

IV. Conclusion

I have tried to show in this chapter that the hypothesis developed from the study of the BSP – a caste-based party, mobilizing a minority ethnic category – provides an illuminating explanation for the performance of parties mobilizing ethnic categories of other types and different sizes within India. In each case, the hypothesis proposed in this book provides a more convincing explanation than the alternatives. But the argument remains to be investigated systematically for ethnic parties within and outside India.

Such an investigation requires the collection of data on four variables for each country included in the analysis: the degree to which the country meets the criteria for a patronage-democracy, the relevant ethnic demography describing the electorate for a given election, the ethnic profile of the personnel of each political party in that election, and the organizational structure of each political party during the period prior to the election. Data on these variables are not available "off the shelf" but must be constructed from primary sources for each country in question. While that is beyond the scope of this book, I hope to have made the case that the investment of time and resources required to collect these data is worthwhile.

---

[60] Basu, *Jharkhand Movement: Ethnicity and Culture of Silence*, 64.

13

Ethnic Head Counts and Democratic Stability

There is a general sense of disquiet among political scientists, and among the newspaper-reading public more generally, about the impact that a politics of ethnic head counts can have on democratic stability. At the heart of this disquiet is the notion that ethnic head counting leads to the creation of "permanent" majorities and minorities, predetermined by ethnic demography. As Horowitz puts it, "absent some dramatic change in group demography... the result of the election is likely to hold for the next election and for every election thereafter."[1] The permanent exclusion of minorities from power, where it occurs, is likely to lead to escalating violence between minority and majority groups and put the survival of the democratic system at risk.[2]

The argument of this book suggests, however, that it is precisely *because* the rise of ethnic parties is determined by ethnic demography that we may have reason to be less pessimistic. The strong incentives that political elites have to manipulate the definition of ethnic categories in patronage-democracies may prevent the emergence of "permanent" results. And where electoral outcomes can be transformed by political manipulation, we are less likely to see the permanent exclusion of minority groups and the destabilizing violence associated with permanent exclusion. I develop this suggestion here, drawing upon examples of such heresthetical maneuvers by politicians in India.

---

[1] Donald Horowitz, *Ethnic Groups in Conflict* (Berkeley: University of California Press, 1985), 84.

[2] The link between permanent exclusion and destabilizing violence is developed in the models of ethnic "outbidding" proposed by Alvin Rabushka and Kenneth Shepsle, *Politics in Plural Societies* (Columbus, OH: Charles E. Merrill, 1972), and in Horowitz, *Ethnic Groups in Conflict*.

If voters prefer elites and parties that represent their "own" category, then one way in which political entrepreneurs can manipulate electoral outcomes is to pass as members of the voter's "own" category. The many ambiguities that shroud the origin and markers of ethnic categories make such "passing" possible. One example of such an attempt comes from the struggle for the votes of the Pasi caste, one of the many Scheduled Caste categories in Uttar Pradesh. Pasi elites, as I pointed out in Chapter 8, were weakly represented in the Bahujan Samaj Party (BSP), even though the BSP attempted to market itself as the party of all Scheduled Castes. As a consequence, the BSP's support base among Pasis was vulnerable to incursions by other politicians.

At a caste meeting of Pasis in 1997, Ram Vilas Paswan, then in the Janata Dal, attempted to exploit this vulnerability by presenting himself to Pasis as one of their "own."[3] Paswan was known to be a Scheduled Caste politician from Bihar. Although the category "Pasi" exists as a census category in both Bihar and Uttar Pradesh, there is little sense of common identity between those classified as "Pasi" in the two states. Further, although his name signaled a possible Pasi identity, it was not clear whether Paswan was truly a Pasi or belonged to some other Scheduled Caste category in Bihar. Paswan's supporters at the meeting attempted to play down his regional identity as a Bihari and to establish his bona fides as a Pasi. The BSP, however, acted quickly to sabotage Paswan's move. A Pasi office-bearer from the BSP, who secured the right to speak at the meeting in her capacity as a community leader, was succinct in her message to those assembled:

I would like to put two things before you: First, if there is anything that has been done for the Pasi community in the fifty years since independence, it has been done by Mayawati [the BSP leader, who belonged to the Chamar category among Scheduled Castes]. Second I would like to say that respected Ram Vilas Paswan, who has graciously given us his time, is not a Pasi.

The BSP delegate did not get any further. She was forcibly removed from the dais and narrowly escaped being beaten as she left the meeting. However, her remarks had had their intended effect, casting doubt on whether Paswan was truly one of the Pasis' "own." Pasis constitute the second largest Scheduled Caste in Uttar Pradesh, after Chamars. A successful attempt at marketing itself as a Pasi party on the part of the Janata Dal would have shifted the preferences of a sufficiently large number of voters to undercut

---

[3] *Pasi Sammelan*, Lucknow, November 16, 1997.

the BSP's winning margins in several constituencies in eastern Uttar Pradesh. It is no wonder, then, that the BSP was quick to repel the attack.

In this example, Paswan attempted to transform the electoral outcome by passing into the voters' "own" category. A second strategy that political entrepreneurs might use is to encourage voters to pass into *their* "own" category instead. The actions of Rajput entrepreneurs in Gujarat provide one of the many examples of this second strategy. The category "Rajput" is generally used interchangeably with the category "Kshatriya" to describe those who belong to the "twice-born" warrior caste. Prior to independence, Rajputs or Kshatriyas constituted 5 percent of Gujarat's population.[4] The majority of Gujarat's population consisted of "lower" castes, traditionally engaged in farming or menial occupations. With the onset of competitive elections in post-independence India, "it was clear that voter numbers were going to be crucial for winning elections and thus for state power and patronage."[5] Rajput politicians could hardly hope to emerge as a significant force in Gujarat politics with only 5 percent of the population. Rather than bowing to the "predetermined" fate of a minority group, however, these politicians engaged in a large-scale attempt to swell the numbers of their "own" ethnic category by relaxing the strict criteria for membership. As one such entrepreneur openly admitted:

We have taken all the backward people who are martial by nature and called them Kshatriyas. Bhils, Ahirs, Bariyas and Dharalas are all Kshatriyas. Congress has taken up the Harijans, so we have taken up these people. *Those people who have intense nationalism, they are Kshatriyas* [italics mine]. It is not a question of blood but of spirit and action. Kshatriyas have upper and lower classes. We say that if the Bhils are brave enough we will call them Kshatriyas. . . . Anyone can call himself Kshatriya if he wants to. Dharalas don't like that name to be used. I tell them they can use any name they want. What is it if a man uses a Rajput name? There are Rajput clan names like Solanki and Chauhan. Anyone can use them. And if people want to intermarry, that is all right too.[6]

The strategy transformed the nature of politics in Gujarat. By 1984, "Kshatriyas" constituted approximately 29 percent of Gujarat's electorate, and those who classified themselves as "Kshatriyas" dominated local and state-level governments in Gujarat on the basis of the numerical strength

---

[4] 1931 census, cited in Atul Kohli, *Democracy and Discontent* (Cambridge: Cambridge University Press, 1990), 241.

[5] Kohli, *Democracy and Discontent*, 244.

[6] Myron Weiner, *Party Building in a New Nation: The Indian National Congress* (Chicago: University of Chicago Press, 1991), 99.

of "their" community.[7] Such a political outcome could not have been predicted from preexisting census figures. Nor should we expect it to persist,
given the fierce competition by political entrepreneurs in Gujarat to activate
new categories based on both caste and religion.

A third strategy through which political entrepreneurs might manipulate political outcomes based on ethnic demography is to combine small
ethnic blocs into larger aggregates, or to break down such aggregates into
smaller units. Political party competition in India is replete with examples of both types of strategies. In Gujarat in the 1970s, Indira Gandhi's
Congress (I) attempted to orchestrate a winning coalition by aggregating
Kshatriyas, Harijans, Adivasis, and Muslims into the KHAM political coalition. In Uttar Pradesh in the 1960s and 1970s, Charan Singh attempted to
forge the political aggregate AJGAR out of the Ahir, Jat, and Gujjar categories. The Samajwadi Party (SP) in Uttar Pradesh and the Rashtriya Janata
Dal (RJD) in Bihar both aggregated the support of the Muslims and Yadavs
into what is now commonly described as the "MY" coalition. Perhaps the
most striking example of the aggregation of small ethnic blocs to produce
electoral victory for one side and ensure defeat for another is the Janata
Dal's activation of the other backward classes (OBC) category. In 1990, the
Janata Dal announced its decision to set aside 27 percent of the jobs in central government employment for the "other backward classes (OBC)." The
Janata Dal's announcement resulted in the overnight transformation of "a
rather careless bureaucratic nomenclature" into " a vibrant and subjectively
experienced political community"[8] composed of hundreds of previously
disparate castes. The OBC aggregate, however, was just as quickly broken down by subsequent political competition. In Uttar Pradesh, parties
that stood to lose from the consolidation of lower castes behind the OBC
category attempted to carve out from it the new categories of the "most
backward castes" (MBC) and the "forwards among backwards." In this and
previous examples, it would have been difficult to predict in advance how
politicians might combine and disaggregate ethnic building blocks into a
winning coalition. And once created, it would be difficult to predict how
long any aggregate might last.

[7] John R. Wood, "Congress Restored? The "Kham" Strategy and Congress (I) Recruitment in
Gujarat," in John R. Wood, ed., *State Politics in Contemporary India* (Boulder, CO: Westview
Press, 1984), 197–227.
[8] Yogendra Yadav, "Reconfiguration in Indian Politics," *Economic and Political Weekly*, January
13–20, 1996: 102.

A fourth way in which politicians can manipulate electoral outcomes is by redefining the politically relevant categorizations themselves. One example of such a heresthetical maneuver comes from the state of Punjab. In Punjab, party politics in the 1980s was defined by the religious divide separating Hindus from Sikhs. Beginning in 1984, the rise of the BSP in Punjab cut into both the Sikh "majority" and the Hindu "minority" in Punjab by activating caste as a politically salient identity. In 1997, however, an alliance between the pro-Sikh Akali Dal and the pro-Hindu BJP activated instead a regional identity as "Punjabi." The simultaneous availability of at least three politically salient identities around which voters could mobilize rendered electoral outcomes in Punjab deeply uncertain.

In all these examples, the strategies of political entrepreneurs were dictated entirely by ethnic demography. Ethnic demography, however, enabled rather than restricted political competition. At the same time, it is worth emphasizing that the freedom to manipulate ethnic demography is not likely to be present in equal measure across and within patronage-democracies. My examples here have all been drawn from within India. And even within India, all attempts at category construction have not been equally successful. While the category "OBC," proposed by the Janata Dal, obtained an immediate membership, we saw that the category "Bahujan," proposed by the BSP, did not. One important area of new research identified by this book for those interested in the relationship between a politics of ethnic head counts and democratic stability, therefore, is a theoretical investigation of the conditions that enable or restrict the ability of political entrepreneurs to redefine ethnic categories.[9]

While this book suggests that we may have reason to be less pessimistic about the politics of ethnic head counts, however, it also highlights a more fundamental source of disquiet. The origins of the politics of ethnic head counts, I have tried to show, lie in the politics of patronage. Elections in a

---

[9] One example of a country in which ethnic political competition has not precluded fluidity is Uganda during the 1960s, in which two ethnic parties competed for virtually the same body of voters on the basis of different dimensions of ethnicity: The Kabaka Yekka (KY) attempted to mobilize the population on the basis of their Ganda identity, while the Democratic Party (DP) competed with the KY for the same support base by activating instead their religious identity. Crawford Young, *The Politics of Cultural Pluralism* (Madison: University of Wisconsin Press, 1976), 255. An example of a country in which the character of ethnic political competition has been relatively fixed is Sri Lanka. See Stanley Tambiah, *Sri Lanka: Ethnic Fratricide and the Dismantling of Democracy* (Chicago: University of Chicago Press, 1986).

patronage-democracy are in essence covert auctions in which basic services, which should in principle be available to every citizen, are sold instead to the highest bidder. The conversion of elections into auctions may not threaten the survival of a competitive system, but it does subvert the normative ideal of democratic governance. Indeed, the fear of ethnic politics may have blinded us to this deeper malaise in the character of the *states* in which such politics takes firm root.

Appendix A

Elite Interviews

Elite interviews are critical sources for any study of the BSP, especially for its early history. The party did not attract systematic newspaper coverage until 1993, when it came to power in Uttar Pradesh. The party's own publications are valuable sources of party history. However, I was unable to obtain access to the official archives of the party and so rely mainly on collections from private records and on the more extensive public record from 1993 onward. Elite interviews are, therefore, the most important sources on which I draw.

The data on elite motivations in this book come from 281 interviews with members of the BSP and its competition across Indian states. When citing an interview, I withhold the name and position of the respondent except when he or she is a prominent public figure and/or when the name or position is critical to the interpretation of the data obtained in the interview. All respondent names in the text are pseudonyms. Table A.1 describes the organizations whose members I interviewed and the states where the interviews were conducted.

I address in this appendix some variables that are relevant to assessing the quality of the data obtained from these interviews.

The majority of these interviews were conducted in party offices or in the homes of politicians. There were typically other people present or within calling distance, including family members, political associates, and favour seekers. During or before each interview, I introduced myself as a doctoral student based in the United States. I took detailed notes during and after each interview. The use of a tape recorder, however, made many respondents uncomfortable, and I typically did not even propose taping the interview except when interviewing MPs, MLAs, or other party functionaries who were used to having their statements recorded.

Table A.1. *Elite interviews by state and organization*

State	BSP and Related Organizations	Congress	BJP	Other Parties[a]	Other[b]	Total
		Organization				
Delhi	28	3	3	4	5	43
Karnataka	26	1	2	7	19	55
Madhya Pradesh	6	2	1	0	0	9
Punjab	24	11	3	9	12	59
Uttar Pradesh	45	9	5	9	24	92
Other[c]	1	5	8	3	6	23
TOTAL	130	31	22	32	66	281

[a] Other parties include the Janata Dal, CPI, CPM, Akali Dal, SP, and RPI.
[b] "Other" includes bureaucrats, academics, journalists, and political activists.
[c] Other states include Maharashtra, Gujarat, Bihar, and West Bengal.

Among the many variables that might influence the quality of information that I obtained, perhaps the most relevant is my own repertoire of ethnic identities. And among these, caste was the most salient in my interviews with BSP elites. I am a nominal member of the "Bania" caste category, normally counted among the three Hindu upper castes. Most BSP elites asked openly about my caste identity (as I did about theirs) early in our conversation, and I responded by listing the relevant caste and subcaste labels that applied to my family. Except in a few cases, this made no difference in their willingness to talk with me, although it is certainly a relevant variable in the content of our conversations.

A second relevant variable is whether I was perceived as being on the side of any political party. Although I devoted most of my time to interviewing leaders and workers from the BSP, I typically attempted to interview at least one member from every political party in every constituency that I visited, and to accompany workers from all sides in their election campaigns. It is not possible to do this inconspicuously: In most constituencies, party offices were clustered in a small area, and all outsiders attracted attention. With one exception, my presence at the offices and in the campaigns of competing parties was not a cause for concern. In part, this may have been because party workers are used to journalists' interviewing all sides during an election campaign and placed me in a similar slot.

In the states of Delhi, Madhya Pradesh, and Uttar Pradesh – all states in which the majority of the population speaks Hindi – I conducted the interviews in Hindi, in which I am fluent. In the state of Punjab, the two main languages are Punjabi and Hindi. Although Punjabi is written in the Gurmukhi script and Hindi in the Devanagri script, the two languages are mutually comprehensible in spoken form. I have a listening knowledge of Punjabi, although I do not speak or write it myself. The interviews in Punjab, therefore, were conducted in a combination of Hindi and Punjabi. The principal regional language in the state of Karnataka is Kannada, which I neither comprehend nor speak. Most of my respondents in Karnataka, however, also spoke English. The interviews in Karnataka, therefore, were conducted mainly in English. In the case of the small pool of respondents who did not have a working knowledge of English, associates or family members stepped in as interpreters.

I asked two types of questions during my interviews with BSP activists. The first type concerned background variables such as age, caste, district of origin, date of joining the party, activity before joining the party, trajectory after joining the party, and so on. The answers to these questions were entered into a database later and serve as an informal elite survey. The second type included open-ended questions on party strategy, party organization, voter support, and sociological information about the caste or ethnic group to which the activist belonged. Here the precise questions I selected varied based on the position of the respondent and the circumstances of the interview.

I took the answers to the questions on background variables at face value. The answers to the open-ended questions, however, required some rules of interpretation in order to ensure their reliability. The two standard ways of ensuring the reliability of data obtained from elite interviews are (1) to cross-check information with more than one respondent and (2) to corroborate the information with written sources. I employed the first method when possible. However, since the BSP is a highly centralized party, there was often only one person who was in a position to give me the information that I needed. Cross-checking in this case would not produce greater reliability, since I did not have a reasonable expectation that other individuals had access to the same information. The second option was typically unavailable because of the scarcity of written sources.

In order to obtain and assess reliable information based on a single source, therefore, I employed two rules. (1) I asked specific rather than broad questions. To find out how the BSP mobilized voters in a particular state, for example, I did not ask the respondent what the ideology of the party was. Instead, I asked for the points emphasized in a particular speech, or for the wording of particular slogans, and reconstructed the broader picture from the specific details. (2) In assessing the reliability of answers, I searched for an incentive to lie or obfuscate. If I could identify an incentive to lie or obfuscate, I did not use the evidence unless I could cross-check it with a second source. If I could not identify an incentive to lie or obfuscate, I treated it as fact. For example, if a Chamar party member told me that there were many Pasis in the BSP organization, I would expect that he had an incentive to say so in order to portray the BSP as a broad, inclusive organization and would therefore discount the statement. If a Pasi party member gave me the same information, however, I would treat the information as reliable, since my expectation is that Pasi party members in the BSP would have an incentive to underestimate rather than overestimate the Pasi presence in the party.

Appendix B

Ethnographies of Election Campaigns

Since census data in India are not available at the constituency level, it is not possible to obtain a precise measure of the urban population in a constituency. I classify a constituency as "urban" here if (1) the urban population in the district in which it is contained is higher than the average urban population of India as a whole (25.7 percent, according to the 1991 census) and (2) if it contains one or more towns in the district. Parliamentary constituencies can often span more than one district. However, those listed here are almost all completely contained within district boundaries, although the district itself may contain more than one parliamentary constituency. Most urban constituencies here are likely to have large (sometimes majority) rural populations. However, the urban clusters they contain make them different from constituencies that are entirely rural.

Table B.1. *Constituency studies during parliamentary and assembly election campaigns, 1996–98*

Constituency	1991 District	State	Region	Urban/Rural
Parliamentary			*(within India)*	
Bangalore North	Bangalore	Karnataka	South	Urban
Bombay	Greater Bombay	Maharashtra	West	Urban
Dausa	Jaipur	Rajasthan	North	Rural
Dhanduka	Ahmedabad	Gujarat	West	Urban
Dharwar North	Dharwad	Karnataka	South	Urban
Jadavpur	24 Parganas	West Bengal	East	Urban
Latur	Osmanabad	Maharashtra	West	Urban
Mainpuri	Mainpuri	Uttar Pradesh	East	Rural
Sahranpur	Sahranpur	Uttar Pradesh	East	Urban
Ujjain	Ujjain	Madhya Pradesh	Central	Urban
Gonda	Gonda	Uttar Pradesh	East	Rural
Assembly			*(within State)*	
Katra Bazaar	Gonda	Uttar Pradesh	East	Rural
Garhshankar	Hoshiarpur	Punjab	North	Rural
Mahilpur	Hoshiarpur	Punjab	North	Rural
Hoshiarpur	Hoshiarpur	Punjab	North	Rural
Sham Chaurasi	Hoshiarpur	Punjab	North	Rural
Tanda	Hoshiarpur	Punjab	North	Rural
Garhdiwala	Hoshiarpur	Punjab	North	Rural
Dasuya	Hoshiarpur	Punjab	North	Rural
Mukerian	Hoshiarpur	Punjab	North	Rural

Appendix C

Content Analysis

Table C.1. *Words or phrases included in main issue categories in content analysis*

Good Governance	Price Rise	Corruption	Nationalism	Social Justice	Other
Stability	Price rise	Corruption	Slow globalization	Anti-casteism	Women's Reservation Bill
Tradition	Control [of] inflation	*Hawala*	*Swadeshi*	Social justice	Pro-farmers
Danger [of] instability	Anti-devaluation of the rupee	Clean government	Uniform Civil Code	Reservations for Dalit Christians	Pro-agriculture
Capable/responsible government		Honest government	Nuclear deterrent	Reservations for backward castes	Rural industries
Experience		*Suchitra*	Kashmir	Economic justice	Federalism
Prosperity		*Lokayukta*	Economic sovereignty	Income gap	Human rights
Progress			National security	Pro-vulnerable sections	National unity
Peace			Infiltration	Pro-poor	Restrict MNC entry
Performance			National safety	Social equality	Article 356
Good government			*Ramrajya*	Social harmony	Electoral reforms
Law and order			*Hindutva*	*Samrasta*	*Uttarakhand*
Rural development			Cultural nationalism	Social transformation	Autonomy for states
Other development programmes			Strong India	Share in power	River water disputes
Purchasing power			Ram temple		Status of Chandigarh
Employment			Justice for all, appeasement of none		Syl Canal dispute
Social welfare			Purulia arms scandal		
Economic development			Pakistani threat		
Investment			Cow slaughter		
Housing			Minorities Commission		
Literacy			Article 370		
Education			Article 30		
Anti-poverty					
Priority [to] agriculture					
Higher procurement prices					
Subsidy					
Child mortality					
Welfare					
Farmers					
Secularism					
Anti-communalism					
Pro-minorities Commission					
Protection against riots					

300

Economic liberalization
Economic growth
Lower taxes
Lower debt
Rise in foreign exchange reserves
Pro-coalition government
Instability good for government
Anti-capitalism
Land reforms
Criminalization of politics
Failure [of] Congress
Anti-Congress policies
Change in government
Swarjya
Child labour
Economy free from exploitation
Economic development
Economic backwardness
Criticism [of] economic reforms
Criticize debt burden
Free water
Free electricity
Free education
Pension
Health
Other benefits
Price subsidies
Land acquisition
Land reclamation
Canal irrigation schemes

301

Appendix D

Description of Survey Data

Table D.1 lists the survey data used in this book. All surveys were conducted by the Centre for the Study of Developing Societies (Delhi) as part of the Indian National Election Studies Project. The survey data are used here with the permission of the National Election Studies Project.

For each survey, the sample was selected using a multistage random sampling procedure. The sample sizes for individual states, and for subgroups, are reported in individual tables throughout. For a detailed description of the methodology of the 1996 surveys, which formed the model for subsequent survey designs, see Subrata K. Mitra and V. B. Singh, *Democracy and Social Change in India: A Cross-Sectional Analysis of the National Electorate* (Delhi: Sage, 1999).

Table D.1. *Description of election surveys*

Year	Type of Election	Name of Survey	Coverage
1996	Parliamentary	Pre-poll	National
1996	Parliamentary	Midcampaign	National
1996	Parliamentary	Post-poll	National
1996	Assembly	Exit poll	Uttar Pradesh
1997	Assembly	Exit poll	Punjab
1998	Parliamentary	Midcampaign	National
1998	Parliamentary	Post-poll	National
1996–98	Parliamentary	Panel	National

Appendix E

Description of the Ecological Inference (EI) Method

The purpose of this appendix is to provide the reader with sufficient information on the ecological inference (EI) method to evaluate the method with which I arrive at the estimates of Scheduled Caste support for the BSP (section I), to evaluate the use of these estimates for the second-stage analysis of strategic voting (Section II), and to underline the possibilities for research on ethnic politics created by EI (section III). It would be most useful for the reader if read in combination with King's *A Solution to the Ecological Inference Problem* (Princeton: Princeton University Press, 1997).

I. Use of EI to Generate Constituency-Level Estimates of Scheduled Caste Voting Behaviour

The ecological inference problem that I address here is how to estimate the proportion of Scheduled Castes who voted for the BSP in each constituency. King's method solves this problem in two iterations. In the first iteration, it is used to estimate the proportion of Scheduled Castes who turned out in each constituency. The logic of the method is as follows. For any constituency, we can compute deterministic bounds on turnout rates for Scheduled Castes and non–Scheduled Castes in the population. Once we have these deterministic bounds for each constituency, EI computes a probabilistic model showing where the turnout rates are likely to lie by "borrowing strength" from all constituencies in order to produce estimates for each. Using King's notation, the ecological inference problem at iteration 1 is as follows:

	Vote	~Vote	
SC	β_i^b	$1 - \beta_i^b$	X_i
~SC	β_i^w	$1 - \beta_i^w$	$1 - X_i$
	T_i	$1 - T_i$	

X_i = Proportion of SCs in the electorate in constituency i

$1 - X_i$ = Proportion of non-SCs in the electorate in constituency i

T_i = Proportion of electors who turn out to vote in constituency i

$1 - T_i$ = Proportion of electors who do not turn out in constituency i

β_i^b = Proportion of Scheduled Castes who turn out in constituency i

$1 - \beta_i^b$ = Proportion of Scheduled Castes who do not turn out in constituency i

β_i^w = Proportion of non–Scheduled Castes who turn out in constituency i

$1 - \beta_i^w$ = Proportion of non–Scheduled Castes who do not turn out in constituency i

The known quantities at iteration 1 are X_i (the proportion of SCs in the electorate) and T_i (the proportion of all voters who turn out). In this iteration, I use EI to estimate β_i^b (the proportion of Scheduled Castes who turn out) and β_i^w. All of the other quantities can be calculated from these four.

The proportion of Scheduled Caste voters (i.e., electors who turned out) who voted for the BSP is then calculated in the second iteration. The estimates of β_i^b and β_i^w enter the second iteration as follows:

	BSP	non-BSP	Subtotal
SC	λ_i^b	$1 - \lambda_i^b$	β_i^b
non-SC	λ_i^w	$1 - \lambda_i^w$	β_i^w
	D_i		T_i

λ_i^b = Proportion of Scheduled Castes who vote for the BSP in constituency i

$1 - \lambda_i^b$ = Proportion of Scheduled Castes who vote for non-BSP parties in constituency i

λ_i^w = Proportion of non–Scheduled Castes who vote for the BSP in constituency i

$1 - \lambda_i^w$ = Proportion of non–Scheduled Castes who vote for non-BSP parties in constituency i

T_i = Proportion of all voters who turn out in constituency i

D_i = Proportion of all voters who vote for the BSP

This second iteration of EI gives us the ultimate quantities of interest: λ_i^b (proportion of Scheduled Castes who vote for the BSP in constituency i) and λ_i^w (proportion of non–Scheduled Castes who vote for the BSP in constituency i).

Assumptions of the EI Method

The method is based on three assumptions, which I will address at some length, since it is important to understand them in assessing the reliability of the estimates and of the use of EI estimates in models of strategic voting.

First, the method assumes that β^b and β^w and λ_i^b and λ_i^w are generated from a truncated bivariate normal distribution. In other words, in the first iteration, it assumes that Scheduled Caste turnout rates do not differ systematically across different clusters of constituencies. In the second iteration, similarly, it assumes that the proportion of Scheduled Castes who vote for the BSP does not differ systematically across different clusters of constituencies.

Second, EI assumes that there is no aggregation bias in the data. In other words, it assumes that the percentage of Scheduled Castes who turn out in each constituency is independent of the percentage of Scheduled Castes in the electorate. Further, it assumes that the percentage of Scheduled Castes who vote for the BSP in each constituency is independent of the percentage of Scheduled Castes who turn out.

Third, EI assumes that there is no spatial dependence between constituencies. In other words, the percentage of Scheduled Castes who turn out and vote for the BSP in any given constituency is independent of the percentage of Scheduled Castes who turn out and vote for the BSP in proximate constituencies.

Violations of the third assumption are inconsequential. However, violations of the first two, if not corrected for, are likely to produce estimates

305

that are both biased and imprecise. King outlines a series of diagnostics that can be used to detect violations of the method's assumptions and a series of steps that can be taken to address such violations.

Procedure for Obtaining EI Estimates

EI diagnostics for the data I use here did not reveal violations of either of the first two assumptions. However, the capacity of the diagnostics to reveal violations depends upon the quality of the data. This data set has a narrow range on X: The percentage of Scheduled Castes in each constituency varies within a limited range, rarely going above 40 percent. With such data sets, King warns that EI may not perform very well, since the data are not good enough to reveal violations of the method's assumptions. In fact, running the basic model produced aggregate estimates of Scheduled Caste turnout rates that were substantially lower than the survey estimates that I used to check EI results. The bias in the estimates produced by the basic EI model indicated that the data violated one or more of its basic assumptions, even though the diagnostics did not reveal such violations.

I corrected for these violations by using survey data to suggest the extent of aggregation bias and by running an extended model that incorporated data estimating this bias in its priors. By pooling survey data from the 1996 and 1997 exit polls in UP and Punjab, I obtained constituency-level estimates of turnout rates among Scheduled Castes based on between 100 and 200 individual observations for each of 66 constituencies. Running a bivariate regression on the percentage of Scheduled Castes and the turnout rates across these sixty-six constituencies yielded a quantitative measure of the correlation between X_i and β_i. I included this correlation in the priors in the extended model. The scatterplots of X_i and T_i with maximum likelihood contours superimposed, and tomography plots, indicate that the model fits the data. The aggregate estimates produced by the extended model approximated the estimates in the survey data, thus suggesting that the constituency-level estimates are more reliable. Further checks using ethnographic data for eight constituencies in Uttar Pradesh indicated that the estimates produced by the extended model are reliable. However, while the estimates for non–Scheduled Caste turnout rates are relatively precise, the estimates of Scheduled Caste turnout rates are highly uncertain.

Once constituency-level turnout rates were generated in the first iteration of EI, I used additional qualitative information to estimate the proportion of voters who voted for the BSP. Evidence from interviews with BSP candidates and activists indicated that most BSP votes during the 1984–91 period came from Scheduled Caste voters. This information is reliable for two reasons. First, the BSP is an ethnic party that relied heavily during its 1989 and 1991 election campaigns on a strategy of polarization that identified upper castes as the enemy. We can reasonably assume, therefore, that no upper castes voted for the BSP in those elections (although this would not be true of more recent elections). Second, although the BSP attempted to include other minority groups (Muslims and backward castes) in its projected electoral coalition, BSP workers readily admit that they were not successful in that effort in the initial stages. According to these candidates and activists, where the BSP put up Scheduled Caste candidates, they obtained the support only of Scheduled Caste voters. And where they put up non–Scheduled Caste candidates, they obtained mostly Scheduled Caste votes, coupled with some additional votes from those who shared the ethnic identity of the candidate. In general, BSP workers have every incentive to overreport their level of support among non–Scheduled Castes to an interviewer in order to present the party as more socially inclusive and successful than it is actually. The widespread and repeated admission of failure, therefore, should be treated as especially reliable. Based on this additional qualitative information, we know that λ_i^w is close to zero.

However, EI does not permit the user to set a limit on the value of λ_i^w. Rather than run the second iteration, therefore, I simply set $\lambda_i^w = 0$ and calculated λ_i^b (the proportion of Scheduled Castes voting for the BSP) by calculating the total votes obtained by the BSP as a proportion of the total number of Scheduled Castes who turned out. Although this procedure might generate overestimates of Scheduled Caste support for the BSP in those constituencies where the BSP has fielded a non–Scheduled Caste candidate, it is still better than running the second iteration of EI, which would certainly produce higher values values for λ_i^w and lower values for λ_i^b than we know are reasonable. The uncertainty estimates for λ_i^b are identical to those for β_i^b. The uncertainty of these estimates should be taken into account in evaluating the test of strategic voting presented here.

II. Using EI Estimates in a Second-Stage Analysis of Strategic Voting

There is a logical contradiction in using EI estimates to test for strategic voting. In this section, I describe this contradiction and the way in which I have addressed it here.

307

If substantial numbers of Scheduled Caste voters vote strategically in the manner that I have described, then the data are likely to violate both the distributional assumption of the EI method and the assumption of no aggregation bias. If Scheduled Castes vote strategically, then we should expect support for the BSP to be systematically higher in those clusters of constituencies where it has leverage, as opposed to those where it does not. This violates the distributional assumption of the model. Second, if Scheduled Castes vote strategically, then support for the BSP should be correlated with the percentage of Scheduled Castes in each constituency. This violates the assumption of no aggregation bias. If not corrected for, EI would produce biased estimates. These estimates, input into a test for strategic voting, would not tell us very much.

The principal way in which to correct for these violations is to incorporate external information on Scheduled Caste voting behaviour. If we suspect strategic voting on the part of Scheduled Castes, then one solution suggested by King is to include a covariate that models the suspected relationship between X_i and β_i^b and then between β_i^b and λ_i^b, in the first and second iteration respectively. However, the problem with this method, if we are interested in testing for strategic voting, is that we would then incorporate the same information into the production of our estimates that we want to test for. In other words, the test for strategic voting at the second stage would be "rigged," because the estimates were produced by a process that already assumed that Scheduled Castes were voting strategically.

I have addressed this contradiction here in two ways. First, I corrected for possible aggregation bias in the first iteration, not by incorporating any expectation about strategic voting on the part of Scheduled Castes, but by incorporating independently generated information from survey data. This ensured that the estimates of Scheduled Caste turnout rates have been produced by a process independent of the hypothesis of strategic voting. Second, because I did not rerun the EI model to estimate the proportion of Scheduled Castes who voted for the BSP at the second iteration, but rather estimated this proportion using simple algebra, possible aggregation bias in the second iteration does not affect the estimates. In other studies that probe for strategic voting among ethnic groups, it is similarly important to use methods of correcting for model violations that are independent of the hypothesized voting behaviour.

III. Possibilities for Research on Ethnic Politics

King points to the general advantages of EI for all political science research where individual-level survey data are unavailable or unreliable. In this section, I underline the particular advantages that EI has for investigations into ethnic politics.

The field of ethnic politics is particularly marked by a bias toward macro-level studies that emphasize the importance of economic and historical forces affecting ethnic mobilization but neglect the microprocesses that underlie these broad theories. This is in part due to the lack of micro-level data on how ethnic groups behave. The relatively recent development of the survey as a research tool means that survey data that would allow us to identify historical patterns in ethnic group political behaviour simply do not exist. And in many cases where surveys do exist, the size of the samples or the categories used do not permit analyses of the particular ethnic categories of interest. EI opens up significant possibilities for procuring data on ethnic participation and voting behaviour for micro-units across space and across time, which should lead to the development of better theory.

In addition, EI may be an even better tool than survey data for allowing us to design tests of constructivist hypotheses of ethnic group behaviour. Surveys typically use identity codes for individuals that reflect the politically salient identity categories at the time the survey is conducted. For scholars interested in testing whether the salient identity categories themselves change across time and space, survey data are often of little use. EI, however, permits the researcher to impose the categories, and then probe to see whether certain categories reflect distinct voting patterns while others do not. The principal constraint on using EI to test constructivist hypotheses is whether demographic data are available on the categories of interest. But even with this constraint, EI provides greater opportunities to explore such hypotheses than have existed previously.

It is precisely because of these advantages of EI that the problems in its application, documented in some detail in this appendix, deserve careful attention.

Appendix F

Method Used to Estimate Ethnic Voting Patterns

The estimates for the percentage of Scheduled Castes voting for the BSP, of Hindus voting for the BJP, of Tamils voting for the DMK, and of Jharkhandis voting for the JMM are arrived at in the following way: I assume that (1) all the votes of the ethnic party in question came from members of its target ethnic category, (2) the percentage of the target ethnic category in the electorate is the same as the percentage in the population, and (3) turnout rates across ethnic categories are equal. Based on these three assumptions, I arrive at estimates of the percentage of the ethnic category supporting the ethnic party in question by calculating the percentage of the vote obtained by the ethnic party as a proportion of the percentage of the target ethnic category in the population. The data on which these estimates are based are summarized in the accompanying tables.

I detail here how I use this method for calculating Scheduled Caste voting patterns for the BSP. In the absence of survey data on individual-level voting patterns, or of sufficiently detailed data to permit an EI analysis, this is the simplest and most transparent way of assessing the degree of support for an ethnic party among its target ethnic group. The possible biases that these assumptions introduce are identified below. If we know that these assumptions are violated in particular cases, we can adjust them accordingly, or at least estimate the direction of bias.

In estimating the percentage of Scheduled Castes voting for the BSP across states, I assume that (1) all of the BSP's votes in each state come from Scheduled Castes, (2) the percentage of Scheduled Castes in the electorate is identical to that in the population, and (3) the turnout rates of Scheduled Castes and the rest of the population are equal. Based on these assumptions, I arrive at the estimates by calculating the average vote for the BSP across the five *parliamentary* elections (1984, 1989, 1991, 1996, and 1998) as a proportion of the overall Scheduled Caste population in the state. For example, if the BSP obtains an average of 10 percent of the vote in a state in which 20 percent of the population is from the Scheduled Castes, I would estimate that 50 percent of the Scheduled Castes in the state, on average, supported the BSP.

The first assumption is empirically justified by evidence collected from interviews with BSP workers across seven states, who readily admitted that their vote base is composed mainly of Scheduled Castes for the period under study. However, it results in a slight overestimate of the level of Scheduled Caste support for the BSP, since there are pockets in which the BSP also obtained some support from other ethnic categories, particularly in 1996 and 1998. This assumption may also be violated in those elections in which the BSP had alliances. However, I expect the inaccuracy introduced by alliances to be marginal. The BSP had alliances in only two states in two parliamentary elections (Punjab and Jammu and Kashmir) in the parliamentary elections during the period under analysis. Even in these two states, alliances are likely to have affected the pattern of concentration of votes but not necessarily the overall vote percentage. What the party gains in additional votes in the seats that it contested may have been offset by the loss of votes from the seats it did not contest.

Although the second assumption cannot be verified, it is reasonable. The electorate is composed of all individuals resident in the district who are eighteen years of age or older. The census does not report data separately on the population over the age of eighteen. However, there is no reason to expect that the age profile of Scheduled Castes is different from that of any other ethnic category in India.

The third assumption is perhaps the most contested. On the one hand, studies of minority voting behaviour suggest that to the extent that minority ethnic categories in India are more politically conscious than other categories, the turnout rates of Scheduled Castes should be higher than those of other categories. On the other hand, exit polls in some states indicate that the turnout rates among Scheduled Castes are somewhat lower than those of other ethnic categories. If Scheduled Caste turnout rates are higher than those of other ethnic categories, then the estimates that I arrive at here are biased upward (i.e., are higher than the "true" values). If Scheduled Caste turnout rates are lower than those of other ethnic categories, then the estimates that I arrive at here are biased downward (i.e., are lower than the "true" values).

Even with these sources of bias, the method used here is the best method for estimating the dependent variable across time. National exit polls and post-poll surveys have not been conducted for all election years, or for all states during the 1984–97 period, and the sample size and design do not permit estimates for the state level in some cases. While I draw on these surveys for studies of particular elections in this book, they are not useful for describing the range of variation of the dependent variable across space and time. The ecological inference method, which I used to estimate constituency-level data in Chapter 10, is also not reliable in this case. The population of Scheduled Castes varies very little across constituencies and so does not provide sufficient variation to generate reliable EI estimates. In this case, EI is a useful research strategy only when used in addition to survey data that can be used to compensate for the lack of information. In the EI estimates in Chapter 10, I was able to use survey data to generate reliable estimates. However, such data do not exist for most of the parliamentary elections shown in Map 1.2 or in the remaining maps.

Table F.1. *Performance of the Bahujan Samaj Party (BSP) by state, 1984–98 parliamentary elections*[a]

Region/State	% SC Population	1984 Vote for BSP[b] (%)	1989 Vote for BSP (%)	1991 Vote for BSP (%)	1996 Vote for BSP (%)	1998 Vote for BSP (%)	Average Vote for BSP[c] (%)	% SCs Who Voted for BSP (Average)
North								
Haryana	19.7	0.26	1.62	1.79	6.59	7.68	3.59	18.21
Himachal Pradesh	25.3	0.43	0.84	0	0.69	1.45	0.68	2.70
Jammu & Kashmir	8.3	0.44	4.06	0	5.95	5.05	3.88	46.69
Madhya Pradesh	14.5	1.2	4.28	3.54	8.18	8.7	5.18	35.72
Punjab	28.3	3.1	8.62	19.71	9.35	12.65	10.69	37.76
Rajasthan	17.3	0.1	0.3	0.11	1.35	2.12	0.80	4.60
Uttar Pradesh	21	1.73	9.93	8.7	20.61	20.9	12.37	58.92
Delhi	19.1	0.23	4.25	0.92	0	2.34	1.55	8.10
West								
Goa	2.1	0	1.29	0.61	0	0	0.38	18.10
Gujarat	7.4	0.25	0.06	0.02	0.38	0	0.14	1.92
Maharashtra	11.1	0.61	0.67	0.48	0.29	0.75	0.56	5.05
South								
Andhra Pradesh	15.9	0	0.49	0.38	0.04	0.21	0.22	1.41
Karnataka	16.4	0	0	0.03	0.15	0.56	0.15	0.90
Kerala	9.9	0	0.12	0.16	0.15	0.13	0.11	1.13
Tamil Nadu	19.2	0	0	0.02	0	0.23	0.05	0.26
East								
Bihar	14.6	0	0.11	0.14	0.63	0.54	0.28	1.95
Orissa	16.2	0.31	0.14	0.64	0	0.32	0.28	1.74
West Bengal	23.6	0	0.31	0.37	0.11	0.24	0.21	0.87

(continued)

313

Table F.1 (continued)

Region/State	% SC Population	1984 Vote for BSP[b] (%)	1989 Vote for BSP (%)	1991 Vote for BSP (%)	1996 Vote for BSP (%)	1998 Vote for BSP (%)	Average Vote for BSP[c] (%)	% SCs Who Voted for BSP (Average)
Northeast								
Arunachal Pradesh	0.5	0	0	0	0	0	0.00	0.00
Assam	7.4	0	0	0	0	0	0.00	0.00
Manipur	2	0	0	0	0	0	0.00	0.00
Meghalaya	0.5	0	0	0	0	0	0.00	0.00
Mizoram	0.1	0	0	0	0	0	0.00	0.00
Nagaland	0	0	0	0	0	0	0.00	0.00
Sikkim	5.9	0	0	0	0	0	0.00	0.00
Tripura	16.4	0	0	0	0	0	0.00	0.00
TOTAL	16.5	0.5	2.07	1.8	4.01	4.68	2.35	15.83

[a] The 1984 and 1991 Lok Sabha election results have been adjusted to incorporate the results of the Punjab Lok Sabha elections, which were held separately, in 1985 and 1992, respectively. Official data are not available for BSP performance by state in the 1984 elections, since the BSP was not a registered party and the BSP candidates contested the 1984 elections as independents. The 1984 election results are taken from the BSP publications *Oppresed Indian*, April 1985, which reported the number of votes obtained by BSP candidates in each state in which the BSP contested (except Punjab); and *Babujan Samgathak*, March 24, 1986, which reported the number of votes obtained by BSP candidates in Punjab.

[b] Here and in the data for the remaining elections, a vote percentage of 0 means that the BSP did not contest these elections.

[c] The average is calculated here across the five elections for every state except Jammu and Kashmir. Where the BSP did not contest, I take the vote percentage to be 0% and include it in the calculation for the average. Because elections in Jammu and Kashmir were not held in 1991, the average for Jammu and Kashmir is calcuated on the basis of four elections.

Source: Compiled from *Census of India 1991, Census District Handbook; Census of India 1991, Primary Census Abstract: Scheduled Castes; Report on the Eighth General Elections to the House of the People in India 1984* (New Delhi: Election Commission of India, 1985); *Report on the Eighth General Election to the House of the People from Assam and Punjab and on the Bye-Elections to That House Held in 1985* (New Delhi: Election Commission of India, 1986); *Report on the Ninth General Elections to the House of the People in India* (New Delhi: Election Commission of India, n.d.); *Report on the Tenth General Elections to the House of the People in India* (New Delhi: Election Commission of India, n.d.); *Report on the General Election to the House of the People from Punjab State 1992 and Statistical Report on General Elections 1996 to the Eleventh Lok Sabha* (New Delhi: Election Commission of India, n.d.).

Method Used to Estimate Ethnic Voting Patterns

Table F.2. *Performance of the Bharatiya Janata Party (BJP) by state, 1991 parliamentary elections*

State	% Hindu Population	1991 Vote for the BJP (%)	% Hindus Who Voted for the BJP
Andhra Pradesh	89.14	9.63	10.80
Arunachal Pradesh	37.04	6.11	16.50
Assam	67.13	9.60	14.30
Bihar	82.42	15.95	19.35
Goa	64.68	15.61	24.13
Gujarat	89.48	50.37	56.29
Haryana	89.21	10.17	11.40
Himachal Pradesh	95.90	42.79	44.62
Jammu and Kashmir[a]	32.24[b]		
Karnataka	85.45	28.78	33.68
Kerala	57.28	4.61	8.05
Madhya Pradesh	92.80	41.88	45.13
Maharashtra	81.12	20.20	24.90
Manipur	57.67	8.10	14.05
Meghalaya	14.67	6.89	46.97
Mizoram	5.05	0.00	0.00
Nagaland	10.12	3.00	29.64
Orissa	94.67	9.50	10.03
Rajasthan	89.08	40.88	45.89
Sikkim	68.37	0.00	0.00
Tamil Nadu	88.67	1.65	1.86
Tripura	86.50	2.99	3.46
Uttar Pradesh	81.74	32.83	40.16
West Bengal	74.72	11.67	15.62
TOTAL	82.41	20.1	24.44

[a] Parliamentary elections were not held in Jammu and Kashmir in 1991 and were postponed in Punjab until 1992.
[b] 1981 census figures.

Source: Compiled from *Census of India 1991*; *Census of India 1981*; *Report on the Tenth General Elections to the House of the People in India* (New Delhi: Election Commission of India, n.d.).

Table F.3. *Performance of the DMK in Tamil Nadu by district, 1967 legislative assembly elections*

District	% Tamil Population	1967 Vote for the DMK (%)	% Tamils Who Voted for the DMK
Madras	70.94	48.8	68.79
Chingleput	82.88	56.1	67.69
North Arcot	81.48	48.2	59.15
South Arcot	92.75	50	53.91
Salem	75.28	47.4	62.96
Coimbatore	67.54	36.9	54.63
Nilgiris	38.56	21	54.46
Madurai	78.98	35.3	44.69
Tiruchirapalli	90.72	44.3	48.83
Thanjavur	96.57	33.3	34.48
Ramanathapuram	89.49	26.7	29.83
Tirunelveli	93.51	36.5	39.03
Kanyakumari	86.63	9.1	10.50
TOTAL	83.15	40.6	48.83

Source: Census of India 1961; Craig Baxter, *District Voting Trends in India* (New York: Columbia University Press, 1969).

Table F.4. *Performance of the Jharkhand Mukti Morcha (JMM) in Jharkhand by district, 2000 legislative assembly elections*

District	2000 Vote for the JMM (%)
Godda	17.09
Sahebganj	22.63
Dumka	32.63
Deoghar	29.49
Dhanbad	11.32
Giridih	15.00
Hazaribagh	12.76
Palamu	2.47
Lohardaga	3.08
Gumla	10.86
Ranchi	4.66
East Singhbhum	22.31
West Singhbhum	21.49
TOTAL	15.93

Source: Calculated from *Census of India 1991;* Election Commission of India, *Statistical Report on the General Election, 2000 to the Legislative Assembly of Bihar.*

Bibliography

Government Publications

Census of India 1971: Series 1, & Punjab Part II-C(ii), C-V Part A.
Census of India Atlas 1981: Series 17, Punjab Part Xii.
Census of India 1991: 1991 Census District Handbook.
Census of India 1991: General Population Tables and Primary Census Abstract 1991 (Punjab), Part II-A and Part II-B, Statement 8.
Census of India 1991: Primary Census Abstract for Scheduled Castes.
Election Commission of India. 1976. *Delimitation of Parliamentary and Assembly Constituencies Order, 1976.*
Election Commission of India. n.d. *Report on the General Elections to the Legislative Assemblies 1979–1980.*
Election Commission of India. n.d. *Report on the Eighth General Elections to the House of the People in India 1984.*
Election Commission of India. n.d. *Report on the Eighth General Election to the House of the People from Assam and Punjab, 1985.*
Election Commission of India. n.d. *Report on the General Elections to the Legislative Assemblies of Andhra Pradesh, Assam, Bihar, Gujarat, Himachal Pradesh, Karnataka, Madhya Pradesh, Maharashtra, Manipur, Orissa, Punjab, Rajasthan, Sikkim, Tamil Nadu, Uttar Pradesh, Arunachal Pradesh, Goa, Daman and Diu and Pondicherry, 1984–5, Vols. I–III.*
Election Commission of India. n.d. *Report on the Ninth General Elections to the House of the People in India, 1989.*
Election Commission of India. n.d. *Report on the General Elections to the Legislative Assemblies of Andhra Pradesh, Arunachal Pradesh, Bihar, Goa, Gujarat, Himachal Pradesh, Karnataka, Madhya Pradesh, Maharashtra, Manipur, Orissa, Rajasthan, Sikkim, Uttar Pradesh and Pondicherry, 1989–90 and Bye-Elections to the Legislative Assemblies Held in 1989–90, Vols. I–II.*
Election Commission of India. n.d. *Report on the Tenth General Elections to the House of the People in India, 1991.*
Election Commission of India. n.d. *Report on the General Election to the House of the People from Punjab State 1992.*

Election Commission of India. n.d. *Report on the General Elections to the Legislative Assemblies of Delhi, Himachal Pradesh, Madhya Pradesh, Meghalaya, Mizoram, Nagaland, Rajasthan, Tripura and Uttar Pradesh Held in 1993 and By-Elections to the Legislative Assemblies in 1993–1994, Vols. I–II.*

Election Commission of India. n.d. *Report on the General Elections to the Legislative Assemblies of Andhra Pradesh, Goa, Karnataka and Sikkim Held in 1994.*

Election Commission of India. 1995. *Manual of Election Law, Vols. I–II.*

Election Commission of India. n.d. *Statistical Report on General Elections, 1996 to the Eleventh Lok Sabha, Vols. I–III.*

Election Commission of India. n.d. *Statistical Report on General Elections, 1996 to the Legislative Assembly of Uttar Pradesh.*

Election Commission of India. n.d. *Statistical Report on General Elections 1997 to the Legislative Assembly of Punjab.*

Election Commission of India. 1997. *Handbook for Counting Agents.*

Election Commission of India. n.d. *Statistical Report on General Elections, 1998 to the Twelfth Lok Sabha, Vols. I–II.*

Election Commission of India. 1998. *Model Code of Conduct for the Guidance of Political Parties and Candidates.*

Election Commission of India. 1998. *Handbook for Returning Officers.*

Government of India. n.d. *Mandal Commission Report of the Backward Classes Commission, 1980.*

Government of India. n.d. *Basic Rural Statistics, 1996.*

Government of Punjab. 1996. *Statistical Abstract of Punjab.* Chandigarh: Economic Adviser to Government.

Government of Punjab. n.d. *Special Component Plan for Scheduled Castes 1996–1997.*

Ministry of Finance. 1997. *Report of the Fifth Central Pay Commission, Volumes I–III.*

Twenty-Ninth Report of the Commissioner for Linguistic Minorities in India, 1991.

Newspapers and Serials

Deccan Herald
Economic Times
Frontline
Hindu
India Annual
India Today
Indian Express
Journal of Parliamentary Information
Pioneer
Times of India
Tribune

Party Periodicals and Other Documents

Bahujan Sangathak
Oppressed Indian
Rajan, Ambeth. *My Bahujan Samaj Party.* New Delhi: ABCDE, 1994.

Bibliography

Recorded Texts of Election Rallies, Caste Conventions, and Other Public Meetings

BJP Election Rally, Hubli, Karnataka, April 18, 1996.
National Front/Left Front Rally, Bombay North, Maharashtra, April 23, 1996.
National Front/Left Front Rally, Kanpur, April 1996.
BSP Election Rally, Karmagaon, Allahabad, April 29, 1996.
BJP Election Meeting, Jadavpur, West Bengal, May 1996.
BSP Rally, Dabri Palam, Delhi, December 8, 1996.
Pichda Varg Mahasammelan, Lucknow, December 16, 1996.
Congress Party Rally, Allahabad, November 14, 1997.
Pasi Sammelan, Lucknow, November 16, 1997.
BSP Election Rally, Hoshiarpur, January 25, 1997.
BSP Election Rally, Sahranpur, February 14, 1998.
BSP Election Rally, Gonda, February 18, 1998.
Bharatiya Janata Party Election Rally, Sahranpur, February 14, 1998.
Samajwadi Party Election Rally, Sahranpur February 14, 1998.

Books and Articles

Ahluwalia, Montek S. "Economic Performance of States in Post-Reforms Period." *Economic and Political Weekly*, May 6, 2000: 1637–1648.
Akerlof, George A. "The Market for 'Lemons': Quality Uncertainty and the Market Mechanism." *Quarterly Journal of Economics*, Vol. 84, No. 3 (1970): 488–500.
Akerlof, George. "The Economics of Caste and of the Rat Race and Other Woeful Tales." *Quarterly Journal of Economics*, Vol. 90, No. 4 (1976): 599–617.
Albo, Xavier. "And from Kataristas to MNRistas?" In Donna Lee Van Cott, ed. *Indigenous Peoples and Democracy in Latin America*. New York: St. Martin's Press, 1994: 55–82.
Aldrich, John. "Rational Choice and Turnout." *American Journal of Political Science*, Vol. 37, No. 1 (1993): 246–278.
Ambedkar, B. R. *What Congress and Gandhi Have Done to the Untouchables*. Bombay: Thacker & Co., 1945.
Ames, Barry. *Political Survival: Politicians and Public Policy in Latin America*. Berkeley: University of California Press, 1987.
Ames, Barry. "The Reverse Coattails Effect: Local Party Organization in the 1989 Brazilian Presidential Election." *The American Political Science Review*, Vol. 88, No. 1 (1994): 95–111.
Amin, Shahid, and Dipesh Chakrabarty. *Subaltern Studies IX*. Delhi: Oxford University Press, 1996.
Andersen, Benedict. *Imagined Communities*. London: Verso, 1983.
Anderson, Walter K., and Shridhar D. Damle. *The Brotherhood in Saffron*. Delhi: Vistaar Publications, 1987.
Arrow, Kenneth. "Models of Job Discrimination." In Anthony Pascal, ed. *Racial Discrimination in Economic Life*. Lexington, MA: Lexington Books, 1972: 83–102.

Arrow, Kenneth. "Some Mathematical Models of Race in the Labor Market." In Anthony Pascal, ed. *Racial Discrimination in Economic Life*. Lexington, MA: Lexington Books, 1972: 187–204.

Assadi, Muzaffar. "Karnataka: Changing Shape of Caste Conflict." *Economic and Political Weekly*, May 6–12, 2000: 1–5.

Auyero, Javier. *Poor People's Politics: Peronist Survival Networks and the Legacy of Evita*. Durham, NC: Duke University Press, 2000.

Axelrod, Robert. *The Evolution of Cooperation*. New York: Basic Books, 1984.

Banton, Michael. *Racial and Ethnic Competition*. Cambridge: Cambridge University Press, 1983.

Bardhan, Pranab. *The Political Economy of Development in India*. Oxford: Basil Blackwell, 1984.

Barnett, Marguerite Ross. *The Politics of Cultural Nationalism in South India*. Princeton, NJ: Princeton University Press, 1976.

Barth, Frederik, ed. *Ethnic Groups and Boundaries*. Prospect Heights, IL: Waveland Press, 1969.

Basu, Amrita, and Atul Kohli, eds. *Community Conflicts and the State in India*. Delhi: Oxford University Press, 1998.

Basu, Sajal. *Jharkhand Movement: Ethnicity and Culture of Silence*. Shimla: Indian Institute of Advanced Study, 1994.

Bates, Robert. "Ethnic Competition and Modernization in Contemporary Africa." *Comparative Political Studies*, Vol. 6, No. 4 (1974): 457–483.

Bates, Robert. *Markets and States in Tropical Africa*. Berkeley: University of California Press, 1981.

Bates, Robert. "Comparative Politics and Rational Choice: A Review Essay." *American Political Science Review*, Vol. 91, No. 3 (1997).

Bates, Robert. "Ethnicity, Capital Formation and Conflict." Paper presented at the festschrift conference for Myron Weiner, September 24–26, Kellogg Institute, University of Notre Dame, 1999.

Bates, Robert H., Rui J. P. de Figueiredo, Jr., and Barry R. Weingast. "The Politics of Interpretation: Rationality, Culture and Transition." *Politics and Society*, Vol. 26, No. 4 (1998): 603–642.

Baxter, Craig. *District Voting Trends in India*. New York and London: Columbia University Press, 1969.

Baxter, Craig. *The Jana Sangh*. Philadelphia: University of Pennsylvania Press, 1969.

Bayley, David H. *The Police and Political Development in India*. Princeton, NJ: Princeton University Press, 1969.

Benton, Allyson Lucinda, "Patronage Games: Economic Reform, Political Institutions, and the Decline of Party Stability in Latin America." Ph.D. dissertation, University of California at Los Angeles, 2001.

Bhagwati, Jagdish. *India in Transition*. Oxford: Clarendon Press, 1993.

Bienen, Henry. *Kenya: The Politics of Participation and Control*. Princeton, NJ: Princeton University Press, 1974.

Birnbach, Lisa. *Preppy Handbook*. New York: Workman Publishing, 1980.

Boltanski, Luc. *The Making of a Class*. Cambridge: Cambridge University Press, 1987.

Bibliography

Bonner, Arthur. *Averting the Apocalypse*. Durham, NC: Duke University Press, 1990.

Bouton, Marshall, and Philip Oldenburg. *India Briefing, 1989*. Boulder, CO: Westview Press, 1990.

Bouton, Marshall, and Philip Oldenburg. *India Briefing, 1990*. Boulder, CO: Westview Press, 1990.

Brass, Paul. *Factional Politics in an Indian State*. Berkeley: University of California Press, 1965.

Brass, Paul. *Language, Religion and Politics in North India*. Cambridge: Cambridge University Press, 1974.

Brass, Paul. "Ethnic Cleavages in the Punjab Party System 1952–1972." In Myron Weiner and John Osgood Fields, eds. *Electoral Politics in the Indian States, Vol. IV*. Delhi: Manohar, 1975: 7–69.

Brass, Paul. "National Power and Local Politics in India: A Twenty-Year Perspective." *Modern Asian Studies*, Vol. 18, No. 1 (1984): 89–118.

Brass, Paul R. *The Politics of India since Independence*. Delhi: Cambridge University Press, 1990.

Brass, Paul. "General Elections 1996 in Uttar Pradesh." *Economic and Political Weekly*, September 20, 1997: 2403–2421.

Brass, Paul R. *Theft of an Idol*. Calcutta: Seagull Books, 1998.

Breton, Albert. "The Economics of Nationalism." *Journal of Political Economy*, Vol. 72, No. 4 (1964): 376–386.

Budge, Ian, Ivor Crewe, and Denis Farlie. *Party Identification and Beyond*. London: Wiley, 1976.

Budge, Ian, and Dennis Farlie. *Voting and Party Competition*. London: Wiley, 1977.

Budge, Ian, David Robertson, and Derek J. Hearl, eds. *Ideology, Strategy and Party Change: Spatial Analyses of Post-War Election Programmes in 19 Democracies*. Cambridge: Cambridge University Press, 1987.

Bueno de Mesquita, Bruce. *Strategy, Risk and Personality in Coalition Politics*. Cambridge: Cambridge University Press, 1975.

Burger, Angela Sutherland. *Opposition in a Dominant-Party System*. Berkeley: University of California Press, 1969.

Burgwal, Gerritt. *Caciquismo, Paralelismo and Clientelismo: The History of a Quito Squatter Settlement*. (Urban Research Working Papers no. 32.) Amsterdam: Institute of Cultural Anthropology/Sociology of Development, Vrije Universiteit, 1993.

Butler, David, Ashok Lahiri, and Prannoy Roy. *India Decides: Elections 1952–1995*. New Delhi: Living Media, 1995.

Castles, Francis, and Peter Mair. 1984. "Left-Right Political Scales: Some Expert Judgments." *European Journal of Political Research*, Vol. 12 (1984): 73–88.

Chabal, Patrick, and Jean-Pascal Daloz. *Africa Works*. Oxford: International African Institute, 1999.

Chakravarty, Kalyan Kumar. *Tribal Identity in India: Extinction or Adaptation*. Bhopal: Indira Gandhi Rashtriya Manav Sangrahalaya, 1996.

Chandra, Kanchan. "Inside the BJP: Political Actors and Ideological Choices." Paper presented at the 1994 meeting of the Association of Asian Studies, Boston, March 1994.

Chandra, Kanchan. "Mobilizing the Excluded." *Seminar*, Vol. 430 (August 1999): 46–51.

Chandra, Kanchan. "Post-Congress Politics in Uttar Pradesh: The Ethnification of the Party System and Its Consequences." In Paul Wallace and Ramashray Roy, eds. *Indian Politics and the 1998 Election*. New Delhi: Sage, 1999: 55–104.

Chandra, Kanchan. "Elite Incorporation in Multi-Ethnic Societies." *Asian Survey*, Vol. 40, No. 5 (2000): 836–855.

Chandra, Kanchan. "The Transformation of Ethnic Politics in India: The Decline of Congress and the Rise of the Bahujan Samaj Party in Hoshiarpur." *Journal of Asian Studies*, Vol. 59, No. 1 (2000): 26–61.

Chandra, Kanchan, ed. "Cumulative Findings in the Study of Ethnic Politics." *APSA-CP*, Vol. 12, No. 1 (Winter 2001): 7–11.

Chandra, Kanchan. "Ethnic Bargains, Group Instability and Social Choice Theory." *Politics and Society*, Vol. 29, No. 3 (2001): 337–362.

Chandra, Kanchan. "Ethnic Parties and Democratic Stability." Unpublished Manuscript, 2002.

Chandra, Kanchan, and Chandrika Parmar. "Party Strategies in the Uttar Pradesh Assembly Elections 1996." *Economic and Political Weekly*, February 1, 1997: 214–222.

Charsley, Simon, and G. K. Karanth, eds. *Challenging Untouchability*. New Delhi: Sage, 1998.

Chhibber, Pradeep. *Democracy without Associations*. Ann Arbor: University of Michigan Press, 1999.

Christiansen, Thomas. "Plaid Cymru: Dilemmas and Ambiguities of Welsh Regional Nationalism." In Lieven de Winter and Huri Tursan, eds. *Regionalist Parties in Western Europe*. London: Routledge, 1998: 124–142.

Chubb, Judith. *Patronage, Power and Poverty in Southern Italy: A Tale of Two Cities*. Cambridge: Cambridge University Press, 1982.

Cohn, Bernard. *An Anthropologist among the Historians and Other Essays*. Delhi: Oxford University Press, 1987.

Collier, David. "Translating Quantitative Methods for Qualitative Researchers: The Case of Selection Bias." *American Political Science Review*, Vol. 89, No. 2 (1995): 461–466.

Corbridge, Stuart. "The Ideology of Tribal Economy and Society: Politics in the Jharkhand, 1950–1980." *Modern Asian Studies*, Vol. 22, No. 1 (1988): 1–42.

Corbridge, Stuart. "Competing Inequalities: The Scheduled Tribes and the Reservations System in India's Jharkhand." *Journal of Asian Studies*, Vol. 59, No. 1 (2000): 62–85.

Corbridge, Stuart, and John Harriss. *Reinventing India*. Polity Press, 2000.

Cox, Gary. *Making Votes Count*. Cambridge: Cambridge University Press, 1997.

Crook, Richard C., and James Manor. *Democracy and Decentralisation in South Asia and West Africa: Participation, Accountability and Performance*. Cambridge: Cambridge University Press, 1998.

Dahl, Robert. *Polyarchy*. New Haven, CT: Yale University Press, 1971.

Dahya, Badr. "The Nature of Pakistani Ethnicity in Industrial Cities in Britain." In Abner Cohen, ed. *Urban Ethnicity*. London: Tavistock, 1974: 77–118.

Bibliography

Das, S. K. *Civil Service Reform and Structural Adjustment*. Delhi: Oxford University Press, 1998.

Das, S. K. *Public Office, Private Interest*. Delhi: Oxford University Press, 2001.

Das, Victor. *Jharkhand Castle over the Graves*. Delhi: Inter-India Publications, 1992.

Deliège, Robert. *The World of the 'Untouchables'*. Delhi: Oxford University Press, 1997.

Devalle, Susanna B. C. *Discourses of Ethnicity*. New Delhi: Sage, 1992.

De Zwart, Frank. *The Bureaucratic Merry-Go-Round: Manipulating the Transfer of Indian Civil Servants*. Amsterdam: Amsterdam University Press, 1994.

Dirks, Nicholas B. *Castes of Mind*. Princeton, NJ: Princeton University Press, 2000.

Downs, Anthony. *An Economic Theory of Democracy*. New York: Harper and Brothers, 1957.

Dreze, Jean, and Haris Gazdar. "Uttar Pradesh: The Burden of Inertia." In Jean Dreze and Amartya Sen, eds. *Indian Development: Selected Regional Perspectives*. Delhi: Oxford University Press, 1998: 33–128.

Dreze, Jean, and Amartya Sen, eds. *Indian Development: Selected Regional Perspectives*. Delhi: Oxford University Press, 1998.

Dube, Siddharth. *In the Land of Poverty*. London and New York: Zed Books, 1961.

Duncan, Ian. "Dalits and Politics in Rural North India: The Bahujan Samaj Party in Uttar Pradesh." *The Journal of Peasant Studies*, Vol. 27, No. 1 (1999): 35–60.

Dushkin, Lelah. "Scheduled Caste Politics." In J. Michael Mahar, ed. *The Untouchables in Contemporary India*. Tucson: University of Arizona Press, 1972.

Echeverri-Gent, John. *The State and the Poor*. Berkeley: University of California Press, 1993.

Eldersveld, Samuel J., and Bashiruddin Ahmad. *Citizens and Politics: Mass Political Behaviour in India*. Chicago: University of Chicago Press, 1978.

Eldersveld, Samuel J., V. Jagannadham, and A. P. Barnabas. *The Citizen and the Administrator in a Developing Democracy*. Glenview, IL: Scott, Foresman, 1967.

Elster, Jon, ed. *Rational Choice*. Oxford: Blackwell, 1986.

Ernst, Robert. *Immigrant Life in New York City*. New York: King's Crown Press, 1949.

Fearon, James. "Commitment Problems and the Spread of Ethnic Conflict." In David A. Lake and Donald Rothchild, eds. *The International Spread of Ethnic Conflict*. Princeton, NJ: Princeton University Press, 1998: 107–126.

Fearon, James. "Why Ethnic Politics and Pork Go Together." Paper presented at the SSRC-Macarthur Workshop on Ethnic Politics and Democratic Stability, Wilder House, University of Chicago, May 22–23, 1999.

Fearon, James, and David Laitin. "Explaining Interethnic Cooperation." *American Political Science Review*, Vol. 90, No. 4 (1996): 715–736.

Ferejohn, John, and James H. Kuklinski, eds. *Information and Democratic Processes*. Urbana and Chicago: University of Illinois Press, 1990.

Fernandes, Walter. *The Emerging Dalit Identity: The Re-Assertion of the Subalterns*. Delhi: Indian Social Institute, 1996.

Ferree, Karen. "Ethnicity and Strategic Behavior: Split Ticket Voting in Durban 1994." Paper presented at the Laboratory in Comparative Ethnic Processes, Duke University, March 23, 2000.

Fey, Mark. "Stability and Coordination in Duverger's Law: A Formal Model of Pre-election Polls and Strategic Voting." *American Political Science Review*, Vol. 91, No. 1 (1997): 135–147.

Fiorina, Morris P. "The Voting Decision: Instrumental and Expressive Aspects." *The Journal of Politics*, Vol. 38, No. 2 (1976): 390–413.

Fiorina, Morris P. *Retrospective Voting in American National Elections*. New Haven, CT: Yale University Press, 1981.

Foner, Philip. *History of the Labor Movement in the United States, Vol. 1*. New York: International Publishers, 1972.

Fox, Jonathan. "The Difficult Transition from Clientelism to Citizenship: Lessons from Mexico." *World Politics*, Vol. 46, No. 2 (1994): 151–184.

Fox, Richard. *Lions of the Punjab: Culture in the Making*. Berkeley: University of California Press, 1985.

Frankel, Francine. *India's Political Economy 1947–1977*. Princeton, NJ: Princeton University Press, 1978.

Frankel, Francine and M. S. A. Rao. *Dominance and State Power in Modern India, Vol. I*. Delhi: Oxford University Press, 1989.

Frankel, Francine R. and M. S. A. Rao. *Dominance and State Power in Modern India, Vol. II*. Delhi: Oxford University Press, 1990.

Fuller, C. J., ed. *Caste Today*. Delhi: Oxford University Press, 1997.

Fussell, Paul. *Class: A Guide through the American Status System*. New York: Summit Books, 1983.

Gaiha, Raghav, P. D. Kaushik, and Vani Kulkarni. "Jawahar Rozgar Yojana, Panchayats and the Rural Poor in India." *Asian Survey*, Vol. 37, No. 10 (1998): 928–949.

Gaiha, Raghav, P. D. Kaushik, and Vani Kulkarni. "Participation or Empowerment of the Rural Poor: The Case of Panchayats in India." Unpublished paper, 1999.

Galanter, Marc. *Competing Equalities*. Berkeley: University of California Press, 1984.

Galbraith, John W., and Nicol C. Rae. "A Test of the Importance of Tactical Voting: Great Britain 1987." *British Journal of Political Science*, Vol. 19 (1989): 126–137.

Gay, Robert. *Popular Organization and Democracy in Rio de Janeiro: A Tale of Two Favelas*. Philadelphia: Temple University Press, 1994.

Gay, Robert. "Between Clientelism and Citizenship: Exchanges, Gifts and Rights in Contemporary Brazil." Paper presented at Conference on Citizen-Politician Linkages in Democratic Politics, Duke University, March 30–April 1, 2001.

Geddes, Barbara. *Politician's Dilemma: Building State Capacity in Latin America*. Berkeley: University of California Press, 1994.

Geertz, Clifford. *The Interpretation of Cultures*. New York: Basic Books, 1973.

Gellner, Ernest. *Nations and Nationalism*. Ithaca, NY: Cornell University Press, 1983.

Ghatak, Maitreya, and Maitreesh Ghatak. "Grassroots Democracy: A Study of the Panchayat System in West Bengal." Paper presented at the Conference on Experiments in Empowered Deliberative Democracy, University of Wisconsin–Madison, 2000.

Bibliography

Ghosh, Amitav. *In an Antique Land*. New York: Vintage, 1992.

Ghosh, Arunabha. *Jharkhand Movement*. Calcutta: Minerva Associates, 1998.

Gil-White, Francisco J. "How Thick Is Blood? The Plot Thickens... If Ethnic Actors Are Primordialists, What Remains of the Circumstantialist/Primordialist Controversy?" *Ethnic and Racial Studies*, Vol. 22, No. 5 (1999): 789–820.

Glenny, Misha. *The Fall of Yugoslavia: The Third Balkan War*. New York: Penguin, 1992.

Goffman, Erving. *Stigma*. Englewood Cliffs, NJ: Prentice-Hall, 1963.

Gould, Harold A. *Grassroots Politics in India*. New Delhi: Oxford and IBH Publishing, 1994.

Graham, B. D. *Hindu Nationalism and Indian Politics*. Cambridge: Cambridge University Press, 1993.

Granovetter, Mark S. *Getting a Job*. Cambridge, MA: Harvard University Press, 1974.

Green, Donald P., and Ian Shapiro. *Pathologies of Rational Choice Theory*. New Haven, CT: Yale University Press, 1994.

Greif, Avner. "Reputation and Coalitions in Medieval Trade: Evidence on the Maghribi Traders." *Journal of Economic History*, Vol. 49, No. 4 (1989): 857–882.

Greif, Avner. "Contract Enforceability and Economic Institutions in Early Trade: The Maghribi Traders' Coalition." *The American Economic Review*, Vol. 83, No. 3 (1993): 525–548.

Greif, Avner. *Historical Institutional Analysis*. Cambridge University Press, forthcoming.

Grofman, Bernard. *Information, Participation, and Choice*. Ann Arbor: University of Michigan Press, 1996.

Gupta, Akhil. *Postcolonial Developments: Agriculture in the Making of Modern India*. Durham, NC: Duke University Press, 1998.

Gupta, Dipankar. *Rivalry and Brotherhood: Politics in the Life of Farmers in Northern India*. Delhi: Oxford University Press, 1997.

Gupta, Dipankar. *Interrogating Caste*. Delhi: Penguin, 2000.

Hannerz, Ulf. "Ethnicity and Opportunity in Urban America." In Abner Cohen, ed. *Urban Ethnicity*. London: Tavistock, 1974: 37–76.

Hansen, Thomas Blom, and Christophe Jaffrelot, eds. *The BJP and the Compulsions of Politics in India*. Delhi: Oxford University Press, 1998.

Haq, Mahbub, and Khadija Haq. *Human Development in South Asia 1998*. Karachi: Oxford University Press, 1998.

Hardgrave. Robert L., Jr. *The Dravidian Movement*. Bombay: Popular Prakashan, 1965.

Hardgrave, Robert L., Jr. *The Nadars of Tamilnad*. Berkeley: University of California Press, 1969.

Hardgrave, Robert L., Jr. "The Kerala Communists: Contradictions of Power." In Paul R. Brass and Marcus F. Franda, eds. *Radical Politics in South Asia*. Cambridge, MA: MIT Press, 1973: 119–180.

Hardin, Russell. *One for All: The Logic of Group Conflict*. Princeton, NJ: Princeton University Press, 1995.

Harrison, Selig. "Caste and the Andhra Communists." *American Political Science Review*, Vol. 50, No. 2 (1956): 378–404.

Harriss, John. "Comparing Political Regimes across Indian States." *Economic and Political Weekly*, November 27, 1999: 1–9.

Hasan, Zoya, "Power and Mobilization: Patterns of Resilience and Change in Uttar Pradesh Politics." In Francine Frankel and M. S. A. Rao, eds. *Dominance and State Power in Modern India*, Vol. I. Delhi and New York: Oxford University Press, 1989: 133–203.

Hasan, Zoya. *Quest for Power: Oppositional Movements and Post-Congress Politics in Uttar Pradesh*. Delhi: Oxford University Press, 1998.

Hasan, Zoya. *Politics and the State in India*. Delhi: Sage, 2000.

Hearl, Derek J., Ian Budge, and Bernard Pearson. "Distinctiveness of Regional Voting: A Comparative Analysis across the European Community (1979–1993)." *Electoral Studies*, Vol. 15, No. 2 (1996): 167–182.

Hechter, Michael. "The Political Economy of Ethnic Change." *American Journal of Sociology*, Vol. 79, No. 5 (1974): 1151–1178.

Hechter, Michael. *Internal Colonialism*. Berkeley: University of California Press, 1975.

Hechter, Michael. "Group Formation and the Cultural Division of Labor." *American Journal of Sociology*, Vol. 84, No. 2 (1978): 293–318.

Hechter, Michael. "Internal Colonialism Revisited." In Edward A. Tiryakiain and Ronald Rogowski, eds. *New Nationalisms of the Developed West*. Boston: Allen and Unwin, 1985.

Hinich, Melvin J., and Michael C. Munger. *Ideology and the Theory of Political Choice*. Ann Arbor: University of Michigan Press, 1994.

Hirschman, Albert. *Exit, Voice and Loyalty*. Cambridge, MA: Harvard University Press, 1970.

Hirschman, Albert. "Social Conflicts as Pillars of Democratic Market Society." *Political Theory*, Vol. 22, No. 2 (1994): 203–218.

Horowitz, Donald. *Ethnic Groups in Conflict*. Berkeley: University of California Press, 1985.

Horowitz, Donald. *A Democratic South Africa? Constitutional Engineering in a Divided Society*. Berkeley: University of California Press, 1991.

Horowitz, Donald. "Democracy in Divided Societies." *Journal of Democracy*, Vol. 4, No. 4 (1993): 18–38.

Hotelling, Harold. "Stability in Competition." *The Economic Journal*, Vol. 39 (1929): 41–57.

Huber, John, and Ronald Inglehart. "Expert Interpretations of Party Space and Party Locations in 42 Societies." *Party Politics*, Vol. 1, No. 1 (1995): 73–111.

Huntington, Samuel. *Political Order in Changing Societies*. New Haven, CT: Yale University Press, 1965.

Huntington, Samuel. *The Third Wave: Democratization in the Late Twentieth Century*. Norman: University of Oklahoma Press, 1991.

Ilaiah, Kancha. *Why I Am Not a Hindu*. Calcutta: Samya, 1996.

Bibliography

Isaac, Thomas. *Campaign for Democratic Decentralization in Kerala*. Paper presented at the Conference on Experiments in Empowered Deliberative Democracy, University of Wisconsin–Madison, 2000.

Isaacs, Harold. *India's Ex-Untouchables*. New York: John Day, 1965.

Jaffrelot, Christophe. *The BJP and the 1996 General Election*. Paper presented at the National Seminar on Political Sociology of India's Democracy, New Delhi, November 14–16, 1996.

Jaffrelot, Christophe. *The Hindu Nationalist Movement and Indian Politics 1925 to the 1990s*. New York: Viking, 1996.

Jaffrelot, Christophe. "The Bahujan Samaj Party in North India." *Comparative Studies of South Asia, Africa and the Middle East*, Vol. 18, No. 1 (1998): 35–52.

Jaffrelot, Christophe. "The Sangh Parivar between Sanskritization and Social Engineering." In Thomas Blom Hansen and Christophe Jaffrelot, eds. *The BJP and the Compulsions of Politics in India*. Delhi: Oxford University Press, 1998: 22–71.

Jaffrelot, Christophe. "The Rise of the Other Backward Classes in North India." *Journal of Asian Studies*, Vol. 59, No. 1 (February 2000): 86–108.

Jalal, Ayesha. *The Sole Spokesman*. Cambridge: Cambridge University Press, 1985.

Jalali, Rita. "The State and the Political Mobilization of the Disadvantaged: The Case of the Scheduled Castes in India." Ph.D. dissertation, Stanford University, 1990.

Jenkins, Rob. "The Developmental Implications of India's Federal Institutions." Paper presented at the Annual Meeting of the American Political Science Association, Washington, DC, August 28–31, 1997.

Jones-Correa, Michael. *Between Two Nations: The Political Predicament of Latinos in New York City*. Ithaca, NY: Cornell University Press, 1998.

Joseph, Richard. *Democracy and Prebendal Politics in Nigeria*. Cambridge: Cambridge University Press, 1987.

Joshi, Barbara R. *Democracy in Search of Equality: Untouchable Politics and Indian Social Change*. Delhi: Hindustan Publishing Corporation, 1982.

Joshi, Barbara R., ed. *Untouchable!* London: Zed Books, 1986.

Kantowicz, Edward T. "Voting and Parties." In Michael Walzer et al., *The Politics of Ethnicity*. Cambridge, MA: Belknap Press, 1982: 29–68.

Kasfir, Nelson. *The Shrinking Political Agenda*. Berkeley: University of California Press, 1976.

Kasfir, Nelson. "Explaining Ethnic Political Participation." *World Politics*, Vol. 31, No. 3 (1979): 365–388.

Katznelson, Ira. *City Trenches: Urban Politics and the Patterning of Class in the United States*. New York: Pantheon, 1981.

Kearney, Robert. *The Politics of Ceylon (Sri Lanka)*. Ithaca, NY: Cornell University Press, 1973.

Keer, Dhananjay. *Dr. Ambedkar, Life and Mission*. Bombay: Popular Prakashan, 1954.

Keer, Dhananjay. *Mahatma Jotirao Phooley*. Bombay: Popular Prakashan, 1964.

Keer, Dhananjay. *Shahu Chhatrapati*. Bombay: Popular Prakashan, 1976.

Khare, R. S. *The Untouchable as Himself*. Cambridge: Cambridge University Press, 1984.

Khemani, Stuti. "Political Cycles in a Developing Economy." Washington, DC: World Bank Policy Research Working Papers, September 2000.

King, Gary, Robert Keohane, and Sidney Verba. *Designing Social Inquiry*. Princeton, NJ: Princeton University Press, 1994.

King, Gary. *A Solution to the Ecological Inference Problem*. Princeton, NJ: Princeton University Press, 1997.

Knoke, David. *Political Networks*. Cambridge: Cambridge University Press, 1990.

Kohli, Atul. *India's Democracy*. Princeton, NJ: Princeton University Press, 1988.

Kohli, Atul. *Democracy and Discontent*. Cambridge: Cambridge University Press, 1990.

Kothari, Rajni, ed. *Caste in Indian Politics*. Hyderabad: Orient Longman, 1970.

Krueger, Anne. "The Political Economy of the Rent-Seeking Society." *The American Economic Review*, Vol. 64, No. 3 (1974): 291–303.

Krugman, Paul. "History versus Expectations." *Quarterly Journal of Economics*, Vol. 106, No. 2 (1991): 651–667.

Kshirsagar, R. K. *Dalit Movement in India and Its Leaders*. New Delhi: M D Publications, 1994.

Kuklinski, James H., and Norman L. Hurley. "On Hearing and Interpreting Political Messages: A Cautionary Tale of Citizen Cue-Taking." *The Journal of Politics*, Vol. 56, No. 3 (1994): 729–751.

Kumar, Pradeep. "Dalits and the BSP in Uttar Pradesh: Issues and Challenges." *Economic and Political Weekly*, April 3, 1999.

Kumar, Purushottam. *History and Aministration of Tribal Chotanagpur*. Delhi: Atma Ram and Sons, 1994.

Laakso, Marku, and Rein Taagepera. "Effective Number of Parties: A Measure with Application to Western Europe." *Comparative Political Studies*, Vol. 12, No. 1 (1979): 3–27.

Laitin, David. *Identity in Formation*. Ithaca, NY: Cornell University Press, 1998.

Laitin, David. *Hegemony and Culture*. Chicago: University of Chicago Press, 1986.

Laitin, David D. "Disciplining Political Science." *American Political Science Review*, Vol. 89, No. 2 (1995): 454–460.

Laitin, David D. "Marginality: A Microperspective." *Rationality and Society*, Vol. 7, No. 1 (1995): 31–57.

Lal, Manohar. *The Munda Elites*. Delhi: Amar Prakashan, 1983.

Landa, Janet Tai. *Trust, Ethnicity, and Identity*. Ann Arbor: University of Michigan Press, 2001.

Lanjouw, Peter, and Nicholas Stern, eds. *Economic Development in Palanpur over Five Decades*. Delhi: Oxford University Press, 1998.

Lemarchand, Rene. "Political Clientelism and Ethnicity in Tropical Africa: Competing Solidarities in Nation-Building." *American Political Science Review*, Vol. 66, No. 1 (1972): 68–90.

Levi, Margaret, and Michael Hechter. "A Rational Choice Approach to the Rise and Decline of Ethnoregional Political Parties." In Edward A. Tiryakian and Ronald Rogowski, eds. *New Nationalisms of the Developed West*. Boston: Allen and Unwin., 1985: 128–146.

Bibliography

Levine, Stephen, and Nigel S. Roberts. "Elections and Expectations: Evidence from Electoral Surveys in New Zealand." *Journal of Commonwealth and Comparative Politics*, Vol. 29, No. 2 (1991): 129–152.

Lijphart, Arend. *Democracy in Plural Societies*. New Haven, CT: Yale University Press, 1977.

Lourduswamy, Stan. *Jharkhandi's Claim for Self-Rule*. Delhi: Indian Social Institute, 1997.

Ludden, David, ed. *Making Indian Hindu*. Delhi: Oxford University Press, 1996.

Lupia, Arthur, and Mathew D. McCubbins. *The Democratic Dilemma*. Cambridge: Cambridge University Press, 1998.

Lupia, Arthur. "Busy Voters, Agenda Control, and the Power of Information." *American Political Science Review*, Vol. 86, No. 2 (1992): 390–403.

Lupia, Arthur. "Shortcuts versus Encyclopedias: Information and Voting Behavior in California Insurance Reform Elections." *The American Political Science Review*, Vol. 88, No. 1 (1994): 63–76.

Lupia, Arthur, Mathew D. McCubbins, and Samuel L. Popkin. *Elements of Reason*. Cambridge: Cambridge University Press, 2000.

Lynch, Owen. *The Politics of Untouchability*. New York: Columbia University Press, 1969.

Mackintosh, John P. *Nigerian Government and Politics*. London: George Allen and Unwin, 1976.

Malkki, Liisa H. *Purity and Exile*. Chicago: University of Chicago Press, 1995.

Martz, John. *The Politics of Clientelism*. New Brunswick, NJ: Transaction Publishers, 1997.

McCourt, Frank. *'Tis*. New York: Scribner, 1999.

Meguid, Bonnie. "Understanding Policy Failure: The Overlooked Role of Ethnic Credibility in Party Strategic Success." Paper presented at the annual meeting of the American Political Science Association, Washington, D.C., September 2000.

Melson, Robert, and Howard Wolpe. "Modernization and the Politics of Communalism: A Theoretical Perspective." *American Political Science Review*, Vol. 64, No. 4 (1970): 1112–1130.

Mendelsohn, Oliver, and Upendra Baxi, eds. *The Rights of Subordinated Peoples*. Delhi: Oxford University Press, 1994.

Mendelsohn, Oliver, and Marika Vicziany. *The Untouchables: Subordination, Poverty and the State in Modern India*. Cambridge: Cambridge University Press, 1998.

Meyer, Ralph. "How Do Indians Vote?" *Asian Survey*, Vol. 29, No. 12 (1989): 1111–1122.

Mill, John Stuart. *Considerations on Representative Government*. New York: Liberal Arts Press, 1961.

Mitchell, J. C. "Perceptions of Ethnicity and Ethnic Behaviour: An Empirical Exploration." In Abner Cohen, ed. *Urban Ethnicity*. London: Tavistock, 1974: 1–36.

Mitra, Subrata K., and V. B. Singh. *Democracy and Social Change in India*. Delhi: Sage, 1999.

Moss, Philip, and Chris Tilly. *Stories Employers Tell*. New York: Russell Sage Foundation, 2001.

329

Munda, Ram Dayal. *The Jharkhand Movement: Retrospect and Prospect*. Ranchi, Bihar: Jharkhand Co-ordination Committee, 1990.

Nagaraj, D. R. *The Flaming Feet: A Study of the Dalit Movement*. Bangalore: South Forum Press, 1993.

Nandy, Ashis. *The Intimate Enemy: Loss and Recovery of Self under Colonialism*. Delhi: Oxford University Press, 1983.

Nayar, Baldev Raj. *Minority Politics in the Punjab*. Princeton, NJ: Princeton University Press, 1966.

Newell, James L. "The Scottish National Party: Development and Change." In Lieven de Winter and Huri Tursan, eds. *Regionalist Parties in Western Europe*. London: Routledge, 1998: 105–124.

Newman, Saul. *Ethnoregional Conflict in Democracies: Mostly Ballots, Rarely Bullets*. Westport, CT: Greenwood Press, 1996.

Nobles, Melissa. *Shades of Citizenship: Race and the Census in Modern Politics*. Stanford, CA: Stanford University Press, 2000.

North, Douglass. *Institutions, Institutional Change and Economic Performance*. Cambridge: Cambridge University Press, 1990.

Nossiter, T. J. *Communism in Kerala*. Berkeley: University of California Press, 1982.

O'Hanlon, Rosalind. *Caste, Conflict and Ideology*. Cambridge: Cambridge University Press, 1985.

Oldenburg, Philip. *India Briefing 1991*. Boulder, CO: Westview Press, 1991.

Oldenburg, Philip. *India Briefing 1993*. Boulder, CO: Westview Press, 1993.

Oldenburg, Philip. *India Briefing: Staying the Course*. Armonk: M. E. Sharpe, 1995.

Olson, Mancur. *The Logic of Collective Action*. Cambridge, MA: Harvard University Press, 1971.

Omvedt, Gail. *Cultural Revolt in a Colonial Society*. Bombay: Scientific Socialist Education Trust, 1976.

Omvedt, Gail. *Dalits and the Democratic Revolution*. Delhi: Sage, 1994.

Omvedt, Gail. *Dalit Visions: The Anti-Caste Movement and the Construction of an Indian Identity*. New Delhi: Orient Longman Limited, 1995.

Padgett, John F., and Christopher K. Ansell. "Robust Action and the Rise of the Medici, 1400–1434." *American Journal of Sociology*, Vol. 98, No. 6 (1993): 1259–1319.

Pai, Sudha. "Politicization of Dalits and Most Backward Castes." *Economic and Political Weekly*, June 7, 1997: 1356–1361.

Panandiker, V. A. Pai. *The Politics of Backwardness*. Delhi: Konark Publishers, 1997.

Panandiker, V. A. Pai, and S. S. Kshirsagar. *Bureaucracy and Development Administration*. Delhi: Centre for Policy Research, 1978.

Pandey, Gyanendra. *The Construction of Communalism in Colonial North India*. Delhi: Oxford University Press, 1992.

Pandey, Gyanendra. "Which of Us Are Hindus?" In Gyanendra Pandey ed. *Hindus and Others*. Delhi: Viking, 1993: 238–272.

Pascal, Anthony H. *Racial Discrimination in Economic Life*. Lexington, MA: Lexington Books, 1972.

Piatonni, Simona, ed. *Clientelism, Interests and Democratic Representation*. Cambridge: Cambridge University Press, 2001.

Bibliography

Popkin, Samuel. *The Rational Peasant: The Political Economy of Rural Society in Vietnam.* Berkeley: University of California Press, 1979.

Popkin, Samuel L. *The Reasoning Voter.* Chicago: University of Chicago Press, 1991.

Posen, Barry. "The Security Dilemma and Ethnic Conflict." In Michael E. Brown, ed. *Ethnic Conflict and International Security.* Princeton, NJ: Princeton University Press, 1993: 103–125.

Posner, Daniel. "The Institutional Origins of Ethnic Politics in Zambia." Ph.D. dissertation, Harvard University, 1998.

Post, Kenneth. *The Nigerian Federal Election of 1959.* London: Oxford University Press, 1963.

Potter, David C. *India's Political Administrators.* Delhi: Oxford University Press, 1996.

Przeworski, Adam. *Democracy and the Market.* Cambridge: Cambridge University Press, 1991.

Przeworski, Adam, and John Sprague. *Paper Stones: A History of Electoral Socialism.* Chicago: University of Chicago Press, 1986.

Pushpendra. "Dalit Assertion through Electoral Politics." *Economic and Political Weekly,* September 4, 1999: 2609–2618.

Putnam, Robert. *Making Democracy Work.* Princeton, NJ: Princeton University Press, 1993.

Rabushka, Alvin, and Kenneth Shepsle. 1972. *Politics in Plural Societies.* Columbus, OH: Charles E. Merrill, 1972.

Rauch, James E., and Alessandra Casella. *Networks and Markets.* New York: Russell Sage Foundation, 2001.

Rauch, James E., and Vitor Trindade. "Ethnic Chinese Networks in International Trade." Cambridge, MA: NBER Working Paper Series, June 1999.

Riker, William. *Liberalism against Populism.* Prospect Heights, IL: Waveland Press, 1982.

Riker, William. *The Art of Political Manipulation.* New Haven, CT: Yale University Press, 1986.

Riker, William. *Agenda Formation.* Ann Arbor: University of Michigan Press, 1993.

Riordon, William. *Plunkitt of Tammany Hall.* Boston: Bedford Books, 1994.

Robb, Peter, ed. *Dalit Movements and the Meanings of Labour in India.* Delhi: Oxford University Press, 1993.

Robertson, David. *A Theory of Party Competition.* London: Wiley, 1976.

Root, Hilton. "A Liberal India: The Triumph of Hope over Experience." *Asian Survey,* Vol. 37, No. 5 (1998): 510–534.

Rothschild, Joseph. *Ethnopolitics: A Conceptual Framework.* New York: Columbia University Press, 1981.

Roy, Ramashray, and V. B. Singh. *A Study of Harijan Elites.* Delhi: Discovery Publishing House, 1987.

Rudolph, Lloyd I., and Susanne H. Rudolph. *The Modernity of Tradition.* Chicago: University of Chicago Press, 1967.

Rudolph, Lloyd I., and Susanne H. Rudolph. *In Pursuit of Lakshmi.* Chicago: University of Chicago Press, 1987.

331

Rudolph, Susanne. *The Action Arm of the Indian National Congress: The Pradesh Congress Committee*. Cambridge: Center for International Studies, 1955.

Sachs, Jeffrey D., Ashutosh Varshney, and Nirupam Bajpai, eds. *India in the Era of Economic Reforms*. Delhi: Oxford University Press, 1999.

Sainath, P. *Everybody Loves a Good Drought: Stories from India's Poorest Districts*. New Delhi: Penguin, 1996.

Sangh, Bharatiya Jana. *Party Documents: Vol. I*. Delhi: Navchetan Press, 1973.

Schaffer, Frederic C. *Democracy in Translation*. Ithaca, NY: Cornell University Press, 1998.

Schattschneider, E. E. *The Semisovereign People: A Realist's View of Democracy in America*. New York: Holt, Rinehart and Winston, 1960.

Schenk, Hans. "Corruption... What Corruption? Notes on Bribery and Dependency in Urban India." In Peter M. Ward, ed. *Corruption, Development and Inequality: Soft Touch or Hard Graft?* London: Routledge, 1989: 110–122.

Schiavo-Campo, Salvatore, Giulio de Tommaso, and Amitabha Mukherjee. *Government Employment and Pay: A Global and Regional Perspective*. Washington: World Bank, 1997.

Scott, James C. *Comparative Political Corruption*. Englewood, NJ: Prentice-Hall, 1972.

Scott, James C. *Weapons of the Weak*. New Haven, CT: Yale University Press, 1985.

Scott, James C., John Tehranian, and Jeremy Mathias. "The Production of Legal Identities Proper to States: The Case of the Permanent Family Surname." *Comparative Studies in Society and History*, Vol. 44, No. 1 (2002): 4–44.

Sen, Amartya. "Indian Development: Lessons and Non Lessons." *Daedalus* Vol. 118, No. 4 (1989): 369–392.

Sengupta, Nirmal. *Fourth World Dynamics, Jharkhand*. Delhi: Authors Guild Publications, 1982.

Shah, A. M. "The 'Dalit' Category and Its Differentiation." *Economic and Political Weekly*, April 6, 2002: 1–4.

Shah, Ghanshyam. "Tenth Lok Sabha Elections: BJP's Victory in Gujarat." *Economic and Political Weekly*, December 21, 1991: 2921–2924.

Shah, Ghanshyam. "The BJP and Backward Castes in Gujarat." *South Asia Bulletin*, Vol. 14, No. 4 (1994): 57–65.

Shah, Ghanshyam. "BJP's Rise to Power." *Economic and Political Weekly*, January 13–20, 1996.

Shah, Ghanshyam. "The BJP's Riddle in Gujarat: Caste, Factionalism and Hindutva." In Thomas Blom Hansen and Christophe Jaffrelot, eds. *The BJP and the Compulsions of Politics in India*. Delhi: Oxford University Press, 1998: 243–266.

Shah, Ghanshyam. *Dalit Identity and Politics*. Delhi: Sage; London: Thousand Oaks, 2001.

Shah, Ghanshyam. "Caste, Hindutva and Hideousness." *Economic and Political Weekly*, April 13, 2002: 1–6.

Sharma, Miriam. *The Politics of Inequality*. Honolulu: University Press of Hawaii, 1978.

Shastri, Sandeep. *Towards Explaining the Voters' Mandate: An Analysis of the Karnataka Assembly Elections*. Bangalore, 1995.

Bibliography

Singh, Gurharpal. *Ethnic Conflict in India.* Basingstoke: Macmillan, 2000.

Singh, H. D. *543 Faces of India.* New Delhi: Newsmen Publishers, 1996.

Singh, K. S. *People of India, Vol. III.* Delhi: Anthropological Survey of India and Oxford University Press, 1994.

Singh, K. S. *The Scheduled Castes.* Delhi: Anthropological Survey of India and Oxford University Press, 1995.

Singh, K. S. *People of India, Vol. IV.* Delhi: Anthropological Survey of India and Oxford University Press, 1998.

Singh, K. S. *People of India, Vol. V.* Delhi: Anthropological Survey of India and Oxford University Press, 1998.

Singh, K. S. *People of India, Vol. VI.* Delhi: Anthropological Survey of India and Oxford University Press, 1998.

Singh, Upjit Rekhi. *Jharkhand Movement in Bihar.* New Delhi: Nunes Publishers, 1988.

Singh, V. B., and Shankar Bose. *State Elections in India.* Delhi: Sage, 1987–88.

Sisson, Richard, and Ramashray Roy. *Diversity and Dominance in Indian Politics.* Delhi: Sage, 1990.

Sklar, Richard. *Nigerian Political Parties.* Princeton, NJ: Princeton University Press, 1963.

Sklar, Richard. "Nigerian Politics in Perspective." *Government and Opposition*, Vol. 2, No. 4 (1967): 524–539.

Spence, Michael A. *Market Signaling: Informational Transfer in Hiring and Related Screening Processes.* Cambridge, MA: Harvard University Press, 1974.

Stigler, George J. "Information in the Labor Market." *Journal of Political Economy*, Vol. 70, No. 5 (1962): 94–105.

Stigler, George J. "Nobel Lecture: The Process and Progress of Economics." *Journal of Political Economy*, Vol. 91, No. 4 (1983): 529–545.

Stiglitz, Joseph E. "The Contributions of the Economics of Information to Twentieth Century Economics." *Quarterly Journal of Economics*, Vol. 115, No. 4 (2000): 1441–1478.

Stokes, Susan. *Cultures in Conflict: Social Movements and the State in Peru.* Berkeley: University of California Press, 1995.

Stroschein, Sherrill Lea. "Contention and Coexistence." Ph.D. dissertation, Columbia University, 2000.

Subramaniam, V. "Representative Bureaucracy: A Reassessment." *American Political Science Review*, Vol. 61, No. 4 (1967): 1010–1019.

Subramanian, Narendra. *Ethnicity and Populist Mobilization: Political Parties, Citizens and Democracy in South India.* Delhi: Oxford University Press, 1999.

Tajfel, Henri. *The Social Psychology of Minorities.* London: Minority Rights Group, 1971.

Tajfel, Henri, and J. C. Turner. "The Social Identity Theory of Intergroup Behaviour." In S. Worchel and W. G. Austin, eds. *Psychology of Intergroup Relations.* Chicago: Nelson, 1986: 7–24.

Tambiah, Stanley. *Sri Lanka: Ethnic Fratricide and the Dismantling of Democracy.* Chicago: University of Chicago Press, 1986.

Taylor, Charles. *Multiculturalism.* Princeton, NJ: Princeton University Press, 1994.

Taylor, Donald M., and Fathali M. Moghaddam. *Theories of Inter-Group Relations: International Social Psychological Perspectives*, 2nd ed. Westport, CT: Praeger, 1994.

Thapar, Romila. "Imagined Religious Communities? Ancient History and the Modern Search for a Hindu Identity." *Modern Asian Studies*, Vol. 23, No. 2 (1989): 209–231.

Thompson, E. P. *The Making of the English Working Class*. New York: Vintage, 1963.

Vail, Leroy, ed. *The Creation of Tribalism in Southern Africa*. Berkeley: University of California Press, 1989.

Van Cott, Donna Lee. *Indigenous Peoples and Democracy in Latin America*. New York: St. Martin's Press, 1994.

Varshney, Ashutosh. *Democracy, Development and the Countryside*. Cambridge: Cambridge University Press, 1995.

Verba, Sidney, Bashiruddin Ahmad, and Anil Bhatt. *Caste, Race and Politics*. Beverly Hills, CA: Sage, 1971.

Visvanathan, Shiv. "Thinking about Elections." *Seminar*, Vol. 440 (April 1996): 72–75.

Wade, Robert. "Politics and Graft: Recruitment, Appointment, and Promotions to Public Office in India." In Peter Ward, ed. *Corruption, Development and Inequality: Soft Touch or Hard Graft?* New York: Routledge, 1989: 73–109.

Waldinger, Roger. "Social Capital or Social Closure? Immigrant Networks in the Labor Market." UCLA Lewis Center for Regional Policy Studies Working Paper, August 1997.

Wallace, Paul. "Religious and Ethnic Politics: Political Mobilization in Punjab." In Francine Frankel and M. S. A. Rao, eds. *Dominance and State Power in Modern India, Vol. II*. Delhi: Oxford University Press, 1990: 416–481.

Weiner, Myron. *The Politics of Scarcity*. Chicago: University of Chicago Press, 1962.

Weiner, Myron. *Party Building in a New Nation: The Indian National Congress*. Chicago: University of Chicago Press, 1967.

Weiner, Myron. *Sons of the Soil*. Princeton University Press, 1978.

Weiner, Myron. *The Indian Paradox*. Delhi: Sage, 1989.

Weiner, Myron. *The Child and the State in India*. Delhi: Oxford University Press, 1991.

Wilson, A. Jeyaratnam. *Politics in Sri Lanka 1947–79*. London: Macmillan, 1979.

Wishwakarma, R. L. *Public Employment: Its Unit Cost and Socio-Economic Profile*. Delhi: Mittal Publications, 1988.

Wolfinger, Raymond. "The Development and Persistence of Ethnic Voting." *American Political Science Review*, Vol 59, No. 4 (1965): 896–908.

Wolfinger, Raymond. *The Politics of Progress*. Englewood Cliffs, NJ: Prentice Hall, 1974.

Wood, John R. "Congress Restored? The 'Kham' Strategy and Congress (I) Recruitment in Gujarat." In John R. Wood, ed. *State Politics in Contemporary India*. Boulder, CO: Westview Press, 1984: 197–227.

World Bank. *India: Primary Education Achievement and Challenges*. Washington, DC: World Bank, 1996.

Bibliography

World Bank. *India: Achievements and Challenges in Reducing Poverty.* (Report No. 16483-IN). Washington, DC: World Bank, 1997.

World Bank. *India: Sustaining Rapid Economic Growth.* Washington, DC: World Bank, 1997.

World Bank. *1998 World Development Indicators.* Washington, DC: World Bank, 1998.

Yadav, Bhupindra, and Anand Mohan Sharma. *Economic Uplift of Scheduled Castes.* Chandigarh: Institute for Development and Communication, 1995.

Yadav, Yogendra. "Reconfiguration in Indian Politics." *Economic and Political Weekly*, January 13–20, 1996: 95–104.

Yashar, Deborah. "Citizenship Claims and Ethnic Movements: Contentious Politics in an Age of Globalization?" Paper presented at the annual meetings of the American Political Science Association, Atlanta, September 1999.

Yashar, Deborah J. "Democracy, Indigenous Movements, and the Postliberal Challenge in Latin America." *World Politics*, Vol. 51, No. 1 (1999): 76–104.

Young, Crawford. *The Politics of Cultural Pluralism.* Madison: University of Wisconsin Press, 1976.

Zelliot, Eleanor. *From Untouchable to Dalit: Essays on the Ambedkar Movement.* Delhi: Manohar, 1996.

Index

Italic page numbers indicate figures.

Action Group (AG), 5, 9
Adamu, Haroun, 47
Adharmis, 168–9, 190, 191
Adi Dravida, 192
Adi Karnataka, 192
Adivasis, 290
African National Congress (ANC), 5
Ahirs, 289, 290
AJGAR political coalition, 290
Akali Dal, 181, 183, 191, 206, 250–1
Akerlof, George, 34–5
All India Congress Committee (AICC),
  247–9, 248t
Ambedkar, B. R., 144, *153*, 222
Andhra Pradesh, 218, 276
Annadurai, C. N. 279

backward classes, *see* other backward
  classes
Bahadur, Raj, 186
Bahujan, 151, 290
  definition of, 15, 148, 149
  Dalit Sangarsh Samiti (DSS) merging
    with, 166, 193
  Dalit Shoshit Samaj Sangarsh Samiti
    (DS-4) and, 144–5, 149, 192
Bahujan Samaj Party (BSP)
  Bahujan as term in, 148, 149–50
  BAMCEF and, 144–5, 148, 150, 155, 165,
    186, 190
  BJP, alliance against, 241
  BJP, alliance with, 261
  cadre camps of, 150, 155
  campaign message of, 150–8
  candidate level, representation of,
    197–200, 198t, 200t, 232

centralized organization of, 246–7,
  257–61
Chamars and, 22, 143, 145, 151, 168–70,
  188–9, 191–2, 210, 231, 242, 258,
  259–61
Congress party alliance with, 241–2
Congress party versus platform of, 151,
  155, 157–8
Dalit Sangarsh Samiti (DSS) merging
  with, 166, 193
Dalit Shoshit Samaj Sangarsh Samiti
  (DS-4) and, 144–5, 149, 192
diversification of candidate base, 198
elite interviews with, 293–6, 294t
ethnic message abandoned by, 220
from ethnic to multiethnic party, 16, 17
ethnic identity of candidates in, 198,
  216–17, 231–2
fragmentation of, 167–8
grievances and performance of, 170–1
Haryana and, 20f, 21, 146t, 147, 165, 166
in Jammu and Kashmir, 20f, 21, 165, 166
Hindi belt and, 166–7
history of, 143–5, 178
Indian Constitution reserved seats and,
  198
Karnataka, representational openness,
  and failure of, 194–5
language divisions impeding, 166–7
lateral expansion through multiplication
  of monoethnic factions, 258–9, 259f
leverage, voters and, 226–7, 229–34, 232t,
  233t, 236–7
Muslims and, 216–17
organizational history of, 164–6
organizational structure of, 246–7, 257

337

Bahujan Samaj Party (*cont.*)
party versus candidates preference in, 199–200, 200t
Ramdassias and, 145, 189
Samajwadi Party alliance with, 241, 260–1
Sikhs and, 145, 146t
state versus national leadership, 200, 200n1
state-by-state performance of, 19–22, 313–14t
support base, estimates of, 310–12, 313–14t
upper castes and, 136–7, 148, 155–7
variation in representational opportunities in, 22, 29, 260–1
Bahujan Samaj Party (BSP) in Karnataka, 20f, 21, 22, 25, 25f, 29
failure of, 172, 184–5, 193–5, 246–7, 261
launching of, 178, 182, 193
relative representation of Scheduled Castes in, 194–5, 246, 261
SCs and, 159, 159t, 165, 166
Bahujan Samaj Party (BSP) in Punjab, 20f, 21, 22, 25, 25f, 29
alliances, 241
Chamars and Adharmis in, 191–2, 258
launching of, 178, 190–1
relative representation of Scheduled Castes in, 191–2, 255
SCs and, 145, 146t, 147, 158–9, 158f, 163t, 165, 166, 168, 169
Bahujan Samaj Party (BSP) in UP, 20–1, 20f, 22, 24–5, 25f, 29, 136–7
alliances, 241–2, 260–1
Chamars in, 188–9
launching of, 178, 181, 185–6
leadership turnover in, 189
relative representation of Scheduled Castes in, 188–9, 189t
SCs and, 146t, 147, 158–9, 159t, 164, 165, 166, 171
success from representational blockage in Congress party, 172, 186–8, 255
Balimikis, 17, 190, 191
BAMCEF (Backward and Minority Community Employees Federation), 144–5, 148, 150, 155, 164, 165, 186, 192
Bariyas, 289
Barth, Frederik, 37, 95
Bates, Robert, 8
beneficiaries, aggregate, 69–70
beneficiaries, individual, 54, 56, 69–70
Breton, Albert, 8
bhagyadari (share), 206

Bharatiya Janata Party (BJP), 18, 191, 197, 202
backward castes, incorporation of, 268–9, 270–2, 274–5
backward caste vote shifted to, 266, 267, 267t
in Bihar, 262, 270–5, 282
BSP alliance against, 241
BSP coalition with, 261
Congress party's organizational decay and, 266–7
1991 election campaign and, 263
1996 election campaign and, 204–6
founding of, 263
in Gujarat, 264, 268–9, 275
Hindu backlash and, 265–6
Jharkhand and, 282–3
organizational structure of, 23, 30, 272–5
support base, estimates of, 23–5, 264, 315t
upper castes and, 266–7, 267t, 269
Bharatiya Janata Sangh (BJS), 263, 266, 272
Bharatiya Kisan Kamgar Party (BKKP), 241
Bhils, 289
Bhumihar, 250
Bihar, 288, 290
BJP in, 262, 270–5, 282
JMM in, 281–2
Bihar People's Party (BPP), 282
BJP, *see* Bharatiya Janata Party
Bolivia, MRTKL in, 5
Brahmins, 37, 137, 148, 157, 187, 258, 278–9, 278t
Brass, Paul, 126, 126n36, 183, 257
Brazil, 69
bribes, *see* corruption
Britain, *see* United Kingdom
British India, 256
BSP, *see* Bahujan Samaj Party
Buddhists, 149
Bueno de Mesquita, Bruce, 180
Buganda, 10
bureaucrats, *see* public officials
Burundi, 17

Chabal, Patrick, 48, 85
Chamars, 17
as aggregate caste category, 168–9
BSP and, 22, 143, 145, 151, 168–70, 188–9, 231–2, 242, 258, 259–61, 288–9
distribution across Indian states, 162t, 168–9
literacy rates among, 188, 191
in Punjab, 22, 168–9, 190, 191–2, 258
subdivisions among, 168–9, 185, 190
in UP, 22, 185, 188–9, 258–60, 288

Index

Chhibber, Pradeep, 255–6, 266–7
Christian Scheduled Castes, 205
Christians, 149, 278t
class
  consumption patterns, taste and, 37
  dress associated with, 42, 44
  name and, 39
  speech associated with, 41
classes
  (other) backward (OBC), xvii
  as castes, xvii
clientelism, 51
  definition, 51
  distinguished from "patronage," 51
  corporate/collective, 69
coalitions
  differentiated, 97, 220
  minimum winning, 107
  oversize, 107
  uniform, 97, 220
colonial rule
  castes and, 77, 155n32, 252
  ethnic favouritism influenced by, 77–8
Communist Party of India (CPI), 282
Communist Party of India (Marxist) (CPM),
    191, 200, 218–19, 276, 282
Communist Party of India Marxist-Leninist
    (CPI-ML), 218–19, 282
Congress party, 197, 199, 220, 289
  All India Congress Committee (AICC) of,
    247–9, 248t
  alliances of, 241–2, 269, 290
  BJP and organizational decay of, 266–7
  BSP alliance with, 241–2
  centralized organization of, 247–8, 254
  competitive organization of, 246, 247,
    249–51, 253–4, 255
  Congress Working Committee of, 249n4
  constitution (1908) of, 247–8
  constitution (1920) of, 249, 249n4
  corruption alleged against, 205–6, 214
  DMK, Tamil Nadu and, 276, 277–8, 278t
  economic reforms of, 117
  elections in, 249–51, 254
  1996 election campaign, 204–6
  Karnataka and, 246, 253–4
  as multiethnic party, 151, 155, 166
  National Congress Committee of, 247
  Non-Brahmin Federation and, 250–1
  Provincial Committee of, 248–9, 248t
  SC elite blocked in Punjab by, 172, 181,
    184, 190–2, 255
  SC elite blocked in UP by, 172, 180–1,
    184, 186–8, 198–9, 255
  SCs and, 23, 30, 151, 152, 155, 157–8, 225

SCs incorporation, intraparty
    competition and, 251–7
  Sikhs and, 250–1
  split of, into Congress (O) and Congress
    (I), 253–4
  upper castes in, 211, 225, 226, 247,
    249–50
Constitution, Indian, 178, 198
constructivist approaches to ethnic identity,
    2, 45, 62, 91–3, 97–8, 287–92
corruption
  patronage and, 50–1
  rent seeking and, 50–1
Corruption Perception Index, 7n13
Cox, Gary, 244–5

Dahya, Badr, 74
Dalit, xvii, 149, 151
  meaning of, xvii, 149
Dalit Panthers, 149
Dalit Sangarsh Samiti (DSS), 166, 193
Dalit Shoshit Samaj Sangarsh Samiti
    (DS-4), 144–5, 149, 164, 166, 192–3
Daloz, Jean-Pascal, 85
De Zwart, Frank, 130
decentralization, 81, 115, 126n38, 199
democracy, definition of, 6
Democratic Party (of Uganda), 291n9
Dharalas, 289
Dhobis, 258
Dhusia, 258
dikus (outsiders), 281
district superintendent of police (SP), 119,
    120, 129
DMK, *see* Dravida Munnetra Kazagham
Downs, Anthony, 35–6, 95
Dravida Munnetra Kazagham (DMK), 18,
    40
  caste divisions and, 278–80, 278t, 279t
  Congress party versus, 276, 277–8, 278t
  founding of, 275–6
  leadership of, 278
  organizational (competitive) structure of,
    23–4, 278, 280–1, 280t
  representational profile of, 278–9, 278t,
    279t
  target ethnic category of, 23, 262, 276
  variation in vote for, 23, 26f, 27f, 277
Dreze, Jean, 126
DS-4, *see* Dalit Shoshit Samaj Sangarsh
    Samiti

Echeverri-Gent, John, 125
ecological inference (EI) method, 15, 27,
    224, 229–30, 233, 243, 303–9

339

education, 120–1, 128–9, 131
electoral system
 FPTP system and, 14, 87, 98, 145–6
 in India, 145–6
 proportional (PR) system and, 14, 86–7
Election Commission of India, 141, 230
 injunctions against use of caste and
  communal rhetoric, 219
 intraparty elections for parties forced by,
  261n
elites
 definition of, 11–12
 in patronage-democracies, 49
Ernst, Robert, 74
ethnic category
 definition of, 2–3
 redefinition of, 2, 63, 92–6, 97, 148–50,
  287–92
 single and composite, 4, 17
 size of, 2, 14, 29, 62, 81, 91, 97–8
 visibility of, 81
ethnic demography, 244–5, 286, 287,
 288–92
ethnic favouritism
 aggregate beneficiaries and, 69–70
 colonial rule and, 77–8
 culture and, 78–9
 decentralization, limited information and,
  81
 equilibrium of, 12, 49, 64–7
 networks and, 71–6, 81
 ethnic group, see ethnic category
Ethnic Groups in Conflict (Horowitz), 3n3,
 5n6, 8–9
ethnic party
 definition of, 3–5, 3n3
 multiethnic party versus, 4–5, 5n6
 nonethnic party versus, 3–4
expressive voting, definition of, 224
Ezhava, 218

Fiorina, Morris, 83
first-past-the-post (FPTP) system, 14, 87,
 98, 145–6
Foner, Philip, 75
founding elections, 46, 81
Fox, Jonathan, 69–70
Fussell, Paul, 42

Gandhi, Indira, 211, 220, 249, 253, 265,
 266, 290
Gandhi, Rajiv, 152, 153, 157, 265
Gandhi, Sonia, 153
Gangwar, Bhanwar Singh, 152
Gay, Robert, 69

governance, 203, 204, 204t, 205, 206–8,
 209f, 300–1t
Gujarat, 264, 268–9, 275, 289–90
Gujjar, 214, 290
Gupta, Akhil, 137
Gupta, Chandra Bhanu, 253

Harijan, meaning of, xvii
Hardgrave, Robert, 218
Hardin, Russell, 8n17
Harijans, 281, 289, 290
Harrison, Selig, 218
Haryana, 20f, 21, 146t, 147, 165, 166
Hausa-Fulanis, 9
Hechter, Michael, 8
Hindi, 166–7, 276–7, 296–9
Hindus
 BJP vote and, 23, 25f, 215, 263–5, 264n4
 Muslims versus, 215, 265–6
 population, 23, 24f, 25f
 Shiv Sena and, 264, 264n4
Hinich, Melvin, 36
Hispanics, 4
Holeyas, 17, 192
Horowitz, Donald, 2n, 3n3, 5n6, 8–9, 223,
 287
Hoshiarpur, 236–7, 298t
Hotelling, Harold, 95
Huntington, Samuel, 6n11
Hutus, 17
hypothesis construction and testing, 15–16,
 160–1, 286

ideology, as information shortcut, 35–6
Igbos, 9
Indian National Congress, see Congress
 party
information, limited
 definition of, 33
 ethnic categorization and, 29, 33–46
 equilibrium of ethnic favouritism and, 49,
  64–7
 institutional legacies and, 76–9
 networks and, 71–6
Inkatha Freedom Party (IFP), 10
Integrated Rural Development Programme
 (IRDP), 124, 127, 131
Irish, 58–9, 64

Jalali, Rita, 184
Jammu and Kashmir, BSP in, 20f, 21, 165,
 166
Jana Sangh, 264
Janata Dal (JD), 212, 216, 254, 266, 288
 in Bihar, 270–1
 in Gujarat, 268, 269

Index

in Karnataka, 182, 184, 195
Muslims targeted by, 217–18
OBCs and, 290
in UP, 181
Janata Dal (G), 268–9
Janata Dal United JD(U), 282
Janata Party, 211, 221, 263
Jassi, R. L., 190
Jat, 250–1, 290
Jatav, 185, 258
Jawahar Rozgar Yojna (JRY), 125, 128
JD, see Janata Dal.
Jharkhand Mukti Morcha (JMM)
founding of, 281
organizational (centralized) structure of, 24, 285–6
performance (in 2000) of, 23, 28f, 282–4, 285, 316t
as regionalist party, 18, 23, 30, 262–3
Santals and, 284–5
Scheduled Tribes, fragmentation and, 282, 283–5
variation in vote for, 18, 23, 28f, 282–5
Jhusia, 185, 258
Jones-Correa, Michael, 72–3

Kabaka Yekka (KY), 10, 291n9
Kainth, Satnam Singh, 190
Kammas, 218
Kannada, 166, 192, 295
Kasfir, Nelson, 95–6
Katznelson, Ira, 76
Kearney, Robert, 47
Keohane, Robert, 160
Kerala, 126n38, 218, 265, 276
KHAM political coalition, 290
Khare, R. S., 177
King, Gary, 15, 27, 160, 224, 306, 308
Kohli, Atul, 184
Kohli Patels, 215
Koris, 185, 258
Krishna, Gopal, 256
Kshatriya, 268, 269, 289–90
Kshirsagar, S. S., 118–19
Kumar, Meira, 151, *152*, 155, 157, 199
Kureel, 258
Kurmis, 281, 284, 285

Laitin, David, 77, 94n, 160n
Lanjouw, Peter, 124, 126
Levi, Margaret, 9n
Lingayats, 215, 250
literacy
Chamar rates of, 188, 191
in Karnataka, 173–4, 173t, 193
in Punjab, 173t, 176, 254

Scheduled Castes (SCs) and, 173–4, 173t, 176, 188, 191, 251
in UP, 173t, 188, 225
local government, Indian, 124, 129, 131, 133–4, 272
leverage, 2, 86–90, 226, 229–34, 244
Lodh, 275
The Logic of Collective Action (Olson), 53
Lok Dal, 254
Lupia, Arthur, 36

Madigas, 192
Maharashtra, 148, 150, 159, 264, 264n4
Malaysia, National Front in, 5
Mandal Commission, 205, 266
mandal committees, 272–3
Manor, James, 251, 256
Maratha, 216
Mayawati, *152*, *154*, 155, 168, 226
Mazhabis, 190
McCubbins, Matthew, 36
mediated democracy, 68
Meenakshipuram, 265
Mexico, 70
Mishra, Jagannath, 137–8
Mitchell, J. C., 73–4
modernity, 8, 8n17
most backward castes (MBC), 290
Movemiento Revolucionario Tupaj Katari de Liberación (MRTKL), 5
multiethnic party
Congress Party as national, 151, 155, 166, 195
definition of, 3–4
differentiated ethnic coalitions supported by, 87
from ethnic party to, 16, 17
as inherently unstable, 99
Janata Dal as national, 195
Munda, 284
Munger, Michael, 36
Muslims, 149, 285
in Bihar, 270–1
BSP and, 216–17, 261
Congress party and, 268, 270, 290
Hindus versus, 215, 265–6
Janata Dal and, 217
Meenakshipuram and SC conversion to, 265
MY political coalition, Yadavs and, 290
in Tamil Nadu, 278

Nadar, 279
Nairs, 218
National Commission for Scheduled Castes and Scheduled Tribes, 27–8

341

National Democratic Alliance (NDA), 282
National Election Studies (India), 26, 302
National Front/Left Front alliance
  (NF/LF), 5, 197, 199, 200, 205–6, 208,
  217–18
nationalism, 203, 204, 204t, 207t, 209, 209t,
  289, 300t
networks
  ethnic favouritism and, 71–6, 81
  factional, 105–6
  functional superiority of ethnic, 48
  kinship, 72
  organization, 75–6
  spatial (clustering), 72–5
New Haven, Connecticut, 52, 58–9, 85
New York City, 72–3, 75–6
NF/LF, see National Front/Left Front
  alliance
Nigeria, 5, 7, 9, 77–8, 95
nonethnic party
  definition of, 3–4
  differentiated ethnic coalitions supported
  by, 87

OBC, see other backward classes
Olson, Mancur, 53
opinion polls, 90, 245
Oraon, 284
other backward classes (OBC), xvii, 148–9,
  156t, 205, 217, 219, 221
  BJP and, 266–7, 267t, 269, 270–2, 274–5
  BSP and, 217
  DMK and, 279
  forwards among, 290
  JD and, 290, 291
  JMM and, 279
  Mandel Commission, government jobs
  and, 266

Panandikar, V. A., 118–19
panchayat (village council), 124, 129, 140
Pradesh, Madhya, 272
parliamentary election, 239, 242, 242t
parliamentary government, 145
Parsis, 40
party manifestos, 201–2, 212
party organization
  centralized, 108–11, 108f, 199, 246, 286
  competitive, 87–9, 102–8, 103f, 104f, 111,
  246, 247, 249–51, 253–4, 255, 258,
  272–3, 280–1
Pasis, 185, 188, 188t, 261, 288, 296
Paswan, Ram Vilas, 199, 288–9
patronage politics
  clientelism versus, 51
  corruption versus, 50–51

definition of, 1–2, 48–9
  pork barrel politics versus, 51
  rent seeking versus, 50–1
patronage-democracy, definition of, 1–2,
  48–9
patwari, 129
Peru, 69
Pilot, Rajesh, 214
police, 119–20, 126
pork barrel politics, 51
Posner, Daniel, 36, 48, 59, 85
Post, Kenneth, 48
Praja Socialist Party (PSP), 276
princely India, 256
private sector
  public sector versus, 6, 66–7, 116–18,
  117t, 118t, 119, 120t
proportional (PR) system, 14, 86–7
public sector
  growth rate of, 117–18, 118t
  job selection in, 119–21, 119t, 120t
  private sector versus, 6, 66–7, 116–18,
  117t, 118t, 119, 120t

Rabushka, Alvin, 8
Rajputs, 289
Ram, Bali, 186
Ram, Jagjivan, 151, 152
Ram, Kanshi, 143–5, 148, 149–50, 151, 152,
  154, 157, 164–5, 168, 186, 193, 234,
  235–7, 258–60
Ramdassias, 145, 168–9, 189, 190, 191, 192
Ramjanmabhoomi movement, 263
ranked versus unranked social systems,
  17–18
Rashtriya Janta Dal (RJD), 282, 290
Rashtriya Swayamsevak Sangh (RSS), 263,
  274–5
Reddis, 218
rent seeking
  corruption and, 50–1
  Indian patronage-democracy and, 116,
  126–7, 126n38, 129–39
  local government, 131, 133–4
  patronage politics versus, 50–1
  state government and, 132–3
Republican Party of India, 144
RJD, see Rashtriya Janata Dal
Root, Hilton, 137
RSS, see Rashtriya Swayamsevak Sangh
rural credit, 123, 127–8
Rwanda, 17

Saini, 217, 259
Samajwadi Janata Party (SJP), 270–1, 282

Index

Samajwadi Party (SP), 197, 214, 254, 290
  BSP alliance with, 241, 260–1
Samata Party, 282
Samyukta Socialist Party (SSP), 276
Santals, 284, 285
Satnamis, 169
Satyashodhak Samaj, 148
Schaffer, Frederic, 52
Schattschneider, E. E., 93
Scheduled Castes (SCs)
  definition of, 16
  BJP and, 267–9, 267t, 271
  Communist Party and, 219
  Congress party and, 23, 30, 151, *152*, 155, 157–8, 225
  definition of, 16
  DMK, Tamil Nadu and, 278, 278t, 279t
  efficacy of votes, 146t
  fragmentation of, 17, 167–8
  literacy rates of, 173–4, 173t, 176, 188, 251
  population of, 18–19, 19f, 147–9, 151, 156t, 185
Scheduled Tribes, 156, 156t
  BJP and, 267t, 268, 269, 271
  fragmentation of, 284
  JMM and, 281, 283–4
Scottish National Party (SNP), 9n20, 10
SCs, *see* Scheduled Castes
secularism, 214
self-esteem, 9, 9n19, 61–2, 87, 227
Senegal, 7
Seshan, T. N., 140
Shah, Ghanshyam, 269
Sharief, Jaffer, 217
Sharma, Miriam, 126
Shepsle, Kenneth, 8
Shiv Sena, 264, 264n4
Sikh, 39, 145, 149, 167, 215
  Jat, 250–1
  Ramdassia, 168–9, 189, 190, 191, 192
Singh, Charan, 251, 254, 290
Singh, Kalyan, 275
Singh, Manmohan, 137, 215
Singh, Zail, 221
social choice theory, 93
social identity theory, 9
social justice, 203–4, 204t, 205, 206, 207–8, 207t, 300t
Soren, Shibhu, 284, 286
South Africa
  African National Congress in, 5
  Inkatha Freedom Party in, 10

Spence, Michael, 35
Sri Lanka, 10
SSP, *see* Samyukta Socialist Party
Stalin, M. K., 40
Stern, Nicholas, 124, 126
Stokes, Susan, 69
strategic voting
  Chamar voters and, 231–2, 238–9, 242
  definition of, 224
  ecological inference method and, 308–9
  patronage-democracies and, 22, 30, 86–91, 243–5
  Scheduled Caste voters and, 223–4, 232–4, 237, 238–9, 240–3
Subramanian, Narendra, 139
success, definition of, 5–6
Swatantra Party, 276

Tajfel, Henri, 9
taluq committee, 280
Tamil Nadu, 18, 23, 26f, 27f, 167, 262–3, 266, 276
Telugu Desam, 211, 221
Tutsis, 17

Uganda, 10, 291n9
United Kingdom
  class and, 39, 41
  Pakistani immigrants in, 74
  strategic voting in, 244
United States, 8, 41, 72
Urdu, 185, 276

Varshney, Ashutosh, 76
Verba, Sidney, 160
village council, *see panchayat*
Vishwa Hindu Parishad (VHP), 263
Vokkaliga, 217, 250

Wade, Robert, 122, 136
Weiner, Myron, 121, 126, 132n56, 135–6, 184, 257
Wolfinger, Raymond, 52, 58–9, 64, 85

Yadav, Laloo Prasad, 270
Yadav, Mulayam Singh, 137, 214
Yadav, Yogendra, 290n
Yadavs, 137, 150, 214, 290

Zambia, 7, 26, 48, 59, 73–4, 85
zero-sum game, 257
Zulu, 10

Other Books in the Series (continued from page iii)

Geoffrey Garrett, *Partisan Politics in the Global Economy*

Miriam Golden, *Heroic Defeats: The Politics of Job Loss*

Jeff Goodwin, *No Other Way Out: States and Revolutionary Movements, 1945–1991*

Merilee Serrill Grindle, *Changing the State*

Frances Hagopian, *Traditional Politics and Regime Change in Brazil*

J. Rogers Hollingsworth and Robert Boyer, eds., *Contemporary Capitalism: The Embeddedness of Institutions*

Ellen Immergut, *Health Politics: Interests and Institutions in Western Europe*

Torben Iversen, *Contested Economic Institutions*

Torben Iversen, Jonas Pontusson, David Soskice, eds., *Unions, Employers, and Central Banks: Macroeconomic Coordination and Institutional Change in Social Market Economies*

Thomas Janoski and Alexander M. Hicks, eds., *The Comparative Political Economy of the Welfare State*

Pauline Jones Luong, *Institutional Change and Political Continuity in Post-Soviet Central Asia: Power, Perceptions, and Pacts*

David Kang, *Crony Capitalism: Corruption and Development in South Korea and the Philippines*

Junko Kato, *Regressive Taxation and the Welfare State*

Robert O. Keohane and Helen B. Milner, eds., *Internationalization and Domestic Politics*

Herbert Kitschelt, *The Transformation of European Social Democracy*

Herbert Kitschelt, Peter Lange, Gary Marks, and John D. Stephens, eds., *Continuity and Change in Contemporary Capitalism*

Herbert Kitschelt, Zdenka Mansfeldova, Radek Markowski, and Gabor Toka, *Post-Communist Party Systems*

David Knoke, Franz Urban Pappi, Jeffrey Broadbent, and Yutaka Tsujinaka, eds., *Comparing Policy Networks*

Allan Kornberg and Harold D. Clarke, *Citizens and Community: Political Support in a Representative Democracy*

David D. Laitin, *Language Repertories and State Construction in Africa*

Mark Irving Lichbach and Alan S. Zuckerman, eds., *Comparative Politics: Rationality, Culture, and Structure*

Evan S. Lieberman, *Race and Regionalism in the Politics of Taxation in Brazil and South Africa*

James Mahoney and Dietrich Rueschemeyer, eds., *Historical Analysis and the Social Sciences*

Scott Mainwaring and Matthew Soberg Shugart, eds., *Presidentialism and Democracy in Latin America*

Isabela Mares, *The Politics of Social Risk: Business and Welfare State Development*

Anthony W. Marx, *Making Race, Making Nations: A Comparison of South Africa, the United States and Brazil*

Doug McAdam, John McCarthy, and Mayer Zald, eds., *Comparative Perspectives on Social Movements*

Joel Migdal, *State in Society*

Joel S. Migdal, Atul Kohli, and Vivienne Shue, eds., *State Power and Social Forces: Domination and Transformation in the Third World*

Layna Mosley, *Global Capital and National Governments*

Wolfgang C. Muller and Kaare Strom, *Policy, Office, or Votes?*

Maria Victoria Murillo, *Labor Unions, Partisan Coalitions, and Market Reforms in Latin America*

Ton Notermans, *Money, Markets, and the State: Social Democratic Economic Policies since 1918*

Simona Piattoni, ed., *Clientelism, Interests, and Democratic Representation*

Paul Pierson, *Dismantling the Welfare State? Reagan, Thatcher and the Politics of Retrenchment*

Marino Regini, *Uncertain Boundaries: The Social and Political Construction of European Economies*

Lyle Scruggs, *Sustaining Abundance: Environmental Performance in Industrial Democracies*

Other Books in the Series (continued)

Yossi Shain and Juan Linz, eds., *Interim Governments and Democratic Transitions*
Beverley Silver, *Forces of Labor: Workers' Movements and Globalization since 1870*
Theda Skocpol, *Social Revolutions in the Modern World*
David Stark and László Bruszt, *Postsocialist Pathways: Transforming Politics and Property in East Central Europe*
Sven Steinmo, Kathleen Thelan, and Frank Longstreth, eds., *Structuring Politics: Historical Institutionalism in Comparative Analysis*
Susan C. Stokes, *Mandates and Democracy: Neoliberalism by Surprise in Latin America*
Susan C. Stokes, ed., *Public Support for Market Reforms in New Democracies*
Sidney Tarrow, *Power in Movement: Social Movements and Contentious Politics*
Ashutosh Varshney, *Democracy, Development, and the Countryside*
Elisabeth Jean Wood, *Forging Democracy from Below: Insurgent Transitions in South Africa and El Salvador*
Elisabeth Jean Wood, *Insurgent Collective Action in El Salvador*

Printed in the United States
71230LV00004B/1-30